APPROACHES
TO
SEMIOTICS

edited by

THOMAS A. SEBEOK

Research Center for the Language Sciences
Indiana University

56

DR. EUGENE A. NIDA

in his various activities

ON LANGUAGE, CULTURE, AND RELIGION: IN HONOR OF EUGENE A. NIDA

edited by

Matthew Black

UNIVERSITY OF ST. ANDREWS

William A. Smalley

UNITED BIBLE SOCIETIES

1974

MOUTON

THE HAGUE · PARIS

ISBN 90 279 3011 2

Printed in Belgium by N.I.C.I., Ghent

CONTENTS

PART ONE: BIBLICAL STUDIES

EUGENE A. NIDA: AN APPRECIATION

ERIC M. NORTH

This collection of essays with their varied themes has been prepared to honor Eugene A. Nida on his sixtieth birthday. But even the variety of these contributions does not match the many different ways in which these writers and Nida's other friends know him.[1] Academically and professionally he is an anthropological linguist; his position in that field is indicated by the fact that he was President of the Linguistic Society of America (1968). But much as Nida enjoys linguistic inquiry and debate, his primary commitment is to the mission of Bible translation, and to making the cross-cultural communication of the Christian message more relevant and intelligible.

THE EARLY YEARS

Eugene Albert Nida was born November 11, 1914, in Oklahoma City, Oklahoma, where he lived for his first five years. The family later settled in Long Beach, California. His mother was Alma Ruth McCullough Nida; his father, Richard Eugene Nida, was a doctor. At an early age Nida committed his life to Christ and felt called to be a missionary.

In his high school Nida led the debating team to win the southern California championship and was voted the outstanding debater. He began the study of language with Latin and looked forward to translating the Scriptures as a missionary. Botany was also one of his early interests and has continued to be a hobby throughout his life. His higher education began at the University of California in Los Angeles where he majored

Eric M. North is General Secretary (retired) and Consultant of the American Bible Society, New York City, New York.
[1] The writer of this essay is deeply indebted to Eugene Nida's brother, Clarence K. Nida, to his professional colleagues, and to the staff of the American Bible Society for providing data, judgment, and help of many kinds. William A. Smalley, acquainted with Nida's work since 1947, has collaborated in preparing this appreciation.

in Greek with a minor in Latin. He was graduated in 1936 *summa cum laude*, with membership in Phi Beta Kappa and one of the highest ratings in UCLA history.

PROFESSIONAL FORMATION

Eugene Nida had been stimulated by philological aspects of his study at UCLA, but his first contact with modern linguistics and missionary Bible translation came the summer of his graduation from UCLA. W. C. Townsend, one of the founders of the Wycliffe Bible Translators, invited him to attend a session of the Summer Institute of Linguistics, Wycliffe's sister organization. Here Nida found his chief stimulus in the works of Edward Sapir and Leonard Bloomfield.

At the conclusion of the summer session he undertook the linguistic analysis of the language of the Tarahumara Indians of Mexico as a prelude to translating the Bible into Tarahumara. Because of an inadequate diet and the intensity of his work he became ill and had to take some months for recuperation. He then began studies at the University of Southern California, reading most of the Church Fathers in Greek and the Greek poets for pleasure. He received the Master's degree in Greek New Testament in 1939.

Each summer from 1937 to 1953 Nida returned to the Summer Institute of Linguistics (SIL) to teach. By 1939 he and Kenneth L. Pike were the principal teachers, Nida teaching morphology-syntax and Pike teaching phonetics-phonemics. Their names continue to be linked in many people's minds even though it has been twenty years since they worked closely together.

In 1941 Nida took up studies in linguistics under Charles C. Fries at the University of Michigan and two years later he received his Ph. D. His doctoral thesis, *A Synopsis of English Syntax* (Nida 1943), was the only relatively full-scale analysis of a major language by the "immediate constituent" linguistic theory of the time. It was circulated in typescript by interlibrary loan and in several hundred lithoprinted copies before finally being published in 1960.

The year of 1943 was a critical turning point in Nida's life and career for more reasons than the Ph. D. In that year he was ordained to the Christian ministry by the Southern California Association of the Northern Baptist Convention. Also in that year he married Althea Lucille Sprague, who had been teaching at Bacone College, an Indian School in Muskogee,

Oklahoma. Furthermore, in 1943 Nida joined the staff of the American Bible Society.

As General Secretary of the Society I had become aware that there was such an affair as "linguistics", and had secured authority from the Board to add a professional linguist to the staff. The American Bible Society (founded 1816) was rapidly becoming more extensively involved in the publication of Bibles and parts of Bibles in more and more languages of the world. The Society had attempted to exercise some control over the linguistic quality of its publications, but was not in a position to do much. The search for a linguist was an attempt to strengthen this control.

At the recommendation of W. C. Townsend of SIL, Nida was invited to undertake this work on an experimental basis, and this soon led to his appointment as Associate Secretary for Versions from 1944 to 1946, and Executive Secretary for Translations ever since. The American Bible Society has provided the institutional base from which Nida's multi-faceted activities have proceeded.

EMERGING INFLUENCE

After joining the staff of the American Bible Society Eugene Nida continued in association with the Summer Institute of Linguistics, teaching in the SIL program at the University of Oklahoma each summer and serving on SIL governing bodies. At the same time he plunged into a series of extended field trips for the American Bible Society (ABS), spending a few days or a few weeks at a time in one place after another in Africa and Latin America. On these visits he worked with missionary translators or potential translators on linguistic problems which were standing in the way of their learning the various languages, and on the problems in the translations themselves. Many of these missionary translators had been his students at SIL.

Being associated both with SIL and ABS was important to Nida's development and to his quickly establishing himself both in linguistics and in Bible translation. He quickly began to see his role in the ABS not so much as one of checking the value of the translation before publication as a publisher would, but rather as one of educating translators to do better translation, of providing a model of translation with which they could work, and of helping them organize their work to get it done. This could all be done only through traveling to where the translators were, through teaching, through writing, and through organizational administration. These, therefore, have been the complementary tools through which Nida has worked.

The extent of Nida's travels must be mentioned because they have been such an important part of his life. It has only been in recent years that his travel has been reduced to three or four months out of the year. More typical were years when six to eight months were spent on the road. For example, in 1966, twenty years after becoming ABS Executive Secretary for Translations, he spent the first few months of the year in Peru, Paraguay, Brazil, and Mexico, June 29 to July 10 in Congo, July 20 to 21 in Zambia, July 23 to 31 in Lebanon and Egypt, August 3 to 11 in the Philippines, August 12 to September 3 in Japan, then some time conferring in Europe, and December in Mexico.

Another aspect of his emerging influence started when Nida became a delegate to what turned out to be the founding conference of the United Bible Societies at Haywards Heath, England, in May 1946. Contacts there were followed by an important conference hosted by the Netherlands Bible Society at Woudschoten, Holland, in 1947. This brought together Bible Society personnel concerned with translation from Denmark, England, Iceland, the Netherlands, Norway, Scotland, Sweden, Switzerland, and the USA. The discussions covered a score of subjects including texts to be used, orthography, training of translators, linguistic surveys, and lexical problems.

A further step was taken at New York when the Council of the newly formed United Bible Societies (UBS) appointed a "Functional Group on Translation" in which Nida was included. During these years (1946 to 1949) a revolution in the work of translating the Scriptures for the world was taking place, not only establishing cooperation between Bible Societies but also providing practical service to Bible translators the world over. And in this revolution Nida had a large part. In due course the "Functional Group" became a UBS Committee of which Nida is now the chairman. John J. Kijne of the Netherlands Bible Society was one with whom Nida teamed up to help make some of the changes possible, and who has helped in their implementation through the years.

In 1949 the UBS approved of the publication of a quarterly journal, *The Bible Translator*, with Nida as editor. He and Herman Rutgers of the Netherlands Bible Society had prepared a specimen copy which became the first issue. This journal is now one of the cornerstones of the world movement of Bible translation.

NIDA AS WRITER

Nida has always put great importance on his writing because he sees it as a major medium through which to influence Bible translation and to make a professional contribution. The volume and significance of his writing is phenomenal, especially in light of the grueling travel and lecture schedule he has always carried.

An examination of the titles of Nida's books in chronological order shows four rather distinct phases:

(1) the DESCRIPTIVE LINGUISTICS phase, 1943-1951 (*Bible Translating* [1947a] does not belong to this phase, but is a foreshadowing of phase 3)

(2) the CROSS-CULTURAL COMMUNICATION phase, 1952-1960

(3) the TRANSLATION phase, 1961-1973 (*Religion Across Cultures* [1968] and *Communication of the Gospel in Latin America* [1969b] are carry-overs from the previous phase)

(4) the SEMANTICS phase, 1974-

The most significant book of the descriptive linguistics phase was *Morphology* (Nida 1946) in its drastically rewritten second edition of 1949. This textbook has continued to be used long after the changes brought in by the newer transformational grammar and other more recent linguistic theories left it behind in its theoretical orientation. Its durability has come from the amazing array of small linguistic problems collected in the course of Nida's extensive travels. People continue to use the problems, although they approach them from different points of view. It is also interesting that the 1946 edition of *Morphology* in its treatment of morphological processes is probably closer to the viewpoint of transformational grammar than is the 1949 edition. It is clear from Nida's later work that he is more at home with this kind of model of language than he is with the "item and arrangement" of his own 1949 *Morphology*.

The key book of the second phase (cross-cultural communication) is probably *Message and Mission* (1960), although *Customs and Cultures* (1954) has sold more widely. *Message and Mission* probably represents Nida's own outlook and motivation better than any other book, and summarizes the rationale behind all of his work: the effective communication of the Good News about Jesus Christ across all kinds of cultural and linguistic barriers.

The key book of the translation phase is *Toward a Science of Translating* (1964), amended and clarified at many points by the textbook *The Theory and Practice of Translation* (with Charles R. Taber) (1969a).

This was his first book-length attempt to present theories of *dynamic equivalence* translation, which he had been developing through the years of activity in this field. It is broadly based, stimulated by insights from communication theory, psychology, Biblical studies, and especially the developing fields of semantics and transformational grammar within linguistics. Some of the ways in which Nida's thinking had grown may be seen by comparing it with *Bible Translating* (1947a). *Bible Translating* had always been a useful book, but it was oriented to "aboriginal languages" and was a collection of hints and suggestions. *Toward a Science of Translating* is an attempt at a coherent theory of translation called dynamic equivalence translation. The value of this theory can be seen in the far greater understanding with which hundreds of Bible translators now approach their task. Some of the papers in this volume deal with aspects of dynamic equivalence translation which need to be further developed.

As Nida developed and popularized it, dynamic equivalence translation captures the meaning and spirit of the original without being bound to its linguistic structure (formal correspondence). The meaning of the text, the purpose of the original writer, and the relationship of the text to its original cultural setting are guarded as much as possible, and are conveyed by new structures as a new text in the language of the translation. Dynamic equivalence translation should not be equated with "free translation" because it is rigorous in its insistence that the meaning and purpose of the original is to be recaptured insofar as possible within the different language patterns of the translation.

It is too early to select any book as representing the semantics phase. The first one has not come off the press at the time of writing this appreciation. But as with all the other phases, Nida's interest in this particular phase has not been limited to recent years. His list of early published articles includes "A System for the Description of Semantic Elements" (1951a) and "A New Methodology of Biblical Exegesis" (1952). The former was abortive. Nida never tried to carry that scheme farther. The latter, however, was highly seminal. It was also an indication of how he was even then seeing beyond the restraints of the then current linguistic theory, and the ideas he developed from it later became key elements in the theory of dynamic equivalence translation.

Nida's contributions to linguistics proper started with a Bloomfieldian-structuralist period, followed by a later period when interest was concentrated on semantics and deep structure. His major linguistic contributions of the first period were primarily within less than ten years, and were associated with his teaching at SIL. The first significant published indication of the second period was the article, "A New Methodology of Biblical Exegesis" (1952), five years before the publication of Chomsky's *Syntactic Structures*, often considered to mark the beginning of the new emphasis in linguistic theory. Nida's paper brought up questions which have since been discussed in transformational grammar under the headings of deep structure and case grammar. In the meantime, the fifties were years in which Nida was concentrating most heavily on the anthropological side of culture and communication (his phase 2), so that the first major book of the second linguistic period did not come until ten years ago – *Toward a Science of Translating* (1964).

It was not only linguistic theory which changed between the forties and the sixties: the situation in Bible translation also changed. In the forties Bible translators were still primarily expatriates, and Nida's work on the two editions of *Morphology* (1946 and 1949) resulted from his teaching such expatriates to get into the grammatical complications of a foreign language. This was largely pre-translation activity.

In the sixties, while there were still many expatriate missionary translators, particularly in remote areas with low education levels, Nida was concerned more with people translating into their own language. Such people did not need so much to analyze the surface structure of the languages they spoke as to understand what was involved in expressing the same meaning in the grammar and vocabulary of two different languages. They needed to learn to sense the deep structure and semantics of the text they were translating, and idiomatically and effectively to express this in the surface forms of their own languages.

Of the linguistic theories in the sixties and seventies, Nida has found transformational grammar most congenial, particularly generative semantics. But the insights of transformational grammar, significant as they were, could not be taken over wholesale for translation because they were at the same time too narrow and too specific. Transformational grammar did not have the theoretical apparatus for the whole scope of translation, which involves the structure of discourse as well as its social context. Nida's work has been heavily influenced by transformational grammar, but also differs considerably from it and other current theories. His work on *Componential Analysis of Meaning* (i.p. a), however, is well within the framework of modern studies in semantics, but without a great deal of formal apparatus. His work on semantics and discourse structure continues, as well as work on a semantic analysis of the vocabulary of the Greek New Testament.

The majority of Nida's articles were contributions to the journals *The Bible Translator* and *Practical Anthropology*. His relation to the first of these has already been mentioned. He was also one of the primary guiding influences and supporters of the second. During the nineteen years of its publication, *Practical Anthropology* was strongly oriented towards cross-cultural communication, particularly communication of the Christian message. Both journals have been media for Nida's continual efforts to make insights from linguistics and the social sciences available and applicable to the Bible translator, or to anyone else involved in the communication of the Christian message.

NIDA AS EDUCATOR

Although he has never accepted an offer of a professorship at any university, Eugene Nida is genuinely a teacher, with a strong compulsion to share the ideas that are important to him. In the first phase of his productivity he taught linguistics each summer at the Summer Institute of Linguistics. But more typical of his career have been shorter lecture series, teaching at training programs for translators (one week to one month in duration), teaching translators by working with them on their translations for brief periods, and leading discussions in UBS staff workshops.

Some of Nida's books were begun as lecture series at theological seminaries or places like the Toronto Institute of Linguistics. At least *Customs and Cultures* (1954), *Message and Mission* (1960a), and *Religion across Cultures* (1968) developed from lectures. Other books, like *Morphology* (1946) and *The Theory and Practice of Translating* (1969a), were written specifically as textbooks. *Learning a Foreign Language* (1950) was written to help missionaries train themselves in field situations. *Introducing Animism* (1959) was written as a study document for church laymen. And the *Translator's Handbook* series (1961b, 1972a, 1972b, 1973a, 1973b) is being written to serve as ready reference for working translators.

In the earlier days, Nida himself participated in all of the Bible Society-sponsored training programs for translators. Now they are shared by a number of associates. Probably some 4,000 translators and potential translators have attended such programs, including Roman Catholic, Orthodox, and Protestant Christians. The triennial translation staff workshops started years ago in Nida's living room with a handful of associates. At the latest one in 1972 there were sixty present, consisting mostly of people who were not themselves Bible translators, but of consultants of several nationalities and from several different Bible Societies.

NIDA AS ORGANIZER

In addition to his traveling, writing, and lecturing, it has been by attention to organization that Nida has succeeded in getting so much done, and spreading his influence so widely in the field of Bible translation. The team of colleagues he has drawn around him has greatly multiplied his efforts; he has stimulated and guided the organization of several major translations and revisions, establishing the principles on which people of different backgrounds could work together; he has also initiated and helped to organize several major scholarly research projects.

Knowing that his personal field work, however intensive, would not cover all that was needed, Nida began in the mid fifties the program of securing and training translation consultants qualified to assist translators. These were then assigned, as staff members of the ABS Translations Department, to different parts of the world. Among the early appointees still serving in such capacity are William L. Wonderly, William A. Smalley, and William D. Reyburn. Later the work of such men was incorporated into the United Bible Societies, rather than being an American Bible Society service, and was internationalized with other consultants from other countries.

With an increasing number of translation consultants taking over things that Nida had been doing all around the world, Nida was appointed UBS Translations Research Coordinator in 1970. In this capacity he not only carries on his own research, writing, and teaching, but is able to coordinate, stimulate, and criticize that which colleagues are doing – a wide range of activities including discourse analysis, preparing teaching materials for teaching the principles of translation, testing translation theories (and testing translations), and writing translators handbooks (frequently in joint authorship with Nida).

Nida's participation in the organization of major revisions and new translations began with the revision of the Reina-Valera Spanish Bible between 1950 and 1960. For some time he had been aware of unsatisfactory elements in this version which was most widely used by Spanish-speaking Protestants in Latin America and Spain. The ABS had earlier published a different translation of the New Testament, the Hispano-Americana, based largely on the American Standard Version, but this had proved too much of an innovation for the conservative constituency in Spanish-speaking America and too difficult for any normal reader. This time, instead of launching a new version, Nida consulted with many leading clergy of various denominations and then set up a process of locating and correcting defects of the older translation. Sixty consultants were found for the Old Testament, eighty for the New Testament; a central Editorial Committee of six (with whom Nida himself worked) and an editorial secretary with two or more literary consultants were engaged in the project (Nida 1961d).

Successful as was his limited revision of the Reina-Valera within its own frame of reference, however, the rapidly developing theory of dynamic equivalence translation with which Nida was absorbed meant that he soon instigated still another Spanish translation under the leadership of an associate, William L. Wonderly. This was to be a completely new translation on a level of style determined by sociolinguistic principles[2] and aimed at meeting the needs not of the church leaders, but of the Biblically unsophisticated layman. Increasingly, all over the world, Nida was leading the Bible Societies toward this emphasis in translation.

This Spanish Versión Popular New Testament (1966) was a common language translation, one type of dynamic equivalence translation. "Common language", as Nida and his colleagues use the term, is language which is intelligible to readers of minimal education and at the same time acceptable to readers of good education. It is thus the range or core of language which is common to a wide spectrum of readership. The English common language translation, which Nida first proposed in 1961, was designed originally to be used by people for whom English is not a native language. However, the translation of the New Testament which appeared in 1966 under the title *Good News for Modern Man* (Today's English Version) is widely used by native speakers of English who find in it highly readable and refreshingly clear translation. Forty-two million copies had been sold by 1973. The translation was done by Robert G. Bratcher, a close associate of Nida's, together with a group of collaborators. The Old Testament should appear in 1975.

---

[2] These principles have been most fully spelled out in William L. Wonderly, *Bible Translations for Popular Use* (London: United Bible Societies, 1968). Nida's influence is strong in this book, reflecting as it does an approach to translation in which he is the leading figure.

The value and success of the Today's English Version and of the Versión Popular helped to convince translators, church leaders, and Bible Societies of the value of the dynamic equivalence theory of translation and its potential for their various situations even when patterns of language use did not call for common language translations as such.

Traditionally, translations sponsored by the Bible Societies did not include Roman Catholics as translators. However, Roman Catholic concern for the distribution of Scriptures among the laity, expressed in Vatican II and in informal conversations with Roman Catholic leaders and scholars, paved the way for conferences of UBS officers with the Roman Catholic Secretariat for Promoting Christian Unity. From these meetings came a joint document entitled *Guiding Principles for Interconfessional Cooperation in Translating the Bible*, issued in 1968 by the UBS and the Secretariat. It is a keystone in the structure of collaboration, reflecting in good part Nida's experience and that of his colleagues in organizing and expediting translation programs, now expanded to include this wider field of cooperation. By 1973 more than 150 translation projects sponsored by the Bible Societies included the participation of Roman Catholic translators.

Still another area in which Nida's organizational efforts have been of major importance has been in the planning and implementing of several major scholarly projects. The first of these was the Bible Societies' edition of the Greek New Testament, the first such edition to be prepared by an international team of scholars and specifically designed to be of the greatest possible use to translators, rather than just to textual scholars. After initial discussions within the American Bible Society, in which Bruce M. Metzger, authority on the New Testament text and member of the ABS board also participated, Nida approached some other Bible Societies and scholars of various nations in 1955. This was well before the days when cooperation on major matters between Bible Societies was automatic, and before the United Bible Societies was functioning in the way it is today. There was some initial resistance, but finally the American Bible Society, the National Bible Society of Scotland, and the Württemberg Bibelanstalt (later to be joined by the Netherlands Bible Society and the British and Foreign Bible Society) formed a sponsoring group. New Testament textual scholars Kurt Aland, Matthew Black, Bruce M. Metzger, Allen Wikgren, and part of the time Arthur Voöbus became the editorial committee, assisted by ABS staff associates. The first edition was published in 1966, and its preface records Nida's contribution:

... the project was initiated, organized, and administered by Eugene A. Nida who also took part in committee discussions, especially relating to major decisions of policy or method.

Partly in recognition of his part in this major scholarly undertaking he was awarded an honorary Th. D. by the University of Münster (Federal Republic of Germany) in 1967.

The editorial committee is a continuing committee. It brought out a second edition in 1968 and is preparing a third edition. After cooperation with Roman Catholics was instituted in the *Guiding Principles* mentioned above, the Roman Catholic scholar Carlo M. Martini was added to the committee. As a part of the continuing project, Bruce Metzger prepared *A Textual Commentary on the Greek New Testament*[3] which gives the reasoning behind the committee's textual decisions. This is in keeping with another feature of the New Testament text, that decisions are weighted along a scale from highly probable to doubtful, according to the nature of the evidence.

A second major scholarly project, which Nida initiated as the first edition of the Greek New Testament text became a reality, was a Hebrew Old Testament text project. This project is somewhat different from the New Testament project because of the differences in the nature of the problems facing textual scholars in the two cases, but Nida's ultimate objectives are the same – to provide help for the translator. With the success of the Greek New Testament project, the pattern of cooperation with Roman Catholics, and the structure of the United Bible Societies all now established, there was no problem this time in enlisting support. A committee of international reputation was formed consisting of Dominique Barthélemy, A. R. Hulst, Norbert Lohfink, W. D. McHardy, H. P. Rüger, and James A. Sanders. Much to Nida's surprise they made him chairman in recognition of his diplomatic and organizational role, in spite of his lack of qualifications as a Hebraist. The committee held its first meeting in 1969. Its first report, covering preliminary decisions on the Pentateuch, was published in 1973.[4]

A third major international scholarly project which Nida originated and in which he is now engaged is that of preparing a semantic analysis of all of the vocabulary in the Greek New Testament. Here his colleagues are Johannes P. Louw and Rondal B. Smith. In this project Nida wants to bring the insights of modern semantic theory to bear on the vocabulary

---

[3] (London: United Bible Societies, 1971).
[4] *Preliminary and Interim Report on the Hebrew Old Testament Test Project* (London: United Bible Societies, 1973).

of the New Testament, again to help the translator in his task. In this case, of course, Nida is entering into the actual analytical process because the data are within his field of competence.

ALTHEA SPRAGUE NIDA

Any appreciation of Eugene Nida would be quite incomplete if tribute were not paid to his wife. Ever since their marriage in 1943, this lovely lady has aided her husband with her good judgment, professional skills, and warm companionship. She has been with him on most of his long journeys to strange places ("our travel agent insists we go to 'the darndest places' "), caring for the inevitable correspondence and documentation for many projects. She has contributed to the housekeeping and accomodations at many a translators institute and conference. She commented cheerfully after the triennial workshop in 1972 (sixty persons):

Three of us women managed the office (men not only talk a lot, but they want a lot of their talk mimeographed), served coffee breaks, tea breaks, snacks (men also eat a lot).

A missionary wrote of the Nidas' twelve-day visit: "They made a great team. Mrs. Nida worked every minute she was here." In more than one instance her rapport with the wives of translators has alerted Nida to the tensions which opinions on orthographies or translation problems sometimes produce.

Althea Nida has also made her own independent contribution, having served since 1958 as a member of the Board of Managers of the American Baptist Foreign Missions Society, as vice-president of the Society (1966-1967), and as president (1967-1968).

As has been the case with Nida, too, the pace of their life has taken its toll in Mrs. Nida's health. The incessant travel, the long hours of work, the strain of being with different people constantly has worn away at her health, but not at her courage or exuberance.

NIDA AS A PERSON

Hopefully, something of the personality of Eugene Nida has been shown in this recital of his professional contributions and public accomplishments, and I cannot really go further into what he is like in the space that is left. A few miscellaneous details might be mentioned to help round out the picture somewhat. He and his wife are avid bird watchers, both at their unique home in Greenwich, Connecticut (which he helped design and build), and all over the world. Nida's "life list" includes many hundreds of species.

In their Greenwich home Nida built much of the furniture and sculptured some of the art. He is a perceptive photographer, plays the recorder, enjoys vigorous hiking, and in earlier years played volleyball with the same energy that he lectured at institutes and other training programs.

Nida has always been approachable. Students, colleagues, translators, and friends have sought him out to discuss their latest ideas, their professional development, and their religious problems. He gives his time freely to them in spite of the many other pressures on him. A significant number of people all over the world have changed direction because of contact with him. In addition, through their own personal resources and by tapping other funds, Nida and his wife have contributed heavily to helping talented young people in several countries on to advanced training when Nida felt that the young person had an important contribution to make.

Nida's frequent description of what a translation consultant for the United Bible Societies should be like is his own portrait:
(1) a keen intellect with a sense of structure and scientific imagination
(2) a capacity to communicate effectively with others
(3) a fundamental empathy with the cause of communicating the Good News, and with those who do, and a willingness to work closely with all kinds of Christian groups
(4) a warm personal touch and sense of humor with which to relate to others, and not to take himself too seriously.

PUBLICATIONS OF EUGENE A. NIDA

Under books we have listed original publications and recent manuscripts scheduled for publication. Second editions are indicated only when they involve substantial revision. Later printings, printings by other publishers, translations, etc., are not included. Under articles, however, we have listed only a selection (perhaps only one third of Nida's output), including the most important ones and a selection of the others to indicate something of the range of his writings. Many of the articles not listed here may be found in *The Bible Translator* and *Practical Anthropology*.

BOOKS

1943

A Synopsis of English Syntax, doctoral dissertation (Ann Arbor, Mich.: University of Michigan, 1943). Printed in 1960 (Norman, Okla: Summer Institute of Linguistics); revised and reprinted in 1966 (The Hague: Mouton).

1946

Morphology, the Descriptive Analysis of Words (Ann Arbor, Mich.: University of Michigan Press, 1946). Completely new edition printed in 1949 (Ann Arbor, Mich.: University of Michigan Press).

1947

Bible Translating: An Analysis of Principles and Procedures (New York: American Bible Society, 1947a). Revised and reprinted in 1961 (London: United Bible Societies).
Linguistic Interludes (Glendale, Ca.: Summer Institute of Linguistics, 1947b).
A Translator's Commentary on Selected Passages (Glendale, Ca.: Summer Institute of Linguistics, 1947c).

1950

Learning a Foreign Language (New York: Committee on Missionary Personnel of the Foreign Missions Conference of North America, 1950). Revised in 1957 (New York: Friendship Press).

1951

An Outline of Descriptive Syntax (Glendale, Ca.: Summer Institute of Linguistics, 1951).

1952

God's Word in Man's Language (New York: Harper and Row, 1952a).
How the Word is Made Flesh: Communicating the Gospel to Aboriginal Peoples (= *Princeton Pamphlets* 7) (Princeton: Princeton Theological Seminary, 1952b).

1954

Customs and Cultures (New York: Harper and Row, 1954).

1959

Introducing Animism (with William A. Smalley) (New York: Friendship Press, 1959).

1960

Message and Mission (New York: Harper and Row, 1960).

1961

A Translator's Handbook on the Gospel of Mark (with Robert G. Bratcher) (Leiden: E. J. Brill, 1961).

1964

Toward a Science of Translating (Leiden: E. J. Brill, 1964).

1968

Religion Across Cultures (New York: Harper and Row, 1968).

1969

The Theory and Practice of Translation (with Charles R. Taber) (Leiden: E. J. Brill, 1969a).
Communication of the Gospel in Latin America (Cuernavaca, Mexico: Centro Intercultural de Documentación, 1969b).

1972

A Translator's Handbook on The Acts of the Apostles (with Barclay M. Newman) (London: United Bible Societies, 1972a).
Translators' Notes on Literacy Selections (Series A and Series B) (London: United Bible Societies, 1972b).

1973

A Translator's Handbook on Paul's Letter to the Romans (with Barclay M. Newman) (London: United Bible Societies, 1973a).

A Translator's Handbook on the Book of Ruth (with Jan de Waard) (London: United Bible Societies, 1973b).

In press

Componential Analysis of Meaning (The Hague: Mouton, i.p.a.).

Exploring Semantic Structures (München, Federal Republic of Germany: Wilhelm Fink Verlag, i.p.b.).

Articles (partial list)

1945

"Linguistics and Ethnology in Translation Problems", *Word* 1 (1945), 194-208.

1947

"Field Techniques in Descriptive Linguistics", *International Journal of American Linguistics* 13 (1947), 138-146.

1948

"The Analysis of Grammatical Constituents", *Language* 24 (1948a), 168-177.

"The Identification of Morphemes", *Language* 24 (1948b), 414-441.

1949

"Approaching Reading Through the Native Language", *Language Learning* 2 (1949), 16-20.

1950

"Translation or Paraphrase", *The Bible Translator* 1 (1950a), 97-109.

"The Pronominal Series in Maya (Yucatan)" (with C. Moisés Romero), *International Journal of American Linguistics* 16 (1950b), 195-197.

1951

"A System for the Description of Semantic Elements", *Word* 7 (1951a), 1-14.

"Problems of Revision", *The Bible Translator* 2 (1951b), 3-17.

1952

"A New Methodology in Biblical Exegesis", *The Bible Translator* 3 (1952), 97-110.

"Selective Listening", *Language Learning* 4:2-3 (1952-1953), 92-101.

1953

"What Is Phonemics?", *The Bible Translator* 4 (1953), 152-155.

1954

"Practical Limitations to a Phonemic Alphabet", *The Bible Translator* 5 (1954a), 35-39, 58-61.
"What Is a Primitive Language?", *The Bible Translator* 5 (1954b), 106-111.

1955

"Tribal and Trade Languages", *African Studies* 14 (1955), 155-158.

1957

"Language, Culture, and Theology", *Gordon Review* 3 (1957a), 151-167.
"Mariology in Latin America", *Practical Anthropology* 4 (1957b), 69-82.
"The Role of Language in Contemporary Africa", *Practical Anthropology* 4 (1957c), 122-137.
"The Roman Catholic, Communist, and Protestant Approach to Social Structure", *Practical Anthropology* 4 (1957d), 209-219.
"Motivation in Second Language Learning", *Language Learning* 7 (1957e), 11-16.

1958

"Analysis of Meaning and Dictionary Making", *International Journal of American Linguistics* 24 (1958a), 279-292.
"The Relationship of Social Structure to the Problems of Evangelism in Latin America", *Practical Anthropology* 5 (1958b), 101-123.
"Some Psychological Problems in Second Language Learning", *Language Learning* 8 (1958c), 7-15.

1959

"Drunkenness in Indigenous Religious Rites", *Practical Anthropology* 6 (1959a), 20-23.
"Principles of Translation as Exemplified by Bible Translating", in Reuben A. Brower (ed.), *On Translation* (Cambridge, Mass.: Harvard University Press, 1959b), 11-31.
"The Role of Cultural Anthropology in Christian Missions", *Practical Anthropology* 6 (1959c), 110-116.

1960

"Do Tribal Languages Have a Future?", *The Bible Translator* 11 (1960a), 116-123.

"Religion: Communication with the Supernatural", *Practical Anthropology* 7 (1960b), 97-112.

"Some Problems of Semantic Structure and Translational Equivalence", in Benjamin Elson (ed.), *A William Cameron Townsend en el XXV Aniversario del I. L. V.* (Mexico, D. F.: Instituto Linguistico de Verano, 1960c), 313-325.

1961

"Christo-Paganism", *Practical Anthropology* 8 (1961a), 1-15.

"Communication of the Gospel to Latin Americans", *Practical Anthropology* 8 (1961b), 145-156.

"Kerygma and Culture. Underlying Problems in the Communication of the Gospel in Spanish-Speaking Latin America", *Lutheran World* 8 (1961c), 269-280.

"Reina-Valera Spanish Revision of 1960", *The Bible Translator* 12 (1961d), 107-119.

1962

"Diglot Scriptures", *The Bible Translator* 13 (1962a), 1-16. "Opportunities in the Field of Bible Translating", *The Bible Translator* 13 (1962b), 193-200.

"Semantic Components", *Babel* 8 (1962c) 175-181.

1963

"Bible Translating and the Science of Linguistics", *Babel* 9 (1963a), 99-104.

"Linguistic and Semantic Structure", in Albert H. Marckwardt (ed.), *Study in Languages and Linguistics, Festschrift in Honor of Charles C. Fries* (Ann Arbor: English Language Institute, University of Michigan Press, 1963b), 13-33.

"Cultural Differences and the Communication of Christian Values" (with William L. Wonderly), *Practical Anthropology* 10 (1963c), 241-258.

"Linguistics and Christian Missions" (with William L. Wonderly), *Anthropological Linguistics* 5 (1963d).

1966

"African Influence in the Religious Life of Latin America", *Practical Anthropology* 13 (1966a), 133-138.

"Bible Translation in Today's World", *The Bible Translator* 17 (1966b), 59-64.

1967

"Linguistic Dimensions of Literacy and Literature", in Floyd Shacklock (ed.), *World Literacy Manual* (New York: Committee on World Literacy and Literature, 1967a), 142-161.

"Readjustment – An Even Greater Problem", *Practical Anthropology* 14 (1967b), 114-117.

1969

"Science of Translation", *Language* 45 (1969a), 483-498.

"Indigenous Pidgins and Koinés" (with Harold W. Fehderau), *International Journal of American Linguistics* 36 (1969b), 146-155.

1970

"New Religions for Old: A Study of Culture Change", *Practical Anthropology* 18 (1970a), 241-253.

"Formal Correspondence in Translation", *The Bible Translator* 21 (1970b), 105-113.

1971

"Communication Roles of Language in Multilingual Societies" (with William L. Wonderly), in W. H. Whiteley (ed.), *Language Use and Social Change*, published for the International African Institute (Oxford: University Press 1971a), 57-74.

"Language and Communication", in J. Robert Nelson (ed.), *No Man is Alien* (Leiden: E. J. Brill, 1971b), 183-202.

"Sociopsychological Problems in Language Mastery and Retention", in Paul Pimsleur and Terence Quinn (eds.), *The Psychology of Second Language Learning* (= *Papers from the Second International Congress of Applied Linguistics*) (Cambridge: University Press, 1971c), 59-65.

"Semantic Components in Translation Theory", in G. E. Perren and J. I. M. Trim (eds.), *Applications of Linguistics* (Cambridge: University Press, 1971d), 341-348.

"Why Translate the Bible Into 'New Languages'?", *The Bible Translator* 23 (1971e), 412-417.

"Implications of Contemporary Linguistics for Biblical Scholarship", *Journal of Biblical Literature* 91 (1971f), 73-89.

1972

"Varieties of Language", *The Bible Translator* 23 (1972a), 316-322.

"The Fifth Point of the Compass", *Practical Anthropology* 19 (1972b), 274-279.

"Semantic Structures" (with Charles R. Taber), in M. Estelle Smith (ed.), *Studies in Linguistics in Honor of George L. Trager* (The Hague: Mouton, 1972c), 122-141.

1973

"Translation", in Thomas A. Sebeok (ed.), *Linguistics and Adjacent Arts and Sciences* (= *Current Trends in Linguistics* 12) (The Hague: Mouton, 1973).

In the press

"Semantic Relations between Nuclear Structures", in Muhammed Ali Jazayery, Edgar C. Polome, and Verna Winter (eds.), *Linguistic and Literary Studies in Honor of Dr. A. A. Hill* (The Hague: Mouton, i. p.).

Part One

BIBLICAL STUDIES

DER DEUTSCHE PIETISMUS
ALS WEGBEREITER FÜR DIE ARBEIT DER
BIBELGESELLSCHAFTEN

KURT ALAND

Es ist sehr selten, daß man den Beginn einer großen kirchengeschicht-
lichen Bewegung sowohl in seinem Zeitpunkt wie in seinen Umständen
im einzelnen genau festlegen kann. Für den deutschen Pietismus ist
das möglich: er trat zur Frankfurter Buchmesse 1675 mit Philipp
Jacob Speners "Pia Desideria" ins Leben. Ursprünglich handelt es sich
dabei um das Vorwort zu einer Neuausgabe der Postille von Johann
Arnd. Diese Ausgabe war im Frühjahr 1675 erschienen. Aber die Nachfrage nach einem separaten Druck des Vorwortes war so groß, daß
Spener es, durch eine Vorrede erweitert, unter dem angegebenen Titel
im Herbst 1675 als selbständige Schrift erscheinen ließ, als "Herzliches
Verlangen nach gottgefälliger Besserung der wahren evangelischen Kirche",
wie der Untertitel lautet. Das Echo auf die Schrift war ungeheuer:
von allen Seiten gingen Spener Zustimmungserklärungen zu – auch
von späteren Gegnern – und was mehr bedeutet: alsbald sehen wir
überall in Deutschland Gemeinschaften entstehen, welche die program-
matischen Forderungen der "Pia Desideria" zu verwirklichen sich be-
mühen. Sehr bald wird Spener zum geistlichen Haupt des sich immer
weiter ausbreitenden Pietismus, wie die Bewegung zunächst spöttisch
von ihren Gegnern genannt wird, bis sie dann diese Bezeichnung als
Ehrentitel übernimmt, geht es ihr doch um die pietas, die Erweckung
und Verbreitung einer echten Frömmigkeit. Sehr bald wirkt dieser
Pietismus über die Grenzen Deutschlands hinaus, das ist insbesondere
das Verdienst August Hermann Franckes und des Grafen Nikolaus
Ludwig von Zinzendorf: in Rußland wie in Indien und Amerika wirken
alsbald die Sendboten des Pietismus. In Südindien gestaltet sich unter
seinem Einfluß die Kirche der Tamulen, in Nordamerika bedeutet das
Wirken Heinrich Melchior Mühlenbergs einen Neubeginn vor allem
für die Gemeinden in Pennsylvania und Georgia.

Gleich wo dieser Pietismus nun wirkt: in Deutschland, in Indien, in
Nordamerika, überall steht er in der Nachfolge des Programms, das

Spener 1675 in seinen Pia desideria aufgestellt hat. Das ließe sich unter
vielen Gesichtspunkten darlegen; wenn wir uns hier, unserem Thema
entsprechend, nur auf einen beschränken, so befinden wir uns dennoch
im Zentrum des Pietismus, denn die Wiederentdeckung der Bibel ist
eines seiner entscheidenden Charakteristika. Von den sechs Vorschlägen,
die Spener für die Besserung des beklagenswerten Zustandes der Kirche
macht, lautet gleich der erste: "Daß man dahin bedacht wäre, das Wort
Gottes reichlicher unter uns zu bringen."[1] "Je reichlicher das Wort unter
uns wohnen wird, je mehr werden wir den Glauben und dessen Früchte
zuwege bringen."[2] Zwar werde überall von den Kanzeln herab die
Schrift gelesen und ausgelegt. "Aber ich finde nicht", erklärt Spener,
"daß dies genug sei." Denn wenn man einmal alle Texte zusammen neh-
me, die auf diese Weise der Gemeinde im Laufe der Jahre vorgetragen
würden, ergäbe sich, daß ihr hier nur ein kleiner Ausschnitt aus der
Schrift bekannt werde. Das übrige höre die Gemeinde entweder gar
nicht oder doch nur in gelegentlichen Zitaten. Neben den Besuch des
Gottesdienstes gehöre deshalb für jedes Gemeindeglied die häusliche
Schriftlesung, insbesondere des Neuen Testaments. Täglich solle jeder
Hausvater darin lesen oder sich, wenn er des Lesens nicht genügend
kundig sei, wenigstens von anderen daraus vorlesen lassen. Wenn Spener
darüber hinaus fortlaufende Lektüre der Schrift vor versammelter
Gemeinde vorschlägt, entweder ganz ohne Auslegung oder nur mit
summarischer Zusammenfassung des Inhaltes des Gelesenen, so denkt
er vor allem an die, welchen das Lesen schwerfällt oder die selbst keine
eigene Bibel besitzen.[3] Zu diesen Gemeindeversammlungen sollen dann
andere kommen, in denen von den Teilnehmern die Schrift gemeinsam
ausgelegt wird. Diese Bibelstunden – darum handelt es sich praktisch –
sollen zwar von den Pastoren geleitet werden, tragen aber sollen sie die
Laien. Sie sollen hier mit ihren Anliegen zu Wort kommen, der Inhalt
der Schrift soll von ihnen gemeinsam, in Rede und Gegenrede, erarbeitet
werden.[4] Gottes Ehre und das geistliche Wachstum der Teilnehmer[5] sollen
das Ziel dieser Versammlungen sein. Wenn die Christen es lernten, in der
Schrift, im "Buch des Lebens ihre Freude zu suchen",[6] dann werde das
geistliche Leben bei ihnen wachsen und würden sie "zu ganz andern

[1] *Pia desideria*, S. 53.
[2] Ebd. S. 54.
[3] Ebd. S. 55.
[4] Ebd.
[5] Ebd. S. 56.
[6] Ebd. S. 57.
[7] Ebd.

Leuten."[7] Luther und die Reformation hätten es sich im Gegensatz zum Papsttum, welches die Menschen "von der Lesung der Heiligen Schrift abgehalten",[8] besonders angelegen sein lassen, die "Leute zu dem Wort Gottes wieder zu bringen, das fast unter der Bank versteckt gelegen."[9] Wenn die Kirche wieder in einen besseren Stand gebracht werden solle, als sie ihn gegenwärtig besitze, wenn sie das Anliegen der Reformation voll verwirklichen wolle, dann sei das vornehmste Mittel dazu, daß die Schrift wieder die Stellung erlange, die sie einst besessen, daß "herzlicher Eifer zu derselben erweckt werde".[10]

Das ist die programmatische Forderung Speners. Wie sie verwirklicht wurde, können wir am Leben und Wirken August Hermann Franckes verfolgen. "Das aber muß ein Student der Theologie zu seiner Hauptregel nehmen, daß er sich den griechischen und hebräischen Text, jenen im Neuen, diesen im Alten Testament, recht vertraut mache, sonst wird er in seinem Leben zu keiner rechten Solidität im theologischen Studium gelangen", so hat Francke vor seinen Studenten in Halle das Ziel und die Mitte der theologischen Ausbildung definiert.[11] Dementsprechend ist die Arbeit der Theologischen Fakultät in Halle, dem Zentrum des deutschen Pietismus schon vor und insbesondere nach dem Tode Speners, gestaltet. Hier steht die Bibel im Mittelpunkt des theologischen Unterrichts. Anderswo war die Ausbildung der Theologen beherrscht von Philosophie und Dogmatik, genauer gesagt von der Vermischung beider, welche die Praxis der lutherisch-orthodoxen Schultheologie jener Zeit kennzeichnet. Das kann nur wundernehmen, denn im Wittenberg der Reformationszeit war das anders gewesen. Hier hatte Luther die Scholastik vertrieben und an ihre Stelle die Schriftauslegung gesetzt. Die Wittenberger Professoren waren sämtlich Schriftausleger; Luther selbst hat nie eine andere Vorlesung als Auslegungen biblischer Bücher gehalten. In den 150 Jahren seit seinem Tode hatte sich das geändert. Jetzt beherrschte eine neue Scholastik das Feld, wenn

---

[8] Ebd. S. 58.
[9] Ebd.
[10] Ebd.
[11] August Hermann Franckens/ Weil S. Theol. Prof. Past. Vlric. & Schol./ LECTIONES PARAE-/NETICAE,/ Oder/ Oeffentliche/Ansprachen/ An die/ Studiosos Theologiae/ auf der Universität zu Halle/ In dem so genannten/ COLLEGIO PARAENETICO,/ In welchem dieselben,/ Nach Abhandlung verschiedener nöthigen und/ nützlichen Materien, zu einer wahren Bekehrung, zu/ einem exemplarischen Wandel, und zu ordentlichen/ und weislichen Art zu studiren, erwecket/ und aufgemuntert sind/ Der IV. Theil./ Nach des sel. Mannes Tode mit einer/Vorrede/ heraus gegeben/ von/ Gotthilf August Francken/ S./ Theol. Prof. Ord. Insp. im Saalcräise,/ und Pred. zur L. Frauen./ HALLE, im Wäysen-Hause, MDCCXXXI, S. 157.

auch unter dem Vorzeichen der lutherischen Theologie. Was sich unter Francke in Halle endgültig durchsetzt, ist den Vorgängen im Wittenberg der Reformation, zumindest äußerlich gesehen, erstaunlich verwandt. Beide Male geht der Kampf gegen ein erstarrtes Lehrsystem, beide Male steht er unter dem Vorzeichen der Schrift. Schlagartig wendet sich beide Male die Teilnahme der Studenten dem Neuen zu: wer nicht Auslegung der Schrift bietet, kann auf keine Hörer rechnen. Die jungen Theologen erkennt man im Wittenberg der Reformationszeit wie im Leipzig zur Zeit der Auseinandersetzung um den Pietismus und in Halle daran, daß sie das Neue Testament, wenn nicht die ganze Bibel bei sich führen. Sie wird mit solchem Eifer studiert, als ob sie gerade eben erst entdeckt sei – eine theologische Auseinandersetzung, gleich über welchen Gegenstand, ist damals wie im Zeitalter des Pietismus nur unter ständigem Aufschlagen der Schrift möglich. Im Mittelpunkt der Vorlesungen stehen an der Theologischen Fakultät Halle solche zur Auslegung der Schrift. Dabei werden die biblischen Bücher jeweils vollständig behandelt. Vorlesungen, die nur ausgewählte Bibelstellen zugrunde legen, um aus ihnen das dogmatische System abzuleiten oder sie als Material zur Lösung strittiger kirchlicher oder dogmatischer Fragen zu verwenden, sind nicht gestattet. Aus dem Ganzen der biblischen Bücher muß sich alles andere ergeben. Bereits im ersten Universitätsjahr wird vom Theologiestudenten erwartet, daß er das Alte Testament einmal und das Neue Testament zweimal gelesen hat, und zwar im hebräischen bzw. griechischen Urtext.[12] So erwirbt sich der Student von Anfang an eine Bibelkenntnis, die ihm die Grundlage nicht nur für sein Studium, sondern auch für seine ganze kirchliche Wirksamkeit gibt.

Aus diesen Voraussetzungen ist die Arbeit der Cansteinschen Bibelanstalt erwachsen, die Francke im Bunde mit dem Freiherrn Hildebrand von Canstein im Jahre 1710 begründet, fast 100 Jahre, bevor im Anfang des 19. Jahrhunderts zunächst in England und dann in rascher Folge überall in der Welt die modernen Bibelgesellschaften ins Leben treten. Die Entstehungsgeschichte der Cansteinschen Bibelgesellschaft (die heute noch existiert, nach 1945 hat sie ihren Sitz erst nach Ost-Berlin und dann nach Witten/Westfalen verlegt) in kurzen Zügen darzustellen, ist unsere erste Aufgabe. Schon als Pfarrer in Erfurt hat Francke sich die Verbreitung der Schrift angelegen sein lassen. Er fand nach einem zeitgenössischen Bericht[13] hier eine lebhafte Nachfrage nach Bibeln

---

[12] Vgl. dazu Franckens Stiftungen II, S. 178ff.
[13] Das Folgende nach Callenbergs Neuester Kirchenhistorie seit 1689, Archiv der Franckeschen Stiftungen Halle F 30b Bl. 17-19; vgl. G. Kramer, *Beiträge* S. 91ff.

und Neuen Testamenten vor. 200 Stück bestellte Francke daraufhin in Lüneburg; in wenigen Tagen waren sie vergriffen, denn Francke hatte billige Ausgaben zu beschaffen gewußt. Weitere 200 Stück wurden bestellt, "von welchen auch in kurzer Zeit kein einziges übrig blieb". Auch noch weitere 500 Stück "gingen reißend ab". In einer "damaligen Schrift"[14], sagt unsere Quelle, habe Francke das berichtet und hinzugefügt,

gewißlich würden hohe Personen ein sehr nützliches Werk stiften, wenn sie etwa einem Verleger die Unkosten dazu herschießen wollten, daß die armen Leute, ohne dem Verkäufer einen Profit zu geben, zu der ganzen Bibel kommen könnten; welches gewißlich wohl um 10 oder 12 gr. [oschen] geschehen könnte; daß demnach derjenige, welcher solche Unkosten hergeschossen, ohne allen Schaden und Verlust bliebe, und sein Geld wieder kriegte.[15]

In Halle hatte sich Franckes Erfahrung wiederholt: wenn die Gemeinde nur Zugang zu einer Ausgabe des Neuen Testamentes oder der ganzen Bibel bekam, deren Preis einigermaßen ihren finanziellen Möglichkeiten entsprach, war die Nachfrage danach sogleich außerordentlich. So bringt man hier alsbald die Bibel oder wenigstens das Neue Testament zum Gottesdienst mit und schlägt die in der Predigt angeführten Schriftworte nach.[16] Auch zum Katechismusunterricht erscheinen die Kinder mit Bibel oder Neuem Testament,[17] wie es Francke bald nach seinem Amtsantritt seiner Glauchaer Gemeinde empfohlen hatte.[18] In jedem Haus solle eine Bibel vorhanden sein, oder wenigstens ein Neues Testament, wenn das Geld nicht zur Beschaffung einer Vollbibel reiche; diese Forderung Franckes bedeutete ein Programm, das sich selbstverständlich nicht auf Glaucha beschränkte, sondern für alle Gemeinden galt. Es war aber mit den bisherigen Mitteln nicht zu verwirklichen. Denn wenn man die Bibel und das Neue Testament zum Besitz aller machen wollte, mußte eingreifend Neues geschehen.

---

14 Die hier gemeinte Schrift Franckes war bisher nicht feststellbar; handelt es sich um eine Vorstufe seines "Großen Aufsatzes"?
15 Callenberg, a.a.O., Bl. 18v-19r; vgl. G. Kramer, *Beiträge* S. 92.
16 Visitationsbericht von 1700, Archiv der Franckeschen Stiftungen D 66, Bl. 409f; vgl. G. Kramer II, S. 353.
17 Visitationsbericht, a.a.O., Bl. 414v ff; vgl. G. Kramer II, S. 355.
18 Glauchisches/Gedenck-Büchlein/Oder/Einfältiger Unterricht/Für die Christliche Gemeinde/ zu/ Glaucha an Halle,/Die Heiligung der Sonn-Fest-/Apostel-Buß- und Bet-Tage,/ Wie auch/ Die Fasten-Zeit, die Wiederholung der/ Predigten, Catechisation, Wochen-Pre-/digten, Bet-Stunden, und insgemein die/Handlung des Göttlichen Worts/ betreffend, /Von/ M. August Hermann Francken,/ Graec. & Orient. Lingg. P.P. Halens./& Past. Glauch./LEIPZIG und HALLE, M DC XCIII., S. 176.

Francke veröffentlicht 1702 und 1708[19] deshalb Vollbibeln und 1704 ein Neues Testament[20] im eigenen Verlag. Aber er muß einsehen, daß eine Massenverbreitung auf dieser Grundlage nicht möglich ist. Denn auch wenn man auf Gewinn verzichtete, blieben die Herstellungskosten und damit die Preise für die Bibelausgaben doch einfach zu hoch. Wie weit Franckes Pläne der Bibelverbreitung damals bereits gehen, ersieht man daraus, daß er 1709 das Neue Testament in böhmischer Sprache und 1710 das Neue Testament in Neugriechisch[21] publiziert. Angesichts dieser bis in die Ökumene vorstoßenden Pläne nimmt es nicht wunder, daß Francke schon früh nach Mitteln und Wegen sinnt, um die Bibelverbreitung, d. h. praktisch die Bibelherstellung, auf eine neue Grundlage zu stellen.

Das geschieht dann unter dem Datum des 1. März 1710 mit dem "Ohnmaßgeblichen Vorschlag, wie Gottes Wort den Armen zur Erbauung um einen geringen Preis in die Hände zu bringen."[22] Nach einem Rückblick auf die bisherigen Mühen und Erfolge bei der Verbreitung der Bibel heißt es hier, daß nach dem Vorbild einer in Holland erschienenen englischen Bibel der Druck künftig vom "stehenden Satz" erfolgen solle. Wenn das geschehen könne, würden die Kosten des Drucks und damit der Herstellung der Bibel entscheidend gesenkt und damit neue Voraussetzungen für ihre Verbreitung geschaffen. Bedingung dafür sei genügend Kapital zur Beschaffung von so vielen Bleilettern, daß die ganze Bibel auf einmal abgesetzt werden könne – bisher wurde sie in Halle nach keinem anderen Verfahren gedruckt als anderswo auch: der erste Bogen wurde gesetzt und ausgedruckt, dann wurde der Satz aufgelöst, mit dem so zurückgewonnenen Typenmaterial der zweite Bogen gesetzt und ausgedruckt usw.

Hier ist das Prinzip vorweggenommen, nach dem die Bibelgesell-

---

[19] Biblia, das ist, die gantze H. Schrift A.u.N.T. nach der teutschen Übersetzung D. Martin Luthers, mit jedes Capitels kurzen summarien, concordanzien und Joh. Arnd's Informatorio biblico, benebens A. H. Franckens Unterricht, wie mann die H. Schrift zu seiner Erbauung lesen soll. 12⁰. 1702, vgl. A. Schürmann, *Zur Geschichte der Buchhandlung des Waisenhauses und der Cansteinschen Bibelanstalt* (Halle 1898), S. 29f; die Ausgabe von 1708 konnte schon von Schürmann nicht mehr aufgefunden werden, vgl. S. 30f, s. auch Wirtschaftsarchiv der Franckeschen Stiftungen IX/III Nr. 5: Generalia der Buchhandlung Bd. I.

[20] vgl. Schürmann, a.a.O., S. 31.

[21] vgl. die Annales Hallenses ecclesiastici zum Jahre 1710: K. Aland, *Kirchengeschichtliche Entwürfe* (Gütersloh 1960), S. 629. Desgl. D. Cyzevskyj, S. 44ff.

[22] Faksimile-Wiedergabe in: *Die bleibende Bedeutung des Pietismus* (Witten 1960), S. 109-116, hier S. 24-59 auch mein Aufsatz: Der Hallesche Pietismus und die Bibel, auf den ich wegen der ausführlicheren Behandlung des hier zusammengefaßt Vorgetragenen verweisen möchte.

schaften des 19. und 20. Jahrhunderts gearbeitet haben. Nur mit Mühe konnte es in Halle verwirklicht werden: erst 1713 hatte man so viel Geld zusammen, daß das Neue Testament in stehendem Satz zur Verfügung war, 1714 kam der Psalter hinzu, 1717 war es dann soweit, daß Typen für den gesamten Text der Bibel zur Verfügung standen, so daß man sie zu einem auch für Minderbemittelte tragbaren Preis verbreiten konnte. Für den großen Erfolg war allerdings nicht nur der niedrige Preis der Bibeln und der Neuen Testamente verantwortlich, welche die Cansteinsche Bibelanstalt von Halle aus verbreitete, sondern neben der Qualität des Druckes auch – und vor allem – die des Textes. Unter Heranziehung und Vergleichung zahlreicher früherer Ausgaben hatte man sehr viel Mühe aufgewandt, um einen einwandfreien Luthertext zu bieten.[23] Der Lohn dafür blieb nicht aus. Noch zu Lebzeiten Cansteins, d. h. von 1712-1719, hat die Hallesche Bibelanstalt 80 000 Bibeln und 100 000 Neue Testamente verbreitet. Bis zum Jahre 1812, also in den ersten hundert Jahren der Arbeit der Cansteinschen Bibelanstalt, beträgt die Zahl der von ihr gedruckten Vollbibeln fast genau zwei Millionen Stück in über 380 Auflagen, die des Neuen Testaments (zusammen mit dem Psalter) über eine Million, wozu noch rund 100 000 Einzeldrucke des Psalters und des Buches Jesus Sirach kommen.

Diese Zahlen sind ganz außerordentlich. Man hat geschätzt[24], daß die Gesamtzahl sämtlicher in Wittenberg, dem Zentrum des Bibeldruckes

[23] "Diese alten Editionen/ welche man also conferirete/ waren folgende: Die zu Wittenberg gedruckte durch Hans Luft 1534. Eben daselbst 1535. Eben daselbst 1541. Leipzig durch Nic. Wollrab 1543. Wittenberg durch Hans Luft 1545. Unter welchen die drey ersten auß der Königl. Bibliothec zu Berlin zu diesem Zweck allergnädigst communicirt wurden. Diese 5. Bibeln wurden nebst der Stadischen von Anfang bis zu Ende durch gelesen/ die lectiones variantes alle in ein dazu verfertigtes Buch eingetragen/ und nachhero auß denselben diejenigen/ welche dem Grund-Text am nächsten zu seyn schienen/ an statt der in den nach Lutheri Tode gedruckten Bibeln angenommen/ restituiret. Ausser diesen Editionen hat man auch einige Oerter auß den ersten Editionen des Neuen Testaments / so Anno 1522. zu Wittenberg/ Anno 1523. zu Basel/ Anno 1530. zu Erfurth heraußgekommen/ wieder eingeführet. Welche denn alle solche Editionen sind/ die noch bei Lebzeiten des sel. D. Luthers ans Licht gegeben worden. Eine einige Stelle ist davon außzunehmen/ die man nach einer Bibel/ so zu Wittenberg 1564. gedruckt ist/ geändert hat": Umständliche Nachricht/ Von dem/ Neuen Testament/ und Bibeln/ Welche/ Nach einem den 1. Martii 1710 publicirten ohnmaaßgebenden Vorschlage:/ Wie GOttes Wort um einen sehr wohlfeilen/ Preis den Armen in die Hände gebracht/ werden könte;/ Zu Glaucha vor Halle in Sachsen bisher ediret worden/ und/ noch ferner ediret werden sollen:/ Von Anfang des Wercks bis zu Ende des/Monaths Octobris 1714/ ertheilet/ von/ Carl Hildebrand von Canstein, § 8, Faksimile-Wiedergabe in: *Die bleibende Bedeutung des Pietismus* (Witten 1960), S. 121; vgl. dazu die Briefe Cansteins.
[24] Vgl. H. Volz, S. 7 u.ö. Es handelt sich um ca. 100 Auflagen, die Auflage durchschnittlich zu 2000 Exemplaren.

in der Reformationszeit und der lutherischen Orthodoxie, in der Zeit von 1534-1626 erschienenen Vollbibeln ca. 200 000 Stück beträgt. Im selben Zeitraum eines Jahrhunderts hat man in Halle also das Zehnfache gedruckt, und das, obwohl neben Halle andere wohlrenommierte Bibeldruckverlage – etwa derjenige der Gebrüder Stern in Lüneburg – mit großem Erfolg arbeiteten. Dazu kommt, daß die deutsche Bibel in der Reformationszeit – buchhändlerisch gesprochen – praktisch eine absolute Novität war, während sie beim Beginn der Arbeit in Halle schon seit rund 200 Jahren in zahllosen Ausgaben verbreitet war. Natürlich kann man einwenden, daß in der Reformationszeit weite Kreise des Lesens unkundig oder nicht genügend darin geübt waren und daß außerdem der sehr hohe Preis der Verbreitung der Drucke von vornherein eine Grenze setzte. Aber trotzdem bleibt die Zahl der Drucke Halles – 80 000 Bibeln und 100 000 Neue Testamente in sieben Jahren, zwei Millionen Bibeln und über eine Million Neue Testamente in hundert Jahren – so bedeutsam, daß man die Leistung der Cansteinschen Bibelanstalt gleichberechtigt neben die anderen Großtaten des Halleschen Pietismus stellen muß.

Auch mit den Leistungen der zur Zeit des 100jährigen Bestehens der Cansteinschen Bibelanstalt neu entstehenden Bibelgesellschaften lassen sich diese Zahlen durchaus vergleichen. Die größte unter den heutigen deutschen Bibelgesellschaften, die Württembergische Bibelgesellschaft, hat z. B. im ersten Jahrhundert nach ihrer Gründung, in der Zeit von 1812-1912, rund drei Millionen Vollbibeln verbreitet (wobei der nominelle Zuwachs gegenüber den Zahlen der Cansteinschen Bibelanstalt im 18. Jahrhundert mehr als ausgeglichen wird durch die im 19. Jahrhundert weitaus größere Zahl der des Lesens Kundigen). Trotz dieser "Konkurrenz" blieb die Cansteinsche Bibelanstalt weiter außerordentlich erfolgreich. Von 1812-1837, also im ersten Viertel des zweiten Jahrhunderts ihrer Geschichte, hat sie rund 400 000 Exemplare der Vollbibel in 146 Auflagen und rund 100 000 Exemplare des Neuen Testaments in 31 Auflagen hergestellt und verbreitet. Erst später ging ihre Leistungskraft zurück, so daß sie von den anderen deutschen Bibelgesellschaften, insbesondere der Württembergischen Bibelgesellschaft und der Preußischen Hauptbibelgesellschaft, überflügelt wurde.

Mit aller Sorgfalt hat sich der Pietismus bemüht, den originalen Text der Bibelübersetzung Luthers festzustellen und zu reproduzieren. Das war legitim, denn diese Übersetzung wurde damals noch voll verstanden und bereitete auch dem einfachen Menschen keine Schwierigkeiten; jedenfalls hören wir in der Literatur keine Klagen darüber, daß das

Lutherdeutsch der Gemeinde nicht verständlich sei. Dennoch haben führende Vertreter des Pietismus eine Revision der Lutherübersetzung gefordert, A. H. Francke wie auch J. A. Bengel. Der Pietismus hat darüber hinaus eine größere Zahl von Neuübersetzungen der Bibel zustande gebracht. Man kann sogar sagen: mit dem 18. Jahrhundert beginnt eine neue Epoche des deutschen Bibeltexts. Gewiß hat es auch im 16. und 17. Jahrhundert im nichtkatholischen Raum Versuche gegeben, Luthers Übersetzung durch eine andere zu ersetzen. Die Reformierten spielten von Anfang an eine Sonderrolle, sie besaßen in der immer weiter entwickelten Zürcher Bibel eine eigene Übersetzung, zu der 1602 die vierbändige Übersetzung J. Piscators hinzukam (Herborn 1602-1604). Die Socinianer hatten sich ebenfalls in der Übersetzung J. Crells/ J. Stegmanns (Rackau 1630) und Jer. Felbingers (Amsterdam 1660) eine eigene Übersetzung wenigstens des Neuen Testaments zu schaffen versucht. Aber sonst existierten nur noch die Übersetzungen von J. Adam Lonicerus (Frankfurt 1590), Am. Polanus von Polansdorff (Basel 1603) und J. Saubert d. J. (Lüneburg 1666). Das ist für einen Zeitraum von über 150 Jahren seit dem Tode Luthers wahrlich nicht viel. Mit dem Beginn des 18. Jahrhunderts ändert sich die Lage beinahe schlagartig. Im Jahre 1703 werden gleich zwei neue Übersetzungen des Neuen Testaments veröffentlicht, die von J. H. Reitz (Offenbach 1703) und die von C. E. Triller (Amsterdam 1703), von denen die von Reitz bis 1738 fünf Auflagen erlebte. 1704 erschien Hedingers Neues Testament. Zwar hieß es auf dem Titelblatt nur, es sei "nach der Übersetzung des seligen Herrn D. Martin Luther ... nach den besten Exemplaren von vielen eingeschlichenen Fehlern sorgfältig korrigiert und gebessert", aber Hedingers Revision – darum handelte es sich tatsächlich – erregte doch erheblichen Anstoß und gab Anlaß zu einer lebhaften Debatte.[25] 1726 begann die Berleburger Bibel zu erscheinen, die, in regelmäßigen Abständen fortgesetzt, 1742 mit ihrem 8. Band vollständig vorlag. Die sog. Wertheimsche Bibel von J. Lorenz Schmidt kommt zwar über den 1. Band mit dem 1. Buch Mose, der 1735 erscheint, nicht hinaus. Aber zur gleichen Zeit publiziert Timotheus Philadelphus, d.h. J. Kayser, Arzt in Stuttgart, sein "Neues Testament nach dem Sinn des Grundtextes" (1733-1736, 1735 Sonderausgabe des Joh.-Evangeliums, 1739 der Offenbarung). Schon vorher hatte Zinzendorf die Ebersdorfer Ausgabe seines Neuen Testaments (1727) vorgelegt, der 1739 die Büdinger folgte. 1732 hatte J.J. Junckherrot seine Übersetzung veröffentlicht,

---

25 Zu den Einzelheiten vgl. Chr. Kolb S. 67ff.

1748 folgt Ch. A. Heumann (Hannover 1748, 2 Bde, 2. Aufl. 1750). Das sind im ganzen 10 neue Übersetzungen in weniger als 50 Jahren.

Das ist ein bemerkenswertes Faktum, muß man doch bedenken, daß Luthers Bibelübersetzung auch in der Kirche des beginnenden 18. Jahrhunderts noch eine beinahe sakrosankte Stellung besaß. An ihr zweifeln oder sie gar durch eine andere Übersetzung ersetzen, hieß für die lutherischen Theologen und weite Teile der Gemeinde an den Grundlagen des Luthertums, d. h. der wahren Lehre, rütteln und den Bestand der Kirche gefährden. Die Lehre von der Verbalinspiration war in ganz Europa noch unerschüttert, bei den Lutheranern wie bei den Reformierten. Zwar bezog sie sich auf den Urtext der Bibel, den griechischen des Neuen und den hebräischen Text des Alten Testaments, aber faktisch wurde sie im Bereich des Luthertums weithin auch auf Luthers Übersetzung ausgedehnt. Umso bedeutsamer sind die Neuübersetzungen der Bibel durch den Pietismus wie seine Forderung nach einer Revision der Lutherübersetzung, soweit sie den Urtext nicht richtig oder mißverständlich wiedergebe. Diese Revisionsforderung ist gleich doppelt erhoben worden, von August Hermann Francke als dem Wortführer des Halleschen Pietismus und von Johann Albrecht Bengel als prominentem Vertreter des Württembergischen Pietismus. Man muß dieses Faktum nur einmal mit den Schwierigkeiten vergleichen, auf welche die Revision der Lutherübersetzung noch im 20. Jahrhundert gestoßen ist, obwohl hier der Anstoß Franckes und Bengels an der Wiedergabe der griechischen Vorlage in ungleich verstärktem Maße galt. Denn jetzt war der Textus receptus, den Luther zugrundegelegt hatte, endgültig entthront und damit eine neue Textgrundlage gegeben. Außerdem war Luthers Übersetzung der Gemeinde, für die Luther doch seine Übersetzungsarbeit getan hatte, jetzt in vielen Einzelheiten nicht mehr verständlich, weil die deutsche Sprache sich wesentlich weiterentwickelt hatte. Als 1936 das sog. "Probetestament" erschien, d. h. eine von prominenten Vertretern der neutestamentlichen Wissenschaft und des kirchlichen Lebens erarbeitete Revision des Neuen Testaments, stieß sie bereits auf erhebliche Kritik in der Öffentlichkeit. Hier handelte es sich, wie der Name schon besagt, um eine einstweilige Lösung. Als man nach dem 2. Weltkrieg dann daran ging, die Lutherübersetzung der ganzen Bibel den Bedürfnissen der Gegenwart anzupassen, kam es schon innerhalb der dafür eingesetzten Kommission zu schweren Auseinandersetzungen darüber, wie weit diese Anpassung gehen könne. In der neutestamentlichen Kommission gerieten die Vertreter der Wissenschaft und die einer konservativen Haltung, welche den Text Luthers so erhalten wollte, wie er nun einmal war, in einen immer schärferen Gegensatz zueinander, bis diese Kommission schließlich auseinanderfiel. Nur der Autorität von Bischof Otto Dibelius war es möglich, eine neu berufene zweite Kommission, in der er persönlich den Vorsitz übernahm, bis zum Ende der Arbeit zusammenzuhalten und deren Resultat zur offiziellen Annahme bei den Kirchenleitungen zu verhelfen. Diese Revision der Luther-Übersetzung des Neuen Testaments von 1956 konnte verständlicherweise nur von einem Minimalprogramm ausgehen, um nicht die vorangegangenen Auseinandersetzungen zu erneuern. Dementsprechend war das Resultat. Heute versucht eine vom Rat der Evangelischen Kirche in Deutschland neu eingesetzte Kommission das damals Versäumte nachzuholen: Zugrundelegung des von der modernen Wissenschaft erarbeiteten griechischen Textes des Neuen Testaments mit den Folgerungen, die sich daraus ergeben, und Anpassung der Übersetzung Luthers an die Voraussetzungen und das Sprachverständnis der Gegenwart. Bis 1975 hofft die Kommission ihre Arbeit abschließen zu können; welche Aufnahme diese bei den offiziellen kirchlichen Gremien wie in den Gemeinden finden wird, bleibt abzuwarten. Möchte sie auf der Linie der Aufnahme liegen, welche die 1964 erschienene Revision des Alten Testamentes fand, die in ihrer Anpassung der Lutherübersetzung an den Urtext wie an das moderne Verständnis sehr viel weiter ging, als das 1956 in bezug auf das Neue Testament geschah.

Der Widerstand gegen eine Anpassung der Lutherübersetzung an den modernen Erkenntnisstand kommt eben nicht nur aus den Kreisen des konservativen Luthertums in Deutschland, sondern ebenso aus denen des heutigen Pietismus, der vielfach von einem grundsätzlichen Mißtrauen gegen die wissenschaftliche Theologie erfüllt ist. "Die Evangelikalen" in Deutschland – einmal pauschal gesagt – fürchten, "die Theologen" – ebenso pauschal ausgedrückt – würden die Botschaft des Evangeliums entweder verwässern oder gar verfälschen, von daher ihr Widerstand gegen die Änderung des überkommenen deutschen Textes des Neuen Testaments. Die Väter des Pietismus haben ganz anders gedacht und gehandelt. Im Jahre 1712 – also zu der Zeit, als die von ihm ins Leben gerufene Cansteinsche Bibelanstalt sich bemühte, ihre Ausgaben so sorgfältig wie möglich dem Text Luthers anzugleichen – hat August Hermann Francke sein "Kurtzes Proiect unparteyischer privat-Gedancken von einer Emendation der Teutschen Bibel" verfaßt.[26]

---

[26] Veröffentlicht von A. Nebe, *Neue Quellen* S. 26ff; zu den Einzelheiten hier wie in allem folgenden vgl. K. Aland, "Bibel und Bibeltext bei August Hermann Francke und Johann Albrecht Bengel" in: *Pietismus und Bibel*, S. 89-147.

Hier wird festgestellt, daß auch Luthers Übersetzung trotz allerhöchster Anerkennung, die man ihr schulde, nicht von der Überprüfung ausgenommen werden könne,

ob sie mit den Grundsprachen nach deren eigentlichem Inhalt durchgehend übereinstimme und ob sie in sich selbst so deutlich sei, daß sie diejenigen, welche die Grundsprachen nicht verstehen, zu dem notwendigen Nutzen dienen könne.

Denn wenn die Übersetzungen "für Gottes Wort selbst gehalten werden sollen", müßten sie mit dem Urtext aufs Genaueste übereinstimmen. Es liege jedoch am Tage, daß in Luthers Übersetzung

noch hin und wieder viele unrichtige und undeutliche Übersetzungen gefunden werden, welche zum Teil in ganzen Sätzen und zum Teil in einzelnen Worten bestehen.[27]

Wer die Grundsprachen ausreichend verstehe und die Muttersprache recht zu gebrauchen wisse, dem würde eine solche Revision der Übersetzung Luthers möglich sein, die übrigens Luthers Absichten durchaus entspreche.[28]

Ausführlich setzt Francke sich mit allen Einwänden dagegen auseinander und hält ihnen gegenüber seine Forderung aufrecht:

Nur die Ursprachen müssen notwendigerweise bleiben, wie sie sind, weil in ihnen Gottes Wort originaliter enthalten ist. Von einer Übersetzung aber, welche hin und wieder mit den Ursprachen und mit der Reinheit ihrer eigenen Sprache nicht übereinstimmt, kann niemand eine Notwendigkeit behaupten, daß man sie stehen und bleiben lassen müsse, wie sie ist.[29]

Diese Forderung ist umso höher zu bewerten, als Francke im Jahre 1695 bereits einmal einen Vorstoß zur Revision der Luther-Übersetzung gemacht hatte und dabei auf den heftigsten Widerstand gestoßen war. In seinen "Observationes biblicae"[30] hatte er in monatlichen Fortsetzungen jeweils "Anmerkungen über einige Orte der hl. Schrift" vorgetragen,

[27] S. 3f, Nebe S. 27.
[28] S. 7, Nebe S. 31.
[29] S. 10, Nebe S. 34.
[30] OBSERVATIO-/ NES BIBLICAE,/ Anmerckungen über eini-/ge/ Oerter H. Schrifft/ Darinnen die Teutsche Ubersetzung/ des Sel. Lutheri gegen den Original/ Text gehalten und bescheidentlich/ gezeiget wird/ Wo man dem eigentlichen Wort-/ Verstande näher kommen könne/ Solches auch/ Zur Erbauung in der Christl. Lehre/ angewendet/ und im Gebet appliciret/ wird/ ausgefertiget im/ JANUARIO/ (FEBRUARIO usw.) 1695.

darinnen die deutsche Übersetzung des sel. Luther mit dem Originaltext verglichen und bescheidentlich gezeigt wird, wo man dem eigentlichen Wortverständnis näher kommen könne.[31]

33 Stellen des Neuen Testaments hatte Francke hier in den ersten vier Heften (Januar bis April) vorgeführt, an denen Luthers Übersetzung revisionsbedürftig sei – vom fünften Heft ab kann er darin nicht mehr fortfahren, sondern muß sich erst einmal gegen die von allen Seiten kommenden Angriffe zur Wehr setzen. Bei dieser Verteidigung des Unternehmens ist es dann geblieben, bis die "Observationes biblicae" mit dem Septemberheft 1695 ihr Erscheinen einstellen.

Von allen Seiten waren die Angriffe gekommen. Johann Friedrich Mayer, damals Hauptpastor in Hamburg und später Generalsuperintendent, hatte bereits auf das erste Heft der Observationes hin eine Gegenschrift erscheinen lassen, in welcher er Franckes Unternehmen als Satanswerk bezeichnete, das den Untergang des evangelischen Glaubens in Deutschland heraufführen würde. Von den Kanzeln herab griffen die Pastoren in Halle Franckes Arbeit aufs heftigste an, sie beabsichtigten, ihn deswegen beim Konsistorium zu verklagen, überall rüsteten die Gelehrten sich zum Angriff gegen ihn, weiß Francke in seinen Briefen an Spener aus dieser Zeit zu berichten. Spener selbst ist wenig glücklich über Franckes Unternehmen, er schreibt Francke, daß er einen Brief von einem berühmten Theologen erhalten habe, in dem es heiße, daß fromme und gelehrte Männer beinahe in Tränen aufgelöst gewesen seien, als sie davon hörten, daß Francke Luthers Bibelübersetzung angegriffen habe. Aber das alles vermag Francke nicht von seinem Standpunkt abzubringen. Noch im letzten Heft seiner "Observationes" beruft er sich auf Luther selbst und dessen Mitarbeiter an der Bibelübersetzung. Sie hätten alle wissenschaftlichen Hilfsmittel dabei gebraucht und immer von neuem sich bemüht, möglichst klar und deutlich in deutscher Sprache das zum Ausdruck zu bringen, was der Urtext sage. So könne man nicht behaupten, daß eine Revision der Übersetzung Luthers diesen und die anderen Reformatoren betrüben müßte:

Ich meine vielmehr, daß sie sich über die Faulheit ihrer deutschen Landsleute beklagen würden, wenn sie jetzt auferstehen sollten, daß diese ihnen nicht mutiger nachgefolgt seien, obwohl sie ihnen so mutig das Eis gebrochen hätten. Sie würden sich aufs neue gern mit Lust und Freude an die Arbeit machen und uns eine weit herrlichere und vollkommenere Übersetzung der Heiligen Schrift in die Hände geben, weil sie sich nun so vieler Hilfsmittel dafür bedienen könnten, welche sie damals zu ihrer Zeit nicht gehabt hätten.

---

[31] Vgl. Anm. 30

Weil wir nun aber nicht darauf warten können, bis sie von den Toten auferstehen, so obliegt es nun uns, die wir jetzt leben, denen Gott Gnade und Kraft dazu gibt und uns vornehmlich durch unseren äusseren Beruf den Weg dazu bahnt, daß wir keinen Fleiß sparen, den Brief Gottes an die Menschen, nämlich die heilige Schrift, immer heller und klarer darzulegen.[32]

Das ist vor rund 180 Jahren geschrieben und gilt bis auf den heutigen Tag, ja hat seitdem an Gewicht nur noch gewonnen. Francke ist ja auch nicht die einzige der großen Gestalten des Pietismus, die eine solche Forderung erhoben hat. Johann Albrecht Bengel, der Klosterpräzeptor von Denkendorf und einer der bis auf den heutigen Tag fortwirkenden Väter des schwäbischen Pietismus, hat genau die gleiche Haltung wie Francke eingenommen: "Eine Übersetzung muß sich auf einen genau revidierten Urtext gründen" – "Eine deutsche Übersetzung soll ein deutscher Leser verstehen können", das sind die Prinzipien eins und fünf in den grundsätzlichen Darlegungen, die Bengel seiner Übersetzung des Neuen Testaments von 1753 vorausschickt:[33]

Das Neue Testament, zum Wachstum in der Gnade und der Erkenntnis des Herrn Jesu Christi nach dem revidierten Grundtext übersetzt und mit dienlichen Anmerkungen begleitet.

Mit dieser Übersetzung ist Bengel sogar noch über Francke hinausgegangen, denn sie stellt keine Revision des Luthertextes dar, sondern eine zu ihrer Ergänzung bestimmte Neuübersetzung, welche "nicht so (glatt) fließt, aber den echten griechischen Grundtext sorgfältiger ausdrückt".[34]

Möglichst weite Verbreitung der Bibel, deswegen Herstellung zu möglichst niedrigem Preis, Bibelmission, Druck einwandfreier Übersetzungen, Anpassung dieser Übersetzungen an das moderne Verständnis durch Revision, notfalls durch Erstellung neuer Übersetzungen – alle diese Aufgaben einer modernen Bibelgesellschaft finden wir bei den pietistischen Vätern des 17./18. Jahrhunderts bereits, und zwar auf erstaunliche Weise, verwirklicht, man denke z. B. an die große Reichweite der Cansteinschen Bibelanstalt und deren Anwendung modernster Druckmethoden. Wie steht es aber nun mit der Verbreitung des Urtextes und kritischer Ausgaben von ihm, die seit 75 Jahren auch zu den Aufgaben der Bibelgesellschaften gehören, zunächst von der Württembergischen Bibelanstalt wahrgenommen, dann aber auch (durch Übernahme des Nestle-Textes) von der British and Foreign Bible Society, bis sich

[32]   vgl. Anm. 30, S. 887f.
[33]   S. XIII und XXII.
[34]   S. X f.

schließlich die United Bible Societies, auf Initiative der American Bible Society und E. A. Nidas, dieser Aufgabe annahmen. Hat auch hier der Pietismus Leistungen vorzuweisen, welche der Arbeit der Bibelgesellschaften von heute wenigstens ungefähr entsprechen?

Diese Frage kann nur nachdrücklich bejaht werden und zwar sowohl was das Alte wie was das Neue Testament angeht. In Halle ist 1720 die sog. Michaelis-Bibel entstanden,[35] welche für ihre Zeit den Vergleich mit Kittels Biblia hebraica von heute durchaus aufnehmen kann. Sie trägt ihren Namen nach ihrem Hauptbearbeiter, dem Hallenser Professor Heinrich Michaelis, zustande kommen konnte sie aber nur, weil Francke und das von diesem im Halleschen Waisenhaus 1702 begründete und durch alle Schwierigkeiten hin aufrecht erhaltene Collegium orientale theologicum dahinterstand. Noch heute wird die Michaelis-Bibel im kritischen Apparat der Biblia hebraica von Kittel verzeichnet, neben der Bomberg-Bibel von 1524/1525 die einzige Druckausgabe des hebräischen Alten Testaments, für die das gilt. Auch drei der fünf von der Michaelis-Bibel benutzten Erfurter Handschriften sind für den kritischen Apparat von Kittels Biblia hebraica ausgewertet worden.

In bezug auf das griechische Neue Testament geht die Leistung des Pietismus noch über die der modernen Bibelgesellschaften hinaus, denn Bengels Ausgabe des griechischen Neuen Testaments von 1744 überragt in ihrer Größenordnung die Handausgaben der Bibelgesellschaften von heute in jeder Beziehung. Als die Württembergische Bibelanstalt 1898 Eberhard Nestles Novum Testamentum Graece herausbrachte, war damit der entscheidende Schritt zur Brechung der bisherigen Vorherrschaft des Textus receptus getan, zumal als die Britische Bibelgesellschaft 1904 diese Ausgabe übernahm. Faktisch bedeutete sie jedoch nicht mehr als das Fazit – durch mechanische Vergleichung hergestellt – aus den großen Ausgaben des 19. Jahrhunderts. Der kritische Apparat, welchen Erwin Nestle (und K. Aland) in immer größerer Verfeinerung

---

[35] עֶשְׂרִים וְאַרְבַּע סִפְרֵי הַקֹּדֶשׁ / sive/ BIBLIA/ HEBRAICA/ ex aliquot manuscriptis/ et compluribus impressis codicibus, item/ masora tam edita, quam manuscripta,/ aliisque hebraeororum criticis diligenter recensita. Praeter nova lemmata textus s. in Pentateucho, accedunt/ loca scripturae parallela,/ verbalia et realia,/ brevesque adnotationes, quibus/ nucleus graecae LXX. interpretum et 00. versionum exhibetur, diffici-/ les in textu dictiones et phrases explicantur, ac dubia resolvuntur;/ ut succincti commentarii vicem praestare possint./ singulis denique columnis/ selectae, variantes lectiones subiiciuntur:/ cura ac studio/ D.J0. Heinr. Michaelis,/ S.S. Theol. & Gr. ac 00. Lingg. in Acad. Frider. P.P. Ord./ et ex parte opera/ sociorum;/ ut pluribus in praefatione dicetur./ Cum gratia et privilegiis/ Sacrae Caes. Maiestatis, Potentiss. Reg. Polon. ac Porussiae, nec non Elect. Saxon. & Brand./ Halae Magdeburgicae, Typis & sumtibus Orphanotrophei MDCCXX.

diesem Text hinzufügten, machte die Ausgabe zwar zu der in der Welt am meisten benutzten, änderte aber ihren Grundcharakter nicht. Auch das Greek New Testament bedeutet nicht mehr als eine Handausgabe. Wenn hier der Text von den Herausgebern (K. Aland, M. Black, C. Martini, B. Metzger, A. Wikgren) auch selbständig erstellt wurde, war ein textkritischer Apparat doch nur für sehr wenige Stellen gegeben. Das erklärt – und rechtfertigt – sich aus der Zweckbestimmung der Ausgabe für die Übersetzer in den Jungen Kirchen, begrenzt die Ausgabe aber im akademischen Unterricht bestenfalls auf eine Benutzung durch Anfänger. Wenn die 26. Auflage des Nestle-Aland und die Third edition des Greek New Testament vorliegen werden (was für die nahe Zukunft erhofft wird), wird in beiden eine Textangleichung vollzogen sein. Dabei wird der Nestle-Aland mit dem völlig erneuerten und wesentlich ausgebauten textkritischen Apparat nicht nur alles Material bieten, das für den akademischen Unterricht erforderlich ist, sondern auch alle Voraussetzungen erfüllen, welche der Neutestamentler vom Fach für seine tägliche Arbeit braucht. Aber auch dann bleibt der Nestle-Aland noch eine Handausgabe – was Bengel 1744 in einem 900 Seiten starken Quart-Band vorlegte,[36] war eine "editio maior". Sie ist durch Wettsteins große Ausgabe von 1751/1752 bald in den Schatten gestellt worden, das mindert aber weder Anspruch noch Bedeutung der Ausgabe Bengels. Im kritischen Apparat werden die Lesarten nicht nur aufgezählt, sondern auch gewertet: ihre erste Kategorie ist nach Bengel dem überlieferten Textus receptus unbedingt vorzuziehen, die zweite scheint ihm ebenfalls überlegen, die dritte ist ihm gleichzustellen, die vierte Kategorie umfaßt die weniger wahrscheinlichen, die fünfte die, obwohl sie von einigen angenommen werden, zu verwerfenden Lesarten. In der Offenbarung konstituiert Bengel (im wesentlichen nach dem Codex Alexandrinus, der ältesten damals zugänglichen Handschrift) von vornherein einen eigenen Text. Mit seinem Versuch, die Handschriften und Übersetzungen in "Nationen", wie Bengel sie nennt, zu scheiden, ist Bengel der Vater der modernen textgeschichtlichen Arbeit geworden; die von ihm aufgestellte Grundregel für die Textkritik, daß die schwierigere Lesart der glatteren, erleichternden vorzuziehen sei, gilt bis auf den heutigen Tag.

---

[36] H KAINH ΔIAΘHKH/ Novum/ Testamentum/ Graecum/ Ita adornatum/ ut/ textus/ probatarum editionum medullam/ margo/ variantium lextionum/ in suas classes distributarum/ locorumque parallelorum/ delectum/ apparatus subiunctus/ criseos sacrae Millianae praesertim/ compendium, limam, supplementum ac fructum/ exhibeat/ inserviente/ Io. Alberto Bengelio. Tubingae/Sumptibus Io. Georgii Cottae A. D. MDCCXXXIV.

Nun ist diese Ausgabe von den Studenten und den Theologen im Amt der Kirche sicher nur in Ausnahmefällen benutzt worden. Welchen Text gab der Pietismus aber den Studenten in die Hand? Auch auf diese Frage kann eine Antwort gegeben werden, Im Jahre 1702 erschien nämlich in Leipzig eine Ausgabe des griechischen Neuen Testaments mit einer ausführlichen Vorrede Franckes.[37] Es handelt sich dabei um die Ausgabe von John Fell, dem Dean von Christ Church und späteren Bischof von Oxford, die 1675 im Verlag der Oxforder Universität (e theatro sheldoniano) erschienen war. Die Wahl Franckes war bezeichnend für seine Haltung. Denn die Ausgabe Fells ist von allen damals existierenden Handausgaben des griechischen Neuen Testaments die fortschrittlichste und wissenschaftlichste. Gewiß operiert auch sie im wesentlichen mit dem Textus receptus, aber das kann kein Anlaß zur Kritik Fells sein. Denn alle Ausgaben des griechischen Neuen Testaments – unter ihnen die Bengels wie Wettsteins – im 18. und auch noch im beginnenden 19. Jahrhundert verfahren nicht anders. Erst mit Griesbachs, vor allem aber mit Lachmanns Ausgaben von 1831 und 1842/1850 sowie Tischendorfs Ausgaben seit 1841 wird der Textus receptus als Grundlage verlassen. Jene frühen Ausgaben sind also daran zu messen, was sie über den Textus receptus hinaus bieten. Und hier übertrifft Fell all seine Vorgänger: der kritische Apparat seiner Ausgabe bietet die Resultate von Kollationen aus nicht weniger als 100 griechischen Handschriften, dazu die koptische und gotische Überlieferung. Natürlich baut er hier auf den Arbeiten anderer auf, aber er fügt ihnen umfangreiche eigene Kollationen hinzu. Der Codex Alexandrinus (A), der Codex Bezae Cantabrigiensis (D^e), der Codex Claromontanus (D^p), der Codex Laudianus (E^p)), dieser zum ersten Mal verwertet, und rund 20 Minuskeln sind hier verzeichnet, ihnen sind die aus Stephanus, Caryophilus, Wechel, Goode, Courcelles und anderen gesammelten Varianten hinzugefügt.

Für die Neuausgabe war die Vorlage noch einmal kritisch durchgesehen und die Beziehung zwischen Text und Apparat, die oft falsch oder nicht klar genug angegeben war, in Ordnung gebracht worden. Daß Francke gerade diese Ausgabe den Studenten empfiehlt und ihren

---

[37] ΤΗΣ ΚΑΙΝΗΣ/ ΔΙΑΘΗΚΗΣ/ ΑΠΑΝΤΑ./ NOVI TESTAMENTI/ LIBRI OMNES./ Accessuerunt/ Parallela Scripturae Loca/ Nec non/Variantes Lectiones ex plus 100.MSS./ Codicibus,/ Et Antiquis Versionibus Collectae,/ Nunc denuo ad Exemplar Oxonii impressum/ revisae, auctae, atque emendatae./ Cum/ Praefatione Nova/AUGUSTI HERMANNI FRANCKII,/ S.S. Theol. Prof. Ord. in Acad. Hallensi,/ & Pastoris,/De vera ratione tractandi Scripturam S. imprimis/libros N. T./ CUM PRIVILEGIIS./LIPSIAE,/ Sumptibus JOH. CHRISTOPH KÖNIG,/Bibliopolae Goslariens./Excudit JOH. HEINR. RICHTER. A. MDCCII/.

Gebrauch unter den Theologen des Pietismus sanktioniert – anders konnte sein Vorwort nicht verstanden werden – ist charakteristisch. Denn Francke hätte durchaus andere Ausgaben wählen können; selbst die Leipziger Verleger hatten verschiedene anzubieten. Eine davon wurde sogar vom Schwager Speners, dem Leipziger Professor Adam Rechenberg betreut. So hätte es nahegelegen, diese Ausgabe zur offiziellen Ausgabe des Halleschen Pietismus zu erklären. Aber Francke verzichtet auf sie, weil sie keinen kritischen Apparat bietet. Bezeichnend ist, was Johann Albrecht Bengel über die inneren Schwierigkeiten berichtet, die ihm die Ausgabe von 1702 bereitete. Er hatte sie sich als Student gekauft (offensichtlich auf die Empfehlung hin, die ihm Franckes Vorwort bedeutete). Aber die Zweifel und Anfechtungen, welche sich ihm aus der sich im kritischen Apparat der Ausgabe spiegelnden Widersprüche in der Überlieferung des neutestamentlichen Textes ergaben, waren schließlich so groß, daß er auf den Gebrauch dieser Ausgabe verzichtete und sich eine kaufte, die keinen kritischen Apparat enthielt. Erst langsam hat Bengel diesen Zweifel überwunden, bis er schließlich zu einem Meister der Textkritik wurde, dessen Name einen Markstein in ihrer Geschichte bedeutet.

Es ist ganz erstaunlich, in welchem Maße die Arbeit der modernen Bibelgesellschaften im klassischen Pietismus bereits vorgebildet und vorbereitet ist – bis hin zu den Bibelübersetzungen für Junge Kirchen, wovon noch gar nicht gesprochen wurde. Als der Sendbote des Halleschen Pietismus, Bartholomäus Ziegenbalg, am 7.9.1706 in Tranquebar landete, begann er alsbald mit der Übersetzung der Bibel ins Tamulische und mit dem Druck evangelischen Schrifttums in der Sprache der sich schnell immer weiter ausbreitenden Kirche, von Halle dabei durch Lieferung einer eigenen Druckerei unterstützt. Bis zu Ziegenbalgs frühem Tod 1718 war nicht nur die Grundlage der tamulischen Literatur geschaffen, sondern durch Erarbeitung eines Lexikons und einer Grammatik auch die Voraussetzung für ihre weitere Entfaltung. Wieder sind die Parallelen zu der Entwicklung, die sich später überall in der Welt vollzieht, frappierend. Die Erklärung dafür ist einfach und naheliegend: wenn es von August Hermann Francke nach seiner Bekehrung heißt, er sei totus pietate ardens gewesen, so gilt das nicht nur für ihn, sondern auch für alle seine Mitarbeiter und den ganzen Pietismus jener Zeit. Eine solche Frömmigkeit, die in der heiligen Schrift ihr Zentrum hat, strebt mit allen Kräften danach, dem Mitmenschen die Bibel zugänglich zu machen, damit auch er, von ihr erfaßt, den Weg zum Glauben und zum Heil finde. Dafür setzt sie alle Mittel ein, auch alle technischen Hilfsmittel, die ihr zur

Verfügung stehen. Sobald sich die Voraussetzungen wiederholen, wird es auch zu gleichen Konsequenzen kommen: deshalb sind die Ereignisse zur Zeit des Pietismus denen in späterer Zeit parallel – möchte die Kraft, die wir hier wirksam sehen, sich ständig erneuern.

REFERENCES

References to modern works only are included: seventeenth and eighteenth century books (Spener, Francke, etc.) are given in full in the footnotes.
Aland, K.
1960 *Die bleibende Bedeutung des Pietismus* (Witten).
n.d. *Der hallesche Pietismus und die Bibel.*
1960 *Kirchengeschichtliche Entwürfe* (Gütersloh: Gütersloher Verlagshaus, Gerd Mohn).
1964 *Pia desideria* (= *Kleine Texte* 170), 3rd edition.
1970 "Bibel und Bibeltext bei August Hermann Francke und Johann Albrecht Bengel", *Pietismus und Bibel* (= *Arbeiten zur Geschichte des Pietismus* 9) (Witten).
Cyzevskyj, D.
1939 "Der Kreis A. H. Franckes in Halle und seine slavistischen Studien", *Ztschr. f. Slav. Philologie* 16 (Leipzig).
Kolb, C.
1917 *Die Bibel in der Evangelischen Kirche Altwürttembergs* (Stuttgart).
Kramer, G.
1861 *Beiträge zur Geschichte August Hermann Franckes* (Halle).
Nebe, A.
1927 *Neue Quellen zu August Hermann Francke* (Gütersloh).
Schürmann, A.
1898 *Zur Geschichte der Buchhandlung des Waisenhauses und der Cansteinschen Bibelanstalt* (Halle).
Volz, H.
1954 *Hundert Jahre Wittenberger Bibeldruck 1522-1626* (Göttingen).

POURQUOI LA TORAH A-T-ELLE ÉTÉ
TRADUITE EN GREC?

DOMINIQUE BARTHÉLEMY O. P.

Ce volume consacré à Eugene Nida me semble être le lieu le mieux adapté pour une recherche portant sur les conditions dans lesquelles fut réalisée la première de toutes les traductions bibliques: la traduction grecque du Pentateuque.

Admettons d'abord que l'on est en droit de parler d'une œuvre littéraire cohérente de traduction du Pentateuque, les doutes présentés par Kahle en ce domaine étant réfutés par les papyri juifs antérieurs à notre ère.[1] On trouve en effet déjà présentes en ces papyri des particularités ou des erreurs de traduction qui caractérisent tous les témoins de notre 'Septante'.

TRADITIONS JUIVES NON ARISTÉENNES SUR LA
TRADUCTION GRECQUE DE LA TORAH

Si l'on veut tenter de se faire une opinion sur les motifs de cette entreprise de traduction, il faut commencer par rassembler et par discuter les traditions juives concernant les origines du Pentateuque grec. Sous cette désignation, c'est à la lettre du Pseudo-Aristée que l'on pense tout naturellement. Mais on sait qu'après les objections soulevées par Louis Vivès[2] contre l'authenticité de ce document, Humphrey Hody (Humfredus Hodius 1684) démontra de manière décisive que l'auteur de la

---

Dominique Barthélemy O.P. est Professeur d'exégèse de l'Ancien Testament à l'Université de Fribourg, Suisse.

[1] C'est aussi l'opinion de Walters (1973:273-274): "The few fragments of a pre-Christian LXX text, Pap. Rylands 458 and Pap. Fouad 266, both containing parts of Deuteronomy and written about 150ᵃ, notwithstanding some minor variants, display the translation which we still read. Therefore, when speaking about a plurality of translations at the outset, we tend to move in the sphere of mere surmise, unsupported by the evidence".

[2] 'Circumfertur libellus eius (scil.: Aristeae) nomine de LXX interpretibus, confictus, ut puto, ab aliquo recentiore' (Vivès 1522:in XVIII, 42).

'lettre' est un faussaire. Depuis ce moment, les historiens ont généralement renoncé à faire usage de cet écrit comme d'un document historique,
cherchant tout au plus à déterminer ce qui aurait pu motiver la confection
de ce faux vers le dernier quart du 2ᵉ siècle. Aussi vaut-il mieux commencer par laisser en suspens cette pseudo-lettre, en abordant en premier
lieu les données assez succinctes fournies par l'apologiste juif Aristobule[3]
dans les fragments de son 'Exégèse de la loi de Moïse' que Clément[4]
et Eusèbe[5] nous présentent comme ayant été dédiée à Ptolémée Philométor un peu avant 150. Jusqu'à ces dernières années, des juges prudents
pouvaient considérer que le 'cas Aristobule' était dans une impasse.
Contre l'authenticité des fragments d'Aristobule, Paul Wendland
(1895, 1898 et 1902), l'éditeur de Philon, avait construit une puissante
argumentation. Malgré cela, la grande autorité d'Emil Schürer (1909:519,
n. 58) demeurait résolument favorable à l'authenticité. A l'université
de Bonn, vers la même époque, Anton Elter (1894-1895) argumentait
résolument contre l'authenticité, ce qui n'empêcha pas son disciple
Robert Keller (1948) de consacrer, vingt-cinq ans plus tard, une thèse
de doctorat à ce problème en concluant à l'authenticité, mais sans avoir
repris en détail toutes les difficultés soulevées par Wendland.

Ce n'est que récemment qu'est parue sur Aristobule une étude très
approfondie et nuancée de Nikolaus Walter (1964). Après avoir envisagé
sous tous ses aspects la question de l'authenticité des fragments, Walter
(1964:123) conclut que tous les indices convergent pour situer la rédaction de l'ouvrage d'Aristobule dans la communauté judéo-alexandrine
vers le milieu du 2ᵉ siècle avant J. C. Le plus probable est qu'il fut bien
rédigé vers la fin du règne de Ptolémée VI Philométor, ce qui confirme
pleinement la tradition patristique. On peut d'ailleurs admettre comme
parfaitement vraisemblable qu'un lettré juif ait dédié un plaidoyer en
faveur de la loi de Moïse à ce souverain qui témoigna un intérêt bien-
veillant à la communauté juive (Walter 1964:38-40). Le point le plus
original de l'enquête de Walter (1964:141-148) est une étude du développement de l'allégorisme judéo-alexandrin. Il y établit sur des bases
solides la succession chronologique Aristobule, Pseudo-Aristée,[6] Philon
et montre (Walter 1964:148-149) que l'erreur de jugement de Wendland
tient au fait que celui-ci identifia purement et simplement l'allégorisme

---

[3] Ces données d'Aristobule nous sont transmises par Eusèbe, Praeparatio Evangelica,
XIII, 12, 2 (Eusebius 1954: 2ᵉ part, 191, 5-7).
[4] Stromates, I, 150, 1-3 (Clemens 1960:92, 27).
[5] Le passage précédent des Stromates est cité par Eusèbe en Praeparatio Evangelica,
IX, 6, 6 (Eusebius 1954: 1ᵉ part, 493, 9-10).
[6] Pour la date du Pseudo-Aristée, voir Walter (1964:49, n. 1).

judéo-alexandrin avec Philon, sans avoir suffisamment conscience que l'œuvre de celui-ci présuppose bien des tâtonnements, et le franchissement par ses devanciers d'un certain nombre d'étapes préalables.

Cette démonstration de l'authenticité des fragments attribués à Aristobule semble d'une grande importance pour la question de l'origine de la traduction grecque du Pentateuque. En effet, ce n'est plus alors seulement d'un faussaire de la fin du 2ᵉ siècle que nous tenons la tradition d'une version réalisée sur l'initiative de Ptolémée Philadelphe et sous l'influence de Démétrius de Phalère. Vers 150, Aristobule considère cette tradition comme déjà connue des destinataires de son ouvrage et elle lui cause même une difficulté dans son argumentation. Lorsqu'il veut démontrer que Platon s'est inspiré de Moïse, il lui faut en effet dire que le Pentateuque avait déjà été traduit avant que Démétrius de Phalère ne se lançât dans son entreprise bien connue.[7] On ne voit vraiment pas pourquoi Aristobule aurait inventé de placer la traduction du Pentateuque sous les premiers Ptolémées alors qu'il eût bien préféré la placer à une époque plus haute, ce à quoi il s'essaie d'ailleurs en termes vagues. On peut donc dire qu'au milieu du 2ᵉ siècle avant J. C. l'essentiel de la tradition classique sur l'origine de la Septante est suffisamment diffusé à Alexandrie pour gêner un apologète juif qui, prétendant s'adresser à un Ptolémée, ne peut nier cette tradition bien connue de son public.

La lettre du Pseudo-Aristée sera sans doute remplie de nombreux détails fictifs, mais ces détails fictifs sont brodés sur une tradition déjà familière aux lecteurs du faussaire et considérée par eux comme solide. De même, pour que le livre d'Hénoch fut écrit, ne fallait-il pas que le public crût déjà qu'Hénoch avait été enlevé au ciel? Pour que la lettre d'Aristée fût écrite, il fallait aussi que le public alexandrin crût au moins déjà que la loi de Moïse avait été traduite en grec sur l'initiative de l'un des premiers Lagides.

Rappelons-nous aussi que s'il est vrai que Josèphe et la plupart des pères de l'Église dépendent directement ou indirectement du Pseudo-Aristée, nous possédons deux lignes de témoignages qui sont partiellement indépendants de la tradition Aristobule-Aristée. Il s'agit d'un côté de Philon d'Alexandrie et de l'autre d'un groupe constitué par quelques écrits patristiques et rabbiniques.

Philon, en effet, dans le 2ᵉ livre de la Vie de Moïse,[8] nous apprend qu'à son époque une fête annuelle célébrait par une assemblée générale en l'île de Pharos le lieu d'où la loi de Moïse avait commencé son rayon-

---

[7]   Praeparatio Evangelica, XIII, 12, 1 (Eusebius 1954: 2ᵉ part, 190, 18 à 191, 2).
[8]   De Vita Mosis, II, 41-44 (Philo 1902:209, 17 à 210, 10).

nement dans le monde hellénistique. Beaucoup de païens venaient dans l'île rendre grâces avec la communauté juive pour ce bienfait divin déjà ancien qui produisait sans cesse des fruits nouveaux. Faut-il penser que c'est la lettre d'Aristée qui a donné naissance à cette cérémonie ou n'est-il pas plus vraisemblable que c'est la fête annuelle de Pharos liée à une tradition ancienne brièvement rapportée par Aristobule, qui a servi de base à l'auteur de la lettre d'Aristée, assurant d'avance un public à son ouvrage.

Sur une autre ligne traditionnelle on rencontre à la fois Irénée de Lyon,[9] l'auteur anonyme de la *Cohortatio ad Gentiles* (Cap. 23 = 1879: 54-59), et une boraïtha du Talmud de Babylone (Meg. 9a). Ces trois témoignages dépendent d'une même tradition qui se signale par trois éléments caractéristiques: Primo: L'initiative de la traduction y est attribuée à Ptolémée Sôter et non à Philadelphe son fils. Secundo: Afin d'empêcher que les traducteurs puissent se mettre d'accord pour transformer le contenu de la Loi, il les fait enfermer chacun dans une maison, chacun devant traduire toute la Loi. Tertio: Dieu intervient miraculeusement pour inspirer à tous des traductions rigoureusement concordantes. Le seul de nos trois témoins qui nous indique d'où il tient cette tradition est l'auteur de la *Cohortatio ad Gentiles*. Après avoir raconté l'histoire des maisonnettes, il ajoute en effet: 'Ce que nous vous racontons là, grecs, ce n'est pas une fable, ni une histoire inventée. Nous avons été nous-mêmes à Alexandrie et nous avons vu à Pharos ce qu'on a préservé des ruines des maisonnettes. Et la source de nos informations, c'est ce que nous avons entendu raconter par ceux qui habitent là et qui l'avaient reçu de leurs ancêtres' (*Cohortatio* 1879:56-57). Quant à la boraïtha du Talmud de Babylone, elle a pour auteur Rabbi Jehudah ben Elaï qui fit un voyage en Égypte vraisemblablement vers 110 de notre ère, voyage d'où il rapporta des souvenirs du Nil qui nuancent certaines de ses anecdotes, des informations sur le temple d'Onias à Héliopolis qui lui permettent d'affirmer contre Rabbi Méïr que le culte de ce temple n'avait rien d'idolâtrique (Men. 109b), et enfin une admiration sans borne pour la grande synagogue d'Alexandrie: 'Celui, disait-il, qui n'a pas vu le double portique à Alexandrie d'Égypte, celui-là n'a jamais eu l'occasion de voir la gloire d'Israël' (Suk. 51b). Il y a donc toutes raisons de croire que la tradition sur les maisonnettes des traducteurs fut également rapportée par Rabbi Jehudah de son pèlerinage aux lieux saints des juifs d'Alexandrie.

[9]   Contra Haereses, III, 21, 2 (Eusebius 1903: 1ᵉ part, 448, 4 à 450, 5). La forme grecque de ce passage a été préservée par Eusèbe (Histoire Ecclésiastique, V, 8, 11-15).

Nous avons donc des indices très suffisants pour admettre que cette
3e forme, la plus merveilleuse, de la légende des origines de la Septante
s'est développée comme le boniment d'un guide, qui faisait visiter aux
pèlerins le lieu saint de Pharos. En y regardant de plus près, on peut
d'ailleurs noter que Philon, sans mentionner formellement les 72 maisonnettes, voit lui aussi une preuve manifeste de l'assistance divine dans le
fait que, 'dans leur retraite solitaire... chacun n'écrivait pas une chose
différente, mais que tous écrivaient les mêmes noms et les mêmes mots
comme si eût résonné en chacun d'eux la voix d'un invisible souffleur'.[10]
Si donc Philon tire bien l'essentiel de ses données de la lettre d'Aristée,
on peut dire que son affirmation de la coïncidence des traductions et
l'explication de cette coïncidence par l'intervention d'un souffleur divin
présuppose la légende locale des maisonnettes dont il tient certainement
la connaissance de sa fréquentation des fêtes annuelles de Pharos.

Y a-t-il quelque chose d'historique à tirer de cette légende du lieu saint.
Elle nous permet surtout de vérifier la permanence et l'enracinement
populaire d'une tradition que la lettre d'Aristée nous présentait sous
une forme littéraire. Elle nous indique aussi que tout le monde ne suivait
pas Aristobule en attribuant à Ptolémée Philadelphe l'initiative de la
traduction. Les souvenirs locaux parlaient plutôt de Ptolémée Sôter, le
fondateur de la Bibliothèque. Plus tard, Clément d'Alexandrie,[11] héritier
de ces souvenirs, tout spontanément s'accordera avec Irénée dans cette
attribution, en notant toutefois que d'autres parlent de Philadelphe.
Quant à Anatolios de Laodicée, qui naquit lui aussi à Alexandrie vers la
fin de la vie de Clément, il affirme que les Septante ont traduit les Écritures
pour Ptolémée Philadelphe et pour son père.[12] Ces deux lettrés alexandrins
semblent donc soucieux de concilier les traditions populaires locales avec
celle que rapportent Aristobule et, à sa suite, le Pseudo-Aristée. Faut-il
penser que déjà la communauté juive alexandrine avait remplacé dans
ses souvenirs Ptolémée Philadelphe par son père afin de résoudre la
difficulté que présentera pour les érudits actuels la présence de Démétrius
de Phalère aux côtés de Philadelphe son ennemi? Je crois qu'on ne doit
pas imaginer de tels scrupules érudits troublant la cervelle du bon
peuple dans son pèlerinage aux petites maisons. D'ailleurs Démétrius
de Phalère semble n'avoir aucune place dans la légende du lieu saint.

---

[10] De Vita Mosis, II, 37 (Philo 1902:208, 16-21).
[11] Stromates, I, 148, 1 (Clemens 1960:92, 7-8).
[12] Cité par Eusèbe (Histoire Ecclésiastique, VII, 32, 16) (Eusebius 1903: 2e part,
724, 5). Pelletier (Lettre d'Aristée 1962:94) confond cet auteur avec Anatole, patriarche
de Constantinople de 449 à 458, alors qu'il s'agit d'Anatole, élu en 268 à l'évêché de
Laodicée et mort vers 282.

Disons plutôt que, dans la communauté juive d'Alexandrie, on associait l'œuvre de traduction de la Loi aux origines mêmes de la grande bibliothèque qui faisait l'honneur de la ville.

L'essentiel de la tradition sur les origines de la Septante est donc indépendant de l'ouvrage du Pseudo-Aristée. Avant le faussaire, et plus tard dans des milieux qui n'ont sans doute jamais entendu parler de son œuvre, on tenait pour certain que la traduction grecque du Pentateuque était l'ouvrage d'une commission de traducteurs réunie dans l'île de Pharos par l'un des premiers Ptolémées. On peut d'ailleurs, avec Elias Bickerman (1959:9), reconnaître que les probalités internes vont dans le sens de la tradition classique à laquelle se réfèrent les anciens témoins alexandrins.

La théorie de Kahle[13] exprime en effet parfaitement ce qui *se serait* passé si aucune haute autorité n'avait pris en mains la réalisation d'une traduction grecque de la loi de Moïse. Étant donnée la répugnance juive bien connue à mettre le targum par écrit, étant donné d'autre part que l'usage de transcriptions en caractères grecs permettait peut-être à des lecteurs ignorant l'hébreu de continuer à assurer la lecture liturgique de la loi en hébreu, il est vraisemblable qu'on aurait continué pendant des siècles la lecture hébraïque de la Loi sur laquelle auraient brodé ensuite des targums très glosés de haggadah où les interprètes prédicateurs auraient dissimulé sous les légendes édifiantes leur connaissance insuffisante de la langue sacrée. Admettons même que, pour certaines péricopes plus utilisées, on ait tenté de rédiger quelques traductions aide-mémoire. Mais 'c'eût été, comme le dit Bickerman (1959:8), gâcher des sommes et un travail considérables que de traduire, copier et recopier tout l'ensemble du Pentateuque en vue de fournir une aide aux traductions orales occasionnelles de passages isolés de la Torah'. Si les choses s'étaient passées comme Kahle en reconstitue le déroulement, c'est-à-dire si aucune autorité n'était intervenue, les rédactions fragmentaires et divergentes du Pentateuque grec seraient demeurées longtemps dans l'état où nous connaissons les targums samaritains et palestiniens. Elles n'auraient en tout cas pas atteint dès le 2e siècle avant J. C. cette unité textuelle fondamentale que nous constatons dans les plus anciens fragments du Lévitique ou du Deutéronome, et qui, à travers le Pentateuque de Philon et les grands onciaux, subsistera dans les apparats critiques de Brooke-McLean. Pour que l'on pût disposer dès le 2e siècle d'une traduction grecque du Pentateuque, il ne suffit pas que quelques inter-

---

[13] Cette théorie a été bien formulée par Jellicoe (1968:59-63). On en trouve les éléments un peu épars en Kahle (1959:209-264).

prêtes liturgiques aient eu besoin d'aide-mémoire. Il faut que quelqu'un – et qui d'autre que le Roi ? – ait disposé de l'autorité et des moyens nécessaires pour réaliser, malgré les inévitables appréhensions et les résistances probables des autorités juives palestiniennes, un propos ambitieux aux conséquences incalculables : donner pour loi nationale aux juifs vivant sous l'empire des Lagides la loi de Moïse en grec.

MOTIFS DE L'INTÉRÊT ROYAL POUR LA TRADUCTION DE LA TORAH

Quoi qu'on en ait dit, une telle initiative n'a d'ailleurs en soi rien d'invraisemblable, comme Leonhard Rost l'a récemment constaté.[14] L'existence de cours de justice (Tcherikover 1957:32, n. 84) et d'archives autonomes (Fraser 1972:I, 56 et II, 140, n. 157) pour la communauté juive d'Alexandrie est un fait bien attesté. Les spécialistes de l'Égypte ptolémaïque considèrent comme certain que les juifs constituaient à Alexandrie dès la première moitié du 2e siècle un πολίτευμα semi-autonome.[15] Cela suppose qu'un souverain leur a accordé le droit de vivre selon les lois de leurs ancêtres. Antiochus III, lors de sa conquête de Jérusalem en 198 ne fera sans doute que reprendre la précédente

[14] R. Hanhart (1962:161) avait affirmé que: 'ni une réinterprétation de la lettre d'Aristée, ni les autres témoignages ne permettent d'ébranler la thèse assez généralement admise depuis 400 ans selon laquelle, à l'encontre des déclarations de la lettre d'Aristée, la cause à laquelle la Septante doit son origine est à chercher dans les besoins cultuels de la communauté juive de langue grecque à l'époque hellénistique et non dans un ordre venant de l'extérieur, c'est à dire de l'autorité ptolémaïque'. Cette affirmation de Hanhart engagea L. Rost à rechercher ce qui occasionna la traduction en grec de la Torah. Il conclut (1970:43) au contraire que: 'la traduction grecque doit principalement son origine à des motifs de droit public et non pas aux besoins de communautés cultuelles juives de langue grecque. Cette traduction du Pentateuque a été le document de base qui permit dans les états hellénistiques, de réclamer pour la communauté juive des droits particuliers et de les lui accorder sous forme de privilèges. Sa signification consiste en ce qu'elle rendit possible pour la communauté juive de recevoir, à titre de privilège, le droit de citoyenneté, sans avoir à se soumettre aux obligations de la religion d'état.'

[15] Comme le note Schürer (1909:71-72 et 76), cela est formellement attesté pour l'époque du Pseudo-Aristée. Sur les conditions dans lesquelles fut créé ce politeuma, P. M. Fraser fournit les données suivantes: (1) il n'y a pas de raison de mettre en doute l'affirmation de la lettre d'Aristée (§§ 12-13) selon laquelle Ptolémée Sôter a installé dans les environs d'Alexandrie un grand nombre de Juifs faits prisonniers pendant diverses campagnes en Palestine. (2) Le fait même de la traduction de la Torah en grec indique que la population juive était assez nombreuse dès le 3e siècle. (3) À la différence des Égyptiens, les Juifs ne pratiquaient guère l'intermariage avec les Grecs mais ont préservé jusqu'à l'époque romaine dans un état inaltéré leurs coutumes particulières (Fraser, I, 1972:57).

charte lagide, lorsqu'il édictera: 'πολιτευέσθωσαν δὲ πάντες οἱ ἐκ τοῦ ἔθνους κατὰ πατρίους νόμους', formule qui reconnaît officiellement la loi de Moïse comme code propre du politeuma juif, à la manière dont avait agi jadis Artaxerxès II envers les judéens[16] dans son firman à l'authenticité duquel la critique actuelle est de plus en plus favorable.[17]

Que les Lagides aient porté un certain intérêt aux affaires religieuses juives, cela nous est attesté par le fait que Ptolémée III Evergète, dans la 2e moitié du 3e siècle, accorde à une synagogue un droit d'asile (Dittenberger 1903:no. 129) analogue à celui dont il gratifiait les temples égyptiens. Cela nous est encore attesté par la façon dont Ptolémée VI Philométor facilita l'érection du temple d'Onias à Léontopolis au siècle suivant (Schürer 1909:144-145). L'intérêt porté par les Lagides à la loi de Moïse a-t-il pu aller plus loin qu'une simple homologation officielle de ce code? Il faut rappeler ici le précédent de Darius I qui, en 518, avait chargé le satrape Aryandes de rassembler des sages parmi les guerriers, les prêtres, les scribes d'Égypte, afin qu'ils mettent par écrit les anciennes lois de l'Égypte, c'est-à-dire la loi du Pharaon, celles des temples et celles du peuple. La commission de codification n'acheva son travail que 15 ans plus tard et l'édita en démotique et en araméen.[18]

---

[16] Bickermann (1935:27) s'exprime ainsi: 'La locution "les lois des ancêtres" indiquait pour les Juifs et pour les autorités païennes, lorsqu'elles parlaient des choses juives, le code de Moïse... Antiochos III garantit donc en 200 av. J. C. l'inviolabilité des prescriptions de la Torah... Il ne fait aucun doute que le Séleucide suivait en cela l'exemple des Lagides et d'Alexandre, qui, selon Josèphe (Ant. XI, 338), avait concédé aux Juifs "la liberté de vivre conformément aux lois de leurs pères". Par cette concession, Alexandre ne fit d'ailleurs que renouveler l'édit émanant d'Artaxerxès II et apporté à Jérusalem par Esdras en 459.' Voir aussi Tcherikover (1957:6-7): 'Le roi ptolémaïque était la seule source de la loi dans le pays... On peut aisément deviner le droit fondamental assuré aux communautés juives par le roi: c'était sans aucun doute, le droit "de vivre selon leurs lois ancestrales"... Et les "lois ancestrales", quand il s'agissait des Juifs ne pouvaient signifier qu'une seule chose: une organisation juive autonome fondée sur les lois de Moïse. Ainsi la Torah était la loi fondamentale de toutes les communautés juives d'Égypte.'

[17] Les commentateurs récents du livre d'Esdras: Rudolph (1949:75-77), Myers (1965:61-63) et Michaeli (1967:287-88) jugent le firman authentique. Cazelles (1954: 126) conclut d'une étude comparative: 'le fond du firman d'Esdras est donc tout à fait dans la ligne de la politique achéménide'. Bright (1972:386) estime qu'il n'y a pas à mettre en question l'authenticité de ce document araméen'.

[18] Olmstead (1970:142) relate ainsi cette entreprise: 'Avant le 30 décembre 518, Darius écrivait à son satrape, Aryandes qui avait été réinstallé,: "Que l'on m'amène les plus sages d'entre les guerriers, les prêtres et les scribes de l'Égypte, eux qui se sont réunis en venant des temples, et qu'ils mettent par écrit les lois anciennes de l'Égypte jusqu'à la 44e année du Pharaon Amasis. Qu'ils apportent ici la loi de Pharaon, du temple et du peuple". A la différence des recueils de lois antérieurs, celui de Darius n'entendait pas se limiter aux décrets royaux; les pratiques religieuses – ce qu'on pourrait appeler le "droit canon" – et la procédure coutumière jusqu'alors

Cette entreprise était beaucoup plus vaste que la traduction en grec d'une loi juive déjà codifiée.[19] Et puisque nous sommes informés par Plutarque[20] que Démétrius de Phalère a conseillé à Ptolémée de rassembler les livres traitant du gouvernement, et que nous savons d'autre part l'intérêt très nouveau qu'Aristote et ses disciples éprouvèrent pour les νόμιμα βαρβαρικά,[21] il n'y a vraiment rien d'improbable à ce que le souverain ait fait coup double, la traduction permettant à sa curiosité de bibliophile d'avoir accès à un ouvrage célèbre, et permettant en même temps à une importante minorité ethnique de sa capitale de juger selon un code rédigé en grec et non selon des grimoires inaccessibles à l'administration lagide.[22]

Cela présentait en outre pour le roi l'avantage d'helléniser cette importante minorité étrangère résidant en sa capitale, et de lui éviter de se raidir en une sorte d'irrédentisme culturel. Les juifs d'Alexandrie qui avaient peut-être suggéré cette initiative durent saluer avec joie l'hommage rendu par les grecs à leur Torah, et surtout la fin du divorce de plus en plus marqué qui séparait leur parler quotidien, la koiné, d'une langue religieuse dont on ne pouvait jusque là se passer, quoique presque plus personne n'y eût accès. Quant aux autorités religieuses de Jérusalem, n'ayant pas la possibilité de s'opposer efficacement au dessein du roi, elles durent bien prêter la main à l'entreprise ou du moins la tolérer. Ne

---

non écrite devaient aussi être codifiés.' Le document cité par Olmstead figure au dos de la Chronique démotique (Papyrus 215 de la Bibliothèque Nationale de Paris). Sur le travail de cette commission de codification, cf. de Vaux (1937:38-39).

[19] Notons d'ailleurs que les Lagides, à partir de Philadelphe semble-t-il, réunirent régulièrement des synodes de prêtres égyptiens qui avaient des pouvoirs législatifs. Cf. Bouché-Leclerq (1903:266 et 1906:20-21).

[20] Regum Apophthegmata, p. 189 D, cité par Wehrli (1949:18).

[21] L'existence d'un traité d'Aristote consacré aux νόμιμα βαρβαρικά est attesté par des témoignages solides (Moraux 1951:130 n. 44). Cicéron, dans le De finibus, nous dit que Démétrius de Phalère avait été auditeur de Théophraste (V, 19, 54) et que celui-ci avait recueilli les lois des Barbares (V, 4, 11). Cicéron tenait vraisemblablement ces informations d'Antiochus d'Ascalon dont il avait suivi l'enseignement en 79-78 avant J. C. Bayer (1942:97) rappelle qu'en invitant Théophraste à sa cour, Ptolémée Sôter avait tenté de transférer à Alexandrie l'école d'Aristote.

[22] Selon Rost (1970:43), ce dernier motif aurait été dominant pour Ptolémée Philadelphe: 'Ptolémée I avait laissé à son successeur une question non résolue: comment est-ce que pouvait sinon s'intégrer, du moins s'insérer dans un état hellénistique la religion monothéiste d'un groupe théocratique qui avait reçu des Perses le privilège de vivre selon sa loi ancestrale?... Une difficulté demeurait: ce droit particulier privilégié n'était formulé en aucune des langues reçues comme langues d'empire par les Perses. Là-dessus, les Grands Rois avaient fermé les yeux. Mais l'état hellénistique n'était pas disposé à faire de même. Aussi éprouva-t-on la nécessité de posséder une traduction qui pût offrir un équivalent authentique de l'original... Le résultat fut la traduction grecque du Pentateuque à la fois reconnue par l'état et authentifiée par la communauté juive.'

verra-t-on pas, au siècle suivant, les palestiniens tolérer jusqu'à un certain point, sans l'homologuer pleinement, l'initiative beaucoup plus scandaleuse que constitua l'érection par Onias du temple de Léontopolis! Il semble bien qu'à Jérusalem on ait été à l'époque assez divisé entre la crainte d'une émancipation religieuse des coreligionnaires d'Alexandrie et la sympathie qu'éveillaient les initiatives prises par les Lagides qui, dans le plan de la nouvelle cité, attribuaient aux juifs de vastes quartiers proches du palais royal (Josephus 1926:304-307) où ils pouvaient pratiquer leur loi en toute indépendance.

On peut donc résumer de la façon suivante les conclusions de notre étude sur l'origine de la traduction grecque du Pentateuque: les données de la critique textuelle prouvent que notre version n'est pas le produit d'un développement targumique spontané. Il s'est passé quelque chose qui a empêché le processus de se dérouler de la même façon qu'il le fit pour les targums samaritains ou palestiniens, ou encore pour la Vieille Latine. Or nous possédons une tradition externe ancienne et largement diffusée sur cette initiative toute puissante extérieure à Israël qui, triomphant de certains scrupules juifs, rompit le cours normal des choses. Et j'espère avoir montré que l'essentiel de cette tradition ne peut être frappé par le discrédit que Hody a jeté, à bon droit, sur les racontars du Pseudo-Aristée.

Qu'elle ait été ou non suggérée par des conseillers juifs, l'initiative royale instituant une commission de traduction est tellement vraisemblable et tellement largement attestée qu'on peut la considérer comme historiquement certaine. Au cas où Kahle aurait raison d'admettre que les juifs d'Égypte usaient pour la lecture liturgique de transcriptions de l'hébreu en caractères grecs, on peut considérer comme très vraisemblable que l'on fit appel pour la traduction, à des manuscrits hébraïques palestiniens. Le résultat fut une version dont le standing de fidélité était ultrasatisfaisant si on la comparait aux targums liturgiques fragmentaires qui avaient pu la précéder.

MOTIFS DE RÉDACTION DE LA LETTRE D'ARISTÉE

Il semble que très vite l'œuvre des Septante constitua les Saintes Écritures pour les juifs d'Alexandrie et tous leurs frères de la Diaspora grecque, et que dans ces communautés on perdit pratiquement toute référence à la Bible hébraïque.[23] Cependant des contacts incessants liaient la

---

[23] Heinemann (1932:524-526) dit de Philon: 'Dans son exposition de la Loi, il ne

diaspora à Jérusalem. Et il n'est pas douteux que l'acribie vétilleuse des scribes palestiniens n'eut aucune peine à relever dans la traduction certaines inexactitudes. Cela éveilla chez certains alexandrins plus érudits ou plus influençables des doutes à l'égard de l'authenticité de leur Bible grecque et on commença à lui faire subir certaines retouches sur l'hébreu comme nous l'attestent dès le 2e siècle avant J.- C. quelques citations bibliques rapportées par l'apologète Aristobule, citations qui sont plus hébraïsantes que notre Septante actuelle.[24] La Bible alexandrine allait-elle donc se mettre en mouvement? Son unité allait-elle s'éparpiller en tentatives diverses pour se modeler plus fidèlement sur les formes, encore divergentes à cette époque, du texte hébraïque? Mais la traduction des Septante représentait aux yeux de l'autorité lagide la forme homologuée une fois pour toutes de la loi nationale des juifs. Comme nous le prouvent les œuvres de Philon, une jurisprudence caractéristique s'était bâtie sur son texte, même là où ce texte divergeait d'avec l'hébreu.[25] Plus de cent ans d'usage indiscuté dans la juiverie prospère de la grande capitale avaient donné à la Septante de la Loi valeur de norme, et la fierté des leaders de la communauté alexandrine faisant écho au besoin de stabilité légale de l'administration lagide se refusait à voir démanteler la Bible de l'hellénisme par les critiques jalouses des scribes palestiniens.[26]

C'est dans ce contexte qu'il faut placer la rédaction de la lettre d'Aristée. Le but de ce document est de faire cesser les tentatives de recension sur l'hébreu,[27] et pour cela de rendre confiance dans le texte officiel en

---

trahit aucune connaissance de l'hébreu.... Il va de soi que sa Bible est la LXX.... La règle qu'il ne suit que la Bible grecque, et pas l'hébraïque, ne trouve aucune exception dans son exposition de la Loi.' Même jugement chez Frankel (1841:45-47).

[24] Ainsi, en Ex 3.20, comme l'a déjà noté Valckenaer (1806:70), alors que tous les témoins de LXX traduisent le verbe *šlḥ* par ἐκτείνειν, Aristobule témoigne de ἀποστέλλειν, traduction beaucoup plus littérale.

[25] Heinemann (1932:525) groupe quelques exemples de ce type. De nombreux autres sont épars dans tout son ouvrage.

[26] Les rabbins palestiniens considéraient la Septante du Pentateuque comme une traduction faite formellement pour le roi Ptolémée. Du fait qu'elle était destinée à un souverain païen, les traducteurs s'étaient sentis obligés d'expurger leur traduction de certaines expressions qui auraient risqué de le scandaliser et de lui faire croire que les juifs ne professaient pas le monothéisme le plus pur. Il était donc évident que cette traduction 'ad usum delphini' était, aux yeux du rabbinat palestinien, parfaitement inapte à fonder la halacha des juifs alexandrins. Sur cette tradition des corrections faites pour le roi Ptolémée, voir ma communication au colloque de Strasbourg (Barthélemy 1971:59-63)

[27] Gooding (1963:378-379) estime que certains juifs alexandrins pouvaient être au courant du fait que leur Septante se fondait sur un texte hébreu différent de certaines autres formes textuelles dont on faisait usage ailleurs, 'et nous pouvons comprendre pourquoi on a créé une histoire des origines de la Septante qui non seulement glorifie-

en établissant l'authenticité une fois pour toutes... grâce à un faux de première main: un prétendu rapport sur l'œuvre de traduction qui aurait été rédigé par l'un des commissaires grecs désignés par Ptolémée pour cette célèbre entreprise. Ce rapport attestait les garanties qu'on avait prises pour se procurer un texte hébraïque d'une qualité supérieure (§§ 30-31, 176) à tous ceux qui circulaient en Égypte (discrète allusion à l'erreur qu'il y aurait aujourd'hui à vouloir appuyer les recensions sur ces textes courants de qualité douteuse). Le rapport montrait ensuite le soin pris pour recruter les traducteurs (§§ 32, 39, 46-50) puis mettre leur sagesse à l'épreuve par des questions subtiles (§§ 295-296), les conditions de travail idéales qu'on leur avait fournies (§§ 301, 303-307), le sérieux avec lequel ils avaient accompli leur tâche, discutant à fond tous les points sur lesquels ils pouvaient diverger (§ 302). On rappelait ensuite les cérémonies de la promulgation en présence de toute la communauté juive enthousiaste, réunie à Pharos (§§ 308-309). Puis, les anciens avaient garanti la légitimité de l'entreprise et l'exactitude rigoureuse de la traduction (§ 310). Et on mentionnait que la solennité s'était achevée par une malédiction contre quiconque retoucherait la lettre du texte, soit en l'allongeant, soit en l'altérant si peu que ce fût, soit en y retranchant, malédiction que l'on qualifiait d'excellente mesure pour garder le texte à jamais immuable (§ 311). Après la promulgation, le Roi avait donné ordre de prendre des livres le plus grand soin et de veiller scrupuleusement à leur conservation (§ 317).

La lettre d'Aristée semble bien avoir produit l'effet qu'on en attendait: mettre un frein aux tentatives de recension sur l'hébreu. En effet on ne retrouve pas trace dans la Bible de Philon ni en la tradition textuelle postérieure de ces recensions sur l'hébreu[28] qui apparaissaient dans les citations bibliques du 2e siècle ou du début du 1er siècle avant J. C.[29]

---

rait la Loi et la sagesse de ses traducteurs en comparaison de la littérature grecque et de ses sages, mais qui, du même coup, assurerait à la juiverie alexandrine que son texte hébraïque et la traduction grecque faite à partir de ce texte étaient des représentants authentiques de la Loi; ils venaient directement du grand prêtre de Jérusalem avec son autorité et sa bénédiction'. Klijn (1965:155) dit: 'Généralement parlant, on doit se demander si l'auteur défend une traduction déjà existante contre une révision ou une révision contre une ou des traduction(s) déjà existante(s).' Klijn s'appuie sur les §§ 310-311 de la Lettre pour conclure en faveur de la première branche de l'alternative (p. 157).

[28] Les formes textuelles 'hébraïsantes' qu'ont les lemmes dans une partie de la tradition textuelle de Philon sont empruntées à la recension d'Aquila. Voir ma communication au colloque de Lyon (Barthélemy 1967:46-55).

[29] Pour Aristobule, voir ci-dessus, note 24. Vers 100 avant J. C., Ézéchiel le Tragique faisait usage, pour l'Exode, d'un texte Septante ayant subi quelques recensions sur

L'AUTONOMIE DE LA BIBLE GRECQUE

Notons que les arguments employés par le faussaire pour authentifier la traduction sont de type rationnel. Pas plus que son prédécesseur Aristobule ou que le petit-fils de Sirach son contemporain, il ne fait appel à un charisme d'inspiration dont eussent été gratifiés les traducteurs. D'ailleurs la cessation de l'inspiration prophétique depuis la clôture du livre de Malachie était un dogme pour le judaïsme palestinien de l'époque.[30] Sur ce point cependant, la tradition populaire alexandrine aura vite fait de déborder les arguments raisonnables du Pseudo-Aristée. La foule juive d'Alexandrie n'a pas idée des exigences techniques d'une traduction et n'a aucun sens de ce que doit être la qualité d'un texte de base ou des critères auxquels se mesure la compétence d'un traducteur. Mais le miracle des petites maisons garantit pleinement à son chauvinisme fervent que sa Bible porte le sceau de Dieu. Il ne faudrait pas croire pour autant que la confiance absolue des didascales alexandrins en leur Bible grecque se soit fondée sur une légende de pèlerinage ou sur le faux du Pseudo-Aristée. Elle leur est antérieure. Aristobule déjà ne manifeste aucune connaissance du texte hébraïque. Il traite le texte grec qu'il commente comme un texte tenant de lui-même sa propre valeur et non comme une traduction (Walter 1964:131-132). Il en était de même dès la fin du 3e siècle pour Démétrius le Chronographe (Walter 1964:99).

Ce qui a valu si vite à la Septante une telle autorité c'est d'abord le fait que la promulgation ptolémaïque officielle en a fait la forme authentique de la loi des juifs pour le royaume des Lagides, et, en suite de cela, le fait que la Bible grecque dût remplacer très vite la Bible hébraïque dans la lecture synagogale. Un juif d'Alexandrie possédait ainsi sur son coreligionnaire palestinien un grand avantage: il lisait le texte authentique de la Bible dans sa langue de tous les jours. La connaissance de la Bible n'était pas à Alexandrie le privilège d'érudits ayant l'accès d'une langue morte, comme elle l'était à Jérusalem du fait de l'interdiction d'écrire le Targum.[31] À Alexandrie, c'était par la même porte qu'on

---

l'hébreu. Ainsi, en Ex 1.5, il lit 70 et non 75 (Eusebius 1954: 1e part, 525, 4). Vaccari (1957:342) a cru déceler dans le papyrus Fouad 266 (entre 100 et 50 avant J. C.) une correction sur l'hébreu. Wevers (1968:47) en a relevé d'autres dans les fragments de l'Exode trouvés dans la 7e grotte de Qumrân (100 avant J. C.).

[30] C'est affirmé par une boraïtha (Sanh. 11a et parallèles): 'Depuis que les derniers prophètes, Aggée, Zacharie et Malachie sont morts, l'esprit saint s'est retiré d'Israël.'
[31] Le Talmud palestinien (Meg. IV, 1) raconte: 'R. Samuel ben Isaac entra dans une synagogue. Il vit qu'un maître d'école lisait le Targum à partir d'un livre. Il lui dit: "cela t'est interdit. Des mots qui ont été dits oralement doivent être transmis oralement."

avait accès à Moïse et à la culture profane la plus actuelle. Il suffit
de vivre un peu dans l'œuvre de Philon pour savourer la qualité religieuse
et culturelle de ce judaïsme en vêtements alexandrins. À l'époque de
Philon, Alexandrie était certes en relations étroites avec Jérusalem, mais
il y avait bon temps que la fille des bords du Nil avait obtenu son émancipation. Et l'on peut dire que c'est au jour où la Loi fut promulguée
en grec dans l'île de Pharos que l'enfant était sortie de tutelle. On avait
bien conscience de ce fait à Alexandrie, et c'est pourquoi on redoutait
qu'en imposant à la Bible grecque une recension sur l'hébreu, Jérusalem
n'essayât de reprendre barre sur le judaïsme alexandrin. D'où l'importance qu'eût la lettre d'Aristée pour sauver l'autonomie alexandrine en
forçant les recenseurs à renoncer à leur entreprise.

On peut donc dire que la confiance des alexandrins en leur Septante
fut d'abord un fait qui allait de soi. N'était-ce pas entièrement sur
la Bible grecque que s'était développé un judaïsme tout aussi fidèle
que celui des palestiniens et plus éclairé? pourtant un Philon n'en
restera pas là. Sur ce fait, il construira une doctrine, celle de l'inspiration
prophétique des traducteurs. Bien qu'il exprime cette doctrine en un
vocabulaire platonicien, il ne semble pas qu'il faille y voir une contamination extérieure de sa foi juive. Il ne faut pas s'imaginer non plus que
la conviction de Philon sur ce point ait été motivée par la légende des
petites maisons, bien qu'il fasse écho à cette tradition locale. Aux yeux
de Philon, le charisme d'inspiration était requis par la tâche surhumaine
qui incombait aux traducteurs: transposer en un langage nouveau des
lois révélées par Dieu sans rien en retrancher, ajouter ou modifier, mais
en préservant intégralement les concepts de base et ce qu'avait de caractéristique leur expression première. Chargés d'une telle mission, les
traducteurs ne cherchèrent pas l'aide des érudits du Musée ou des ou-
vrages accumulés dans la Bibliothèque Royale. Ils choisirent, hors des
murs, la grève de Pharos et là, dans la seule compagnie des quatre éléments de la nature, ils élevèrent le livre saint vers les cieux, suppliant
Dieu qu'il leur donnât de ne pas faillir à leur tâche. Et Dieu les exauça
si bien que ce fut sous la possession de l'Esprit révélateur lui-même qu'ils
accomplirent leur œuvre.[32]

En reconstituant ainsi l'histoire de l'événement, Philon ne fait que
formuler ce qu'implique à ses yeux l'autonomie indiscutable que s'est
acquise la Septante comme témoin immédiat de la révélation mosaïque.

---

[32] De Vita Mosis II, 36-37 (Philo 1902:208, 11-21).

PRIMAUTÉ DU PENTATEUQUE À ALEXANDRIE

Dans cette étude sur l'origine et l'autorité de la Bible grecque, j'ai limité mon propos au Pentateuque. En effet c'est essentiellement sur lui que portent les traditions et les documents auxquels nous avons fait appel. Et il faut noter que le Pentateuque jouit dans le judaïsme alexandrin d'une primauté beaucoup plus tranchée que celle que lui reconnaissent esséniens ou pharisiens de Palestine. On peut dire qu'à Alexandrie, lorsqu'on passe de la Loi aux Prophètes, il y a vraiment passage d'un ordre à un autre. De cette primauté marquée de la Loi, nous avons de nombreux indices: il suffit de parcourir l'index des citations bibliques de Philon[33] et de voir comment il introduit les rares emplois qu'il fait de livres extérieurs au Pentateuque (Heinemann 1932:527-528), ou de noter que tous les fragments bibliques grecs préchrétiens d'origine égyptienne sûrement identifiés ne contiennent que des textes du Pentateuque.[34] En parcourant le livre de la Sagesse[35] ou les fragments judéo-alexandrins conservés par Eusèbe,[36] on est frappé de voir que tous ces auteurs avaient toujours le Pentateuque sous les yeux, se passionnant pour l'époque des patriarches ou celle de Moïse et ne faisant que de rares allusions aux événements postérieurs. Cette primauté exceptionnellement marquée dont jouit le Pentateuque à Alexandrie ne tient-elle pas à ce que seul il a fait l'objet de la traduction initiale officiellement promulguée? Il acquérait par là une autorité qu'on ne pouvait revendiquer pour aucun autre livre. Lui et lui seul était canonisé.

Le petit-fils de Sirach nous atteste cependant[37] qu'on ne tarda pas à traduire les autres livres que certains milieux palestiniens considéraient comme sacrés. Mais on peut constater que leurs traducteurs gardèrent toujours les yeux fixés sur la traduction du Pentateuque comme sur une norme indiscutée.[38] Et ces livres n'occupèrent jamais qu'une position périphérique aux yeux des vrais lettrés d'Alexandrie comme Aristobule ou Philon.

[33] Dans l'index de Leisegang (1926:29-43) les livres extérieurs au Pentateuque ne représentent que 5% des références bibliques.
[34] Genèse et Deutéronome dans le pap. Fouad 266, Deutéronome dans le pap. Rylands grec 458.
[35] L'auteur de la Sagesse semble familier avec presque tous les écrits de l'Ancien Testament. Mais ce sont la Genèse (en 10. 1-14) et l'Exode (de 10.15 à la fin) qui constituent la trame sur laquelle il brode son midrash.
[36] 'Les écrivains dont Alexandre Polyhistor nous livre des extraits ont surtout exploité les plus anciens récits de la Bible.' (Schürer 1909:482).
[37] Prologue à la traduction grecque du Siracide, versets 24-26.
[38] Thackeray (1909:30) note que:' les traducteurs récents prirent le Pentateuque grec pour modèle'.

On ne saurait dire qu'il en fût de même dans toutes les familles juives de langue grecque. Dans le IVe livre des Maccabées (18:10-19) la mère des jeunes martyrs leur rappelle l'éducation qu'ils ont reçue à la maison:

tant que votre père était en vie, il vous enseignait la Loi et les Prophètes, il vous lisait comment Abel avait été tué par Caïn, le sacrifice d'Isaac et l'emprisonnement de Joseph. Il vous parlait de Phinéés le Zélote et vous enseignait le cantique qu'Ananias, Azarias et Misaël avaient chanté dans le feu. Il rendait gloire à Daniel dans la fosse aux lions et le bénissait. Il vous rappelait les écrits d'Isaïe où il est dit: "même si je passe par le feu, la flamme ne me consumera pas". Il vous chantait les hymnes écrits par David: "Nombreuses sont les angoisses du juste". Et il vous citait cette similitude dite par Salomon: "Il est un arbre de vie pour tous ceux qui font sa volonté". Il vous attestait les oracles d'Ézéchiel qui s'était demandé si ces os-là revivront. Et il n'oubliait pas de vous apprendre le cantique où Moïse enseigne: "C'est moi qui tue et qui fais vivre. Et voici votre vie et ce qui prolongera vos jours."

L'enseignement biblique en famille ignorait donc les distinctions des lettrés et on peut constater que les privilèges du Pentateuque grec n'avaient pas gêné la diffusion des autres livres dans le peuple. Le fait que le Pentateuque et lui seul ait été canonisé par promulgation officielle dès les origines de la communauté alexandrine eut pour conséquence que les autres livres durent pénétrer dans la langue grecque d'une manière quasi-clandestine et comme dans l'ombre de leurs grands aînés. Jamais les lettrés d'Alexandrie ne rouvrirent officiellement leur canon. La présence d'autres livres sacrés autour du Pentateuque demeura toujours officieuse. Aussi ne faut-il pas s'étonner si les limites de la collection scripturaire hellénistique demeurèrent toujours assez floues.

RÉFÉRENCES

Barthélemy, Dominique
   1967   "Est-ce Hoshaya Rabba qui censura le Commentaire Allégorique?", *Philon d'Alexandrie* (Paris: CNRS), 45-78.
   1971   "Eusèbe, la Septante et 'les autres'", *La Bible et les Pères* (Paris: Presses Universitaires), 51-65.
Bayer, Erich
   1942   *Demetrios Phalereus der Athener* (= *Tübinger Beiträge zur Altertumswissenschaft* 36) (Stuttgart: Kohlhammer).
Bickerman(n), Elias J.
   1935   "La charte séleucide de Jérusalem", *Revue des Études Juives* 100 (Paris: Durlacher), 4-35.
   1959   "The Septuagint as a Translation", *Proceedings of the American Academy for Jewish Research* 41 (New York), 1-39.

Bouché-Leclercq, Auguste
1903 *Histoire des Lagides*, 1er tome (Paris: Leroux).
1906 *Histoire des Lagides*, 3e tome (Paris: Leroux).
Bright, John
1972 *A History of Israel*, 2e éd. (Philadelphia: Westminster).
Cazelles, Henri
1954 "La mission d'Esdras", *Vetus Testamentum* 4 (Leiden: Brill), 113-140.
Clemens Alexandrinus
1960 *Stromata* Buch I-VI (= *Die Griechischen Christlichen Schriftsteller der ersten Jahrhunderte, Clemens Alexandrinus*, 2e vol.) éd. par O. Stählin, 3e éd. par L. Früchtel (Berlin: Akademie).
Cohortatio ad Gentiles
1879 *Opera Justini addubitata* (*Justini philosophi et martyris opera quae feruntur omnia...*), 3e éd., 2e tome, éd. par J. C. Th. de Otto (Jéna: Fischer), 18-127.
Dittenberger, Wilhelm
1903 *Orientis Graeci Inscriptiones selectae*, 1er vol. (Leipzig: Hirzel).
Elter, Anton
1894-1895 *De Aristobulo Judaeo* I-V (= *De Gnomologiorum Graecorum historia atque origine commentatio* V-IX) (Bonn: Universitätsprogramme).
Eusebius Caesariensis
1903 *Die Kirchengeschichte*, éd. par Ed. Schwartz (= *Die Griechischen Christlichen Schriftsteller der ersten drei Jahrhunderte, Eusebius Werke*, 2e vol., 1e part; 2e part 1908) (Leipzig: Hinrichs).
1954 *Die Praeparatio Evangelica*, éd. par K. Mras (= *Die Griechischen Christlichen Schriftsteller der ersten Jahrhunderte, Eusebius Werke*, 8e vol., 1e part; 2e part 1956) (Berlin: Akademie).
Frankel, Zacharias
1841 *Vorstudien zu der Septuaginta* (Leipzig: Vogel).
Fraser, Peter M.
1972 *Ptolemaic Alexandria*, 3 vols. (Oxford: Clarendon).
Gooding, David W.
1963 "Aristeas and Septuagint Origins", *Vetus Testamentum* 13 (Leiden: Brill), 357-379.
Hanhart, Robert
1962 "Fragen um die Entstehung der LXX", *Vetus Testamentum* 12 (Leiden: Brill), 139-163.
Heinemann, Isaak
1932 *Philons griechische und jüdische Bildung* (Breslau: Marcus).
Hodius, Humfredus
1684 *Contra historiam Aristeae de LXX interpretibus dissertatio* (Oxford: Lichfield).
Jellicoe, Sidney
1968 *The Septuagint and Modern Study* (Oxford: Clarendon).
Josephus, Flavius
1926 *Against Apion*, éd. par H. St. John Thackeray (= *The Loeb Classical Library, Josephus*, 1er vol.) (London: Heinemann), 161-411.
Kahle, Paul E.
1959 *The Cairo Geniza*, 2e éd. (Oxford: Blackwell).
Keller, Robert
1948 *De Aristobulo Judaeo* (Bonn: Phil. Diss.).
Klijn, Albertus F. J.
1965 "The Letter of Aristeas and the Greek Translation of the Pentateuch in Egypt", *New Testament Studies* 11 (Cambridge: University Press), 154-158.

Leisegang, Hans
    1926   *Indices ad Philonis Alexandrini opera* (= *Philonis Alexandrini opera quae supersunt*, 7ᵉ vol.) (Berlin: de Gruyter).
Lettre d'Aristée à Philocrate
    1962   Éd. par André Pelletier (= *Sources chrétiennes* 89) (Paris: Cerf).
Michaeli, Frank
    1967   *Les livres des Chroniques, d'Esdras et de Néhémie. Commentaire de l'Ancien Testament* (Neuchâtel: Delachaux).
Moraux, Paul
    1951   *Les listes anciennes des ouvrages d'Aristote* (Louvain: Ed. Universitaires).
Myers, Jacob M.
    1965   *Ezra. Nehemia. The Anchor Bible* (New York: Doubleday).
Olmstead, Albert T.
    1970   *History of the Persian Empire*, 6ᵉ ed. (Chicago: University).
Pelletier, André
    1962   (éd.) *Lettre d'Aristée à Philocrate* (= *Sources chrétiennes* 89) (Paris: Cerf).
Philo Alexandrinus
    1902   *Opera quae supersunt*, 4ᵉ vol., éd. par L. Cohn (Berlin: Reimer).
Rost, Leonhard
    1970   "Vermutungen über den Anlass zur griechischen Übersetzung der Tora", dans H. J. Stoebe (éd.), *Wort-Gebot-Glaube* (= *Abhandlungen zur Theologie des Alten und Neuen Testaments* 59) (Zürich: Zwingli), 39-44.
Rudolph, Wilhelm
    1949   *Esra und Nehemia. Handbuch zum Alten Testament* (Tübingen: Mohr).
Schürer, Emil
    1909   *Geschichte des jüdischen Volkes im Zeitalter Jesu Christi*, 4ᵉ éd., 3ᵉ vol. (Leipzig: Hinrichs).
Tcherikover, Victor A.
    1957   *Corpus Papyrorum Judaicarum*, 1ᵉʳ vol. (Harvard: University).
Thackeray, Henry St. John
    1909   *A Grammar of the Old Testament in Greek* (Cambridge: University Press).
Vaccari, Alberto
    1957   "Papiro Fuad. inv. 266", *Studia Patristica* 1 (= *Texte und Untersuchungen zur Geschichte der altchristlichen Literatur* 63) (Berlin: Akademie), 339-342.
Valckenaer, Lodewijk C.
    1806   *Diatribe de Aristobulo* (Leiden: Luchtmans).
Vaux, Roland de
    1937   "Les décrets de Cyrus et de Darius sur la reconstruction du Temple", *Revue Biblique* 46 (Paris: Gabalda), 29-57.
Vives, Ludovicus
    1522   *In Sancti Augustini de Civitate Dei* (Bâle: Froben).
Walter, Nikolaus
    1964   *Der Thoraausleger Aristobulos* (= *Texte und Untersuchungen zur Geschichte der altchristlichen Literatur* 86) (Berlin: Akademie).
Walters, Peter
    1973   *The Text of the Septuagint*, éd. par D. W. Gooding (Cambridge: University Press).
Wehrli, Fritz
    1949   *Demetrios von Phaleron* (= *Die Schule des Aristoteles* 4) Bâle: Schwabe).
Wendland, Paul
    1895   Contribution à *De Aristobulo Judaeo* (= *De Gnomologiorum Graecorum historia atque origine commentatio* IX par Anton Elter) (Bonn: Universitätsprogramm, Index scholarum, Octobre), 229-234.

1898 "Recension de *De Gnomologiorum Graecorum historia atque origine commentatio* par Anton Elter", *Byzantinische Zeitschrift* 7, 445-49.

1902 "Article *Aristobulus of Panaeas*", *The Jewish Encyclopedia* 2 (New York et Londres: Funk and Wagnalls), 97-98.

Wevers, John W.

1968 "Septuaginta Forschungen seit 1954", *Theologische Rundschau* 33 (Tübingen: Mohr), 18-76.

THE PERFECT WITH *WAW* IN 2 SAMUEL 6:16

P. A. H. DE BOER

The usual translation of 2 Sam. 6:16 reads:

As the ark of the Lord was entering the city of David, Saul's daughter Michal looked down through the window and saw king David leaping and dancing before the Lord, and she despised him in her heart.

There are some differences in the modern translations, but these involve the division of the sentence. Dhorme (1910: 323ff.) distinguishes three clauses,

Comme l'arche de Iahvé entrait dans la cité de David, la fille de Saül, Mîcal, regardait par la fenêtre. Elle vit le roi David dansant et gambadant devant Iahvé. Alors elle le méprisa en son cœur.

Kittel (1922) connects the last two clauses and translates,

Während nun die Lade Jahwes in die Stadt Davids einzog, hatte Sauls Tochter Michal durchs Fenster geblickt. Und als sie den König David sah, wie er vor Jahwe hüpfte und tanzte, empfand sie Verachtung für ihn.

It appears that differences in translation exist, too; the rendering of *mᵉp̄azzēz ūmᵉkarkēr* may or may not be in connection with the reading of the parallel text in 1 Chron. 15:29. Those differences will not be considered here.

The following verses (2 Sam. 6: 17-19) continue and complete the story of the bringing up of the ark. Verse 19 ends with the common final line of narratives, "all the people departed every one to his house". In the recension to be found in the Chronicles version, verse 20a, "And David returned to bless his house" is taken into the final sentence of the story. Then follows (2 Sam. 6:20-23) the scene in David's palace. The Chronicler, dropping this scene, adds, after the blessing of the people by David, a long passage of liturgical character, in which large parts of some Psalms – 105, 96, and others – are incorporated. Evidently he could

Dr. P. A. H. de Boer is Professor at Leiden University, Leiden, The Netherlands.

not use David's punishment of Michal in his picture of the chosen king.

Michal's observation of David and her resultant feelings (2 Sam. 6:16b) anticipate the story of her reprobation because of her criticism of David's behaviour. Smith (1912:295) observes,

The verse [16] is designed to prepare for the scene at home. As it breaks the thread of the narrative, and is introduced awkwardly [16a], it is perhaps a redactional insertion.

Budde (1902:231) and Dhorme (1910:323) do not accept Smith's opinion but fail to argue why they take verse 16 as belonging to the original narrative.

Almost every translator and commentator changes the first word of verse 16. Instead of *weḥāyāh*, perfect with *waw*, one reads *wayhî*, imperfect with *waw*.[1] The Revised Version (1884) is an exception in trying to maintain the Masoretic text, rendering, "And it was so, as the ark of the Lord came into the city of David, that...."

The emendation, reading *wayhî* instead of *weḥāyāh*, is supported by the recension in 1 Chron. 15:29 and by the rendering in the Septuagint, while the rendering of the Vulgate, "cumque intrasset arca domini civitatem David" might also reflect the reading *wayhî*. Peshiṭta and Targum, using perfect forms, do not support the Masoretic reading being *whw'* and *whwh* the rendering both of *weḥāyāh* and *wayhî*. Recently a fragment from Qumrân, 4QSam[a], has been found to strengthen the emendation.[2] It seems certain that in the future few people will continue to prefer the Masoretic reading of 2 Sam. 6:16a.

A difficult question remains unanswered, however. Why is an understandable reading changed into a form which at first sight does not make sense? This question is rarely taken into consideration. Klostermann

---

[1]   Without striving for completeness I mention a number of commentaries and translations from the latest time: Klostermann (1887:153); S. R. Driver (1913:270); Het Oude Testament (Leiden Translation) (1899); Smith (1912:295); Budde (1902:231); Dhorme (1910:323); Schulz (1920:72); Kittel (1922); Caspari (1926:473); Das Buch Schmuel (n.d.); Die Heilige Schrift (1931); de Groot (1935:21); Revised Standard Version (1952); de Vaux (1956); Dhorme (1956); Goslinga (1956:78,86f); van den Born (1956:153); Grispino (1965); Hertzberg (1965:226); The New American Bible (1969); The New English Bible (1970).

[2]   See the Notes to the New American Bible. I could check the reading on a xerox of the photograph, kindly made available to me by Professor F. M. Cross, Jr., in view of the Biblia Hebraica Stuttgartensia, Samuel, which is expected to appear in 1974 (de Boer i.p.).

(1887:153) supposes, "*weʰāyāh* ist vermutlich aus *weʰhinnēh* entstellt", but he did not have confidence in his guess; *weʰhinnēh* is wrongly spelled *weʰāyāh*, as appears from his translation "Es geschah aber", as in the reading in 1 Chron. 15:29. Budde (1902:231) suggests as original reading *weʰā'ārôn* instead of *weʰāyāh 'aʰrôn yhwh*. Cod. Vaticanus of the Septuagint, leaving Yahweh unrendered, is no real support for this suggestion because of its καὶ ἐγένετο. Joüon (1947: paragraph 119z, 336) thinks that graphic resemblance between *weʰāyāh* and *wayʰî* "peut expliquer en partie certains *weʰāyāh* anormaux" (1 Sam. 1:12; 10:9; 13:22; 17:48; 25:20; 2 Sam. 6:16; 2 Kings 3:15; Jer. 37:11; Amos 7:2). He adds to 2 Sam. 6:16, "mais parall. 1 Chron. 15:29 correctement *wayʰî*". Joüon's reservation "en partie" discourages real discussion. The supposition of a possible orthographic variant seems to me arbitrary. If *wayʰî* is taken as a variant of *weʰāyāh* in 2 Sam. 6:16 we ought to speak of a real variant reading and not of an orthographic one. The same applies, in my opinion, to the other quoted texts, where the Septuagint renders καὶ ἐγένετο or καὶ ἐγενήθη. Such variants, in most cases emendations, are of the category: *weʰḳataltî* instead of *wayyiḳtōl*. The difficult question, why a perfect with *waw* has been chosen instead of the usual imperfect with *waw*, which is according to the later witnesses a smoother reading, remains unanswered.

Those who maintain the Masoretic reading seem to be compelled to credit *weʰāyāh* here with the meaning of *wayʰî*. Gesenius-Kautzsch (1885) concludes the "Gebrauch des Perfect" in the Grammatik with

Dass jedoch *weʰayah* auch zur Fortführung der Erzählung verwendet werden kann, lehrt Gen. 30: 41; 38: 9; 1 Sam. 13: 22 (überall in Bezug auf eine in der Vergangenheit wiederholte Handlung); 1 Sam. 1: 12; 13: 22; 25: 20; Jer. 3: 9; 37: 11; 38: 28; Hiob 1: 1.

An explanation is not given. Davidson (1902: 81, paragraph 54, Rem. 1 (2)) distinguishes perfect with strong *waw*, and mentions herewith, "Details are often introduced or a new start made in the narrative by *weʰāyāh*." And further on (1902: 85, paragraph 58), "The use of *waw* perf. as freq. is exceedingly free; it may occur in any connexion, introducing an additional trait or an entirely new fact"; and perfect with simple *waw*. In the latter he states that there are many cases where *waw* with perfect appears in simple narrative, and is merely copulative. The usage becomes more common as the language declines and comes under the influence of Aramaic. But Davidson does not dismiss lightly the difficulty by everywhere supposing Aramaic influence.

Even in early style, the form *wehāyah and it was* is not quite rare. Amos 7: 2; 1 Sam. 1: 12; 10: 9; 17: 48; 25: 20; 2 Sam. 6: 16. In Gen. 38: 5³ read *wehî'* with Septuagint (1902: 85).

Davidson's remark in the same paragraph of his important *Syntax* seems to me elucidating," The perfect with *waw* seems occasionally to resume and restate briefly an event previously described in detail; Judg. 7: 13 *wᵉnāpal*; 1 Kings 20: 21; Gen. 15: 6.(?)" He finds Judg. 3: 25 and 2 Sam. 13: 18 to be curious. I shall return to Davidson's remark below.

Joüon (1947: 335) observes,

Même en tenant largement compte des altérations possibles du texte conso- nantique, il reste un assez grand nombre de *wᵉkatalti et j'ai tué* anormaux, c'est-à-dire contraires à l'usage.

Next to the supposition of errors through graphic resemblance concern- ing *wayhî* and *wᵉhāyāh*, in my opinion an impossible idea (see above), he takes into account the influence of Aramaic and post-Biblical Hebrew. But he reckons also with other factors. Paragraph 119z of his useful *Grammaire*, however, does not explain those cases where no influence of Aramaic or post-Biblical Hebrew is supposed.

It is incorrect, in my opinion, to detach the cases of *wᵉhāyāh* in question from the rather many cases of perfect with *waw* in simple narrative. Let us first look at some of those cases. In 2 Kings 23: 4, 5, 10, 12, and 15, five cases occur. They are considered to be incorrect forms and translated as imperfects with *waw*, see Klostermann (1887: 479ff); Benzinger (1899: 192ff), and others. Klostermann supposes in some cases – also in 2 Kings 14: 7 – an original reading *(wᵉ) hû'* plus verb, to get rid of the "impossible perf. cons.". Davidson (1902: 85) considers *waw* here and in similar cases as merely copulative (see also Montgomery-Gehman 1951: 529ff; Gray 1970: 730ff). It is possible that perfect with *waw* in the quoted texts indicates late additions or a late redactional influence. Such seems more likely than to suppose similarity in meaning between the perfect with *waw* forms and the imperfect with *waw* forms. I prefer, however, following Davidson's remark about some other texts quoted above, reckoning with a special meaning of perfect with *waw*: an attempt to express a brief resumption of an event described in detail previously, or to express a kind of conclusion or making a record, a statement, or to indicate the conditions for a following narrative.

³ The Septuagint reading is αὐτὴ δὲ ἦν. καὶ ἦν is usually the rendering of *wayhî* but occurs sometimes as rendering of *wᵉhāyāh*, indicating a durative, see Gen. 38:5; Num. 11:8; Judg. 2:18, and 2 Kings 18:7.

In several studies the additional character of the perfect with *waw* cases in 2 Kings 23 has been proven. But, even as additions to an earlier story, the forms may preserve a special meaning. It seems possible, I think, to paraphrase the verses in question as follows: verse 4, "Well, thus he has carried their ashes to Bethel" – a scoffing allusion to Bethel's cult, anticipating Bethel's destruction mentioned in verses 15ff. Verse 5, "Well, thus he has stopped the heathen priests" (of Jerusalem's surroundings). Verse 10, "Well, thus he has desecrated Tefet." Verse 12, "Well, thus he has thrown their ashes into the wadi Kedron", indicating the definitive end of the cult. Verse 15, "Well, thus he has burnt Ashera", here using intentionally the name of the goddess to state the total destruction of Bethel's cult.

wᵉnāp̄al hā'ōhel, at the end of verse 13 in Judges 7, whether or not it is an addition, is in my opinion another example of a conclusive statement expressed by perfect with *waw*, "Well, thus the tent has collapsed." Similarly preserved is a final statement in 1 Kings 20: 21, "Well, thus he has smitten the Aramaeans with great slaughter" – a resumption of the preceding story. Gen. 15: 6, in Davidson's work mentioned with a question mark, might mean as a record, "Well, he was a believer in Yahweh, therefore he – Yahweh – planned righteousness – blessing – for him."[4]

In Judg. 3: 23 *wᵉnāʿāl* may have the meaning, "Well, thus it – the door – was tied up", a repetition of the idea expressed with the verb *śāgar*, indicating the durative. But in 2 Sam. 13: 18 the use of *wᵉnāʿāl* is curious. Davidson (1902: 85) rightly observes that verse 18 states how the *two* injunctions of verse 17 were literally carried out. It would seem we are forced to suppose here a record of Amnon's definite decision. In Ezek. 37: 2, 7, 10 one may assume a condition, expressed by the construction with perfect with *waw*. I think that Zimmerli (1969: 886) is right in his comments,

eine die Vorbedingung beschreibende Aussage im perf. mit *waw* führt vorbereitend hin zu der eigentlich akzentuierten Hauptaussage.
Man wird also keineswegs schon mit einer völligen Einebnung des perf. mit *waw* in der allgemeinen Gebrauch des perf., wie sie dann etwa in der späten Sprache Kohelets zu finden ist, zu rechnen haben.

---

[4]   The pointing of the Masoretic text, *wᵉhĕ'ᵉmīn* read a hiph. perf. with *waw*. This meaning is found in the Septuagint, moreover adding the name Abraham. See, too, the quotation in Rom. 4:3; Gal. 3:6, and James 2:23. The spelling of the Hebrew text handed down to us suggests a reading *wᵉhāʾᵃmēn*, imperative hiph. Such would give a totally different idea.

Such a condition, expressed in an introductory clause, is usually followed by a nominal sentence, introduced with w^e*hinnēh* or by sentences using imperfect with *waw*. 1 Sam. 5: 7, "Well, thus they have said", and 2 Sam. 16: 5, *ūbā'* picturing a situation which is the condition for the following story, seem to me to be in the same category.

w^e*hāyāh* occurs several times to express frequency, repetition, or iteration: Gen. 38: 9; Exod. 17: 11; 33: 7, 8, 9; Num. 21: 9; Judg. 6: 3; 1 Sam. 16: 23; 17: 48; 2 Sam. 14: 26; 15: 5; 2 Kings 3: 15. In cases as Exod. 17: 11; 33: 7; and 1 Sam. 16: 23, the similarity of the construction with other perfect with *waw* forms is underlined.

w^e*hāyāh* occurs, too, as the indication of a brief resumption. Hannah's prayer, previously mentioned at length, is in 1 Sam. 1: 12 briefly repeated in order to introduce Eli's intervention. Jer. 40: 3, "Therefore this thing is come upon you" is a conclusive sentence, resuming the preceding record. In Jer. 3: 9, "It has been the staff[5] of her infidelity – adultery, metaphorically used – by which she..." is a resumption as well as a condition for what follows (cf. further Jer. 37: 11; Amos 2: 7 (?); 1 Sam. 10: 9; 13: 22). 1 Sam. 25: 20a seems to me also to be a conditional clause, a clear picture of the situation, introducing the unexpected meeting, "then she met him" (verse 20 end). w^e*hāyāh* in verse 20a is followed by further nominal sentences, constructed with participles: she, Abigail, riding and coming down, and David and his men coming down, kept hidden from each other by a hill in between.

It is time to return to our starting point, 2 Sam. 6: 16. If I am right that several perfect with *waw* clauses possess an intentional meaning and are erroneously understood as mistakes or as additions from a period that did not distinguish between perfect and imperfect with *waw*, 2 Sam. 6: 16a also might indicate a brief statement of the situation, resuming the event of the bringing up of the ark previously described in detail. This should be expected after verse 19, the end of the story.

The reading of the Peshitta suggests verse 16a to be a final statement. In cod. Ambrosianus, sixth or seventh century, we find two marks,

---

[5] I read *makkēl* (z^e*nūtāh*), cf. Hos. 4:12. The staff will be used by sorcery . (see AJirku 1914). C. H. Cornill (1905:37ff.) shows that the pointing *makkēl*, instead of the difficult *mikkōl* of the Masoretic text, has been suggested already by J. D. Michaelis (1793), who was followed by Hitzig (1841:26). Michaelis (1793): "Quod, si legatur *makkēl baculus est scortatio eius*: i. e. cum baculo divinatorio (sacris sortibus) scortatur. Confer Hos. IV, 12 '*ammi $b^e c$*ēṣô yis'al ūmakk^{e}lô yaggîd lô*. Nec vero *baculus* h. l. idolum est, sed ut apud Hoseam instrumentum divinatorium, sagitta ex qua vaticinabantur. Egregie confirmant hanc meam interpretationem, verba quae statim sequuntur." The editor, Schleusner, adds a note wherein he declines. Michaelis' reading

—¦— —¦—, to indicate the end of the story. Other ancient manuscripts do not have these marks. But three of the lectionaries available to me, all of the Nestorian rite, support the final character of verse 16a in Syrian use of the Bible.[6] These liturgical books do not contain the Michal episode. One of the lectionaries mentioned[7] continues the reading after 2 Sam. 6: 16a with 2 Sam. 7: 1 - 5 and 8 - 11. "Thus was the ark of the Lord in David's house" is considered to be the end of the story of the bringing up of the ark.

The Peshitta version gives us a slightly deviating text. The Hebrew *bā*' is not rendered and instead of "town of David" Peshitta reads "house of David". The dropping of *bā*' can be caused by taking verse 16a as a final statement. The variant "house (palace) of David" might be a correction of the Hebrew tradition, or a reminiscent of a lost tradition. A survey of the term *'îr dāwid* suggests that the term is not original in the Books of Samuel. In the story of David's capture of the strong-hold Șiyyôn, 2 Sam. 5: 7, "this is David's town" is evidently a gloss. In 2 Sam. 5: 9 the clause, David giving the stronghold Șiyyôn the name "David's town", is secondary. The stronghold is named *after* David, not *by* David, as appears from the many occurrences of the term in the stories about the time following, preserved in the Books of Kings. Finally, in 2 Sam. 6: 10 and 12, the term is not at all required, but is mere adornment.

2 Sam. 6: 16 is unnecessary for the scene at David's house in verses 20 to 23. This, together with a consideration of the place at which it interrupts the story of the bringing up of the ark, indicates its secondary character. The placement might have been influenced by the description of David's and the people's exuberant behaviour (verses 13-15). We should not forget that the author is writing in glorification of king David. The composer, who might have added verse 16 to connect the story of the bringing up of the ark with the scene at David's house, shows his religious zeal in giving David's cultic behaviour as the reason for Michal's contempt. The story of Michal's criticism of the chosen king and David's humiliation of Saul's daughter aims at dishonour for the house of Saul, diminishing, almost dissolving, David's connection with the clan of the rejected king. The context exhibits the glorification of David as founder of the cult in Jerusalem.

---

[6]　These lectionaria have the sigla 13/1, 15/1 and 16/2 in the Leiden edition of the Peshitta (de Boer i.p.).

[7]　13/1.

Saul's daughter Michal saw king David leaping and dancing before the Lord, and she despised him. 2 Sam. 6: 16a seems to preserve an intentional construction, a perfect with *waw* followed by two participles, expressing the condition by picturing the situation and introducing the verbal clause – she despised him. "Well, thus it was, the ark of the Lord coming into David's city, and Michal, Saul's daughter, looking down through the window...."

REFERENCES

Translations

The Revised Version (Oxford: The University Press, 1884).
Het Oude Testament (Leiden Translation) (Leiden: Brill, 1899).
Die Heilige Schrift des Alten Testaments, E. Kautzsch and A. Bertholet (eds.), 4th ed. (Tübingen: Mohr, 1922).
Das Buch Schmuel, by M. Buber and F. Rosenzweig (Berlin: Schneider, n.d.).
Die Heilige Schrift (Zürich: Zwingli Verlag, 1931).
Revised Standard Version (New York: Oxford Press, 1952).
La Sainte Bible (Bible de Jérusalem) (Paris: du Cerf, 1956).
La Bible, Ed. Pléiade (Paris: Gallimard, 1956).
Confraternity Version (New York: Guild Press, 1965).
The New American Bible (Paterson: St. Anthony Guild Press, 1969).
The New English Bible (Oxford and Cambridge: University Press, 1970).

Other Literature

Benzinger, I.
1899 "Die Bücher der Könige", in K. Marti (ed.), *Kurzer Hand-Commentar* (Freiburg i. B.: Mohr).
Boer, P. A. H. de (ed.)
i.p. The Old Testament in Syriac. Peshiṭta Version, publication on behalf of the International Organization for the Study of the Old Testament by Peshiṭta Institute, Leiden University (Leiden: Brill).
Boer, P. A. H. de
i.p. Samuel. Biblia Hebraica Stuttgartensia (Stuttgart: Württembergische Bibelanstalt).
Born van den
1956 "Samuël" in van den Born, Grossouw, and van der Ploeg (eds.), *De Boeken van het Oude Testament* (Roermond: Romen).
Budde, K.
1902 "Die Bücher Samuel", in K. Marti (ed.), *Kurzer Hand-Commentar* (Freiburg i. B.: Mohr).
Caspari, W.
1926 "Die Samuelbücher", in E. Sellin (ed.), *Kommentar zum Alten Testament* (Leipzig: Deichert).
Cornill, C. H.
1905 *Das Buch Jeremia* (Leipzig: Tauchnitz).
Cross, F. M.
1969 "Textual Notes to the Books of Samuel", (*The New American Bible*) (Paterson: St. Anthony Guild Press).

Davidson, A. B.
    1902 *Hebrew Syntax*, 3rd ed. (Edinburgh: Clark).
Dhorme, P. (E.)
    1910 *Les Livres de Samuel* (Paris: Gabalda).
    1956 Translator of La Bible, Ed. Pléiade (see Translations above).
Driver, S. R.
    1913 *Notes on the Hebrew Text and the Topography of the Books of Samuel*, 2nd ed. (Oxford: Clarendon).
Gesenius, W., — Kautzsch E.
    1885 *Hebräische Grammatik*, 24th ed. (Leipzig: Vogel).
Goslinga, C. J.
    1956 "De Boeken Samuël", *Korte Verklaring der Heilige Schrift* (Kampen: Kok).
Gray, J.
    1970 *I and II Kings* (London: SCM Press).
Grispino, J. A.
    1965 Translator of the Books of Samuel in the Confraternity Version (see Translations above).
Groot, de
    1935 "II Samuël", *Tekst en Uitleg* (Groningen: Wolters).
Hertzberg, H. W.
    1965 "Die Samuelbücher", *Das Alte Testament Deutsch* 10 (Göttingen: Vandenhoeck and Ruprecht).
Hitzig, F.
    1841 "Der Prophet Jeremia", *Kurzgefasstes exegetisches Handbuch* (Leipzig: Weidmann).
Jirku, A.
    1914 *Materialien zur Volksreligion Israels* (Leipzig: Diechert). Reprinted in *Von Jerusalem nach Ugarit, Gesammelte Schriften* (Graz: Akademische Druck- und Verlagsanstalt, 1966).
Joüon, P.
    1947 *Grammaire de l'hébreu biblique*, 2nd ed. (Rome: Institut Biblique Pontifical).
Kittel, R.
    1922 Translator of the Books of Samuel in Die Heilige Schrift des Alten Testaments (see Translations above).
Klostermann, A.
    1887 "Die Bücher Samuelis", in H. Strack and O. Zöckler (eds.), *Kurzgefasster Kommentar* (Nordlingen: Beck).
Michaelis, J. D.
    1793 "Observationes philologicae et criticae in Jeremiae Vaticinia et Threnos" J. F. Schleusner (ed.), (Göttingen: Vandenhoeck and Ruprecht).
Montgomery, J., — H. S. Gehman
    1951 "The Books of Kings", *The International Critical Commentary* (Edinburgh: Clark).
Schleusner, J. F. (ed.)
    1793 see Michaelis.
Schulz, A.
    1920 "Die Bücher Samuel", in J. Nikel (ed.), *Exegetisches Handbuch* (Münster in Westf.: Aschendorff).
Skehan, P. W.
    1969 "Textual Notes to the Books of Samuel", (*The New American Bible*) (Paterson: St. Anthony Guild Press).

Smith, H. P.
  1912 "The Books of Samuel", *The International Critical Commentary*, 3rd ed.
        (Edinburgh: Clark).
Vaux, R. de
  1956 Translator of the Books of Samuel in La Sainte Bible (See Translations
        above).
Wellhausen, J.
  1871 *Der Text der Bücher Samuelis* (Göttingen: Vandenhoeck and Ruprecht).
Zimmerli, W.
  1969 "Ezechiel", *Biblischer Kommentar* (Neukirchen-Vluyn: Neukirchener Verlag).

OBSERVATIONS ON THE TIḲḲÛNÊ SÔPᵉRÎM

WILLIAM McKANE

I

The attestations of the *tiḳḳûnê sôpᵉrîm* which are considered in this article come from the following sources: (a) Mechilta on Exod. 15: 7 (Lauterbach 1949), (b) Siphre on Num. 10: 35 (Friedmann 1864), (c) Yalkut Shimeoni on Exod. 15: 7 (Warsaw 1876), (d) Midrash Tanchuma on Exod. 15: 7 (Wilna 1833), (e) Manuscript Oriental 1425 (Ginsburg 1897: 351), (f) The Massorah Magna of the St. Petersburg Codex of the Prophets at Ezek. 8: 17 and Zech. 2: 12 (Strack 1876), (g) The Massorah of Manuscripts BM Oriental 1379, 2349 and 2365 (Ginsburg 1897: 350, 641 ff., 685 ff.). I shall give each example the same number in all the lists which are reproduced and this will enable us to see easily the extent of attestation which exists for each example. It will also establish that the traditional number of eighteen is made up of different items in the several lists.

(a) The Mechilta of R. Ishmael is a Halakhic midrash on the book of Exodus which was compiled in Palestine and which is not earlier than the end of the fourth century A. D. (Roth, 2, 1972: 1267-1269). The following list of *tiḳḳûnê sôpᵉrîm* appears at Exod. 15: 7:

1. Zech. 2: 12
2. Mal. 1: 13
3. 1 Sam. 3: 13
4. Job 7: 20
5. Hab. 1: 12
6. Jer. 2: 11
7. Ps. 106: 20
8. Num. 11: 15
9. 2 Sam. 20: 1
10. Ezek. 8: 17
11. Num. 12: 12

In respect of all of these we find the statement that the original text has been adjusted (*kynh hktwb*), but only in the case of Num. 12: 12 is the

William McKane is Professor of Hebrew and Oriental Languages at St. Mary's College in The University of St. Andrews, Scotland.

alleged original reproduced (*'mnw hyh lw lwmr*). Hence for Num. 12: 12 we are told that *'immēnû* has been corrected to *'immô*. There is no doubt that number 9 (above) is 2 Sam. 20: 1 rather than 1 Kings 12: 16 or 2 Chron. 10: 16 since *'ên lānû ḥēleḳ*, which is cited, occurs only in the Samuel passage over against *mah lānû* in the other two.

(b) Siphre is a Halakhic midrash on Numbers and Deuteronomy which was probably compiled in Palestine and which is not earlier than the end of the fourth century A. D. (Roth, 14, 1972: 1519-1521). The list, which is shorter than that of the Mechilta, appears at Num. 10: 35. The order of the Mechilta list is maintained except for Ezek. 8: 17, but there are gaps in the series – 2, 3, 6, 9 are missing, that is, Mal. 1: 13, 1 Sam. 3: 13, Jer. 2: 11, 2 Sam. 20: 1.

1. Zech. 2: 12	7. Ps. 106: 20
4. Job 7: 20	8. Num. 11: 15
10. Ezek. 8: 17	11. Num. 12: 12
5. Hab. 1: 12	

(c) Yalkut Shimeoni is a midrashic anthology which covers the whole of the Old Testament. It has been attributed to Simeon ha-Darshan (thirteenth century A. D.), but it did not circulate widely before the end of the fifteenth century (Roth, 16, 1972: 707-709). The following list appears in connection with the midrash on Exod. 15: 7:

1. Zech. 2: 12	7. Ps. 106: 20
2. Mal. 1: 13	9. 2 Sam. 20: 1
3. 1 Sam. 3: 13	11. Num. 12: 12
5. Hab. 1: 12	10. Ezek. 8: 17
6. Jer. 2: 11	

The order of the Mechilta list is preserved except for the reversal of the order of Ezek. 8: 17 and Num. 12: 12. Job 7: 20 and Num. 11: 15, which appear in the preceding two lists, are missing here. No indications of the original text are given either in this or the Siphre list.

(d) Midrash Tanchuma is a homiletical midrash on the entire Pentateuch which was first published in Constantinople in 1522. The genre probably developed in the ninth and tenth centuries A. D., drawing on old as well as more recent sources, which were attributed to R. Tanchuma bar abba, a Palestinian *amora* of the second half of the fourth century A. D. (Roth, 15, 1973: 793-796; cf. Barthélemy 1963: 288). This differs from the preceding lists in two important respects: it probably contains eighteen examples – the "canonical" number of *tikkûnê sôpᵉrîm* – and it gives the alleged original reading in a high proportion of cases.

1. Zech. 2: 12, original *ᶜênî*
2. Mal. 1: 13, original *ᶜôtî*
3. 1 Sam. 3: 13, original not given
4. Job. 7: 20, original *ᶜālêkā*
5. Hab. 1: 12, original *yāmût*
6. Jer. 2: 11, original *kᵉbôdî*
7. Ps. 106: 20, original *kᵉbôdî*
12. Hos. 4: 7, original *kᵉbôdî*
13. Job 32: 3, original not given

14. Gen. 18: 22, original not given
8. Num. 11: 15, original not given
11. Num. 12:12, original *ᶜimmēnû*
11a. Num. 12:12, original *bᵉśārēnû*
15. 1 Kings 12: 16, original *lē'lôhāw*
16. 2 Chron. 10: 16, original *lē'lôhāw*
17. Lam. 3: 20, original not given
18. 2 Sam. 16: 12, original *bᵉᶜênāw*
10. Ezek. 8: 17, original *'appî*

It will be seen that the order of the first seven items is the same as that of the Mechilta list. Hos. 4: 7 has been associated with Jer. 2: 11 and Ps. 106: 20 for the obvious reason that it involves the same kind of *tikkûn* and requires the restoration of a first person suffix with *kābôd*. Beyond this a comparison of the order with that of the Mechilta list is not worth pursuing. There are seven indisputable new items in this list (Hos. 4: 7; Job 32: 3; Gen. 18: 22; 1 Kings 12: 16; 2 Chron. 10: 16; Lam. 3: 20; 2 Sam. 16: 12). Ginsburg (1897: 349) says that there are six new instances and the explanation of this may be that he has overlooked 2 Chron. 10: 16. The text which is cited in the list (*mah lānû ḥēlek bᵉdāwîd* and so on) is 1 Kings 12: 16. This is followed by *ûbᵉdibᵉrê yāmîm* and then the postulated original, *lē'lôhāw*. This means that the original is being given as *lē'lôhāw* in both 1 Kings 12: 16 and the parallel passage 2 Chron. 10: 16. Ginsburg supposes that the number of items in the list is seventeen, but I suggest that we should assume a figure of eighteen and understand that this is meant to be a "complete" list of *tikkûnê sôpᵉrîm*. The figure of eighteen is achieved by counting two *tikkûnîm* – *'immēnû* (11) and *bᵉśārēnû* (11a) – at Num. 12: 12. The artificiality of the number eighteen or, at least, the different ways in which it is computed is shown by the circumstance that elsewhere (in the Massorah Magna of the St. Petersburg Codex of the Prophets) two *tikkûnîm* are counted for each of 1 Kings 12: 16 and 2 Chron. 10: 16. The reason for this is that if *lē'lôhāw* is accepted as the original of *lᵉ'ōhālāw* it follows that *lᵉōhālêkā* must become *lē'lôhêkā*. If, however, this procedure had been followed in the Tanchuma list, the total would have come out as twenty rather than eighteen.

(e) The list which appears in Manuscript Oriental 1425 (Ginsburg

1897: 351) has the heading *tikkûn sôpᵉrîm ᶜezrāʾ ûnᵉhemyāh* and is constituted as follows:

14. Gen. 18: 22, original *wYHWH ᶜômēḏ lᵉpānāy*
8. Num. 11: 15, original *bᵉrāᶜāṭēk*
11. Num. 12: 12, original *ʾimmēnû*
3. 1 Sam. 3: 13, original *lô*

9. 2 Sam. 20: 1, original *lēʾlôhāw*
6. Jer. 2: 11, original *kᵉḇôḏî*

10. Ezek. 8: 17, original *ʾappî*

1. Zech. 12: 12, original *ᶜênî*

19. Mal. 1: 12, original *ʾôṭî*

2. Mal. 1: 13, original *ʾôṭî*
4. Job 7: 20, original *ᶜālēkā*
18. 2 Sam. 16: 12, original *bᵉᶜênāw*
17. Lam. 3: 20, original *napšô*
11a. Num. 12: 12, original *bᵉśārēnû*
13. Job 32: 3, original *šēm šamāyim*

(Number 13 would seem to be a circumlocution for the actual reading, *ʾelôhîm*, according to Ginsburg 1897: 361.)

There is a complete lack of correspondence between the order of this list and that which has been more or less observable in the lists already considered. It would seem that a new principle is operating here and that the items appear in the order of the books of the Hebrew Bible. This accounts perfectly for the order of the first ten items but not for the final four. This list includes a verse which has not appeared in the lists previously considered (Mal. 1: 12) and it supplies six additional "original" readings (1 Sam. 3: 13; Num. 11: 15; 2 Sam. 20: 1; Job 32: 3; Gen. 18: 22; Lam. 3: 20). There is no doubt that it is 2 Sam. 20: 1 which is being cited and not 1 Kings 12: 16 or 2 Chron. 10: 16 since *ʾîš lᵉʾôhālāw yiśrāʾēl* is attributable only to the Samuel passage. Further the circumstance that the two *tikkûnîm* from Num. 12: 12 are recorded separately, one near the beginning of the list and the other near the end, tends to support the view which I have advanced that these should be counted as two in the Tanchuma list.

(f) This list is taken from the Massorah Magna of the St. Petersburg Codex of the Prophets (916 A. D.), where it appears at Ezek. 8: 17 and Zech. 2: 12 (Strack 1876; Ginsburg, 2, 1883: 710, List 205).

14. Gen. 18: 22, *wᵉʾaḇrāhām*

8. Num. 11: 15, *bᵉrāᶜāṭî*

11. Num. 12: 12, *mērehem ʾimmô*
3. 1 Sam. 3: 13, *mᵉkallᵉlîm*
10. Ezek. 8: 17, *hazzᵉmôrāh*
5. Hab. 1: 12, *lôʾnāmûṭ*

6. Jer. 2: 11, *hēmîr kᵉḇôḏô*.

15. 1 Kings 12: 16, *'îš lᵉ'ōhālêḵā yiśrā'ēl*

20. 1 Kings 12: 16, *b bw* = 'a second example in it', referring to *lᵉ'ōhālāw*

16. 2 Chron. 10: 16, *wᵉhaḇrô*, referring to *'îš lᵉ'ōhālêḵā yiśrā'ēl*

21. 2 Chron. 10: 16, *b bw*, referring to *lᵉ'ōhālāw*

13. Job 32: 3, *wayyaršî'û*

4. Job 7: 20, *wā'ehyeh*

19. Mal. 1: 12, *mᵉhallᵉlîm*

2. Mal. 1: 13, *wᵉhippaḥtem*

7. Ps. 106: 20, *wayyāmîrû*

21. Mal. 3: 8, *ḳôḇᵉʿîm*

1. Zech. 2: 12, *bᵉḇāḇaṭ ʿênô*

This list like Ginsburg's List 204 (Ginsburg, 2, 1883: 710) has the heading "Eighteen Examples of the Corrections of the Scribes" and the arithmetic works out correctly for both lists if two items are allowed for each of 1 Kings 12: 16 and 2 Chron. 10: 16. In neither of these lists is any "original" reading reproduced, but an indication is given of where in the verse the *tikkūn* has been made. Items in the Tanchuma list which are absent from the St. Petersburg Codex list (and from Ginsburg's List 204) are numbers 12, 17, 18, 11a (Hos. 4: 7; Lam.3: 20; 2 Sam. 16: 12; the second *tikkūn* of Num. 12: 12). Items additional to the Tanchuma list are numbers 19, 20, 21, 22 (Mal. 1: 12; the second *tikkūn* of 1 Kings 12: 16; the second *tikkūn* of 2 Chron. 10: 16; Mal. 3: 8). No principle is discernible in the ordering of the items of the St. Petersburg Codex list and in this it contrasts with Ginsburg's List 204 which follows the order of the Hebrew Bible. One can say of our list that the first four items follow the order of the Hebrew Bible, but the remainder have a random order in relation to the Hebrew Bible. It is understandable that 2 Chron. 10: 16 should be linked to 1 Kings 12: 16, but not that Ezekiel and Habakkuk should precede Jeremiah, nor that Job should precede Zechariah, Malachi, and Psalms; nor that Malachi should precede Zechariah, nor that Mal. 3: 8 should be separated from Mal. 1: 12, 13 by Ps. 106: 20.

The fragment of the verse which is cited does not always point precisely to the area of the *tikkūn*. Thus 1 Sam. 3: 13 is accompanied by *mᵉḳallᵉlîm*, but the *tikkūn* involves the following word which according to Oriental 1425 was *lô* and not *lāhem*. Ezek. 8: 17 is accompanied by *hazzᵉmôrāh*, and the *tikkūn* according to Tanchuma and Oriental 1425 involves *'appām* which was originally *'appî*. With Job 32: 3 *wayyaršî'û* appears and the *tikkun* according to Oriental 1425 is connected with *'îyôḇ* which is said to have been substituted for *'elōhîm* (see above p. 56). *wā'ehyeh* appears with Job 7: 20, but Tanchuma and Oriental 1425

indicate that ʿālāy has been substituted for ʿālêḵā. The original of Mal.
1: 12 is given as 'ôṯî by Tanchuma and that of Mal. 1: 13 as 'ôṯî by
Oriental 1425. All that appears in the St. Petersburg Codex list for Mal.
1: 12 is mᵉhallᵉlîm and for Mal. 1: 13, wᵉhippaḥtem. Finally wayyāmîrû,
which appears with Ps. 106: 20, does not give an exact indication that
the tikkûn is concerned with the suffix of kāḇôḏ which, according to
Tanchuma, was originally first person singular (kᵉḇôḏî instead of kᵉ-
ḇôḏām).

Mal. 3: 8 is accompanied by kôḇeʿîm and the practice of the list in
respect of 1 Sam. 3: 13, Ezek. 8: 17, Job 7: 20, Mal. 1: 12, 13, and Ps.
106: 20 would suggest that the tikkûn concerns the suffix which follows
kôḇeʿîm, that is, 'ôṯî. This is confirmed by the circumstance that kôḇeʿîm
'ôṯî appears with Mal. 3: 8 in Ginsburg's List 204. Hence Ginsburg
(1897: 363) is wrong in supposing that the verse in question is Mal.
3: 9 rather than 3: 8. It is by no means clear, however, what the motivation of the tikkûn could have been and Mal. 3: 8, whose corrected text
is said to be 'ôṯî, stands apart from those examples where the motivation
would be the desire to avoid a first person suffix which was thought to
encroach on the majesty of God (Jer. 2: 11; Ps. 106: 20; Hos. 4: 7;
Ezek. 8: 17; Mal. 1: 12, 13; Zech. 2: 12). In Mal. 3: 8 the extant text
contains a bold expression, namely, that Yahweh is being robbed with
violence ("in that you rob me with violence") and we should therefore
have expected any tikkûn to have removed the first person suffix.

(g) This list represents the Massorah which appears at Num. 12: 12 in
three Yemenite manuscripts (BM Oriental 1379, 2349, and 2365) and
is Ginsburg's List 208 (Ginsburg, 2, 1883: 710; cf. 1897: 350). One
important difference between this list and the two Massoretic lists already
considered is that the alleged original is given here for each item.

14. Gen. 18: 22, original wYHWH
    ôḏennû ʿômēḏ lipᵉnê 'aḇrāhām

8. Num. 11: 15, original bᵉrāʿāṯēk

11. Num. 12: 12, original 'immēnû

11a. Num. 12: 12, original bᵉśārēnû

3. 1 Sam. 3: 13, original lô

18. 2 Sam. 16: 12, original
    bᵉʿênênû

15. 1 Kings 12: 16, original
    lēʾlôhêḵā

16. 2 Chron. 10: 16, original
    lēʾlôhāw

10. Ezek. 8: 17, original 'appî

2. Mal. 1: 13, original 'ôṯî

1. Zech. 2: 12, original ʿênî

6. Jer. 2: 11, original kᵉḇôḏî

12. Hos. 4: 7, original kᵉḇôḏî

5. Hab. 1: 12, original tāmûṯ

4. Job 7: 20, original ʿālêḵā

13. Job 32: 3, original *'eṭ haddîn*   17. Lam. 3: 20, original *ᶜālêkā*
    (another circumlocution for
    'ᵉlôhîm, see above p. 56)   7. Ps. 106: 20, original *kᵉḇôḏî*

This list follows the order of the Hebrew Bible for the first seven items. The eighth item is 2 Chron. 10: 16 and its association with 1 Kings 12: 16 is understandable for the reasons already given. It is difficult to find any principle behind the ordering of the remaining ten items. The list diverges in its composition from the two other Massoretic lists which have been reviewed and is exactly the same as the list of Tanchuma. Of the original readings which are indicated the only ones which deviate from those which appear in Tanchuma and/or Oriental 1425 concern 2 Sam. 16: 12, Hab 1: 12, Job 32: 3, Lam. 3: 20. For 2 Sam. 16: 12 the original is given as *bᵉᶜênênû* (*bᵉᶜênāw*); for Hab. 1: 12 it is *tāmûṭ* (*yāmûṭ*); for Job 32: 3 *'eṭ haddîn* (see above p. 59); and for Lam. 3: 20 *ᶜālêkā* (*napšô*). The list reckons two *tikkûnîm* for Num. 12: 12 and appears to show an awareness that there are two in each of 1 Kings 12: 16 and 2 Chron. 10: 16, since it cites one of them for 1 Kings 12: 16 (*lê'lôhêkā*) and the other for 2 Chron. 10: 16 (*lê'lôhāw*). Rather inconsistently, or so it would seem, it only reckons one to each of 1 Kings 12: 16 and 2 Chron. 10: 16, and the explanation of this is probably that eighteen was the desiderated number and that the computation of the selected passages had to be so organized as to achieve this total.

What we have learned from these lists of *tikkûnê sôpᵉrîm* may be gathered together in the following way:

(a) The total number attested in all the lists is twenty-three and these, with the serial numbers which I have attached to them are:

1. Zech. 2: 12	12. Hos. 4: 7
2. Mal. 1: 13	13. Job 32: 3
3. 1 Sam. 3: 13	14. Gen. 18: 22
4. Job 7: 20	15. 1 Kings 12: 16
5. Hab. 1: 12	16. 2 Chron. 10: 16
6. Jer. 2: 11	17. Lam. 3: 20
7. Ps. 106: 20	18. 2 Sam. 16: 12
8. Num. 11: 15	19. Mal. 1: 12
9. 2 Sam. 20: 1	20. 1 Kings 12: 16
10. Ezek. 8: 17	21. 2 Chron. 10: 16
11. Num. 12: 12	22. Mal. 3: 8
11a. Num. 12: 12	

(b) Three items appear in all the lists: Zech. 2: 12; Ezek. 8: 17; Num. 12: 12.

(c) Three items appear in all the lists except Siphre: Mal. 1: 13; 1 Sam. 3: 13; Jer. 2: 11.

(d) Two items appear in all the lists except Yalkut: Job 7: 20; Num. 11: 15.

(e) Two items appear in all the lists except Oriental 1425: Hab. 1: 12; Ps. 106: 20.

(f) Two items appear in Tanchuma, Oriental 1425, Ginsburg's Lists 204, 205, 206: Job 32: 3; Gen. 18:22.

(g) Two items appear in Tanchuma, Lists 204, 205, 206: 1 Kings 12: 16; 2 Chron. 10: 16.

(h) Two items appear in Tanchuma, Oriental 1425, and List 206: Lam. 3: 20; 2 Sam. 16: 12.

(i) One item appears in Mechilta, Siphre, and Oriental 1425: 2 Sam. 20: 1.

(j) One item appears in Oriental 1425 and Lists 204 and 205: Mal. 1: 12.

(k) One item appears in Tanchuma and List 206: Hos. 4: 7.

(l) One item appears in Lists 204 and 205: Mal. 3: 8.

(m) Two items are reckoned for Num. 12: 12 in Tanchuma and Lists 204 and 205.

(n) Two items are reckoned for each of 1 Kings 12: 16 and 2 Chron. 10: 16 in Lists 204 and 205.

(o) There are four complete lists of eighteen items; of these Tanchuma has the same composition as List 206, while a different set of eighteen appears in Lists 204 and 205.

II

When one looks more closely at the kind of alteration which is being postulated in these *tikkûnê sôperîm*, one finds that the principle which is alleged to have influenced the scribes is the avoidance of anthropomorphisms and anthropopathisms which were thought to be theologically improper because they encroached in one way or another on the majesty of God. The following groups can be formed:

(1) The alteration of *kebôdî*, where the first person suffix refers to God (Jer. 2: 11; Ps. 106: 20; Hos. 4: 7). The exchanging or bartering of Yahweh's *kābôd* (the Hiphil of *mwr* occurs in all three passages) is

thought to be an offensive idea and so it is removed by attaching a third person suffix to *kābôd*, singular in the case of Jer. 2: 11 and plural in the case of Ps. 106: 20 and Hos. 4: 7.

(2) Related to (1) are the alleged alterations of first person suffixes referring to God. Thus "You are profaning me" (*wᵉ'attem mᵉhallᵉlîm 'ôtî* has been changed to "You are profaning it", where "it" (*'ôtô*) refers to Yahweh's name (Mal. 1: 12). Similarly in Mal. 1: 13 *wᵉhippaḥtem 'ôtô*, with *'ôtô* referring to *šulḥān* "table", is said to have been substituted for *wᵉhippaḥtem 'ôtî* "you sniff at me". In Zech. 2: 12 "touching the apple of my eye" (with Yahweh the speaker) was thought to be too daring and *'ênî* was altered to *'ênô*, "He who touches you touches the apple of his (own) eye", that is, does himself a vital injury. Both Zech. 2: 12 and Ezek. 8: 17, where *'appî* is said to have been changed to *'appām*, are treated in more detail in the final section of the article.

(3) Another group of still basically the same kind, in which alterations of suffixes are involved, consists of 1 Sam. 3: 13, Job 7: 20, Num. 11: 15, Num. 12: 12, Lam. 3: 20 and 2 Sam. 16: 12. I shall state the motives which are alleged for these changes where they are sufficiently transparent, without necessarily indicating my own attitude to the postulated originals.

(a) In 1 Sam. 3: 13 *mᵉkallᵉlîm lāhem* used of Saul's sons might mean that they were bringing a curse down on their own heads, provided that *lāhem* can be translated "with respect to themselves". There is, however, as Ginsburg has pointed out (1897: 354), some doubt whether *killēl* can be construed with the dative in the sense "bring a curse down on someone". In view of the reading of LXX (ὅτι κακολογοῦντες θεὸν υἱοὶ αὐτοῦ) Ginsburg's suggestion that the original was *'ᵉlôhîm* is attractive. Ginsburg holds that this is, nevertheless, a *tikkûn* – an excision of a reference to the sons of Eli cursing God – but it could reasonably be regarded as an accidental corruption resulting from the omission of *alep* (*'lhm* becoming *lhm*).

(b) The motive for the *tikkûn* in Job 7: 20 would be an unwillingness to tolerate the representation that Yahweh was using Job as a target and hence *'ālêkā* was altered to *'ālay*. It is certainly true that *wā'ehyeh 'ālay lᵉmaśśā'* makes poor sense and that the alteration, which furnishes a parallel to *lᵉmipgā' lāk* is necessary for this reason. It cannot, however, be satisfactorily elucidated as a *tikkûn*, because *lᵉmipgā' lāk* is precisely the same representation as *'ālêkā lᵉmaśśā'* and if scrupulosity produced an alteration in the one it should have brought about a similar alteration in the other.

(c) It is said that the original in Num. 11: 15 was *wᵉ'al 'er'eh bᵉrā'ātek*

"If I should win your favour, let me not experience your ill-will". The thought of Yahweh's malice was too much and *bᵉrāʿāṭēḵ* was altered to *bᵉrāʾāṭî* "If I should win your favour, let me not look on my misfortune".

(d) A satisfactory elucidation of the alleged *tikkûnîm* is lacking in Num. 12:12, where I find the original postulated by Ginsburg unintelligible: "Let her not, I pray, be as the dead born child which when proceeding from *our mother's* womb the half of *our flesh* is consumed" (1897: 353). Ginsburg (1897: 354) observes,

This was regarded as derogatory to the mother of the great lawgiver by depicting her as having given birth to a partially decomposed body. The simile was, therefore, altered from the first person plural into the impersonal

Better sense can be had out of Num. 12: 12 if the extant text is read. Miriam has been struck with leprosy and Aaron says to Moses, "Let her not be as the child which is dead when it comes from its mother's womb, with half of its flesh eaten away". Miriam in her leprous condition is likened to a malformed foetus which is stillborn.

(e) The matter in Lam. 3: 20 is complicated by a Kᵉrê- Kᵉtîb (*tāšôaḥ – tāšîaḥ*) and by the circumstance that Oriental 1425 gives the original as *napšô* (MT *napšî*), whereas List 206 gives it as ʿ*ālêḵā* (MT ʿ*ālay*). Geiger (1857: 315) and Ginsburg (1897: 361) assume an original *napšᵉḵā* which does not, however, seem to be attested (Hillers 1972: 55f.). The Greek translator (LXX) vocalized the Hebrew as *tāšîaḥ* which he took as third feminine singular in agreement with *napšî* (with καταδολεσχήσει compare ἠδολέσχησα which is the rendering of ʾ*āśîḥāh* in Ps. 77: 4). Hillers supposes that both the verbs in 3: 20 are third person singular in agreement with *napšî* and that *tāšôaḥ* (Kᵉrê) is a Qal of *šḥḥ*. He translates, "Within myself I surely remember and am despondent". Ginsburg's rendering ("Thy soul will mourn over me" or "will condescend unto me") takes *tāšîaḥ* (Kᵉtîb) as a Hiphil of *šwḥ* and assumes an original *napšᵉḵā* and NEB's rendering ("Remember, o remember and stoop down to me") rests on the same text and grammar. Judgment on philological particulars is influenced by the general exegetical view which is taken of verses 19 to 21, and Hillers, though he has the support of LXX, would seem to me to be wrong in his view that verse 20 is lament and that verse 21 looks forward to verse 22 and not backwards to verse 20. The fact that Hillers translates *zôʾṭ* (beginning of verse 21) as "Yet one thing" is an indication that a special effort has to be made to establish the connection between verses 21 and 22. *zôʾṭ* must refer to verse 20 and, while *wtšyḥ npšy* is obscure, *zāḵôr tizkôr* must be translated "You will not fail to remember". Hence verse 20 marks the beginning'of the recovery of hope and the grounds for it are elaborated in verses 22ff. (so NEB). Neither of the two attested "originals" (*napšô* and *ʿālêḵā*) would seem to me to have much contribution to make to the elucidation of the obscure verse 20. In the case of the first the effective subject would be Yahweh and in the case of the second the subject would be "I": "He will certainly remember and stoop down (to help) me" (both verbs third person feminine singular in agreement with *napšô*); or, "I (Yahweh) will certainly remember and will stoop down (to help) you" (both verbs third person feminine singular in agreement with *napšî*).

(f) In 2 Sam. 16: 12 there is again the complication of a Kᵉrê-Kᵉtîb (*bᵉʿênî* – *baʿᵃwônî*). The "original" is given by Tanchuma and Oriental 1425 as *bᵉʿênāw* and by List 206 as *bᵉênênû*. If *bᵉʿênāw* were the original, the motivation of the *tikkûn* would be to eliminate the anthropomorphism – Yahweh seeing with his eyes. Another consideration, however, is that LXX ἐν τῇ ταπεινώσι μου may point to *bᵉʿonyî* "in my distress" (Ginsburg 1897: 355), although this could possibly be explained on the basis of Kᵉtîb *baʿᵃwônî* "on my punishment".

(4) A group is constituted by alterations involving *YHWH* or *ʾᵉlôhîm* (2 Sam. 20: 1; 1 Kings 12: 16; 2 Chron. 10: 16). If the testimony of LXX were accepted, 1 Sam. 3: 13 could also belong to this group (see above p. 61).

(a) 2 Sam. 20: 1; 1 Kings 12: 16; 2 Chron. 10: 16. In all of these it is alleged that *ʾᵉlôhîm* has been altered to *ʾôhel* and the implication apparently is that *lēʾlôhêḵā* and *lēʾlôhāw* (1 Kings 12: 16; 2 Chron. 10: 1 6) and *lēʾlôhāw* (2 Sam. 20: 1) contained an allusion to idolatry. Sheba advised the northern tribes to rebel from David and his God and to give allegiance to their own gods.

(b) The original which is indicated for Job 32: 3 by Oriental 1425 and List 206 is either *YHWH* or *ʾᵉlôhîm*. As it stands, the verse states that Elihu was angry with Job's three friends because of the unsatisfactory nature of the answers which they had supplied and because they "condemned Job" or "pronounced Job to be guilty". As such the sense of MT is not noticeably defective, although Elihu's solicitude for Job is somewhat unexpected in view of the statement in verse 2 that he was angry with Job because he had made himself more righteous than God. Hence there is some exegetical point in the suggestion that the original was "and because they condemned God", and that the *tikkûn* was made because the thought of bringing in a verdict of "guilty" against God was considered to be blasphemous.

(c) The motivation of the *tikkûn* in Gen. 18: 22 would be the removal of an anthropomorphism – the representation that Yahweh was standing in Abraham's presence – and the safeguarding of Yahweh's transcendence. This is not done by removing anything from the verse but by altering the grammar so that "Abraham" becomes the subject and *YHWH* is governed by *lip^enê* (that is, the grammatical functions of "Abraham" and *YHWH* are reversed). There would appear to be no such deficiency of sense in MT as to justify the assumption of a *tikkûn*.

(5) There is one case (Hab. 1: 12) where the person of a verb is said to have been altered. MT reads, "Are you not my God from of old, O Yahweh, the Holy One, We shall not die". The sense is poor and it is alleged that *nāmût* is a *tikkûn*, but there is disagreement between Tanchuma (*yāmût*) and List 206 (*tāmût*) as to the original. *lô' yāmût* would have to be connected with *'^elôhê kodšî*, "The God of my holiness (who) does not die", or, idiomatically, "My God, the Holy and Immortal One". *lô' tāmût*, on the other hand, would connect with all that precedes in the verse (*halô' 'attāh mikkedem YHWH '^elôhê kodšî*), but the sense would be the same: "Are you not my God from of old, O Yahweh, the Holy and Immortal One". The reason for the *tikkûn* would be the desire to suppress even the barest suggestion that Yahweh might be subject to death.

Barthélemy's contention (1963a: 294 ff.) that there are other cases of alterations to the Old Testament text whose motivation is similar to that of the *tikkûnê sôp^erîm* is in general reasonable and unexceptionable, and he has produced a few interesting examples. In 2 Sam. 12: 14, where the sense is defective, he suggests that *'ôy^ebê* has been inserted because the thought of David's despising Yahweh was found offensive. The motivation which he formulates for the insertion of *'ôy^ebê* at 1 Sam. 25: 22 is not so transparent – it deflects the possibility of the curse away from David himself. The insertion may be related rather to the difficulty which was felt with David's reference to himself in the third person (cf. NEB, "God do the same to *me*"). With regard to 1 Sam. 2: 17, which appears in a Qumran fragment without *hā'^anāšîm* (Cross 1958: Plate 19), it is doubtful whether the motive of a *tikkûn* is discernible. Barthélemy suggests that it is a deliberate attempt to separate "despise" from "Yahweh's sacrifice", but the mere specification of the subject of "despise" and the inserting of it between *nā'^asû* and *minhat YHWH* is not an effective way of doing this.

The most interesting and complicated of Barthélemy's examples is Deut. 32: 8ff., where *b^enê yiśrā'ēl* (MT) contrasts with ἀγγέλων θεοῦ

(LXX) and *benê 'elôhîm* of a Qumran fragment (Skehan 1954: 12; 1959: 21). This can be explained convincingly as a *tikkûn*: the polytheistic implications of *benê 'elôhîm* were unacceptable and so *'elôhîm* was suppressed. Of particular interest are the exegetical consequences which Barthélemy attempts to trace. The key phrase is *yaṣṣēḇ geḇûlôt 'ammîm lemispar benê yiśrā'ēl* which was understood as the formulation of an equation between the number of the *benê yiśrā'ēl* and the number of the nations. The number seventy which is given for the nations in Bk. Jub. 44: 33ff. includes five descendants of Joseph. Further light is thrown on this by the circumstance that the number of the *benê yiśrā'ēl* in Egypt is given as seventy by MT at Gen. 46: 27, Exod. 1: 5 (a Qumran fragment gives seventy-five at Exod. 1: 5; Cross 1958: Plate 18), and Deut. 10: 22. Only in the last of these passages does LXX agree with MT; in Gen. 46: 27 and Exod. 1: 5 it gives the number as seventy-five. In Gen. 46: 27 (LXX) the number is made up of sixty-seven plus nine and the nine are the sons who were born to Joseph in Egypt. So far as I understand Barthélemy, I take him to say that the two groups of seventy were achieved by Jubilees through the expedient of deducting five of Joseph's sons from the LXX list of seventy five and attaching them to the Gentile nations. Hence Barthélemy appears to argue that seventy has replaced an original seventy-five in the MT of Gen. 46: 27 and Exod. 1: 5, and in the MT and LXX of Deut. 10: 22, and that these are alterations which are consequential on a particular exegesis of *yaṣṣēḇ geḇûlôt 'ammîm lemispar benê yiśrā'ēl*, namely, that it refers to seventy *benê yiśrā'ēl* and seventy nations. It should be noted, however, that the seventy of Gen. 46: 27 (MT) has a different basis of computation from the seventy-five of Gen. 46: 27 (LXX). The latter consists of sixty-six descendants of Jacob and nine sons born to Joseph in Egypt, while the former consists of sixty-six descendants of Jacob along with Jacob, Joseph, Ephraim, and Manasseh. It does not therefore seem to me that seventy-five could have been the original in MT of Gen. 46: 27.

Barthélemy draws wider conclusions about *tikkûnê sôperîm* from his consideration of Deut. 32: 8. He attributes the exegesis of that verse which is reflected in Bk. Jub. 44: 33ff. to priestly and pietist circles who were active at the beginning of the Hasmonaean dynasty. This suggests to him that the correction to *benê yiśrā'ēl* may have originated at this time and he finds further support for this in the circumstance that an exegesis of Deut. 32: 8 resting on *benê yiśrā'ēl* occurs (along with an exegesis resting on ἀγγέλων θεοῦ) in a work (Targum Pseudo-Jonathan) in which he detects a favourable allusion to John Hyrcanus at Deut. 33:

11. Since "original" readings are found in Qumran fragments (Exod. 1: 5; Deut. 32: 8; 1 Sam. 2: 17) and since in his view the schism which brought the Qumran sect into being took place at the beginning of the reign of John Hyrcanus, he holds that those responsible for the *tikkûnê sôperîm* were Sadducaean scribes active during the reign of John Hyrcanus. Hence on his view of the matter the Qumran schism took place before the corrections had been made and this explains the presence of the "originals" in the fragments. The Pharisees, who came to power around 75 B. C., inherited the corrections and accepted them as part of the normative text, although they were not themselves correctors. The text became fixed during this period and divergent forms were suppressed.

My own impression of the attested *tikkûnîm* is that the balance of advantage as between the extant text and the alleged original is sometimes far from clear, that the description of the motivation of the *tikkûn* sometimes lacks cogency, and that a distinction has to be drawn between passages which make good sense as they stand and those whose sense is so poor that there is a *prima facie* case for postulating an "original". I illustrate these points and draw together this section of the article by investigating the attitude of two English translations, the RSV and the NEB, to the attested *tikkûnîm* which I have listed.

		RSV	NEB
1.	Zech. 2: 12 (8)	"apple of his eye"	"apple of his eye"
2.	Mal. 1: 13	"and you sniff at me"	"you sniff at it"
3.	1 Sam. 3: 13	"because his sons were blaspheming God"	"because he knew of his sons' blasphemies against God"
4.	Job 7: 20	"Why have I become a burden to thee?"	"Why have I become thy target?"
5.	Hab. 1: 12	"We shall not die"	"My God, the holy, the immortal"
6.	Jer. 2: 11	"have changed their glory"	"have changed their glory"
7.	Ps. 106:20	"They exchanged the glory of God"	"they exchanged their glory", footnote, "or *the glory of God*"
8.	Num. 11: 15	"that I may not see my wretchedness"	"let me suffer this trouble at thy hand no longer"
9.	2 Sam. 20: 1	"every man to his tents"	"away to your homes"

		RSV	NEB
10.	Ezek. 8: 17	"They put the branch to their nose"	"even while they seek to appease me", footnote, lit. *"hold twigs to their nostrils"*
11. 11a.	} Num. 12: 12	"of whom the flesh is half consumed when it comes out of his mother's womb"	"whose flesh is half eaten away when it comes from the womb"
12.	Hos. 4: 7	"I will change their glory into shame"	"their dignity I will turn into dishonour"
13.	Job 32: 3	"although they had declared Job to be in the wrong"	"and had let God appear wrong"
14.	Gen. 18: 22	"but Abraham still stood before the Lord"	"Abraham remained standing before the Lord"
15. 16. 20. 21.	1 Kings 12:16 2 Chron. 10:16	"to your tents" "to their tents"	"to your homes" "to their homes"
17.	Lam. 3: 20	"and (my soul) is bowed down within me"	"and stoop down to me"
18.	2 Sam. 16: 12	"look upon my affliction"	"will mark my sufferings"
19.	Mal. 1: 12	"But you profane it"	"But you profane it"
22.	Mal. 3: 8	"you are robbing me"	"that you defraud me"

The following points should be noted:

(1) Out of the twenty three examples there is not a single one in which both RSV and NEB adopt the alleged original of a *tikkûn*.

(2) RSV accepts the presence of a *tikkûn* only in Mal. 1: 13, where it adopts the "original" contained in the lists (*'otî*).

(3) NEB acknowledges *tikkûnîm* in five instances (Num. 11: 15; Hab. 1: 12; Job 7: 20; 32: 3; Lam. 3: 20).

(4) RSV and NEB agree in adopting the reading of LXX at 1 Sam. 3: 13 and 2 Sam. 16: 12. In so far as *'ᵉlôhîm* can be regarded as an "original" which has been corrected for doctrinal reasons (see above p. 61.), 1 Sam. 3: 13 can be regarded as a second case where RSV and NEB agree in the acknowledgement of a *tikkûn*.

The slight extent to which these English translations have been influenced by alleged originals of *tikkûnê sôp^erîm* reinforces the observations which I have already made under two heads. In the first place I have noted that the account which is given of how the changes were motivated is not always convincing (see my remarks on Job 7: 20 and Mal. 3: 8), and I have pointed to one instance where it is hardly intelligible (Num. 12: 12). The second consideration was whether or not there was a poorness of sense in the extant text which constituted a *prima facie* case for giving serious attention to the possibility of an "original" which had been suppressed. The attitude of RSV is almost entirely negative and that of NEB only moderately hospitable towards the postulating of *tikkûnê sôp^erîm*. In a number of cases there are no pressing linguistic or exegetical reasons for postulating *tikkûnîm* (2 Sam. 20: 1; 1 Kings 12: 16; 2 Chron. 10: 16; Num. 12: 12; Gen. 18: 22). There are others which have not been invoked by NEB, but which, nevertheless, seem to deserve serious consideration and I devote the third part of this article to a detailed treatment of two of the more interesting of these: Zech. 2: 12 and Ezek. 8: 17.

III

Zech. 2: 12 (8 EVV). The text is obscure: BHS says that *'aḥar kāḇôḏ š^elāḥanî* is corrupt and may be an addition and that *kî hannôḡēa' bāḵem nôḡēa' b^eḇāḇat 'ênô* may also be an addition. *'aḥar kāḇôḏ š^elāḥanî*, which makes poor sense, is reproduced by the versions (LXX, Vulg., Targ., Pesh.), being expanded by Targ. into "after the glory which he has promised to bring on you". It is elucidated by Ibn Ezra as "after the sending of his glory to me" and by Kimchi as "after the glory which made you feel secure". Both Kimchi and Abranavel (1641) relate *kāḇôḏ* to the last part of verse 9 (*ûl^eḵāḇôḏ 'ehyeh b^etôḵāh*) and thus Abranavel remarks: "After he said to me that Jerusalem would have glory in her midst as he mentioned above at the end of his prophecy against the nations which despoil you". *'aḥar kāḇôḏ* has given just as much trouble to commentators nearer our own times. The emendation of Sellin (1930), *'^ašer k^eḇôḏô š^elāḥanî* "whose glory sent me", was adopted by Horst (1964) and is possibly the emendation reflected in the rendering of NEB ("when he sent me on a glorious mission to the nations"). Ehrlich (1912) would emend to *'aḥar kāḇôḏ š^elaḥtîḵā* "I sent you after treasure" (*kāḇôḏ* "treasure"), but neither this nor the proposal that *'aḥar kāḇôḏ* should be rendered "with insistence" (Chary 1969) commands assent.

With regard to the alleged *tikkûn* there is support for an original *ʿênî* in Vulg. (*tangit pupillam oculi mei*) and also in Codex Washingtonensis (τῆς κόρης τοῦ ὀφθαλμοῦ μου) and Tertullian (Ziegler 1943). Barthélemy (1963b: 136-139) in a discussion of Zech. 2: 12 argues that Origen substituted a Palestinian Greek recension for the "ancient Septuagint" in his Quinta, and that he did this because the former was nearer to the Hebrew text. The Vulg. reading (*oculi mei*) has been taken by Jerome from the Quinta on which, according to Barthélemy, Jerome's Greek quotations from the book of the Twelve Prophets are based (1963b: 213-217). Barthélemy further argues that the fragments of the Twelve Prophets which were said to have come from a cave south of the Wadi Murabbaʿat (1963b: 163) and which he published (1963b: 170-178) belong to the Palestinian Greek καίγε recension which Origen substituted for the "ancient Septuagint" in the Quinta.

The Codex Washingtonensis also features in this argument (Barthélemy 1963b: 239-245), since the postulated Palestinian Greek recension of the first century A. D. (R) is held to be the source of the "Hebraizing glosses" in the first and second hands of Codex Washingtonensis, and Zech. 2: 12 (which is not among the fragments discovered) is noted by Barthélemy as one of these glosses (1963b: 241). Hence if a Palestinian Greek recension made by the authority of the Rabbinate in the first half of the first century A. D. (1963b: 189) restored an original *ʿênî* (τοῦ ὀφθαλμοῦ μου), a *tikkûn* which was already in the "ancient Septuagint", this *tikkûn* (*ʿênô*; τοῦ ὀφθαλμοῦ αὐτοῦ) must, in all probability, have originated prior to the end of the second century B. C. (Barthélemy 1963b: 291ff.). This connects with the argument advanced by Barthélemy in another work (1963a; see above p. 66) that Sadducaean scribes active in the reign of John Hyrcanus were responsible for the *tikkûnîm*.

There is no mention of a *tikkûn* at Zech. 2: 12 in Rashi or Ibn Ezra or Kimchi, and although *Mᵉṣûḏaṯ Dāwîḏ* mentions that it is one of the *tikkûnê sôpᵉrîm* he does not assume *ʿênî* for his exegesis. Two different interpretations of *ʿênô* are represented. According to Kimchi it means "his own eye":

He who touches you will not go unpunished, like the man who touches the pupil of his eye. It is the *'îšôn hāʾayin* which one pierces if one touches it heavily *(bhzkh)*. So anyone who molests you will hurt himself.

Mᵉṣûḏaṯ Dāwîḏ and Abranavel, on the other hand, explain *ʿênô* as *ʿênô šelᵉhammāḳôm*, that is, "God's eye". Both these interpretations of *ʿênô* are to be found in later commentators: the first of them is nicely expounded by an English scholar (Blayney 1797: 10 of notes) who remarks:

This has sometimes been misunderstood as if God's eye was meant and both Vulgate and two Jewish commentators here read ʿênî, oculi mei. But the meaning certainly is that he who meddled with the Jews to hurt them would be doing himself the most essential hurt, wounding himself in the tenderest part.

Among others who have followed this view are Hitzig (1852), Nowack (1897), von Orelli (1908), and Ehrlich (1912).

The second interpretation of ʿênô "God's eye" is already present in the reading noted by Ziegler (Justin, ὀφθαλ. θεοῦ; 534, ὀφθαλ. τοῦ κυρίου). It is not clear to me why Barthélemy says (1963b: 211) that Justin's τῆς κόρης τοῦ ὀφθαλ. θεοῦ seems to rest on a revised translation of ὀφθαλμοῦ μου. On the contrary it presupposes ʿênô (τοῦ ὀφθαλ. αὐτοῦ) which it interprets as "God's eye".

The question whether ʿênî (Marti 1904; Sellin 1930; Elliger 1951; Horst 1964; Petitjean 1969) or ʿênô is the better reading cannot be settled in separation from the general view which is taken of verses 12 and 13. If Yahweh's speech does not begin until verse 13 (Marti 1904; Mitchell 1912; Sellin 1930; Elliger 1951; Horst 1964; Petitjean 1969), ʿênî is ruled out. The solution of Keil (1868) to the problem of the structure of verses 12 and 13 is not commendable, but it does rest on a true appreciation of the main difficulty. If the prophet is the speaker at the beginning of verse 12 (šᵉlāḥanî seems to make this conclusion inevitable), then a transition to speech of Yahweh, at whatever point it is made, whether at hannôgēaʿ or at the beginning of verse 13, is awkward. Keil cut the knot by saying that the speaker throughout is malʾak YHWH and that the speech begins where we would normally expect it to do so, namely after the introductory formula. This solution will not do and there are two remaining alternatives:

(a) "For he who touches you touches the apple of his eye" is parenthetical and is spoken by the prophet. As I have said this rules out ʿênî which would only be appropriate if these words were spoken by Yahweh, but it does not resolve the ambiguity of ʿênô. This can be illustrated by the NEB rendering which depends on this understanding of the syntactical structure: "for whoever touches you touches the apple of his eye". This could mean either "his own eye" or "Yahweh's eye", but those who postulate a tiḳḳûn and who suppose that the original was ʿênî are bound to assume that the scribes who made the correction intended "his own eye", since the scandal would not be removed by substituting "Yahweh's eye" for "my eye".

(b) But the scribes could only have made this correction on the under-standing that the speech of Yahweh begins with *hannôgēaʿ* (Ehrlich 1912; Petitjean 1969). On this view of the matter the obscure *'aḥar kāḇôḏ šᵉlāḥani 'el haggôyîm haššôlᵉlîm 'eṯᵉḵem* is inserted parenthetically by the prophet after the introductory formula and then the message from Yahweh opens with *kî hannôgēaʿ* and closes with *lᵉʿaḇᵉḏêhem*. In that case *kî* (both instances) cannot be a conjunction introducing motive clauses and must be regarded as asseverative ("surely"). Only if the structure of verses 12 and 13 is so described can a cogent argument be presented for an original *ʿênî* over against MT *ʿênô*:

Surely he who touches you touches the apple of my eye. I shall raise my hand against them without fail and they will be despoiled by theiɪ own slaves.

The concluding clause of verse 13 ("Then you will know that *YHWH Ṣᵉḇā'ôṯ* has sent me") comes from the prophet himself.

Ezek. 8:17. The difficulty of assessing the textual value of the alleged original *'appî* is compounded by the obscurity of *zᵉmôrāh*. Attempts at a new philological departure which have been made by Gordis (1936) and Sarna (1964) must be judged unsuccessful. Gordis supposes that *zᵉmôrāh* "branch" has here the specialized sense of "thorn" and that "proffering a thorn to my nose" (adopting *'appî*) refers to a gesture which causes intense irritation to Yahweh. The other proposal by Sarna has a highly improbable appearance. It is not in doubt that *zmr* can mean "strength" in Biblical Hebrew or that it has such a sense in Ugaritic, but what must be contested is the suggestion that Ezek. 8:17 becomes more intelligible when this assumption is made for *zᵉmôrāh*. The render-ing "and they provoke me still more, for see they send out the strong men to execute their anger" (*'appām*), or "to anger me" (*'appî*) will not win many adherents, nor will the exegesis, "The reference would be to the manner by which the rich forcibly dispossessed the poor through the employment of hired thugs or strong men".

The pattern of exegesis is largely set by the versions and the mediaeval commentators, and the obscurity of *šôlᵉḥîm 'eṯ hazzᵉmôrāh 'el 'appām* is seen in the versions. The summarizing paraphrase of LXX^B (ὡς μυκ-τηρίζοντες) indicates *'appām* rather than *'appî*. It is a fair conclusion that the Greek translator was unsure about the exact sense of *zᵉmôrāh*, but was convinced that the whole expression was idiomatic or proverbial and was indicative of a contemptuous or derisory gesture. Hence his paraphrase, "as though turning up their noses (in disdain)".

The later Greek versions, which all indicate *'appām*, are divided over their understanding of $z^e m \hat{o} r \bar{a} h$ (the material is taken from Ziegler 1952). $z^e m \hat{o} r \bar{a} h$ is understood as "branch" by Theod. (probably also by Aq., although the attestation is incomplete), and as "song" by Symm. Vulg. (*Et ecce applicant ramum ad nares suas*) agrees with Theod. (καὶ ἰδοὺ αὐτοὶ ἐκτείνουσι τὸ κλῆμα εἰς τὸν μύκτηρα αὐτῶν; cf. Aq. πρὸς μύκτηρα αὐτῶν). Pesh. has a rendering (*whnwn mpk̲yn bnḥryhwn* "and behold they snort with their nostrils") which looks like a paraphrase derived from the more explicit translation of Symm. (καὶ ἰδοὺ αὐτοὶ ὡς ἀφίεντες εἰσιν ἦχον ὡς ᾆσμα διὰ τῶν μυκτήρων αὐτῶν, "it is as if they were emitting a sound like a song through their nostrils"). Jerome reproduces Symm. as *quasi emittentes sonitum per nares suas* and remarks, *Symmachi autem interpretatio, foedum raucumque sonitum de naribus procedentem in Dei contemptum significat* "The interpretation of Symmachus signifies an unseemly and raucous sound coming from the nostrils in contempt of God".

Among later commentators Newcombe (1788) follows Symm. and Pesh. ("And lo they sent forth a scornful noise through their nostrils"), while Cooke (1936) follows Theod. and Vulg. ("They hold forth the twig to their nose"). This, according to Cooke, refers to an offensive and idolatrous rite.

The rendering of Targ. (*wh' 'ynwn mytn bht' l 'pyhwn* "and behold they bring shame on themselves") marks a new departure which is influential for subsequent exegesis. Cooke's rendering of Targ. ("they bring forth the stench to their noses") would establish an even more precise connection between Targ. and the mediaeval Jewish commentators, but the rendering is illegitimate. Aramaic *bht* is the equivalent of Hebrew *bwš* and not of Hebrew *b'š* and the sense "smell" is not attested for *bht* in Aramaic. The sense of Targ. is the quite general one that they bring shame on their own heads (hence *'appām* and not *'appî* is presupposed), and "shame" is then particularized by Rashi in terms of the stench associated with farting or *excreta* – they suffer the indignity of having to put up with their own disgusting smells. This is also found in *M^e ṣûḏaṭ Dāwîḏ* who associates the bad smell with diarrhoea.

Kimchi retains the sense of "smell" for $z^e m \hat{o} r \bar{a} h$, but he offers a different kind of interpretation based on the adoption of *'appî*:

They are offering incense in my house and sending the smell of their offerings of incense to my nostrils, apart from the contempt which they do to me in turning their back on my house [referring to verse 16].

With this should be compared Kraetzschmar's [*Opfer-*]*gestank zu 'meiner' Nase* (1900) and his explanation that the reference is to sacrifices offered at sanctuaries other than Jerusalem in defiance of the Deuteronomic law of centralization. Kimchi's influence in a less precise form and resting on the basic similarities *zᵉmôrāh* "smell", and *'appî* rather than *'appām*, is found in Bertholet (1936), Eichrodt (1959), and Zimmerli (1969). Zimmerli's emphasizing of the obscurity of the philology of *zᵉmôrāh* (he leaves a blank in his translation) along with his conviction that the expression of which it is a part must be idiomatic or proverbial has some similarity to the general feeling for *wᵉhinnām šôlᵉḥîm 'eṭ hazzᵉmôrāh 'el 'appām* which is represented by LXX^B (καὶ ἰδοὺ αὐτοὶ ὡς μυκτηρίζοντες). The difference is that Zimmerli's "proverb" assumes *'appî*, while the sense of LXX^B is "turning up their noses" (*'appām*), and this describes a self-contained, derisive gesture rather than one which is specifically directed towards Yahweh as a calculated insult (*'appî*). This thought of an insult offered to Yahweh by way of an obscene gesture made to Him appears in Herrmann's exegesis (1924). The expression *šôlᵉḥîm 'eṭ hazzᵉmôrāh 'el 'appî* is proverbial and what is indicated is a *Körperhaltung* which is a deliberate affront to Yahweh.

Jahn (1905) exhibits a similar reticence about the sense of *zᵉmôrāh* but observes that the expression of which it formed a part referred to something unseemly. He notes, as does Bertholet, the suggestion that *zᵉmôrāh* might mean "penis" and makes the interesting observation that *zirmāh* (Ezek. 23: 20) has been translated as αἰδοῖα "genitals" by LXX. The view that *zirmāh* is to be associated with *zerem* "torrential rain" is still maintained by NEB ("and whose seed came in floods like that of horses"), but in view of what precedes ("She was infatuated by their male prostitutes whose members were like those of asses") there are strong reasons for following *KB³* (1967) and rendering "whose genitals were like those of horses" (whether we suppose that the metathesis of *m* and *r* is a philological phenomenon as *KB³* does, *zrmh* < *zmrh*; or that the transposition of *m* and *r* is accidental and that *ûzᵉmôraṭ* and *zᵉmôrāṭām* should be read). On this view, which seems to me to be a reasonable one, we can say that *zᵉmôrāh* "penis" or "genitals" is attested in the book of Ezekiel as well as in post-Biblical Hebrew (Jastrow 1926: *s. v. zᵉmôrāh*), but even if this sense were adopted in Ezek. 8: 17 it would still be an open question whether we have to reckon with a proverbial expression (sticking one's penis in someone's face), which refers to the contriving of the most deadly kind of insult, or with a phallic rite.

The question of a phallic rite is, however, bound up with the more general question whether a new rite is described in verse 17 or whether (as Kimchi supposed) Yahweh is indicating how deep an insult the people of Jerusalem offer him when they turn their backs on the temple and worship the sun (verse 16). Both Herrmann and Gordis follow Kimchi in this respect, although it is possible that the rite described in verse 14 is also included in what is described as *šôlᵉḥîm 'eṭ hazzᵉmôrāh 'el 'appî* in verse 17. Zimmerli also holds that the "proverb" of verse 17 refers back to verse 16 in the way that Kimchi supposes, but he also speaks of four depictions of sinful acts (verses 5, 10ff., 14, 16) which are summed up by the "proverb" in verse 17. That verse 17 does introduce a new rite is supposed by Cooke ("some offensive idolatrous rite") and this possibility in phallic terms is entertained by Bertholet who suggests a lewd, domestic cult which defiles the whole land (verse 17) and not merely the sanctuary.

Finally the theories which postulate Persian, Egyptian, or Mesopotamian rites all assume that verse 17 introduces something new and are all based on the retention of MT *'appām*. The Persian theory is already found in Michaelis (1792: 633), and it supposes that those mentioned in verse 17 are holding a bundle of twigs to their faces in the way that worshippers of the Persian sun god shielded their impure breath from the deity by placing a bundle of twigs of date palm, or of tamarisk or pomegranate trees to their mouths. Michaelis says, *virgas sacras emittunt ad vultum suum, i. e., solem adorantes vultui praetendunt*, and notes that the Persian name for such a bundle of twigs is *Bersam* (1792: 633). Smend (1880) considers the possibility of emending *zᵉmôrāh* to *brzm*, but he adds that even if *zᵉmôrāh* means "vine", a vine branch is appropriate in the context of sun worship (so also Hengstenberg 1869 and Fohrer 1955). Von Orelli (1896), who does not adopt the theory, nevertheless holds that *zᵉmôrāh* means "vine branch". Fohrer's view is based on de Buck (1951) and he explains verse 17 in terms of an Egyptian rite in which a flower or vegetable symbol of the rising sun – in Palestine this would be a branch of the vine – was held up to the face. Saggs (1960: 318-329) has noted that the putting of a branch to the nose is a rite paralleled in Mesopotamia and that it occurs there in the context of sun worship. In so far as all these theories describe the rite in verse 17 as an aspect of sun worship, they establish a continuity between verses 16 and 17.

The conclusions which I draw after this somewhat complicated discussion are as follows:

(1) The reading *'appî* is to be preferred to *'appām*.

(2) With regard to the obscure *zᵉmôrāh* there is more to be said for

the sense "penis" than for any other suggestion, but this is not indicative of a phallic rite.

3. *wᵉhinnām sôlᵉḥîm 'eṭ hazzᵉmôrāh 'el 'appî* is an idiomatic expression or proverb which signifies the offering of a deadly insult to Yahweh. The proverb may be "sticking one's penis in someone's face", that is, offering a deadly affront to someone, but the details of the proverb are uncertain because of the obscurity which surrounds *zᵉmôrāh*.

REFERENCES

Abbreviations:

VTS	*Supplements to Vetus Testamentum*
KHCAT	*Kurzer Handcommentar zum Alten Testament*
HAT	*Handbuch zum Alten Testament*
OTS	*Oudtestamentische Studien*
ICC	*International Critical Commentary*
ATD	*Das Alte Testament Deutsch*
JTS	*Journal of Theological Studies*
KAT	*Kommentar zum Alten Testament*
HKAT	*Handkommentar zum Alten Testament*
HTR	*The Harvard Theological Review*
BASOR	*Bulletin of the American Schools of Oriental Research*
JBL	*Journal of Biblical Literature*
BKAT	*Biblischer Kommentar Altes Testament*

LITERATURE

Abranavel, I.
    1641 *pyrwš 'al nby'ym 'ḥrnym.*
Barthélemy, D.
    1963a "LES TIQQUNÊ SOPHERIM ET LA CRITIQUE TEXTUELLE DE L'ANCIEN TESTAMENT", *VTS* 9, 285-304.
    1963b *Les Devanciers D'Aquila* (= *VTS* 10).
Bertholet, A.
    1897 *Hesekiel, KHCAT.*
    1936 *Hesekiel, HAT.*
Blayney, B.
    1797 *Zechariah: A New Translation with Notes, Critical, Philological and Explanatory.*
Buck, A. de
    1951 "La fleur au front du grandprêtre", *OTS* 9, 18-29.
Chary, T.
    1969 *Aggée-Zacharie-Malachie*, Sources Bibliques.
Cooke, G. A.
    1936 *A Critical and Exegetical Commentary on the Book of Ezekiel, ICC.*

Cross, F. M., Jr.
1958   *The Ancient Library of Qumran and Modern Biblical Studies.*
Ehrlich, A. B.
1912   *Ezechiel und die kleinen Propheten: Randglossen zur Hebräischen Bibel, Textkritisches, Sprachliches und Sachliches* 5. Reissued in 1968.
Eichrodt, W.
1959   *Der Prophet Hesekiel, ATD* 22:1. English trans. by C. Quin, *Ezekiel*, Old Testament Library (1970).
Elliger, K.
1951   *Das Buch der zwölf kleinen Propheten, ATD* 25:2, 2nd ed.
1971   *Liber Ezechiel* (Biblia Hebraica Stuttgartensia). Cited as BHS.
Fohrer, G.
1955   *Ezechiel, HAT* 1:13.
Friedmann, M.
1864   *mdrš spry dby rby, der älteste hagadische Midrasch zu Numeri und Deuteronomium.*
Geiger, A.
1857   *Urschrift und Uebersetzungen der Bibel in ihrer Abhängigkeit von den innern Entwicklung des Judenthums.*
Ginsburg, C. D.
1883   *The Massorah, Compiled from Manuscripts Alphabetically and Lexically Arranged,* Vol. 2.
1896   *Introduction to the Massoretico-Critical Edition of the Hebrew Bible.* Reissued with a Prolegomenon by H. M. Orlinsky (1966).
Gordis, R.
1936   " 'The Branch to the Nose'. A Note on Ezekiel viii 17", *JTS* 37, 284-288.
Hengstenberg, E. W.
1869   *The Prophecies of the Prophet Ezekiel Elucidated.*
Herrmann, J.
1924   *Ezechiel, KAT.*
Hillers, D. R.
1972   *Lamentations: A New Translation with Introduction and Commentary* (Anchor Bible).
Hitzig, F.
1852   *Die zwölf kleinen Propheten, Kurzgefasstes exegetisches Handbuch zum Alten Testament,* 2nd ed.
Horst, F.
1964   *Die zwölf kleinen Propheton, HAT,* 3rd ed.
Jahn, G.
1905   *Das Buch Ezechiel.*
Keil, C. F.
1868   *Biblical Commentary on the Old Testament. The Twelve Minor Prophets* 2.
Koehler, L., and W. Baumgartner
1967   *Hebräisches und Aramäisches Lexicon zum Alten Testament,* unter Mitarbeit von Hartmann B. und Kutscher E. Y., Lieferung I. Cited as KB^3.
Kraetzschmar, R.
1900   *Das Buch Ezechiel, HKAT.*
Lauterbach, J. Z.
1949   *Mekilta de Rabbi Ishmael. A Critical Edition on the basis of the manuscripts and early editions with an English Translation, Introduction and Notes* 2.
Marti, K.
1904   *Das Dodekapropheton, KHCAT* 13.
Michaelis, J. D.
1972   *Supplementa ad Lexica Hebraica,* edited by T. C. Tychsen.

Migne, J. P. (ed.)
  1865   *Sancti Eusebii Hieronymi, Opera Omnia*, tom. 5 (= *Patrologiae Latinae*, tom. 20:5).
mikr'wt gdwlwt nby'ym 'hrwnym
  1959   The source for Rashi, Kimchi, Ibn Ezra, and M^eṣûḍaṭ Dāwîḍ.
Mitchell, H. G.
  1912   *Haggai and Zechariah, ICC.*
Newcombe, W.
  1788   *An Attempt towards an improved Version, a metrical Arrangement and an Explanation of the Prophet Ezekiel.*
Nowack, W.
  1897   *Die kleinen Propheten, HKAT.*
Orelli, C. von
  1896   *Das Buch Ezechiel, Kurzgefasster Kommentar zu den heiligen Schriften Alten und Neuen Testamentes.*
  1908   *Die zwölf kleinen Propheten*, 3rd ed.
Petitjean, A.
  1969   *Les Oracles du Proto-Zacharie.*
Roth, C. (ed.)
  1972   *Encyclopaedia Judaica* 1-16.
Saggs, H. W. F.
  1960   "The Branch to the Nose", *JTS* 11, 318-329.
Sarna, N. M.
  1964   "Ezekiel 8:17: A Fresh Examination", *HTR* 57, 347-352.
Sellin, E.
  1930   *Das Zwölfprophetenbuch, KAT.*
Skehan, P. W.
  1954   "A Fragment of the 'Song of Moses' (Deut. 32) from Qumran", *BASOR* 136, 12-15.
  1959   "Qumran and the Present state of Old Testament Text Studies: The Masoretic Text", *JBL* 78, 21-24.
Smend, R.
  1880   *Der Prophet Ezechiel*, 2nd ed.
Strack, H. L.
  1876   *Prophetarum Posteriorum Codex Babylonicus Petropolitanus.*
Ziegler, J.
  1943   *Septuaginta Vetus Testamentum Graecum Auctoritate Societatis Litterarum Gottingensis editum: Duodecim prophetae* 13.
  1952   *ibid, Ezechiel* 16: pars 1.
Zimmerli, W.
  1969   *Ezechiel, BKAT* 13: 1.

Postscript: Since the article was written Brockington's book indicating the readings adopted by the NEB translators has appeared (Brockington L.H., *The Hebrew Text of the Old Testament*, 1973). This shows that the reading, adopted by the NEB translators at Zech. 2:12 is *'ōrah kāḇôḏ* not *'ᵃšer kᵉḇôḏô* (see above p. 68).

THE QUMRAN PSALMS SCROLL (11QPsa) REVIEWED

JAMES A. SANDERS

It has been a little more than a decade since the first publications based on the large scroll of Psalms from Qumran Cave 11 first appeared. In that period over eighty titles, including text editions, reviews, and specific studies on the texts have appeared. I am pleased to take the occasion this volume affords to provide in one locus the necessary bibliographical data stemming from the discussion which the scroll has occasioned, and to offer some comment on certain aspects of the discussion. I know from personal conversation that, though Qumraniana are not strictly at the center of his scholarly interest, Eugene Nida has been keenly interested in work being done on the scroll and in its significance for understanding the Biblical Psalter. I take great pleasure, joining with others, in paying homage to Eugene Nida's own scholarship as well as to his dedication to the quest today of the most reliable text available of the Bible, especially of the Psalter.

Because this study is in large measure bibliographical, the order generally followed will here be reversed – the bibliography will come first instead of last. It will be arranged alphabetically by author; where needed, a brief indication of its subject matter will accompany an entry. Such a procedure seems here to be preferable to arranging the titles primarily by their subject matter as was done in the Cornell edition on the scroll (Sanders 1967: 151-153). In point of fact, the present list grows out of the earlier one and includes all the pertinent titles from it. The list intends to include all pertinent scholarly discussions, insofar as possible; the writer would be most grateful to receive both corrigenda and addenda from readers. Since the list of *editiones principes* of all Palestinian manuscripts (Sanders 1973a) includes the text editions of all Psalms fragments, as well as 11QPsa, titles not strictly pertaining to the large Psalms scroll are not included here.

Ackroyd, P. R.
1966 "Notes and Studies", *Journal of Theological Studies* 17, 396-399. On col. 16
Ahlström, G. W.
1967 *Journal of Religion* 47, 72-73. Review of Sanders 1965b.
Albright, W. F.
1966 *Bulletin of American Schools of Oriental Research* 182, 54. Review of Sanders 1965.
Anderson, A. A.
1967 *Journal of Semitic Studies* 12, 142-143. Review of Sanders 1965b.
Bardtke, H.
1970 *Theologische Literaturzeitung* 95, cols 2-4. Review of Sanders 1967.
Barthélemy, D., and O. Rickenbacher
1973 *Konkordanz zum Hebräischen Sirah* (Göttingen: Vanderhoeck and Ruprecht).
Brownlee, W. H.
1963 "The 11Q Counterpart to Psalm 151, 1-5", *Revue de Qumran* 15, 379-387.
Bruce, F. F.
1966 *Palestine Exploration Quarterly* 98, 118-189. Review of Sanders 1965b.
1970 *Palestine Exploration Quarterly* 102, 71-72. Review of Sanders 1967.
Carmignac, J.
1963 "La Forme poétique du Psaume 151 de la grotte 11", *Revue de Qumran* 15, 371-378.
1965 "Précisions sur la forme poétique du Psaume 151", *Revue de Qumran* 18, 249-252.
Cross, F. M.
1964 *Harvard Theological Review* 57, 286. On 11QPs[a] and canon.
Dahood, M.
1966 *Biblica* 47, 142ff. Review of Sanders 1965b.
Delcor, M.
1966 "Zum Psalter von Qumran", *Biblische Zeitschrift* 10, 15-29. On Psalms 151, 154, and 155.
1967 "L'Hymne à Sion du rouleau des psaumes de la grotte 11 de Qumran (11 QPs[a])", *Revue de Qumran* 21, 71-88.
1968 "Le Texte hébreu du cantique de Siracide LI, 13 et ss. et les anciennes versions", *Textus* 6, 27-47.
Driver, G. R.
1969 "Psalm 118:27 – 'asurê ḥag", *Textus* 7, 130-131.
Dupont-Sommer, A.
1964a "Le Psaume cli dans 11QPs[a] et le problème de son origine essénienne", *Semitica* 14, 25-62.
1964b "David et Orphée", *Séance publique annuelle des Cinq Académies* (lundi, 26 octobre). On Psalm 151.
1964c "Le Psaume hébreu extra-canonique (11QPs[a] xxviii)", *Annuaire du Collège de France* 64, 317-320.
1965 "Notes quomraniennes", *Semitica* 15, 74-77. On col. 22, the Apostrophe to Zion.
1966 "The Psalms Scroll of Qumran Cave 11 (11QPs[a])", *Annuaire du Collège de France* 66, 358-367. Review of Sanders 1965b.
1967 "The Psalms Scroll of Qumran Cave 11 (11QPs[a]) col. xxi-xxii", *Annuaire du Collège de France* 67, 364-368. On the Sirach acrostic.
1969 *Annuaire du Collège de France* 69, 383-409. Review essay on Sanders 1967.
Eissfeldt, O.
1968 *Orientalistische Literaturzeitung* 63:3-4, cols. 148-149. Review of Sanders 1965b.

1970   *Orientalistische Literaturzeitung* 65:3-4, cols. 149-150. Review of Sanders 1967.

Flusser, D.

1966   "Qumran and Jewish 'Apotropaic' Prayers", *Israel Exploration Journal* 16, 194-205. On col. 19, Plea for Deliverance.

Fohrer G.

1966   *Zeitschrift fur die alttestamentliche Wissenschaft* 78, 124. Review of Sanders 1965b.

1967   *Zeitschrift fur die alttestamentliche Wissenschaft* 79, 272-273. Review of Sanders 1967.

Goldstein, J. A.

1967   *Journal of Near Eastern Studies* 26, 302-309. Review of Sanders 1965b.

Goshen-Gottstein, M. H.

1966   "The Psalms Scroll (11QPsᵃ): A Problem of Canon and Text", *Textus* 5, 22-33.

Gurewicz, S. B.

1967   "Hebrew Apocryphal Psalms from Qumran", *Australian Biblical Review* 15, 13-20.

Hoenig, S. B.

1966   "The Qumran Liturgic Psalms", *Jewish Quarterly Review* 57, 327-332.

1967   *Jewish Quarterly Review* 58, 162-163. Review of Sanders 1967.

Hurvitz, A.

1965a   "The Form of the Expression 'Lord of the Universe' and Its Appearance in Psalm 151 from Qumran" (in Hebrew), *Tarbitz* 34, 224-227.

1965b   "Observations on the Language of the Third Apocryphal Psalm from Qumran", *Revue de Qumran* 18, 225-232. On Psalm 155.

1967   "The Language and Date of Ps. 151 from Qumran" (in Hebrew), *Eretz Israel* 8, 82-87.

1971   *Israel Exploration Journal* 21, 182-184. Review of Sanders 1967.

Jongeling, B.

1972   *Journal of Semitic Studies* 27, 271-272. Review of Sanders 1967.

Laperrousaz, E. M.

1967   "Publication en Israel d'un fragment du 'Rouleau des Psaumes' provenant de la grotte 11Q de Qumran, et autres publications récentes de fragments de psaumes découverts dans les grottes 11Q et 4Q", *Revue de l'Histoire des Religions* 171, 101-108.

Lehmann, M. R.

1966   *Tradition* 8, 76-78. Review of Sanders 1965b.

Lella, A. di

1966   *Catholic Biblical Quarterly* 28, 92-95. Review of Sanders 1965b.

1967   *Catholic Biblical Quarterly* 29, 284-286. Review of Sanders 1967.

Heureux, C. E. l'

1967   "The Biblical Sources of the 'Apostrophe to Zion' ", *Catholic Biblical Quarterly* 29, 60-74.

Lührmann, D.

1968   "Ein Weisheitspsalm aus Qumran (11QPsᵃ xviii)", *Zeitschrift fur die alttestamentliche Wissenschaft* 80, 87-98. On Psalm 154.

MacKenzie, R. A. F.

1970   "Psalm 148bc: Conclusion or Title?", *Biblica* 51, 221-224.

Meyer, R.

1967   "Die Septuaginta-Fassung von Psalm 151:1-5 als Ergebnis einer dogmatischen Korrektur", in F. Maass (ed.), *Das Ferne und Nahe Wort (Leonard Rost Festschrift)* (Berlin: Töpelmann), 164-172.

1968 "Bemerkungen zum vorkanonischen Text des Alten Testaments", in M. Weise (ed.), *Wort und Welt* (*Erich Hertzsch Festschrift*) (Berlin: Ev. Verlagsanstalt), 213-219.

Osswald, E.
1966 *Theologische Literaturzeitung* 91, cols. 729-734. Review of Sanders 1965b.

Ouellette, J.
1969 "Variantes qumraniennes du Livre des Psaumes", *Revue de Qumran* 25, 105-123.

Ovadia, A.
1968 "The Synagogue at Gaza" (in Hebrew), *Qadmoniyot* 1, 124-127. On the Orphic David in Ps 151. See *Orientalia* 35 (1966), 35.

Philonenko, M.
1967 "David-Orphée sur une mosaïque de Gaza", *Revue d'histoire et de philosophie religieuses* 47, 355-357. On Psalm 151.

Ploeg, J. P. M. van der
1966 *Bibliotheca Orientalis* 23, 133-142. Review of Sanders 1965b.

Polzin, R.
1967 "Notes on the Dating of the Non-Massoretic Psalms of 11QPsa", *Harvard Theological Review* 60, 468-476.

Priest, J.
1966 *Journal of Biblical Literature* 85, 515-517. Review of Sanders 1965b.

Qimron, E.
1970 "The Psalms Scroll of Qumran – A Linguistic Study" (in Hebrew), *Leshonenu* 35, 99-116.

Rabinowitz, I.
1964 "The Alleged Orphism of 11QPss 28, 3-12", *Zeitschrift für die alttestamentliche Wissenschaft* 76, 193-200. On Psalm 151.
1971 "The Qumran Hebrew Original of Ben Sira's Concluding Acrostic on Wisdom", *Hebrew Union College Annual* 42, 173-184.

Roberts, B. J.
1966 *Book List of the British Society for Old Testament Study* 60. Review of Sanders 1965b.
1967 *Journal of Theological Studies* 18, 183-185. Review of Sanders 1965b.
1969 *Journal of Theological Studies* 20, 573. Review of Sanders 1967.

Sanders, J. A.
1962 "The Scroll of Psalms from Cave 11 (11QPss): A Preliminary Report", *Bulletin of the American Schools of Oriental Research* 165, 11-15.
1963 "Ps 151 in 11QPsa", *Zeitschrift für die alttestamentliche Wissenschaft* 75, 73-86.
1964 "Two Non-Canonical Psalms in 11QPsa", *Zeitschrift für die alttestamentliche Wissenschaft* 76, 57-75. On Psalms 154 and 155.
1965a "Pre-Masoretic Psalter Texts", *Catholic Biblical Quarterly* 27, 114-123.
1965b "The Psalms Scroll of Qumran Cave 11", *Discoveries in the Judaean Desert* 4 (Oxford: Clarendon). *Editio princeps.*
1966 "Variorum in the Psalms Scroll (11QPsa)", *Harvard Theological Review* 59, 83-94.
1967 *The Dead Sea Psalms Scroll* (Ithaca New York: Cornell University Press). *Editio secunda.*
1968 "Cave 11 Surprises and the Question of Canon", *McCormick Quarterly* 21, 284-298. Republished in D. N. Freedman and J. C. Greenfield (eds.), *New Directions in Biblical Archaeology* (Garden City: Doubleday, 1969), 101-116.

1971 "The Sirach 51 Acrostic", in M. Philonenko and J. Caguot (eds.), *Hommages à André Dupont-Sommer* (Paris: Librairie d'Amérique et d'Orient), 429-438.

1972 *Torah and Canon* (Philadelphia: Fortress).

1973a "Palestinian Manuscripts 1947-1972", *Journal of Jewish Studies* 24, 74-83.

1973b "The Dead Sea Scrolls - - A Quarter Century of Study", *Biblical Archaeologist* 36, 110-148.

Segert, S.

1967 *Archiv Orientálni* 35, 129-133. Review of Sanders 1965b.

Shenkel, J. D.

1967 *Theological Studies* 28, 836-837. Review of Sanders 1967.

Siegel, J. P.

1969 "Final *mem* in medial position and medial *mem* in final position in 11QPsᵃ: Some Observations", *Revue de Qumran* 25, 125-130.

1971 *Hebrew Union College Annual* 42, 159-172.

Skehan, P. W.

1963 "The Apocryphal Psalm 151", *Catholic Biblical Quarterly* 25, 407-409.

1965a "A Broken Acrostic and Psalm 9", *Catholic Biblical Quarterly* 27, 1 ff. On Psalm 155.

1965b "The Biblical Scrolls from Qumran and the Text of the Old Testament", *Biblical Archaeologist* 23, 87-100.

1971 "The Acrostic Poem in Sirach 51:13-30", *Harvard Theological Review* 64, 387-400.

1973 "A Liturgical Complex in 11QPsᵃ", *Catholic Biblical Quarterly* 35, 195-205.

Strugnell, J.

1965 "More Psalms of 'David' ", *Catholic Biblical Quarterly* 27, 207-216. On Pseudo-Philo para. 59.

1966 "Notes on the Text and Transmission of the Apocryphal Psalms 151, 154 and 155", *Harvard Theological Review* 59, 257-281.

Talmon, S.

1966 "The Apocryphal Psalms in Hebrew from Qumran" (in Hebrew), *Tarbitz* 35, 214-234. Republished in English: "Pisqah Be'emsa' Pasuq and 11QPsᵃ", *Textus* 5 (1966), 11-21.

1967 *Tarbitz* 37, 99-104. Review of Sanders 1965b.

Tournay, R.

1966 *Revue biblique* 73, 258-265. Review of Sanders 1965b.

1967 *Revue biblique* 74, 605. Review of Sanders 1967.

Ufenheimer, B.

1964 "Psalms 152 and 153 from Qumran: Two More Apocryphal Psalms" (in Hebrew), *Môlad* 22:191-192, 328-342.

Weiss, R.

1962 *Ḥerut* of 28 Sept. On Preliminary Report.

1963 *Ha-Boqer* of 28 May, 5-6. On Psalm 151.

1964 *Ḥerut* of 1 May. *Massa* of 15 May and 7 August. On Psalms 151 and 154.

1965 *Massa* of 29 January. On Psalm 151.

Yadin, Y.

1966 "Another Fragment (E) of the Psalms Scroll from Qumran Cave 11 (11QPsᵃ)", *Textus* 5, 1-10. First edition.

1964 "Psalms from a Qumran Cave", *Môlad* 22: 193-194, 463-465. Critique of Ufenheimer.

PSALM 151

The first text from the Psalms Scroll published was that of Psalm 151, from column 28 (Sanders 1963). The text itself immediately attracted interest and the treatment some considerable reaction. Within a year five studies had appeared, two agreeing in substance with the writer's treatment, two modifying it at crucial points, and one disagreeing rather strongly (Rabinowitz 1964). Soon thereafter one of the scholars who had agreed with the original treatment revised his reading of the psalm to meet Rabinowitz' objections (Carmignac 1965). All these titles are grouped together, for the student's convenience, in the Cornell edition of the scroll (Sanders 1967: 152). Insofar as major studies of the psalm are concerned, the list there is complete except for an article by Professor Rudolf Meyer (1967).

In the Cornell edition of the scroll the writer presented the several studies of Psalm 151 which had appeared at the time of writing (Sanders 1967; 94-103). Those were still early days, and I attempted to present each reading, side by side with mine, as objectively as possible, leaving it to the student himself to judge as to which reading most fits texts and context. I did not press my own case over the others but was content to suggest that, while not abandoning my reading, I recognized other possibilities which had their own integrity. Indeed, I still see three basic ways possible to scan the text of the psalm, as indicated in the Cornell edition discussion. But, far from conceding the other readings premier lieu, I now, after a decade of discussion and review, wish to take this opportunity to respond to the major objections advanced to my reading, as well as to reaffirm the latter as the most valid rendering.

B. Jongeling (1972) in his review of the Cornell edition concentrates on Psalm 151. The effect of his criticism is that I did not pay sufficient attention to the earlier critics. What I have found, by contrast, is that reviewers have overlooked the fresh arguments I advanced for my reading in the notes in the Cornell edition (Sanders 1967: 96-97, 100-102). The most consistent critique in the reviews of the Cornell edition has been that it is not truly a popular edition, as announced, but has much technical material in it. I must concede that I used the *editio secunda* as a means of advancing the scholarly discussions of particular texts in the scroll.

The student who comes fresh to the dispute must first realize that the text of Psalm 151 itself does not settle the crucial questions: no two scholars agree on all the crucial readings involved, but rather tend to cancel each other out, point by point. Hence the student should also be aware that there is no single grouping of scholars reading the text consistently over against the original rendering. What this situation signifies, above all else, is that the poem found in the scroll (in contrast to that received in the versions) lends itself to more than one mode of scansion. The versions, however, beginning with the Greek, present a greatly condensed recension of the poem; all scholars agree that the Hebrew psalm in the scroll is the original. It still seems to me that no other reading or treatment of Psalm 151A sufficiently accounts for the reduced recension lying back of the versions.

My first response to the various critics, therefore, is that it would appear that insufficient attention has been paid in the variant renderings to comparison with the Greek text. It was for this reason that I provided, a second time, a synoptic line by line juxtaposition of the Hebrew and Greek texts (Sanders 1967: 96). Why does the recension omit the portions contained in the original, especially lines 5 and 6 of column 28 of the scroll? Clearly the omission was not due to mechanical or scribal accidental means. Equally clearly some other reason must be advanced.

Tempting, of course, is the possibility of reading all the personal pronominal suffixes in those two lines, beyond *benafshi*, consistently either *waw* or *yod*, including the reading *'alaw* (defectivum) (as Strugnell 1966) or *'ālay* (as Rabinowitz 1964) instead of *'illû*. But tempting as consistency may be, it has little place in vocalization of ancient Hebrew poetry. More important, in this instance, it rids the poem of the potentially offensive statements which would explain the recensional activity. A number of critics have objected to the poem's saying that hills and flocks cannot or do not witness to God, because the Bible so often says they do. One is tempted to suggest that some modern scholars have precisely expressed, in this regard, the thinking of the ancient revisionist. Is there any evidence elsewhere, therefore, that would suggest such an offense in antiquity? Professor John Strugnell found the answer to that question in an Arabic poem published in 1909 by O. C. Krarup (Sanders 1967: 100, n. 20):

O David, if the mountains did not glorify me then would I surely pluck them out. And if the trees did not glorify me then would I surely reduce their fruit. But there is nothing which does not render me glory.... Act so then, ye people, for I see everything ....

As Strugnell has remarked, "Our Arab had access to Psalm 151A and corrected 'David's' unorthodox thoughts." Strugnell's own rendering concurs essentially with ours in this respect (Strugnell 1966).

The Arabic poem agrees with Psalm 151A that God sees everything, if one follows the rendering here reaffirmed. Some scholars, including Weiss (1964) and Rabinowitz (1964) and others who have followed them, read the words 'adôn and 'ĕlôah of line 7 of the scroll as construct to the word ha-kôl which follows each, rendering the phrases "Lord of the Universe" and "God of the Universe". This is, of course, quite possible though to do so quite alters the scansion of the lines and renders the syntax awkward. Here, however, we have not only the Arabic poem to support our original reading but also the Sinaiticus manuscript of the Septuagint and a portion of the Old Latin tradition of Psalm 151 in both of which ha-kôl is translated as accusative of the verb "to hear" in LXX Ps. 151: 3. Actually most scholars agree with us here. The introduction of the idea of the Lord of the Universe into a poetic midrash, on 1 Samuel 16, which clearly stressed the Biblical idea of God's seeing everything, even what was in David's heart, or, in the poem, in his *nefesh*, is both unnecessary and inappropriate. It is, in fact, because it is so clear that this was the very purpose of the original poem that the recensionist preserved it. Far from being offensive like lines 5 and 6, this aspect of the whole poem, and God's consequent action of choosing David over his brothers, made it indeed worth keeping. The question whether the recension took place in Hebrew before translation into Greek or took place in the process of translation is difficult to answer. At this point one can only conjecture that the reason we have had it all along in recension and not in the original is that it was the latter which took place, but there is no clear evidence either way. Orthodox thinkers in antiquity apparently chose, because of the offensive nature of the poem, either to expurgate it or to revise it (R. Meyer 1967 agrees on this point).

The most disputed reading in the original rendering is that of ʿillû in line 6 of the scroll. Other renderings of ʿillû have been ʿālay, ʿālāw, and ʿălê. They are all quite possible but seem to me (a) to render the scansion difficult, and (b), for reasons cited above, to abort the central reason for the recensional activity resulting in the versions. This dispute lies at the crux, as I see it, of the offense of the poem. Normal scansion would indicate that the word be read as a verb serving a double function with the phrase which follows. The one verb available in the Hebrew of the period, and in the Qumran literature (CD v 5), is the *piʿel* form of the verb ʿālāh. It occurs only rarely in the literature, as we stressed from the beginning, but it fits the context perfectly: "The trees have cherished (or, appreciated, or, held in esteem) my words and the flock my works." This reading provides the contrast indicated to the first offense, that nature, or the mountains and hills, cannot or do not witness to or proclaim God; and it provides the second and greater offense to later or non-Qumran orthodox sensibilities. But to the original author I am confident that these two observations, offensive as they might be to other eyes and ears, were quite in line with another point of view which in its own eyes was as "conservative" as any other (Sanders 1967: 94-100, 157-159). Mountains and hills, like nature in general, cannot witness, as man can, to the mighty acts of God. Who actually remembers and recites the epic history of God's dealings with Israel – such as the choice of leaders and kings (2 Samuel 7)? Man can, Israel ought to, and David did so – out on the mountains and hills amongst the trees and his flocks, by creating a lyre and composing psalms about those wonderful deeds in his mind (line 5), and singing them in such a manner that the plants and the animals listened in rapt attention. He did what the mountains and hills could not do. He created, already in his mind (or heart or soul), the Psalter which later came to be written down in so many copies including 11QPsᵃ. But at that early moment, as much as later, Israel and especially the faithful at Qumran came to appreciate every psalm he wrote (4,050 according to the preceding co-lumn), only the trees and the grazing flocks had the great privilege of hearing him compose his earliest psalms and sing out in his shepherd's lone-liness.

This, it seemed to me, was the genius of the poem which later dis-turbed those who no longer shared the vision of the lonely shepherd whose music in praise of God's mighty acts was so wondrous as to arrest the attention of mute nature about him, and whose intention in composing it was so pure as to arrest the attention of God who looks upon the heart. Surely what God saw in David's soul was *not* a com-plaint that nature did not bear witness to his, David's, words and deeds, and a plea that someone would recount his deeds (Rabinowitz 1964; Carmignac 1965). It is clearly more in line with normal usage for the phrase "Said I within my soul" to introduce something which follows it rather than to complete a preceding thought. But that usage also indicates the sense "I had wrongly thought"; and then follow the "wrong" thoughts. But most of the scholars who have insisted that the phrase must introduce what follows have also expunged in the text the offense of what follows. And if what he thought was wrong, was the thought in his mind the basis for his divine selection (1 Samuel 16)? All of this left me with the somewhat uncomfortable but far preferable alternative of attaching the phrase "Said I within my soul" to the clear expression of intent of composing psalms in the preceding phrase. The one improvement I might make at this juncture would be to render that preceding phrase, "And (so) may I render glory to the Lord" (with Sanders 1963), instead of "And (so) have I rendered glory to the Lord" (Sanders 1967).

Such a poetic image of David as the shepherd-musician *par excellence*, based precisely upon 1 Samuel 16-17, cannot but call to mind Hellenistic traditions of the period about Orpheus so well attested to David in later art forms (Sanders 1963; Ovadia 1968; Philonenko 1967). Is it not a form of apologia thus to coopt (and deny) a facet of the mythical figure of Orpheus in order to laud the historical figure of David?

THE SIRACH 51 ACROSTIC

It will not be possible here to deal with all the features of the scroll which have aroused interest. There is a growing consensus following Hurvitz (1965b) and Polzin (1967) that though the non-Massoretic psalms in the scroll are somewhat archaizing in form, that is, scan more like Biblical psalms than like the Thanksgiving Hymns from Qumran, the language would indicate a comparatively late dating, for most if not all of them, probably postexilic Persian to early Hellenistic times. W. F. Albright (1966) at one point suggested a seventh to sixth century B. C. dating for Psalm 151, but he never developed the idea. The discussions about dating will continue, but their direction seems indicated.

In the space remaining here, remarks will be limited to two other issues arising out of the scroll and its contents.

In 1971 three quite independent studies of the acrostic poem in columns 21 and 22 were published (Skehan, Rabinowitz, and Sanders). None of the three was aware that the others were working on the same material and hence was not able to take advantage of the others' findings. Earlier studies of this particular text were those of Dupont-Sommer (1967), which none of the three mentioned above had apparently seen, and of M. Delcor (1968) which Skehan does not mention. In addition to these, the reviews of Sanders 1965b by M. Dahood (1966) and by A. di Lella (1966) should be mentioned since both contain important statements concerning this acrostic poem. Following the *editio princeps* (Sanders 1965) the regnant position (as Rabinowitz puts it) anent the poem, with only di Lella's voice dissenting, has been that it, like a number of

Biblical passages, was poetically composed in *mots à double entente* bearing both erotic and pious meanings, and that it was most probably not written by Ben Sira, author of the first fifty chapters of Ecclesiasticus, or his grandson. While there are considerable differences in readings and scansion between Skehan (1971) and Rabinowitz (1971), and while Rabinowitz does not attempt, like Skehan and me (Sanders 1971), to reconstruct the second half of the poem, they both agree, following di Lella, that neither of these major conclusions about the poem are correct. Neither perceives any erotic ambiguity in it, and both defend Ben Sira as its author. Skehan does not, like Rabinowitz, stress these points, but it is clear from his work that he wants to be counted on the side of his student, di Lella. Also unlike Rabinowitz' paper, Skehan's is quite free of rhetoric and constitutes a serious challenge to the so-called regnant position.

I feel it in order to try to respond to Professor Rabinowitz' comments which are of a general nature. First of all, I am genuinely sorry that my work has now twice provoked a colleague to the sort of response Rabinowitz has made (Rabinowitz 1964; 1971). I have always appreciated his work and read it with care. I have not been able to agree with the position concerning the scrolls which Rabinowitz took rather early – that the Qumran sect were a pre-Maccabean group who viewed any and all Hellenizing influence as highly heterodox. While he has modified this position, one can only assume that the rhetoric, to the measure that it was present in his response (Rabinowitz 1964) to my work on Psalm 151 (Sanders 1963), was in reaction to the thesis advanced that Psalm 151 reflected tenuously an Orphic image of the shepherd David. A decade of discussion of this point has not erased that possibility, as I think the above discussion of the psalm has shown.

Rabinowitz's phrases of a similar nature in his study of the Sirach acrostic poem are even more puzzling. In his paper he rightly brackets the work of Delcor (1968) with mine, which "though differing here and there, are in thorough agreement in main conception". He might also have bracketed Dupont-Sommer (1967) and Dahood (1966) with us. In fact, most of the conversations I have had with colleagues about this "precious fragment of the Hebrew original" (di Lella 1966, followed by Rabinowitz) have made me feel I had been entirely too reluctant to see the full amount of erotic overtone in this stirringly beautiful poem. I am grateful, incidentally, to Rabinowitz (1971: 184) for pointing out that well before the discovery of the scroll, W. Baumgartner, on the basis of the Cairo manuscripts and the versions, was the first to advocate the position later advanced on the basis of the original. It is difficult to know how to handle phrases in Rabinowitz's study, such as "bowdlerization of the 'obscene' original", "fundamentally (and grossly) mistaken", and "to thus convict Ben Sira of ungentlemanliness". My response to such rhetoric, when seen in Rabinowitz (1964), was to bide the time and let scholarly discussion take its course.

In the present instance I deem it better, because others are more directly involved and because the original text has now been available for some nine years, to respond more directly. It should be made quite clear that no one has at any point suggested that this poem is in any sense obscene. Delcor, Dupont-Sommer, and I have all insisted that it, like some Biblical poetry and like other poetry of the highest quality, far from being obscene, takes the language of natural love and presses it into the service of piety. We have stressed, that, like much poetry of the greatest artistic ability, it bears most admirably the burden of literary ambiguity. The student needs but to refer to the studies cited, reading not only the interpretive comments but also the apparatus to words and phrases in the text. Rabinowitz reports that Delcor and I take *tuḇ* in the *zayin* verse in "the restricted meaning 'pleasure'". On the contrary, with great care, as in the case of the numerous other occasions of ambiguity, it was pointed out that the word meant both "pleasure" and "good" – the meaning Rabinowitz prefers.

With caution I have underscored in all three of my publications of the poem (1965b; 1967; 1971) that the task of translation of such literary ambiguities is fraught with difficulty, even painful in the sense that the receptor modern language rarely carries in one word the same dual burden. As Dahood avers in his critique (1966), I have erred (sic) on the side of piety rather than eros in much of my own effort. In fact, it is not certain, since Dahood and others who have discussed the poem with me personally have not published direct studies of the text, whether there might not be some scholars who would, in contrast to Rabinowitz and Skehan, want to deny the side of the ambiguity which the latter two wish to affirm alone! For my part, I would continue to insist on the high quality of literary ambiguity in the poem with the attendant translational difficulties. The man whom we honor in this volume knows better the translational difficulties of such material than those of us whose linguistics are limited to certain disciplines.

At no point has there been the least suggestion that the author – Ben Sira or another – was ungentlemanly in his thoughts in composing the poem. Professor Rabinowitz must, I suppose, decide for himself if

Ben Sira himself was ungentlemanly when he composed the metaphoric poetry in Sirach 24, or the authors of Proverbs in chs. 8 and 9, or the author of Wisdom of Solomon 8 (Sanders 1967: 114-117).... Song of Songs?

Finally, one somewhat begs the question of authorship if he turns to passages in Sirach itself, as Rabinowitz does in his notes, to contest the meaning of particular passages and whether or not they bear the literary ambiguities. Monsignor Skehan's appendix to his article, a reconstruction of Sirach 6: 18-37, bears a number of similarities to the acrostic poem in question; and, though he does not state it, I am sure he intends to offer the passage as indication of authorship of the acrostic. But aside from the short passage in Sirach 24: 19-22, which pursues the same metaphor of Wisdom as a harlot, as does Proverb 9, there is nothing in all of Sirach which displays the delicate balance of literary ambiguity which our acrostic poem maintains so admirably. On the contrary, as I have argued from the beginning, such passages in Sirach show clearly why the poem would become attached to the work of Ben Sira. This problem is now illuminated by the appearance of Barthélemy and Rickenbacher (1973). (See also R. Meyer 1968: 217.) Finally, neither Rabinowitz nor Skehan addresses the obvious question of how a poem known to have been by Ben Sira was included at Qumran in a Davidic Psalter (see especially Skehan 1973: 195).

Let us turn now to the text itself, with the 1971 studies of it by Skehan and Rabinowitz in hand, to discern the improvements which should be made to my efforts of 1965b, 1967, and 1971. All scholars who have worked on the text agree that (a) the scroll presents the original Hebrew of the poem where it is extant, and (b) the medieval Cairo Hebrew is, following Israel Lévi (Sanders 1971: 437, n. 1), in principle, a retroversion from the Syriac version. The minor points of difference which do not touch on the basic meaning of the text will be by-passed in favor of putting in relief the essential differences among us and the judgments which they require. After careful study of the work of both colleagues, I must reaffirm all of my earlier readings of the extant portion of the poem in the scroll but am pleased to acknowledge indebtedness to Professor Skehan for points of improvement in the scansion. Skehan and I disagree on three readings of the scroll text; Rabinowitz and I disagree in our readings at four points. In only one of these do my colleagues agree with each other.

In the *waw* verse of the acrostic Skehan and Rabinowitz both read *hôdô* against my *hôdî*. 11QPsᵃ, as Rabinowitz rightly notes, does not distinguish clearly between *waw* (their reading) and *yod* (mine). Mechanically speaking it can be read either way. Skehan (also Delcor) reads it as the noun "praise" with 3pm suffix, citing pertinent Biblical parallels, but translates it simply "grateful praise", presumably meaning praise due God. Rabinowitz reads it as a verbal noun, citing rare parallels in Isaiah and CD, and translates it simply as "praise". Both readings disrupt the *Verlauf* of first person suffixes throughout the poem and seem to me to avoid the obvious. *Hôdî* here means both "the praise I have to offer" and the poet's ardour in quest of wisdom.

In the *zayin* verse the second verb in the scroll all agree reads *W'SHQH*. I take this, with the immediately preceding *zammôtî*, in hendiadys to mean "I lusted to play". Skehan says that the verb *śāḥaq* here is "incongruous", and emends the text, following the Cairo B reading (which he admits is secondary) to *va'eḥśĕqah* and adds to the text *bah*, translating this innovation, "I became resolutely devoted to her". Rabinowitz, who fails to recognize the hendiadys construction, keeps the textual consonants but reads *va'ešḥāqeha*, translating it (by adding a word not in the text) "and constantly trod her (path)". I see no reason for either of these efforts to avoid what the text says. I, on the other hand, am willing to alter my 1971 translation and revert to the earlier, "I purposed to make sport", referring the student to the critical notes of my earlier publications.

In the *ṭeṭ* verse Skehan agrees with me that *ṭāratî* derives from *ṭārad*, whereas Rabinowitz takes the verb to have been *ṭāraḥti*. Neither, of course, agrees with Delcor and me that the sense of the phrase is "I bestirred my desire for her".

In the same *ṭeṭ* verse Rabinowitz agrees completely with my reading of the second colon whereas Skehan deems *ûberûmèha* (note printer's error in Sanders 1971: 432) to be "meaningless" and emends the text to read *ûberômemāh*, a complementary infinitive construction which he translates, "never weary of extolling her". I completely agree with Rabinowitz that the phrase, on the contrary, means, "and on her heights I am not at ease". Of course, I maintain that the phrase bears a double meaning including Rabinowitz's, while he would understand only the sense of not "free from the never-ending labor imposed upon all who would reach wisdom's heights".

In the *yod* verse Skehan and I agree on the reading of the letters which are at the decomposed bottom of column 21 of the scroll, and I deem his judgment to be correct, against the possibility of the reading di Lella advanced and Rabinowitz sustains. The third word of that line

I reconstructed from the Syriac as *šaʿărèhā*. Skehan is surely right that it should read the singular, *šaʿărāh*, rather than the plural. My translation should, therefore, be altered to read, "My hand opened her gate", with all my various explanatory notes standing as to its double meaning and significance.

The second colon of the *yod* verse begins with the word *ûmaʿărumèhā*. Skehan and Rabinowitz read the preposition *bet* between the conjunction and the noun. Skehan seems to claim he can see the top of it on the leather (though his comments are not clear here); Rabinowitz does not claim so but puts the preposition with the conjunction before the bracket, in lacuna. I do not think the *bet* is there at all, either on the leather or by assumption. Whereas they see only the sense of "secrets" in the noun I see also the sense of "secret parts".

Only the first colon of the *caf* verse is discernible on the leather. Skehan and I read it exactly the same except that I think the accusative of the phrase should read "my hand" and he "my hands". Rabinowitz's readings here are far afield.

Rabinowitz does not attempt to reconstruct the second half of the poem. Therefore the remainder of these comments will deal with the differences between Skehan and myself in our attempted rehabilitations of the remaining verses, and in the improvements I am grateful to accept from his work.

In the second colon of the *caf* verse Skehan by-passes the Cairo B reading *ûbeṭāhărāh* for his own *ûbeniqqayôn*. There is a certain sensitivity in Skehan's further decision that the purity involved is "her wooer's" rather than "Wisdom's". From the context it might indeed seem that Wisdom could not be entirely pure if she lets herself be pursued in the manner the poem has indicated. And it should again be stressed that while Skehan nowhere actually states his recognition of the poem as in any sense a *Liebesgeschichte*, in a few covert hints, as here, he clearly refrains from denying this aspect of it. Since Wisdom's purity, in all such texts as this, is ever new, ever fresh, and ever available to all wooers, I prefer to keep the Cairo reading and point the *hē* at the end as feminine suffix. (Note the printer's error in *ʾěʿezvennāh* in Sanders 1971: 432 in the *lamed* verse.)

I am truly puzzled, however, by Skehan's rejection of the first colon of the *mem* verse in Cairo B in favor of his own creation. He is, of course, right, on the other hand, to reject the suggestion of D. W. Thomas (Sanders 1971: 429-431), who completely ignored the scroll in his consideration of the phrase. My arguments remain the same.

For this verse as a whole, however, I am grateful to follow Skehan's lead in his manner of scansion of the *alef, gimmel, nun,* and *resh* verses and see this one also (which he fails to do) as composed of three colons, instead of two:

My loins would burn like a firepot
　　from gazing upon her,
　　hence I took her as a pleasant possession.

Similarly, in the *alef* verse *beṭerem tā*ʿ *îtî* should be taken as the second of three colons; in the *gimmel* verse *bibšôl*ʿ *ănābîm* as the second of three colons; in the *nun* verse *śākār śiftôtāy* as the second of three colons; in the *resh* verse *kî qāṭān hāyîtî* as the second of three colons; and in the *shin* verse *limmûdî bin*ʿ*ûray.*

In the *samek* verse I think Skehan's *petāyîm* preferable to my *sekālîm* but would suggest the typical 11QPsᵃ orthography, *petāʾîm.* As indicated in Sanders (1971: 435), I was not able at the time to decide between them. I am pleased now to follow Skehan in this reading. With Segal, however, I prefer to retain *bet midrāšî* rather than Skehan's *bet mûsār.*

In the *qof* verse Skehan's *yimṣāʾ ehā* is clearly preferable to the periphrastic *môṣāʾ ʾôtāh.* But while I accept Skehan's scansion of the *resh* verse, as already indicated, I would for the reasons advanced (1971: 436), retain my reconstruction of the verse.

The *shin* verse, as indicated above, should now be seen as a tricolon. Whether the last word of the verse should read *bāh* with Skehan or *bî* as in my reconstruction is difficult to decide. Either will serve.

I see no basis on which to change the *taw* verse and hence it should remain as is. Skehan's reading completely overlooks the reference of this verse back to the poem as a whole. By contrast, I am inclined to accept Skehan's coda verse, with the exception of one word, in place of my own. His own work elsewhere, which he does not mention in this article, has shown that such coda verses often begin with *pe.* Thus his *paʿălû paʿălekem* would suit well. And in the second colon my *vehûʾ nôtēn lākem* (Cairo) must give way to Skehan's far simpler and better, *veyittēn.* But I consider *beṣedeq* at the end of the first colon more preferable than *beʿittô.* The verse would now read, "Work your work in righteousness and he will grant your reward in due season."

I permit myself to quote, in concluding this review of work on this remarkable poem, my earlier estimates of the acrostic as a whole:

The strong indication, therefore, is that the last part of the song was an exhortation by the supposed Wisdom teacher to his students that they follow his

example and in their puberty dedicate themselves also to the pursuit and acqui-
sition of Wisdom, so that as they mature they, like their teacher, may direct
their human passions toward righteousness! (Sanders 1967: 117).

The first part of the poem is the Wisdom teacher's confession of his youthful
experience with Wisdom as his nurse, teacher and mistress, a commendable
manner of sublimation in celibacy and undoubtedly highly meaningful in every
spiritual sense for the celibate at Qumran (Sanders 1965b: 84).

THE QUESTION OF CANON

The concluding part of this review of work done on the Psalms Scroll
will concern its place in the canonical process as it relates to the Psalter.
I have dealt with this question on three other occasions (Sanders 1967:
157-159; 1968; and 1973b: 134ff.), and shall not here repeat what is
available elsewhere except when clarification concerning the general
thesis seems needed. The principal reason I wish to deal here with the
problems raised by the Psalms Scroll in regard to canon, aside from
the immense importance of the subject, is that Professor Skehan has
recently published a significant study which deals directly with the question (Skehan 1973).

Skehan continues in this article the work begun in Sanders (1966),
and especially in Sanders (1968), and in large measure builds upon it.
He has succeeded where we did not, however, in making some significant
redaction-critical observations about the scroll, and in passing, about
the Massoretic Psalter as well. Skehan, who is charged with the publication of most of the Cave 4 Psalms manuscripts, has been intensely
interested in the Cave 11 Psalter materials and has been a gracious
consultant for my work since the beginning. For a listing of what he has
published to date of Cave 4 Psalter texts, as well as of all Qumran
Psalter texts, see Sanders (1973); for a catalog and index to all pre-
Massoretic Psalter texts, published and unpublished, see Sanders (1967:
143-149).

Skehan early on (Skehan 1965b: 100), followed by me (Sanders
1967: 10 ff., 157 ff.; 1968: 3 ff.), suggested that explanations needed
to be sought for the variant order and content, as well as addenda
(over against the Massoretic Psalter), in the Qumran Psalter. With the
subsequent publications of 4QPs^d, 4QPs^f, 11QPs^b, and 11QPsAp^a
(see Sanders 1967: 144-145) it was clear that 11QPs^a was not a private
or maverick collection but indicated a valid, variant Psalter. But it still
was not clear how one was to relate the Qumran Psalter to the later

Massoretic Psalter. In 1966 M. H. Goshen-Gottstein and S. Talmon suggested that it represented the earliest example of a Jewish Prayerbook. Talmon, at least, has abandoned this position and in a public conference in Jerusalem on May 30, 1973, announced that he now agrees with the position I had advanced that the Qumran Psalter was viewed at Qumran as "canonical" and that it was, as we know it, an open-ended Psalter.

Skehan prefers to call 11QPs^a a "Library Edition" of the Psalter which presupposes the Psalter as we know it in the Massoretic Text. Such a thesis would be quite viable, it seems to me, if 11QPs^a were the only copy of the Qumran Psalter which we possess. But it is not. It is not at all clear to the writer, from the catalog and index compiled of all published and unpublished Psalter manuscripts from Qumran (Sanders 1967: 143-149) and from transcriptions of unpublished Psalter texts in Skehan's care (e.g. 4QPs^k and 4QPs^n), how many different arrangements of the Psalter there were in the Qumran library; but it is quite clear that 11QPs^a was not a unique, single issue there. Skehan's thesis is that this scroll presupposes the order and content of the MT-150 collection (my term, not his). I sincerely wish that this were as clear to me as it is to him.

Skehan's article (1973) probes deeply into the redactional and liturgical aspects of the scroll, and offers some valuable suggestions as to the arrangement of Massoretic psalms in it, "addenda" within them, and their relation to the non-Massoretic psalms included in the scroll. His overall conclusion (1973: 201, n. 24) is that "what we have basically in 11QPs^a is a collection of Pss 101-150 with liturgical regroupings and 'library edition' expansions". There is not the space here to enter into details. Suffice it to say that some of his work is extremely helpful: it is the sort that should be applied to that other liturgical collection of psalms, the MT-150 collection! Other observations are doubtful, however, and the whole study will have to be scrutinized carefully at another opportunity. Some of his observations I had already made in the earlier efforts cited. But there should be no doubt in the student's mind that Skehan has considerably advanced the cause of search for the liturgical sense of the scroll.

But I must still demur as to Skehan's assertion that "the standard collection of 150 Psalms was fixed before the 11Q form was derived from it". It could well have been that what we know as the MT-150 collection was already known, and indeed that copies of it, too, existed in the Qumran library. We shall have to wait until we have photographs of all the Cave 4 Psalter fragments, and of all the Cave 4 hymnic fragments, to determine that question. Certainly what is clear is that even if the MT-150 collection was already current it was not viewed at Qumran as "standard" and so "canonical" that it could not be added to or subtracted from! Professor Y. Yadin, who is editing the Temple Scroll from Cave 11, is convinced that it was viewed as canonical at Qumran. In the same sense, I am convinced, the Qumran Psalter was viewed as canonical at Qumran. The argument that since the tetragrammaton always appears in the scroll in the archaizing palaeo-Hebrew script it was not held to be Biblical or canonical at Qumran has fallen of its own weight (Sanders 1968: 288, n. 10; J. P. Siegel 1971: 159-172). The manner in which the scroll was copied by the scribe argues on the contrary that there is no facile way in which it can be set aside; on the contrary, it challenges our assumptions about the canonical process by which the Psalter came to be limited to the 150 psalms ordered in the received manner. Rudolf Meyer (1968) has argued this point in an extremely forceful way which cannot be easily dismissed. His name must now be added to those already mentioned (Sanders 1968: 288, n. 10).

It is our current view of "canon" which needs to be modified in treating these materials. It was largely out of dissatisfaction with the currently available approach to the whole concept of canon, and especially as it pertains to the Psalter, that I called recently for serious, fresh efforts in canonical criticism (Sanders 1972). That effort will be supplemented shortly by two forthcoming essays. And I am pleased to say that the quarterly *Interpretation* plans to respond to the call by assigning a number of articles to the topic in forthcoming volumes. I am convinced that the Psalter at Qumran was open-ended. It was not yet closed in its latter third. It was a working Psalter, as I think Skehan's work clearly indicates. What is not clear from Skehan's findings is his confidence that the MT-150 lay back of the Qumran Psalter as a "standard" or closed Psalter. On the contrary, one can take each of his valuable findings and state the opposite, that 11QPs^a lies back of the Massoretic Psalter which developed out of the fuller edition, paring down unnecessary liturgical matter. One can almost detect our current bias for the post-A. D. 70 situation in that I am sure all of us ask the question, "Why did the Qumran sect add x, y, and z?" We have to exercise special scientific caution to admit also of the question, "Why did the MT omit x, y, and z?" And yet we must attempt to do so.

S. Talmon, in the May 30, 1973, public address mentioned above, suggested some comparisons with the Chronicler. One of the many ancient sources of the Chronicler was the work of the Deuteronomistic history we have in the books of Kings. In fact, says Talmon, Chronicles could be described as a midrash on his sources. In like manner, he suggests, the Qumran Psalter might be viewed as a midrash on its sources. See, for instance, the psalm in 1 Chron. 16: 8-36 which is made up of portions of Psalms 105, 96 and 106; and note also the liturgical bits of poetry in 1 Chron. 29: 10-13 and 2 Chron. 6: 41-42. I think especially interesting the notations in 2 Chron. 5: 13 and 20: 21 where the familiar refrain from Ps. 118: 1 and 29 (11QPs^a xvi 1-2, 5-6) is cited as sung at the dedication of the Temple: "Give thanks to the Lord, for he is good, for his mercy endures forever". Also pertinent is the note in Ezra 3: 10-11 that psalms were recited and sung "in the manner of David". Is it not possible that some Psalters included these notations of the fifth century which were later excised in the MT-150 Psalter? It seems to me that one must not assume that such floating bits and portions of liturgical literature are FROM the MT Psalter psalms. The most one should say is that they are also found there, but in different arrangements and combinations. Our first reaction quite understandably is that the psalm in columns 26 and 27 of the Qumran scroll, identical (so far as we know) with 2 Sam. 23: 1-7, was taken from Samuel and added to the Qumran Psalter. Is it not just possible that in the canonical process moving toward the MT-150 collection it had been present in many Psalter collections but was finally omitted, whereas Psalm 18, almost identical with 2 Samuel 22, was for other reasons kept? Similarly, one is gravely tempted to ask why the Qumran Psalter added the constant refrain it has to each verse of Psalm 145. Should not one also ask, scientifically speaking, whether it was not the process leading to the MT-150 Psalter which dropped the refrain in a tendency toward a leaner collection. And should one not ask why the MT retains the refrain of Psalm 136 (11QPs^a xv)? Even a leaner edition of the Psalter, such as the MT, cannot omit a refrain so integral to the psalm.

I would refer the student once more to our earlier position taken in Sanders (1968). Until proved otherwise, I would hold open the questions there posed, especially that of the "canonical priority" of the MT Psalter. In the meantime I should say that I think the field is moving toward affirming that the Qumran Psalter, represented by 11QPs^a but also by other more fragmentary Psalter manuscripts from Cave 4 and 11, was revered at Qumran as authoritative as any other Psalter present there: it was "canonical" at Qumran though by no means closed; on the contrary, it was, while authoritative, still open-ended. And, following Skehan's recent study, I would stress a point I have made earlier: certain smaller groupings of psalms, such as the Songs of Ascents and the

Passover Hallel, were possibly in some collections viewed as units, but in others, such as the Qumran Psalter, clearly had not yet attained the status of fixed groupings. Is not this in reality a more sober, rather in fact more "conservative", view than that the faithful at Qumran rearranged their sectarian Psalter at will out of various materials including an already fixed Psalter? I am convinced that we much need thorough, careful work in canonical criticism, to disembarrass ourselves of post-A. D. 70 assumptions about "canon". It seems to me that the Qumran Psalter manuscripts indicate that in the first century B. C. and early first century A. D. Judaism had simply not yet arrived at that uniform point for the Psalter, just as it had not yet arrived at stabilisation of the remainder of the Hagiographa or Ketubim.

THE USE OF REPETITION IN THE PROPHECY OF JOEL

JOHN A. THOMPSON

On the value of repetition Eisenson (Eisenson, Auer, and Irwin (1963: 239-240) writes:

Repetition, within limits, has high attention value. Its advantages lie in the added strength given to the stimulus by repeating it and in the consequent increase in our sensitivity to the stimulus.... The possibility of monotony may be avoided and even greater potency often achieved if the repeated stimulus is varied slightly in form while retaining the central theme. This application of repetition is a hallmark of good design and composition.

Though in most languages repetition strengthens, as Eisenson says, in some languages of the South Pacific, Dr. Eugene A. Nida informs me, repetition weakens and expresses doubt or disparagement.

OTHER STUDIES OF REPETITION

A comprehensive outline of the different kinds of repetition, according to Latin and Greek rhetoricians, is given by Lausberg (1960: 310-345). König (1900: 152-157) lists cases of repetition in the Bible including some in Joel. Types of words and phrases repeated in Isaiah 40-66 are treated by Muilenburg (1956: 389). Thompson (1956: 730) studies the purpose and function of repetition in the book of Joel, and that study is revised and much amplified in this paper.

This paper deals with meaningful repetition in Joel. It does not deal with some repetitions which are the inevitable result of Hebrew poetic parallelism, e.g. "hear", "give ear" (1:2). Also not treated are alliterative repetitions of syllables such as are found in the Hebrew of 1:7, 10, 15. This study covers the significant repetition of words, of synonyms, of phrases, and of ideas. The first translations given are

John A. Thompson is Research Consultant for the American Bible Society, Princeton, New Jersey.

those of the Revised Standard Version, and occasionally alternative translations, preceded by "or", immediately follow those of the Revised Standard Version. The Scripture references are in Joel unless otherwise indicated.

FUNCTIONS OF REPETITION IN JOEL

1. *Emphasis* (Lausberg 1960: 450-453)

The most common use of repetition is for emphasis, and this function extends into most of the other categories which follow.

The most obvious example of repetition in Joel is "multitudes, multitudes" (3: 14, Hebrew 4: 14). This doubling of words in immediate succession is called *geminatio* by the Latin rhetoricians (Lausberg 1960: 312-313). Here the repetition emphasizes the great number of people who are gathered for judgment.

Many repetitions are used in describing the locusts. The great number and organization of the locusts are emphasized by the metaphors "nation" (1: 6) and the synonym "people" (2: 2), by "army" three times (2: 5, 11, 25) and the synonym "host" (2: 11). The destructive capability of the locusts appears in "powerful" four times (1: 6; 2: 2, 5, 11). Both numbers and power are implied in "great" (2: 2, 11, 25).

The coming of the locusts is made vivid by many synonyms or related verbs of motion: "come up" (1: 6; see section 2. *Correspondence* below), "run" (2: 4, 9), "leap" (2: 5, 9), "charge" (2: 7), "scale" (2: 7), "climb up" (2: 9, same Hebrew verb as the preceding), "march" (2: 7), "marches (2: 8), "burst through" (2: 8), and "enter" (2: 9; see section 4. *Climax* below).

Similarly the coming of the armies of the nations for the last battle is described by repeated words and synonyms: "stir up" (3: 7, Hebrew 4: 7), "bestir" (3: 12, Hebrew 4: 12, same Hebrew verb as preceding), "draw near" (3: 9; Hebrew 4: 9), "come up" (3: 9, 12; Hebrew 4: 9, 12; see section 2. *Correspondence* below), "hasten" (3: 11, Hebrew 4: 11), "come" (3: 11; Hebrew 4: 11), and "gather" (3: 11, Hebrew 4: 11).

The destruction caused by the locusts is expressed by many synonymous expressions (on the use of synonyms see Lausberg 1960: 329-332). The devastation of the plants and of the crops is shown by the following: "cut off" (1: 5, 9, 16), "laid waste" (1: 7, 10), "splintered" (1: 7), "stripped" (1: 7), "destroyed" (1: 10), "perished" (1: 11), the metaphors "fire devours" and "flame burns" (2: 3), and "desolate wilderness" (2: 3).

The destruction caused by the drought, simultaneous with the locust plague, is also indicated by repeated phrases of similar meaning: "fails" or "dries up" (1: 10), "failed" or "dried up" (1: 17), "dried up" (1: 20), and, with the same Hebrew verb as the three just listed, "withers" and "are withered" (1: 12), "shrivels" (1: 17), the metaphors "fire has devoured" and "flame has burned" (1: 20).

Many synonyms are repeated to describe the sorrow of the people because of the locust plague and the drought. These words for sorrow include: "weep" (1: 5; 2: 17), "weeping" (2: 12,) "wail" (1: 5, 13), "lament" (1: 8, 13), "mourn" (1: 9), "mourning" (2: 12), "in anguish" and "faces grow pale" (2: 6). The idea of sorrow is also repeated by twice negating the opposite – joy (1: 12, 16, on negation of the opposite Lausberg 1960: 217). These repeated expressions of similar meaning not only emphasize the seriousness of the suffering but also, with different subjects, show its universality, including all classes of people, animals, and even, by personification, "the ground" (1: 10).

Similarly synonyms for supplication to God for deliverance are repeated to show the earnestness of the prayers. All people "cry" or "call" (1: 14); the prophet says, "I cry" (1: 19, a different Hebrew verb from the preceding); even the beasts are said with personification to "cry" or "pant" to God (1: 20, a different Hebrew verb than either of the preceding). The varied subjects of these synonymous verbs indicate the universality of the prayers (see section 2. *Correspondence* below).

The promise of the spirit is assured by being repeated, "I will pour out my spirit" (2: 28, 29, Hebrew 3:1, 2). This promise opens and closes the famous section on the giving of the spirit, which Peter quoted at Pentecost (Acts 2: 18, 19). On this enclosing structure, x....x, called in Latin *redditio*, see Lausberg (1960: 317-318).

The certainty of God's final judgment is expressed by such repetitions as: "I will enter into judgment" (3: 2, Hebrew 4:2), "I will sit to judge" (3: 12, Hebrew 4: 12), and "valley of decision ... valley of decision" (3: 14, Hebrew 4: 14). "Valley of Jehoshaphat" (3: 2, 12, Hebrew 4: 2, 12) produces in Hebrew a repetition of the thought of God's judgment which does not appear in the English transliteration of the name Jehoshaphat, which means "Yahweh has judged".

2. *Correspondence*

In Joel many elements in the present judgment through the locusts are repeated by corresponding elements in the final future judgment.

The repeated references to the present time of judgment as a "day" (1: 15; 2: 2) and "the day of the Lord" (1: 15; 2: 1, 11) correspond to the repeated references to the final "day of the Lord" (2: 31, Hebrew 3: 4; 3: 14, Hebrew 4: 14; see section 4. *Climax* below). The present day of the Lord corresponds to the future day of the Lord not only because both are times of God's judgment and of deliverance, but also because some specific elements are similar in each, as indicated below.

The attack of the locusts corresponds to the attack of the human enemies of Israel (see section 1. *Emphasis* above and section 4. *Climax* below). Particularly significant for correspondence is the repeated use of "come up" of the locusts (1: 6) and of the attacking nations (3: 9, 12, Hebrew 4: 9, 12). This verb is often used of attacking armies, e.g. Num. 13: 31; Judg. 6: 3; 1 Sam. 7: 7; 1 Kings 14: 25.

"The earth quakes" and "the heavens tremble" at the time of the locust plague (2: 10), and, with chiastic variation in order "the heavens and the earth shake" (3: 16, Hebrew 4: 16) during the final day of the Lord. During a locust plague the advancing hordes of locusts on the ground give the impression that the earth is moving (Thompson 1956: 746), and the flying locusts give a shimmering and trembling effect in the sky (Driver 1901: 48-49). The shaking in 3: 16, Hebrew 4: 16, doubtless refers not to appearance (as with the locusts) but to the actual heavens and earth themselves (compare Isa. 13: 13).

Another characteristic associated with the day of the Lord is the darkening of the heavenly bodies (Isa. 13: 10). In the first part of Joel (1: 1-2: 27) the "day" is characterized by "darkness", "gloom", "thick darkness" (2: 2) and by the darkening of the sun, moon, and stars (2: 10). In the second part of Joel (2: 28-3: 21, Hebrew 3: 1-4: 21), as an element of the final day of judgment, the sun becomes dark (2:30, Hebrew 3:4), and the sun, moon, and stars are darkened (3: 15, Hebrew 4: 15, an exact duplication of 2: 10b). As with the shaking of the earth and heavens mentioned above, the darkness of the present and future days of the Lord are described with similar words, but the realities are probably different. The darkness of the present day of judgment is probably the result of the flying locusts, which actually do becloud the heavenly bodies (Thompson 1956: 746). The means of darkening in the final "day" is not specified.

Another feature of the present day of the Lord, with a corresponding element in the future "day", is "the Lord utters his voice" (2: 11; 3: 16, Hebrew 4: 16). This is sometimes a metaphor for thunder (Ps. 18: 13, Hebrew 18: 14; Ps. 68: 33, Hebrew 68: 34), and this interpretation is probable in Joel 2: 11.

Attention has already been called to the repetition of synonyms for supplication to God in connection with the present locust plague and drought (see section 1. *Emphasis* above). In the second part of the book this idea is repeated: "all who call upon the name of the Lord shall be delivered" (2: 32, Hebrew 3: 5). In both the present and the future judgment the way to salvation is through calling on God.

Joel 2: 27 gives the assurance that Israel will know that the Lord is their God when the locusts are removed, rain is given, and fertility is restored. In 3: 17, Hebrew 4: 17, is the balancing identical assurance in connection with the deliverance of Israel in the last battle and the last judgment. The King James Version, the Jerusalem Bible, and the New American Bible are correct is giving the same translation of this clause in each of the two verses. The slightly different translations of the Revised Standard Version, "I, the Lord am your God" (2: 27) and "I am the Lord your God" (3: 17, Hebrew 4:17) are both possible, but obscure the correspondence of the clauses in the Hebrew.

3. *Contrast* (Lausberg 1960: 241-242, 389-390)

In chapter two the grain, wine, and oil (2: 19, 24), the pastures, trees, fig trees, and vines (2: 22) are restored. This specification in restoration contrasts with chapter one where the same products and plants are destroyed by the locusts and the drought: grain, wine, and oil (1: 10, note same order as in 2: 19, 24), pastures (1: 18, 19, 20), fig trees (1: 7, 12), and vines (1: 7, 12).

Two words are each used twice to express joy at the restored fertility: "be glad" (2: 21, 23) and "rejoice" (2: 21, 23). Also a near opposite is negated twice: "fear not" (2: 21, 22). These positive and negative elements are contrasted to the repeated expressions of sorrow and the negation of the opposite in chapter one (see section 1. *Emphasis*).

In several cases contrast is achieved by repeating a verb with a different subject. Examples are: "return [addressed to the people] to the Lord" (2: 13) and "whether he [the Lord] will not turn" (2: 14, in Hebrew same verb as "return"); "for he [the locust army] has done great things [in destruction]" (2: 20) and "for the Lord has done great things [in driving away the locusts]" (2:21); "all who call upon the name of the Lord" and "the Lord calls" (2:32, Hebrew 3:5); "you [Tyre, Sidon, Philistia] have sold" (3:6, 7, Hebrew 4:6, 7) and "I [the Lord] will sell" and "they [the sons of Judah] will sell" (3:8, Hebrew 4:8).

4. *Climax* (Lausberg 1960: 246-247, 311)

The many synonymous verbs describing the attack of the locusts (see section 1. *Emphasis* above) reach a climax in "they enter through the windows" (2:9).

The repeated references to "the day" and "the day of the Lord" have already been listed (see section 2. *Correspondence* above). The references to the day of the Lord as a present, limited judgment prepare for the climax, the future, great day of the Lord when the judgment will be general and final (2:31, Hebrew 3:4; 3:14, Hebrew 4:14).

5. *Succession*

The Greek rhetoricians called the linked repetition of words to show succession *anadiplosis*, and Latin writers called it *reduplicatio* (Lausberg 1960: 314-315).

Such a chain of repetition is found in 1:2, "your children ... your children ... their children ... their children". Here, of course, the repetition is connected with the passing on of the story of the locust plague from one generation to another.

In 1:4 and 2:25 four names of insects are given which have been variously interpreted. Koehler (Koehler and Baumgartner 1951: 178, 82, 383, 319, respectively) thinks that *gāzām* is probably a caterpillar, *'arbeh* is the adult locust, *yeleq* is the pupa stage of the locust, and *ḥāsîl* is the cockroach (order of 1:4). Many recent commentators think that the four words refer to four stages of the desert locust, the species that most frequently attacks Palestine, cf. Kapelrud (1948: 17), Thompson (1956: 737), Myers (1959: 77), Wood (1968: 440), Wolff (1969: 30-31), Murphy "probably" (1971: 462). It is likely that 1:4 gives the historical order in which the stages of locust attacked Judea in the plague described by Joel. Joel 2:25 repeats the same names in a different order, but in the same relative order if a cycle of successive stages is involved. Perhaps 2:25 gives the logical order beginning with the adult (Thompson: 1956: 751). The Revised Standard Version attempts to translate the names from etymology: "cutting locust", "swarming locust", "hopping locust", "destroying locust" (order of 1:4). Two problems with these translations are that some of the etymologies are uncertain and that the idea of stages is not conveyed. In non-scientific English the stages in 1: 4 might be expressed by :"young locusts", "mature locusts", "newly-hatched locusts", and "growing locusts". If the names refer to successive stages, 1: 4 becomes illuminating: the first wave of locusts, the "young locusts", ate some of the vegetation; these developed into "mature locusts" which ate more; these produced a wave of "newly-hatched locusts" which ate more; finally the latter developed into "growing locusts" which finished eating the plants. In any case, the repetition of the two middle names in 1: 4 produces a chain indicating successive swarms of locusts.

6. *Irony* (Lausberg 1960: 446-450)

In 3: 4, Hebrew 4: 4, God asks the surrounding nations, "Are you paying me back?" (by attacking the land of God's special people). Contrary to the expectation of the nations, God goes on to state twice, "I will requite your deed upon your own head" (3: 4, 7, Hebrew 4: 3, 7). "Requite" translates the same Hebrew verb as "pay back", and this repetition points up the irony.

7. *Anaphora, Beginning a Section* (Lausberg 1960: 318-319)

Identical clauses, "Blow the trumpet in Zion", are used at the beginning of two sections (2: 1, 15). Though the same words are used, the actual significance is slightly different: the first blast of the ram's horn warns the people of the locust plague; the second blast calls the people to prayer and repentance.

8. *Epiphora, Ending a Section* (Lausberg 1960: 320-321)

Three times Joel closes a section by repeating some significant element of that section.

In 1: 20 Joel repeats the clause "fire has devoured the pastures of the wilderness", which is also found in 1: 19. The repetition of this metaphor ends a section which deals with the devastation of vegetation by the locusts and, particularly in this clause, by drought.

In 2: 27 Joel ends the first main part of the book with "and my people shall never again be put to shame", an exact repetition of 2: 26c. Two themes of 1: 1-2: 27 are here repeated: the shaming of Israel by the

judgment of the locust plague and drought, and the assurance that
Israel will never be so punished again.

In 3: 21, Hebrew 4: 21, the book ends on an encouraging note:
"the Lord dwells in Zion". In Hebrew "dwells in Zion" is identical with
"who dwell in Zion" of 3: 17, Hebrew 4: 17. This is the sum of the
blessings promised to Israel in 2: 28-3: 21, Hebrew 3: 1-4: 21, that the
Lord, the source of all their blessings, will be in their midst.

CONCLUSIONS

1. The first conclusion of this study of the use of repetition in prophecy
of Joel is that the book is the product of conscious literary art. Wolff
(1969: 9) says: "Here is an artistic literary creation. It uses forms that
are almost exclusively rhetorical." This statement came to my attention
after I had reached a similar conclusion.

2. The study of the repetitions in Joel is an aid to interpretation.
For example, what is "my army" in 2: 11? The immediate context does
not tell. In 2: 25 the context clearly shows that "my great army" refers
to the locusts, and the similar phrase in 2: 11 probably does also (see
also 2: 5).

3. The use of repetitions favors the general unity of the book. Some
scholars, like Robinson (1954: 55-56), attribute all of 2: 28-3: 21,
Hebrew 3: 1-4: 21, to unknown authors later than Joel. The repetitions
which produce many correspondences between the first and second parts
of the book support unity of authorship for the book as a whole. Bewer
(1911: 49-56) relegates all references to the day of the Lord to an apo-
calyptist later than Joel. The fact that these references conform to the
style of the rest of the book, particularly in repetition and correspondences, supports the presumption that the passages on the day of the
Lord are an integral part of the original work.

4. An understanding of Joel's repetitious style has a bearing on text
criticism. The critical notes of *Biblia Hebraica* (Kittel 1962: 910-916)
indicate that some scholars propose deleting the following passages
because they are repetitions: "their children and their children" (1: 3,
see section 5. *Succession*), "for he has done great things" (2: 20, see
section 3. *Contrast*), "and my people shall never again be put to shame"
(2: 26, see section 8. *Epiphora*), "in the valley of decision" (second
occurrence in 3: 14, Hebrew 4: 14, see section 1. *Emphasis*), and "and
the heavens and the earth shake" (3: 16, Hebrew 4: 16, see section 2.

Correspondence). Each one of these phrases has been shown above to fit into Joel's stylistic pattern of repetition, and therefore the very repetition argues for the originality of the phrases.

5. Since repetition is characteristic of rituals, the prevalence of repetition in Joel may give some limited support to the thesis of Engnell and Kapelrud (Kapelrud 1948: 4, 13, 192-195) that the book is essentially a liturgy.

6. Finally the incidence of the repetitions gives some indication of what Joel considered important. According to the number of repetitions involved, the important subjects are: the day of the Lord, the attack by the locusts, the devastation caused by the locusts and the drought, the mourning of the people, the restoration of fertility, the pouring out of God's spirit, the attack by human enemies, God's judgment, and God's promises to Israel.

REFERENCES

Bewer, Julius A.
   1911   *A Critical and Exegetical Commentary on Obadiah and Joel*, *The International Critical Commentary* (New York: Scribner's).
Driver, Samuel R.
   1901   *The Books of Joel and Amos*, *The Cambridge Bible* (Cambridge: University Press).
Eisenson, Jon, J. Jeffry Auer, and John V. Irwin
   1963   *The Psychology of Communication* (New York: Appleton-Century-Crofts).
Kapelrud, Arvid S.
   1948   *Joel Studies* (= *Uppsala Universitets Arsskrift* 1948:4) (Uppsala: A. B. Lundequistska Bokhandeln).
Kittel, Rudolf, et al. (eds.)
   1962   *Biblia Hebraica*, 3rd edition, 13th printing (Stuttgart: Württembergische Bibelanstalt).
Koehler, Ludwig, and Walter Baumgartner
   1951   *Lexicon in Veteris Testamenti Libros* (Leiden: E. J. Brill).
König, Eduard
   1900   *Stilistik, Rhetorik, Poetik in Bezug auf die biblische Litteratur* (Leipzig: Dieterich'sche Verlagsbuchhandlung).
Lausberg, Heinrich
   1960   *Handbuch der literarischen Rhetorik*, 2 vols. (München: Max Hueber Verlag).
Muilenburg, James
   1956   "The Book of Isaiah, Chapters 40-66, Introduction and Exegesis", *The Interpreter's Bible* 5 (Nashville: Abingdon), 381-773.
Murphy, Roland E.
   1971   "The Book of Joel", *The Interpreter's One-Volume Commentary on the Bible* (Nashville: Abingdon), 461-464.
Myers, Jacob M.
   1959   *Hosea, Joel, Amos, Obadiah, Jonah, The Layman's Commentary* (Richmond: John Knox Press).

Robinson, Theodore M.
  1954 *Die zwölf kleinen Propheten, Hosea bis Micha*, zweite Auflage, *Handbuch zum Alten Testament* (Tübingen: J. C. B. Mohr).
Thompson, John A.
  1956 "The Book of Joel, Introduction and Exegesis", *The Interpreter's Bible* 6 (Nashville: Abingdon), 729-760.
Wolff, Hans W.
  1969 *Dodekapropheton* 2: *Joel und Amos, Biblischer Kommentar Altes Testament* (Neukirchen-Vluyn: Neukirchener Verlag).
Wood, Geoffry F.
  1968 "Joel Obadiah", *The Jerome Biblical Commentary* (Englewood Cliffs: Prentice-Hall), 439-446.

A GREEK TRANSLATION-TECHNICAL TREATMENT
OF AMOS 1: 15

JAN DE WAARD

The last sentence of the fourth element in the highly structured message to Ammon (Amos 1: 13-15) which gives a description of the particular way in which God's judgment will be executed, runs in the MT as follows:

wᵉhālak malkām bagōlāh hū̕ wᵉśārāyw yaḥdāw

or, in a formal equivalence translation, "and their king shall go into exile, he and his princes together".

It has long been noted that Greek translations of this sentence show a number of surprising variants (Touzard 1909), but insufficient attention has been paid to the variants themselves as well as to their character. Biblia Hebraica (Kittel 1937) mentions one variant reading though the information is incomplete and the variant orthographically wrong. However, Biblia Hebraica Stuttgartensia (Elliger 1970) has omitted even this bare minimum of information. In some commentaries and special studies the Greek translational problems are passed over in silence (Cripps 1969; Maag 1951; Weiser 1956), in others they are dealt with but in a rather superficial and unsatisfactory manner since no extensive survey of all the existing Greek texts has been made. For this reason, a complete survey of the Greek texts is given in the diagram in order to provide a reliable scientific basis for discussion.[1]

Dr. Jan de Waard is Translation Consultant for the United Bible Societies, Aix-en-Provence, France.
[1] For this diagram Ziegler's (1967) text and critical apparatus have been used as well as the conventional *sigla* of the Göttinger Septuagint.

Amos 1:15a

	καὶ	πορεύσονται	οἱ	βασιλεῖς	αὐτῆς	ἐν	αἰχμαλωσίᾳ
130′ 407^txt	×	×	×	×	αυτων	×	×
86^mg 2	×	πορευθησονται	×	×	αυτων	×	×
86^txt	×	πορευθησονται	×	×	×	×	×
86^mg 1 L′ — 407^mg	×	πορευσεται		μελχομ	∅	×	×
46′ C — 68	×	×	∅	×	×	×	×
36^c	×	×	×	×	∅	×	×

α′ σ′ πορευσεται μελχομ

Amos 1:15b

		οἱ	ἱερεῖς	αὐτῶν	καὶ	οἱ	ἄρχοντες	αὐτῶν	ἐπὶ	τὸ	αὐτό
106	και	×	×	×	×	×	×	×	×	×	×
68		×	×	×	×	×	×	∅	×	×	×
Q^c L — 86^c		×	×	αυτου	×	×	×	αυτου	×	×	×
1 II		×	×	×	×	×	×	× εν	×	×	×
								αιχμαλωσια			

α′ σ′ θ′ pro αυτων 1°: ωσαυτως αυτης; pro αυτων 2°: αυτου

The first question to be answered is how to explain the rendering of
malkām by οἱ βασιλεῖς αὐτῆς. For Wolff (1969: 162) the differences
between source and receptor text (singular noun versus plural noun;
3rd p. plur, masc. suffix versus 3rd p. sg. fem. pronoun) can only be
explained through the assumption of a different, though incorrect,
Hebrew *Vorlage* which probably read *mᵉlākeyāh*. Apart from the fact
that no different source text has yet been found, there are other grounds
to consider such a proposal as highly unlikely. If this were the case,
one should at least expect a "correction" according to the "correct"
Hebrew text. It is, of course, true that a correction of αὐτῆς into αὐτῶν
has taken place in 130′, 407^txt, and 86^mg 2. But it is likewise true that
none of the existing Greek manuscripts changed the plural noun into
a singular. From this one may conclude that οἱ βασιλεῖς αὐτῆς is a

Greek translational variant and that major attention should be given to the pronoun αὐτῆς.

The use of the pronoun αὐτῆς, however, can easily be explained as the result of a translation technical operation. The antecedent of αὐτῆς is Rabbah (verse 14),[2] and this is a much closer antecedent than υἱῶν Αμμων (verse 13). Within the Greek restructuring of the total discourse Amos 1:13-15, the Greek translator of Amos had only two translational possibilities: he could either state the object (υἱῶν Αμμων) explicitly or use a pronoun, in which case he had to make a syntactical adaptation to the nearest possible meaningful antecedent. He may not have felt free to follow the first possibility, so he selected the second. So the translation technical approach seems to offer a much more natural and satisfactory explanation than the assumption of a different *Vorlage*. It might even be added as a more general rule that such an approach will yield better results also elsewhere, since scholars in the area of textual criticism made a basic mistake in operating almost exclusively on the word and sentence level without taking into account the total discourse of the message and the restructuring required by the receptor language.

A number of manuscripts belonging to the Lucianic main and sub-groups as well as 407[mg] present the particular reading πορευσεται μελχομ, a reading followed by Aquila and Symmachus. This reading is, of course, due to a difference of vocalization of the Hebrew consonant text, *milkōm* being read instead of *malkām*. Lucianic manuscripts dealt exactly in the same way with Zeph. 1:5 MT. Especially nineteenth century scholars considered this vocalization to be the original one (Grätz 1893; Kautzsch 1896; S. R. Driver 1897; Nowack 1897; Oort 1900),[3] but this position has rightly been abandoned in more recent research, mainly for reasons of contextual meaning (Keil 1888; van Hoonacker 1908; Touzard 1909; Sellin 1929; van Gelderen 1933; Snaith 1946; Wellhausen 1963; Wolff 1969). The substitution of the national god of Ammon *milkōm* for *malkām* is clearly the result of a secondary interpretation. On the other hand, it should be noted that there is not only a close morphological relationship between the two items, but also a close semantic link. For, regardless of how the form *milkōm* is analyzed morphologically as well as semantically,[4] *milkōm* can always be considered as an extended meaning of *mlk*.[5]

---

[2]   Not, of course, "Ammon" as Snaith (1946:29) maintains.
[3]   This position of older research is reflected in some of the translations belonging to that period such as the Dutch Leidsche Vertaling (Leiden translation).
[4]   Morphologically *milkōm* has been analysed as *mlk* + mimation (de Lagarde 1889: 190) though it should be said that Hebrew possesses neither mimation nor nunation·

The major problem, however, is how to explain the translation of
weśārāyw by οἱ ἱερεῖς αὐτῶν καὶ οἱ ἄρχοντες αὐτῶν in verse 15b.
It is important to note that this reading is supported by all existing
Greek manuscripts if one does not take into account minor variants,
which are mainly obligatory syntactical adaptations of the pronouns in
Lucianic manuscripts. As translation technique, it does not seem to be
justified to say that the nominal phrase οἱ ἱερεῖς αὐτῶν takes the place
of Hebrew *hū᾽* (Wellhausen 1963: 71; Wolff 1969: 162). One should not
forget that the use of the pronoun in the source text may have been
conditioned in more than one way – syntactically by the use of *yaḥdāw*
and the necessity of having a so-called *pronom de reprise* (Joüon 1947:
450), and metrically by the necessity of maintaining the metre 3 + 3.
However, the same conditioning does not exist in the receptor language.

One could, of course, argue that the Septuagint text has an *extra*,
namely the nominal phrase οἱ ἱερεῖς αὐτῶν, and then ask the question
where this extra comes from. One of the answers which has been given
to that question is that this reading has its origin in the (wrong) interpretation of *malkām* as *milkōm* (Wellhausen 1963; Wolff 1969).[6] Here
it becomes abundantly clear that making such general statements
without taking into account the total Greek text tradition is a rather
dangerous procedure. Such an answer could be considered for a minority
of manuscripts, almost exclusively Lucianic, which have the reading
μελχομ in verse 15a, but it cannot be taken seriously for the vast majority
of manuscripts which have the reading οἱ βασιλεῖς in verse 15a and
which read nevertheless οἱ ἱερεῖς αὐτῶν in verse 15b. More strikingly
even, the plural form of the noun βασιλεῖς seems to make any suggestion of an implicit reference to the national god of Ammon at least
improbable.[7]

---

in the singular (Moscati 1969:98) so that the presence of traces of mimation in such
proper names as *Milkōm* remains uncertain. It has also been analysed *milk-* + suffix
-ōm (Brockelmann 1966:396) and as a compound noun, either *mlk ʿm* 'king of the
people' or *mlk ʿm* 'Am is king'.
5   As already stated in a different terminology by van Hoonacker (1908:216): " 'le
roi' dont il était question Amos 1:15 pouvait d'ailleurs aisément devenir Milcom,
qui était en effet le roi suprême du peuple qui l'honorait".
6   Wellhausen (1963:71) states: "Es scheint dass die Lesart *khnyw* dem falschen
Verständnis von *mlkm* als Milkom ihre Entstehung verdankt". Compare also Wolff
(1969:162): "Entsprechend der Deutung von *mlkm* auf den Ammonitergott..."
7   No full attention has ever been paid to the plural οἱ βασιλεῖς. The most natural
explanation is to see here the use of a more generic descriptive term including descendants of the royal house, princes, etc. It seems to go too far to consider the plural
as a reference to both king and national god and the reading μελχομ as a case of

A second solution has been proposed which merits more consideration. It would account for the extra as a conflation due to assimilation to Jer. 49:3 (Snaith 1946:29). In fact, the text reoccurs in a somewhat different form Jer. 49:3 MT:

ki malkām bagōlāh yēlēk kōhanāyw weśārāyw yaḥdāyw

which text has been translated in the Septuagint (Jer. 30:3/19) as follows: ὅτι [Μελχομ] ἐν ἀποικίᾳ βαδιεῖται, οἱ ἱερεῖς αὐτοῦ καὶ οἱ ἄρχοντες αὐτοῦ ἅμα. As some scholars have become the victim of a conflation of ideas, it is not always easy to decide whether they think that such a conflation has already taken place in the source text or only in the receptor. In so far as any conclusion can be made on the basis of mainly fragmentary notes, some researchers at least seem to have been in favour of a conflation of the source text (Kautzsch 1896:63; Wellhausen 1963:71) which comes near to a difference in *Vorlage* (Grätz 1893; Nowack 1897; Harper 1966:35). It goes without saying that such a hypothesis lacks any textual foundation. More serious consideration should be given to the suggestion that the conflation is due to an assimilation to Jer. 30:3/19 LXX (Wolff 1969). However, even this assumption poses many problems. First of all, it is based upon a certain number of presuppositions as to the date of the different translations, etc.,[8] which are difficult to prove. Second, the assimilation must have taken place according to a highly selective process; one glance at the text of Jer. 30:3/19 is sufficient to show that the Greek vocabulary is almost completely different so that in fact only the nominal phrase οἱ ἱερεῖς would have been assimilated. Finally, it seems to be incomprehensible that such a conflation would have left no traces, either in the form of a correction through the omission of οἱ ἱερεῖς αὐτῶν in certain manuscripts of Amos 1:15 or in the form of the introduction of at least some of the vocabulary items of Jer. 30:3/19 LXX into manuscripts of Amos 1:15. As far as the approach itself is concerned, it can be objected that no explanation through a conflation of texts should be tried if a certain text can be explained by itself. This is a question of sound methodology.

Now this method, which has priority over any other, can be applied with rather positive results. There is no need to presuppose a different Hebrew *Vorlage* or a conflation of different Greek texts. It is again the

more specific information. If this were true, one would, of course, face an additional example of the use of translation techniques.

[8] For this see especially Thackeray (1915; 1923) and Jellicoe (1968:67).

translation-technique approach which can provide a fully satisfactory answer to the question where the reading οἱ ἱερεῖς αὐτῶν καὶ οἱ ἄρχοντες αὐτῶν comes from. It should be noted that Hebrew *śar* is a generic term for any being, either supernatural or natural, having any kind of authority, either political, administrative, military, or religious (Brown, Driver, and Briggs 1968: 978). The LXX translator of Amos simply divided this broad group of authorities into two more specific subgroups, one religious (οἱ ἱερεῖς), the other secular (οἱ ἄρχοντες).[9] As a translation technique, this means that nothing has been added in the Septuagint text of Amos 1: 15. This is simply an example of generic source text information versus specific information in the receptor.

For such an answer one turns in vain to modern Biblical scholarship. Remarkably enough, in order to get a clear hint as to the direction of this answer, one should consult an ancient scholar who was himself a gifted translator working along the lines of well-conceived, modern translation principles: Jerome.[10] In his commentary on Amos 1: 15 he wrote:

Sacerdotes in Hebraeo non habetur, sed principes. Addiderunt itaque Septuaginta sacerdotes ut, si velis scire qui sint illi principes, audias sacerdotes.[11]

One could, of course, argue that an overall translation-technique treatment is likewise amazing and that one should expect at least some "corrections" in some Greek manuscripts. However, the fact that the nominal phrases οἱ ἱερεῖς αὐτῶν καὶ οἱ ἄρχοντες αὐτῶν existed in Greek parallel texts may be one of the reasons which can be given for the extraordinary unity of the Greek text tradition.[12]

The translation-technique approach has the methodological advantage of offering a clear explanation of all the surprising variants[13] in the Greek texts of Amos 1: 15 so that it is no longer necessary to have recourse to such diverse operations and factors as differences in *Vorlage* and conflation of texts. Finally, it is the only approach which does full justice to translators.

[9]   Though the Greek ἄρχων is a superordinate term on a rather high level of the Greek taxonomy, it does not seem to refer to religious officers (Liddell and Scott 1951:254; Moulton and Milligan 1963:83).
[10]   On Jerome's translational approach see especially Nida (1964:12ff.).
[11]   *Commentariorum in Amos prophetam libri tres* (P. 1. xxv:989-1096).
[12]   In this sense one could agree with van Hoonacker's (1908:216) observation: "D'autre part le texte de Jérémie a pu influer sur la version grecque du passage d'Amos."
[13]   An additional example of a translation-technique operation in Amos 1.15b is the reading ἐν αἰχμαλωσίᾳ in 1 II which is an example of making implicit source information explicit.

REFERENCES

Brockelmann, Carl
 1966   *Grundriss der vergleichenden Grammatik der semitischen Sprachen I Laut- und Formenlehre* (Hildesheim: Georg Olm).
Brown, Francis, S. R. Driver, and Charles A. Briggs
 1968   *A Hebrew and English Lexicon of the Old Testament* (Oxford: Clarendon Press).
Cripps, Richard S.
 1969   *A Critical and Exegetical Commentary on the Book of Amos* (London: S. P. C. K.).
Driver, S. R.
 1897   *Joel and Amos. The Cambridge Bible for Schools and Colleges.*
Elliger, K.
 1970   Liber XII prophetarum. Biblia Hebraica Stuttgartensia (Stuttgart: Württembergische Bibelanstalt).
Gelderen, C. van
 1933   *Het Boek Amos* (Kampen: Kok).
Grätz, H.
 1893   *Emendationes in plerosque Sacrae Scripturae Veteris Testamenti libros, secundum veterum versiones nec non auxiliis criticis caeteris adhibitis. Fasciculus secundus Ezechielis et Duodecim Prophetarum libros etc. continens.*
Harper, William Rainey
 1966   *A Critical and Exegetical Commentary on Amos and Hosea. The International Critical Commentary* (Edinburgh: Clark).
Hoonacker, A. van
 1908   *Les douze petits prophètes. Études Bibliques* (Paris: Gabalda).
Jellicoe, Sidney
 1968   *The Septuagint and Modern Study* (Oxford: Clarendon Press).
Jerome
 1845   *Commentariorum in Amos prophetam libri tres, Patrologiae Cursus Completus*, ed. J. P. Migne (= *Series Patrum Latinorum* 25) (Paris), 989-1096.
Joüon, Paul
 1947   *Grammaire de l'hébreu biblique* (Rome: Institut Biblique Pontifical).
Kautzsch, E.
 1896   *Die Heilige Schrift des Alten Testaments, Beilagen* (Freiburg, i.B. and Leipzig: Mohr).
Keil, Carl Friedrich
 1888   *Biblischer Commentar über die zwölf kleinen Propheten* (Leipzig: Dörffling und Franke).
Kittel, Rudolph (ed.)
 1937   Biblia Hebraica (Stuttgart: Württembergische Bibelanstalt).
Lagarde, P. de
 1889   *Übersicht über die im Aramäischen übliche Bildung der Nomina.*
Liddell, Henry George, and Robert Scott
 1951   *A Greek-English Lexicon* (Oxford: Clarendon Press).
Maag, Victor
 1951   *Text, Wortschatz und Begriffswelt des Buches Amos* (Leiden: Brill).
Moscati, Sabatino (ed.)
 1969   *An Introduction to the Comparative Grammar of the Semitic Languages. Phonology and Morphology* (Wiesbaden: Harrassowitz).
Moulton, James Hope, and George Milligan
 1963   *The Vocabulary of the Greek Testament* (London: Hodder and Stoughton).

Nida, Eugene A.
  1964 *Toward a Science of Translating* (Leiden: Brill).
Nowack, W.
  1897 *Die kleinen Propheten übersetzt und erklärt. Handkommentar zum Alten Testament.*
Oort, H. (ed.)
  1900 *Textus Hebraici emendationes quibus in vetere testamento neerlandice vertendo usi sunt.*
Sellin, Ernst
  1929 *Das Zwölfprophetenbuch. Erste Hälfte: Hosea – Micha* (Leipzig: Scholl).
Snaith, Norman H.
  1946 *Notes on the Hebrew Text of Amos. Part II: Translation and Notes* (London: Epworth Press).
Thackeray, H. St. John
  1915 "Septuagint", in James Orr (ed.), *International Standard Bible Encyclopaedia* 4 (Chicago), 2722-2732.
  1923 *The Septuagint and Jewish Worship. A Study in Origins* (London).
Touzard, J.
  1909 *Le livre d'Amos* (Paris: Bloud).
Weiser, Arthur
  1956 *Das Buch der zwölf kleinen Propheten. Das Alte Testament Deutsch* (Göttingen: Vandenhoeck and Ruprecht).
Wellhausen, J.
  1963 *Die kleinen Propheten* (Berlin: de Gruyter).
Wolff, Hans Walter
  1969 *Dodecapropheton 2: Joel und Amos. Biblischer Kommentar Altes Testament* (Neukirchen: Verlag des Erziehungsvereins Neukirchen – Vluyn).
Ziegler, Joseph
  1967 *Duodecim prophetae. Septuaginta. Vetus Testamentum Graecum Auctoritate Academiae Litterarum Gottingensis editum* (Göttingen: Vandenhoeck and Ruprecht).

NOTES ON THE LONGER AND THE SHORTER TEXT OF ACTS

MATTHEW BLACK

One of the important results of the magisterial monograph of Carlo Martini on Codex Vaticanus and the Bodmer Papyrus XIV (P 75) has been the recognition of the existence in the second century in Christian Egypt of a text, of the type P75 – B, which had taken shape "in a milieu of rigorous respect for the letter, as also for a certain standard of textual purity", whereas elsewhere in the church, especially in Palestine and Syria, "a text had been preserved and transmitted, with equal veneration, but with tendencies, a little different with regard to the literal sound of the words" and not above "enriching itself with various extraneous, if venerable, elements" (Martini 1966: 151).

It is not difficult to recognise, in this last description, the so-called "Western" text. And the idiosyncrasies and vagaries of that text can nowhere have been more temperately described (cf. W. Knox 1925: xviii-xxvii).

Dr. Martini's further plea – to cease setting one text against the other, but rather to establish a concept of a parallelism of texts, thus adequately representing the diversity of textual tradition in the early church –is entirely in line with recent approaches to the textual criticism of the New Testament. Clark and Parvis in the U.S. and Fascher in Germany have drawn attention to the hermeneutical problems raised by the study of *variae lectiones*; and the most recent book on the "Western" text, that of Eldon Jay Epp, concentrates exclusively – except for some remarks in the introductory chapter – on theological tendencies in "Western" variants. The older search for the "original text", problems of *Textgeschichte*, including the question of the interrelationship of the "Western" and the "B text" are no longer at the centre of these modern textual studies.

The older enquiries, however, can scarcely be abandoned. The fun-

Matthew Black is Professor of Biblical Criticism and Principal of St. Mary's College in The University, St. Andrews, Scotland.

damental question must still be answered, namely, where among these
"parallel" texts are we to look for the text most closely approximating to
the apostolic autographs. No less urgent are problems of the history of
the text and the relationship of "parallel" traditions. The situation in
the New Testament is not quite the same as that of the history of the
Targums: there, the collation of different texts to a basic "text" defeats
every effort, and the only solution is to print the different texts in parallel
columns. But there is in all the New Testament textual traditions a
basic text: there is an "overwhelming majority of textual agreements
among all New Testament texts and textual traditions" (Epp 1966: 40),
so that comparison of texts is not only an unavoidable, but a necessary
process in the search for the "true text".

This procedure is especially important in assessing the comparative
value of the "Western" over against the "B" text. The former, no less
than the latter, has a substantial element with second century support,
even in some of its most characteristic variations (cf. Epp 1966: 2,
note 1). Moreover the textual "profile" of the P75-B tradition is undoubtedly an Egyptian one, whereas the "Western" tradition is not only
attested for Palestine and Syria, but also for Egypt.

The central problem of the relationship of these two "parallel traditions" is the question of the originality of the longer text in the "Western"
tradition or of the shorter text in the "B" tradition. The most significant
study in this connection has been the work of A. C. Clark, whose judgment in favour of the "longer text" was questioned and virtually rejected
by most of his contemporaries. Recent textual discoveries, however,
not to mention exegetical studies, have been vindicating his position in
more than one "Western" variant; the NEB, for instance, has adopted
the reading "Gaius, the Doberian", at Acts 20: 4. That individual
"Western" "additions" as well as variant readings may be original has
not been so widely recognised.

The intention of this paper is to make a modest contribution to the
discussion of this "longer text" vis-a-vis the "shorter text" controversy.
No far-reaching conclusions are drawn, and only those passages have
been selected where some new evidence or consideration, textual or
exegetical, justifies a fresh study of the problem. But the long and the
short of it may well be, in the end, that A. C. Clark was right that the
scribe or scribes responsible for the "B" textual tradition, now exemplified in P75-B, were, in many cases, deliberately abbreviating the
tradition of the "Western" text.

Acts 2: 30-32

The case for a reopening of the question of the longer text at Acts 2:30 rests on both textual and hermeneutical grounds. The words omitted by Bℵ appear in D as κατὰ σάρκα ἀναστῆσαι τὸν Χριστὸν καί, in TR as τὸ κατὰ σάρκα ἀναστήσειν τὸν Χριστόν, and in 1739 as ἀναστήσειν τὸν Χριστόν. The future ἀναστήσειν seems clearly to be a *diorthosis* of the aorist ἀναστῆσαι, and the other variations in the textual tradition of the clause have undoubtedly been occasioned by the same desire for grammatical improvement. D, therefore, has the oldest form of text. How firmly established in textual tradition the words are is shown, not only by the combination of D and the Byzantine standard text, but by the attestation of 1739, which, if it is incorrect to say – as is sometimes claimed – that it represents the text of Origen, is something even more valuable, viz., "a second witness besides Origen, as old as, or even older than he", and "even nearer to the papyrus (P46) than to codex Vaticanus" (Zuntz 1953: 81). These claims for 1739 may not be conceded by all textual critics, but no-one is going to question the authority of 1739, backed up, as it is here, by Origen himself, by the Georgian, the Peshitta and Harclean Syriac, the Old Latin, and the other bilingual manuscript E.

If original, its omission was probably accidental. Without καί it forms a στίχος in D, and the words beginning with *KA* before and after the clause beginning κατὰ σάρκα may account for the scribe's omission of the clause. Similarly D accidentally omits προϊδὼν ἐλάλησεν περὶ τῆς, again probably a single στίχος, but in this case with disastrous consequences, for the resultant text, without these words, is unintelligible. The omission of the κατὰ σάρκα ἀναστῆσαι clause leaves a construable text, but we are then obliged to treat ἐκ καρποῦ τῆς ὀσφύος αὐτοῦ as a partitive construction, corresponding to the Hebrew partitive *min*, a construction which normally means "some from" not "one from". With the κατὰ σάρκα clause we would have a regular use of ἐκ, "to raise up *from* the fruit of his loins". The construction without the clause is arguably a "botching" of the text.

The presence of a Qumran type of hermeneutic in the New Testament is now a well-established fact. Qumran *pesher* appears in Acts, especially in these early chapters (Black 1971-1972: 1 ff.). Thus at Acts 3: 22-23, 26 and at 4: 2, texts which cite or allude to Deut. 15: 18, the "raising up" (3: 22, ἀναστήσει) of the Moses-like prophet, the Lucan application is to the raising up by God of His Servant Jesus, but now in the new sense of ἀνίστημι meaning the raising up of Jesus from the dead as the new Moses-like prophet (Black 1971-1972: 6).

This Christological or Messianic motif of the raising up of the Messiah is especially associated with the promise at 2 Sam. 7: 12 that God will raise up a scion of David (LXX, ἀναστήσω). As Dr. D. C. Duling (1973-1974: 75) has pointed out, an unusually large number of texts from this "promise-tradition" refer to this raising up of the Davidic descendant in the same or closely related terminology. Thus, in addition to the source text at 2 Sam. 7: 12, Jer. 37(30): 9 (cf. Targum), Num. 24: 17 (a sceptre [LXX,a man] shall arise ἀναστήσεται), T. Jud. 24: 1, 5; T. Sim. 7: 1; Ps. Sol. 17: 23; 4 Q Flor. (Amos 9: 11), etc.

There is good reason for believing that ἀνίστημί is probably the earliest term for the resurrection in primitive Christianity (Duling 1973-1974: 75). The predicate κατὰ σάρκα, "to raise up ... according to the flesh", reads like a Christian *pesher* or interpretation of the promise text from 2 Sam. 7: 12: it occurs again at Rom. 1: 3 ἐκ σπέρματος Δαυὶδ κατὰ σάρκα, where the same promise-tradition, based on this same proof text, lies behind this Christian understanding of it (Duling 1973-1974: 77).

Acts 2: 31 expressly applies 2 Sam. 7: 12 to the resurrection of Jesus and his enthronement as Lord and Christ. To omit the element in the promise text which refers to the raising up by God of the Anointed One, and is clearly the basis of the resurrection-to-reign fulfilment in Jesus of Nazareth (verses 31ff.), is to suppress an integral part of the foundation *testimonium*.

The same promise tradition reappears at 13: 22ff. and 13: 33. The Gospel which Paul is proclaiming to his Jewish hearers concerns the promise made to their ancestors (verse 32) which God has fulfilled for them *having raised up Jesus* (verse 33). Here it is not the verse in 2 Samuel which is quoted as the Scriptural promise but Ps. 2: 7; but verse 22 and especially verse 23 imply the version of the promise at 2 Sam. 7: 12: ἤγαγεν (v.l. ἤγειρεν) is a synonym of ἀνέστησεν. Behind 13: 22ff., 32ff., therefore, there also lies the formula of the promise tradition, here again interpreted by a Christian *pesher* of the resurrection of Christ. And this provides further confirmation of the presence of the κατὰ σάρκα clause in the original text, which is the *only complete proof text* from Scripture of the resurrection of Jesus as son of David.

Two explanations of the variant καρδίας for ὀσφύος at verse 30 have been offered presupposing influence of a foreign usage. Haenchen (1970) favours Latin influence: D has *praecordis*, which is ambiguous, and can mean "belly" or "heart". Torrey (1941: 145) suggests Aramaic *beṭen*. A third alternative is that καρδίας represents an alternative translation of the Hebrew word at 2 Sam. 7: 12, viz., *mē'im*: LXX has κοιλιας. The same Hebrew noun is translated by καρδία at Ps. 39(40): 8 (v.l. κοιλία).

Acts 8:39

The longer "Western" reading here is an interesting case textually, since D and its allies are supported by A and the new Coptic papyrus cop^G67 (Epp 1966: ix) it is also a strongly attested "Western" reading, including support from Ephrem. Since it is one of the "Western" texts' "Holy spirit" passages, it is discussed in this connection by Eldon Jay Epp (1966: 117).

When the shorter and longer texts are compared, it is much more difficult to account for the growth or expansion of the BℵJ text out of the shorter form than to explain the latter as a deliberate or accidental shortening of the "Western" reading.

ὅτε δὲ ἀνέβησαν ἐκ τοῦ ὕδατος πνεῦμα [ἅγιον 'επέπεσεν ἐπὶ τὸν εὐνοῦχον, ἄγγελος δὲ] κυρίου ἥρπασεν τὸν Φίλιππον ἀπ' αὐτοῦ...

In favour of an accidental shortening of the text is the variant of the Harclean which read for πνεῦμα ἅγιον, πνεῦμα κυρίου. The scribe's eye may have slipped from the first κυρίου to the second and omitted the intervening words.

Acts 12:25

There are weighty textual reasons for the reading, 'εξ 'Ιερουσαλήμ for the extremely difficult, if not totally impossible, εἰς 'Ιερουσαλήμ. These reasons include the combination of P74 – here against BℵJ – with 1739, and they have evidently led to the introduction of this reading into the Nestlé-Aland text.

As a glance at Metzger's text-critical note will show, the contortions of Greek usage to which exegetes have resorted in defence of the εἰς reading have to be read to be believed. The most widely accepted solution is to take εἰς in the sense of "in" and connect the phrase εἰς 'Ιερουσαλήμ with what follows, not with ὑπέστρεψαν, i.e. "Barnabas and Saul returned (i.e. to Antioch), *after they had fulfilled at Jerusalem their mission*, bringing with them John whose other name was Mark". But with such an expression following ὑπέστρεψαν it would be impossible not to connect it with this verb. As Westcott and Hort (1896: 94) wrote: "εἰς Ἰερουσαλήμ... cannot possibly be right if it is taken with ὑπέστρεψαν."

The Bℵ text has all the appearance of a "botched" text. But where can the εἰς have come from? The reading ἐξ Ἰερουσαλὴμ εἰς Ἀντιόχειαν is attested by E and several minuscules, supported by the Peshitta, the Georgian, Old Latin, and Coptic versions. Coptic manuscripts are cited with the reading εἰς Ἰερουσαλὴμ εἰς Αντιόχειαν. If εἰς Ἀντιόχειαν is original, then its removal and the displacement of EΞ by EIC from this rejected expression would be the simplest way to account for the impossible εἰς Ἰερουσαλήμ.

Acts 18: 18-19: 1

No-one since Clark, so far as I am aware, has sought to defend the longer text at Acts 18: 21, although the tendency in modern commentaries seems to be to support the view, even on the basis of the shorter text, that it was the church in Jerusalem to which St. Paul "went up", and from which he "went down" to Antioch. Thus F. F. Bruce (1951: 350) maintains that, while the ἀναβάς is ambiguous, "the following words κατέβη εἰς Ἀντιόχειαν make it plain that Jerusalem is intended". There does not seem to be any ambiguity in the ἀναβάς (see further below) and Moffatt can hardly be said to "reproduce the ambiguity" by rendering "went up to the capital" (cf. Bruce 1951: 350). Both expressions, as William Neil (1973: 199) points out, support the location of the church in Jerusalem.

If we read the shorter text, nothing in the context expressly points to Jerusalem. The natural sense, as Clark (1933: 309) maintains, is that Paul made a short visit to the church at Caesarea before going to Antioch. This is the view of Lake and Cadbury who interpret ἀναβάς to mean "going from the port to the city" (of Caesarea); they account for Paul's circuitous route from Ephesus to Antioch via Caesarea by the argument that "the winds prevalent in the summer rendered a journey to Caesarea easier than one to Antioch" (Lake and Cadbury 1933). B. H. Streeter (1933: 237), in a review in which he rejects Clark's solution, made the even bolder suggestion that the words which should be read in this longer text are those in D 19: 1: "But though Paul intended, according to his own desire, to go to Jerusalem, the Spirit bade him return to Asia".

Haenchen's position (1970) is not absolutely clear. His caption to

Acts 18: 18-23 is "Paul's Travels", and his translation reads: "... he left Ephesus and landed in Caesarea, went up and greeted the community, went down to Antioch". His comment on verse 22 reads (italics mine): "It is a matter of debate whether Paul visited the Jerusalem congregation or the one in Caesarea. *Luke will have thought of a visit to Jerusalem*". But if Luke did think of a visit to Jerusalem, why, in the shorter text, does he omit direct mention of it? Haenchen reports the reading of "the Western and Antiochene texts", but dismisses it as "an explanation constructed on the model of 19: 21 and 20: 16"; a similar view is also taken by Metzger (1971). No consideration is given to Clark's arguments for the longer text, which, in fact, resolve all doubts and difficulties.

The reference to Paul's vow at verse 18, obviously a Nazirite vow, has "laid up for the commentators serious problems" (Haenchen 1970). The suggestion that it was Aquila not Paul who had his hair cut at Cenchraea is absurd. The fact that the vow had to be discharged within a limited time period in Jerusalem points to the originality of the longer text.

One of the main objections to interpreting ἀναβάς in this context in the shorter form of text as referring to a journey *up to Jerusalem* is that the phrase elsewhere is only found where the noun Jerusalem is expressly mentioned or evident from the context (Haenchen 1970). With the mention of Jerusalem at verse 22 in D this difficulty is entirely removed. The older commentary of Franz Overbeck (1880), who argued for Jerusalem, made the further interesting observation that each of Paul's three journeys (13: 1-14; 15: 40-18: 21; 18: 23-21: 18) starts from Antioch and includes a visit to Jerusalem (1880: 189).

Clark does not include this section of Acts among the passages where, in his opinion, the resultant text, once it had been abbreviated by the removal of a part of the original, shows signs of "botching". This seems to me, however, to be a striking example of a "botched" text. Verse 18, Paul's Nazirite vow, is left without its necessary sequel, the visit to the Temple in Jerusalem in the near future to discharge it. The most convincing evidence of "botching", however, is the use of ἀναβαίνω and καταβαίνω with nothing in the context which allows them their full and idiomatic meaning as virtually *termini technici*, for "going up" or "coming down" from Jerusalem, i.e. quite literally, physically "ascending" and "descending" from the plains to the hill country and vice versa. A non-Jew, unfamiliar with these expressions, would certainly wonder what was meant by "going up" from Caesarea.

Even with the longer text, the extreme brevity of Luke's account of Paul's visit to the Jerusalem church is puzzling. The solution to this problem may well be, as Dr. John Knox (1954: 68) has cogently argued, that this was in fact the real "conference visit", and to be identified with the visit reported at Gal. 2: 1-10. This would oblige us to assume that Luke wished to represent the issue between Jew and Greek as settled early and finally in Paul's missionary career in his "conference visit" which he identifies with the visit at Acts 15. He had left himself, in that case, nothing to say about the real "conference visit". Knox (1954: 68) writes that

if the conference at Jerusalem over the Jewish issue stood in Acts 18 instead of in Acts 15, the major discrepancy between the letters and Acts would disappear, and, along with it, any awkwardness in fitting the Pauline intervals with the Lucan incidents.

Dr. Knox adds (1954: 68 footnote) that "the Greek text (at Acts 18: 22-23) does not include a reference to Jerusalem, but the context strongly indicates that the 'church' was there". Nothing could more eloquently illustrate the dominance of the B𝔑 textual tradition; for by "Greek text" is evidently meant the shorter text. For Dr. Knox the longer text does not exist.

The reinstatement in this verse of the Received Text, supported by the "Western" witnesses, gives a firmer basis for the view that this was, in fact, the "conference visit". The problems which this additional visit to Jerusalem raises, when a comparison is made between the letters and Acts, may also supply the reason for the suppressing of this reference to Jerusalem by the shortening of the original text.

The reading of D has δεῖ με πάντως τὴν ἑορτὴν ἡμέραν ἐρχομένην ποιῆσαι (d *oportet me sollemnen diem advenientem facere*): ἡ ἑορτὴ ἡμέρα is an odd formation, but it corresponds to the Aramaic expression *yoma de^eida*, Prov. 7: 20, except that, as Greek, it defies grammar; d is a grammatically more acceptable expression. The Feast, ἡ ἑορτή *simpliciter* is especially used of the Passover, and the Feast Day could be a synonym for the Day of Unleavened Bread (Luke 22: 7 ἡ ἡμέρα τῶν ἀζύμων); Zahn held that a Passover was here meant. If some Semitic source lies behind the clumsy Greek expression of D, or even if D does no more than reproduce a Jewish-Greek expression, the reading furnishes a fresh piece of evidence for the originality of the longer text.

The variation in the textual tradition earlier at verse 19 points to difficulties of a similar kind. The incongruity of "and he left them here (there)", i.e. in Ephesus, words clearly intended to dismiss Priscilla and Aquila once and for all from the narrative, with "and he himself went into the synagogue" reveals an obvious editorial "patch". The reading of the Syriac versional tradition (Sy^vg.h) at verse 22, "Aquila (and Priscilla) he left in Ephesus, while he himself set sail and arrived in Caesarea" may (as Clark surmised) preserve the original reading: "and he left them there and he himself" looks like a typical abbreviation of the B text, inserted by the redactor at a quite unsuitable point in the narrative; the καὶ αὐτός may have displaced an original ὁ Παῦλος at verse 19 (read by Sy^vg and Sah). The motive for the "addition" of τῷ ἐπιόντι σαββάτῳ at verse 19 is not evident: it seems an appropriate enough circumstantial detail – Paul and his company landed some time in midweek, and "on the following Sabbath Paul entered the synagogue and disputed with the Jews".

In the remainder of these selected verses there are two apparently minor readings (at verses 25 and 28) and two larger "Western" "additions" (at verses 27 and 19:1). 18:25 describes Apollos as one "who had been instructed *in his own country* [ἐν τῇ πατρίδι] in the *word* of the Lord". This last reading, for "in the way of God" (τὴν ὁδὸν τοῦ θεοῦ) may be, as Ropes maintains, "clearly an attempt to make a harder word easier" (cf. Metzger 1971: 466). The implication of the addition of ἐν τῇ πατρίδι, as Metzger points out, would seem to be that the Gospel had reached Alexandria before A.D. 50, so that this is, by no means, an unimportant variant. The D reading διαλεγόμενος καί at at verse 28 is supported by P38, and is, of course, the regular term for "disputing"; it may have been felt to be superfluous, or added from other passages; its preservation in a Papyrus supports the first alternative.

At verse 29 the Bezan text gives a totally different account of the situation there described. According to the shorter Bℵ text it was Apollos's own wish to cross over into Achaea. The Ephesian brethren, wishing to encourage him (or the Achaean churches?) wrote a letter of recommendation for him; when he arrived in Achaea he proved of great assistance "to those who believed by grace". The longer text informs us that it was on the pressing invitation of certain Corinthians in Ephesus that Apollos was invited to cross over with them to Achaea. When his consent had been given, the Ephesian brethren wrote him an accompanying letter of recommendation.

Now certain Corinthians were staying in Ephesus, and having heard him [Apollos] urged him to cross over with them to their own country. And when he had consented the Ephesians wrote to the disciples in Corinth that they should receive the man who, having stayed in Achaea, proved of great assistance in the churches to those who believed by grace.

The longer text at 19:1 is a characteristic "Western" passage about the Holy Spirit: "And although Paul wished, according to his own plan, to go to Jerusalem, the Spirit instructed him (εἶπεν αὐτῷ) to return to Asia; and, when he had traversed the upper regions, he came to Ephesus." The shorter text links this return journey to Ephesus with the preceding chapter: "Now it fell out, while Apollo was in Corinth, Paul, when he had traversed the upper regions, came to Ephesus." Dr. Eldon Epp (1966: 14) includes 19:1 in those passages where the "Western" text "introduces" allusions to the Holy Spirit. The role of the Spirit here is exactly parallel to that at Acts 16:6 (cf. also D 20:3), so that this could be a *Lucan* characteristic of Acts – and 19:1 (D) a genuine Lucan verse. If the festival mentioned at 18:21 was Passover, the festival here which Paul wished to attend could have been Pentecost in the same year.

It is easy to dismiss all these longer texts as secondary tradition, and there is no obvious "botching" in the shorter text in any of the longer passages: but if the Bℵ text at verse 29 is an abridged version, then the author of the recension is guilty of suppressing the truth by his condensed account. The D text is supported there by P38 in its omission of the clause τοῖς πεπιστευκόσιν διὰ τῆς χάριτος, although this is required after συνεβάλλετο, and the omission, therefore, an error. On the whole, it is more difficult to imagine anyone inventing these new facts in order to expand the shorter text than to see in the latter a deliberate abridging of the longer text. The longer passage at 19:1 could be a Lucan text.

Acts 20: 7-13

That the accident to Eutychos was fatal (verse 9, "he was taken up dead") is now generally agreed, in spite of the words St. Paul uses, after falling on the youth and embracing him like a second Elijah, namely, "Do not start to lament, for his life is in him". Modern exegesis insists, rightly, that the command not to lament, meant not to start the lamentation for the dead (cf. Mark 5: 39); and St. Paul is being here represented by Luke as working a miracle of restoring the dead to life, like Elijah (1 Kings 17: 21ff.) and Elisha (2 Kings 4: 34). The story may also be the Pauline counterpart to the revival of Tabitha by Peter (Acts 9: 36-43).

Where difficulties with the narrative arise is with verse 10: the statement that the youth is still alive demands a sequel which it does not receive till verse 12, after the celebration of the eucharist in the "upper room". "The sequence of the narrative is remarkable" (Ramsay), and Harnack maintained that the statement at verse 12 "and they brought the youth alive" should have appeared earlier in the narrative. Cassiodorus, as Clark pointed out (1933: 377), assumes that it did appear after the words ἡ γὰρ ψυχὴ αὐτοῦ ἐν αὐτῷ ἐστιν, and in the Bezan form ἤγαγεν τὸν νεανίσκον ζῶντα κ.τ.λ. The "Western reading" ἀσπαζομένων δὲ αὐτῶν then begins verse 12 - as the congregation was taking leave of Paul who was setting out on foot (πεζεύω) for Assos we, i.e. Luke and his companion, were boarding ship to go by sea and join Paul at Assos.

However slender the basis for this reconstruction, it restores a proper sequence to the narrative. A further suggestion may be worth considering: if this story were told in Aramaic (or Syriac) ἤγαγεν τὸν νεανίσκον ζῶντα would be ʾaiti ḥayyaʿulēma. Was this originally ʾēttaḥi ʿulēma "the youth is restored to life"? The words would then be St. Paul's.

Acts 24: 6-10

Although rejected by Haenchen (1970), support among commentators has rallied in favour of the longer text at Acts 24: 6ff – Clark (1933: xlvii) referred to his case here as *instar omnium*. Haenchen (1970: 653, n. 4) writes:

That the governer would learn everything about which the Jews accused Paul when he questioned him seemed to the Western text (found among others in (E) e gig p syʰ Chrys) so foolish that it referred παρ'οῷ to Lysias and accordingly rewrote vv. 6-8: "whom we seized and wanted to judge according to our law" (use of John 18: 31?). "The tribune Lysias however interfered" (so παρελθών according to *Beg*. IV 299) "and took him away with great force out of our hands (v. 8), commanding his accusers to come to you".

Haenchen, however, notes that Holzmann considered this "addition" genuine, because Lucan expressions are used (e.g., παρελθών). F. F. Bruce (1951: 422) writes:

This addition bears marks of genuineness, and the misleading and reproachful reference to the tribune's "violence" in rescuing Paul is an amusing travesty of the real facts...

and W. Neil (1973: 233):

This [addition] may well be correct, and strengthens Tertullus' case. He blames Lysias – falsely, of course – for interfering in the seemly handling of the matter by the Jews themselves. This points forward to the procurator's decision to postpone judgment until Lysias should appear to give evidence (verse 22).

If the Western text is correct, and unless Tertullus is identifying himself professionally with his Jewish clients, his references to "we" and "our law" would indicate that he was himself a Jew and not a Roman. Furthermore, if we accept the Western text, "examining him" in verse 8 will refer to Lysias and not to Paul, although the word is normally used of examining a prisoner rather than a witness.

The latter objection may be questioned: ἀνακρίνω is used of interrogating witnesses in general, not only the accused (cf. 12: 19).

The textual evidence for the Western reading might seem, on a first glance, to suggest its secondary character: in fact the variants seem to be confined mainly to the two cursives 483 and 424: most manuscripts read κρῖναι and μετὰ πολλῆς βίας ἀπήγαγε. Among Greek evidence 1739 is again present, supported by the Old Latin, Peshitta, Harclean, etc.

Metzger draws attention to the abruptness of Tertullus's ἐκρατήσαμεν which "seems to require some sequel", although this itself may have prompted the desire for addition and completeness. The main case for the longer text, however, rests on the absurdity of a proceeding where Paul is a witness in his own prosecution. Lysias was the star witness of a probably Jewish prosecution. Blass's wry comment (cited by Clark 1933: xlvii) bears repetition:

it is intolerable that, according to ℵ etc. this monster of an orator, after a few words, requests the judge to conduct the rest of the enquiry from the accused.

REFERENCES

Black, Matthew
1971-1972 "The Christological Use of the Old Testament in the New Testament",
       New Testament Studies 18, 1-14.
Bruce, F. F.
    1951   *The Acts of the Apostles: The Greek Text with Introduction and Commentary*
       (London: Tyndale Press).
Clark, A. C.
    1933   *The Acts of the Apostles: A Critical Edition with Introduction and Notes on*
       Selected Passages (Oxford: Clarendon Press).
Duling, D. C.
1973-1974 "The Promises to David and their Entrance into Christianity", *New*
       Testament Studies 20, 55-77.
Epp, Eldon Jay
    1966   *The Theological Tendency of Codex Bezae Cantabrigiensis in Acts* (= Society
       for New Testament Studies Monograph Series 3) (Cambridge: University
       Press).
Fascher, E.
    1953   *Textgeschichte als hermeneutisches Problem* (Halle (Saale): Niemeyer).

Haenchen, Ernst
  1970   *The Acts of the Apostles, A Commentary* (Oxford: Blackwell).
Knox, John
  1954   *Chapters in a Life of Paul* (London: Adam and Charles Black).
Knox, W. L.
  1925   *St. Paul and the Church of Jerusalem* (Cambridge: University Press).
Lake, K., and H. J. Cadbury
  1933   *The Beginnings of Christianity* 4 (London: Macmillan).
Martini, Carlo M.
  1966   *Il Problema della recensionalità del codice B alla luce del papiro Bodmer XIV* (= *Analecta Biblica* 26) (Roma).
Metzger, Bruce M.
  1971   *A Textual Commentary on the Greek New Testament* (London and New York: United Bible Societies).
Neil, William
  1973   *The Acts of the Apostles, New Century Bible* (London: Oliphants).
Overbeck, Franz
  1880   *Kurzgefasstes exegetisches Handbuch zum neuen Testament* 1:4 (Leipzig).
Clark, K. W.
  1953   "Textual Criticism and Doctrine", *Studia Paulina in honorem Johannis De Zwaan septuagenarii* (Haarlem: De Erven F. Bohn), 52-65.
Parvis, M. M.
  1952   "The Nature and Tasks of New Testament Textual Criticism: An Appraisal", *Journal of Religion* 32, 165-174.
Ropes, J. H.
  1926   *The Beginnings of Christianity* 3 (London: Macmillan).
Streeter, B. H.
  1933   "The Primitive Text of the Acts", *Journal of Theological Studies* 34, 232-241.
Torrey, C. C.
  1941   *Documents of the Primitive Church* (New York and London: Harper).
Westcott, B. F., and F. J. A. Hort
  1896   *The New Testament in the Original Greek* (London: Macmillan).
Zuntz, G.
  1953   *The Text of the Epistles* (= *Schweich Lectures* 1946). (London: Oxford University Press for the British Academy).

THE LINGUISTIC BACKGROUND OF "SHAME" IN THE NEW TESTAMENT

HOWARD C. KEE

On first exposure to the brilliant, fascinating lectures of Eugene Nida on linguistics more than twenty-five years ago, I little suspected that I should later have the rewarding opportunity of association with him as a member of the Translations Committee of the American Bible Society. In that venerable institution his genius for linguistics, his skill as an administrator, and his deep commitment to making the Scriptures available in the languages people can understand have converged to the creative benefit of the Bible cause in America and throughout the world. This essay, which is part of a larger endeavor to recover and interpret the thought world of the Gospel of Mark, seeks to trace the changing connotations of a term which, in spite of its seemingly obvious meaning, is something of an enigma in most of the crucial texts where it occurs: shame (αἰσχύνω, ἐπαισχύνω, καταισχύνω, αἰσχύνη, αἰσχρός). How are we to understand this common term in such diverse contexts as, "I am not ashamed of the gospel..." (Rom. 1: 16); "Whoever is ashamed of me... of him will the Son of man also be ashamed" (Mark 8: 38); "... it is my eager expectation and hope that I shall not be at all ashamed" (Phil. 1: 20)? The word "shame", with meanings covering a spectrum running from "humiliation" to "disgrace", scarcely serves adequately to convey what is implied in any of these texts, much less in all of the other comparable New Testament passages where "shame" appears. What is the linguistic background of this important New Testament term?

I

Bultmann, in his study of this word (Kittel 1964: 169ff., 189ff.), discusses the related Greek terms, αἰδώς and αἰσχύνη. The first, he says, meant

Howard C. Kee is Rufus Jones Professor of the History of Religion at Bryn Mawr College, U. S. A.

originally, fear or awe in view of established authority, whether that of kings, parents, elders, one's spouse, or society as a whole. As such, it is the opposite of ὕβρις. Αἰσχύνη on the other hand, means (in its subjective sense) fear or shame, whether as a result of a misdeed or as a consequence of lowly origin or a humiliating destiny. On the objective side, it means "disgrace", or in its verbal form αἰσχύνω, "to bring into disgrace". There are no significant differences between the meaning of the simple root, αἰσχύνω, and those of the compounds, ἐπαισχύνω and καταισχύνω. Bultmann goes on to show that the New Testament usage is largely based on the LXX, where

what is in view is not so much the state of the soul of the αἰσχυνθείς but the situation into which he is brought, and in which he is exposed to shame and has thus to be ashamed.

Accordingly the substantive is seldom used for "the feeling of shame". Mostly it denotes "disgrace" and the primary reference is to divine judgement. In the New Testament, building on the LXX usage, it means – in the active voice – "to bring to shame". Here a prime example is 1 Cor. 1: 27, where it is parallel with καταργήσῃ in 1: 28, and the import is clearly that the prideful powers are rendered inoperative ("brought to nothing"). In the middle voice, the root means something close to "disillusioned" (Phil. 1: 20), as it does in the LXX of Jer. 2: 36. Although Bultmann does not develop it, there is implicit in several of the texts that he cites in this connection the factor of divine vindication, as in Luke 13: 17, where Jesus is vindicated in the face of his enemies, and in 1 Pet. 3: 16, where the faithful witness in the face of impending persecution results in the adversaries' being put to shame.

Although this analysis of the term is largely without exception so far as it goes, its inadequacies are evident in that it cannot provide satisfactory interpretation for such crucial texts as 1 John 2: 28, and simply groups the puzzling texts Rom. 1: 16 and Mark 8: 38 in the general category where the term refers to "being ashamed" of doing something or of being identified with a dubious person. Although the quotation from Isa. 28: 16 in Rom. 9: 33; 10: 11 and 1 Pet. 2: 6 is recognized as important, its fuller significance is not realized and therefore not developed in Bultmann's article in Kittel (1964). The inadequacy of this interpretation is evident if we translate – with only slight overstatement – the passages according to this lexical conclusion:

I am not embarrassed by the gospel of Christ... (Rom. 1: 16).
Whoever is embarrassed concerning me... of him will the Son of man be embarrassed... (Mark 8: 38).

The former of these is of central importance in Paul's great Letter to the Romans, and the latter is a pivotal text for the interpretation of the gospel tradition, whether it is regarded as an authentic saying of Jesus (Bultmann, 1951: 28-30) or as a product of Markan theology (Perrin 1967: 185-193).

Unfortunately the modern speech translations, such as RSV and TEV, do not clarify the meaning, since they simply translate the word as "shame" or some variant of that. In English this is a highly subjective term, but to become aware that far more lies behind these New Testament passages than embarrassment or even disillusionment one has only to look at the connotations of the Hebrew terms in the Old Testament that are translated in LXX by αἰσχύνω and its cognates (Bultmann in Kittel 1964: 189). In addition to bwš, the same or closely related ideas are expressed in the Old Testament by the roots ḥpr and klm. A survey of the Old Testament texts in which bwš and its kindred terms appear, as well as those where αἰσχύνω appears in the LXX yields the following range of meanings.

(1) HUMILIATION

The classic example is the amusing story of the emissaries of David to the Ammonites. Suspected of being spies, they have half their beards shaved off and the upper part of their clothing cut away (2 Sam. 10: 5; 1 Chron. 19: 5). The king permits them to remain at Jericho until their beards have grown back, and the occasion of their humiliation has thus been removed. Here the root is klm,[1] but as we shall see, although this root seems especially to connote embarrassment, it is used in later texts in parallel with bwš, and therefore does not have an exclusively subjective connotation. Comparable in their connotations, though not so dramatically specific in detail are the humiliation of Miriam (Num. 7: 14 – klm, rendered in LXX as ἐντραπήσεται), the embarrassment of Elijah (2 Kings 2: 17 – bwš rendered in LXX αἰσχύνειν), and that of Elisha (2 Kings 8: 11, where the Hebrew and LXX texts are identical with the Elijah passage). Appropriately, the causative force of the hiphil of bwš is translated in the LXX of 2 Sam. 19: 6 as καταισχύνειν in the passage where Joab rebukes David for the lamentation over the death of his son, who was also his enemy: "You have covered with shame the faces of all your servants."

---

[1] klm = ἀτιμάζω in LXX, which confirms the appropriateness of our category (1) humiliation, dishonor, or embarrassment.

The terms *bwš* and *klm* are used frequently in Jeremiah, especially in connection with the shame – or lack of it – in Israel's lack of covenant loyalty, as evidenced by her consorting with the idols: Jer. 3: 3 *(klm)*; 10: 14 *(bwš)*; and 2: 26; 6: 15; 8: 9-12 where both the *qal* and the *hiphil* of *bwš* are found. The same theme in Hos. 2: 5 (verse 7 in MT) is expressed by the *hiphil* of *klm*. An instructive juxtaposition of the terms occurs in Job 19: 3: where God is accused by Job of having "shamed" Job (verse 3a), the root is *klm*; in verse 3b, however, when Job asks if God is not ashamed of the injustice he has done to him, the root is *bwš* *(qal* impf.).

Although these passages clearly are dealing in the subjective realm of embarrassment and humiliation, what is at stake is a failure to perform appropriately, whether in the case of God or man. When the situation is that reliance has been placed on false gods who cannot fulfill their promises, as in the case of the idols, the first set of meanings shifts from humiliation to disillusionment.

(2) DISILLUSIONMENT

The texts dealing with "shame" in the sense of disillusionment are not so much concerned with the state of mind of the one who is "ashamed" as with the circumstances which have led to the disillusionment. The representative contexts in which this idea appears may suggest the range of possible significance. The first and most basic is a sense of having been betrayed as a result of a confidence which turns out to have been unwarranted. For example, in the gruesome story of the assassination of the obese king, Eglon (Judg. 3: 25), the courtiers are disillusioned because their monarch, in whose power and stability they trusted, proved to be weak and vulnerable. The people of Moab rightly see in the death of the king the destruction of the power of the state, and indeed Moab is subjugated to Israel (Judg. 3: 30). *bwš* moves beyond feeling to the continuity of the political order, and to the despair that comes when its center of authority is destroyed.

Analogous to this is Job's disappointment in his supposed friends (Job 6: 20), who are compared to travellers in the desert who look in vain for water at the site of an oasis: so the friends' failure to display fidelity *(ḥsd)* by responding to Job's petition has disillusioned Job. RSV renders *bwš* here as "disappointed", and in parallel is *ḥpr*, which is translated as "confounded". This latter root figures frequently in other passages, e.g. where *bwš* is used to describe the state of God's enemies, or with a negative particle to depict those who have been delivered by His act in their behalf.

Even more completely objective is the use of *bwš* in relation to the created order when it fails to bring forth as expected. Thus in Joel 1: 10, *bwš* is used of the failure of the wine, which in 1: 12, again with the *hiphil* of *bwš*, is attributed to the vine's failure to produce. Placed in parallel with *bwš* are terms, depicting active destruction – "laid waste" *(šdd)*, "destroyed" *('bd)* – so that it is quite appropriately translated as "withered" (1: 12). But then the force of the term, even when allowances are made for the metaphorical nature of the language here, is not that of humiliation but of the effects of divine judgement.

The same point is made in passages concerned with a different aspect of human experience: the contrast in the Proverbs between *bwš* and wisdom, especially *mskyl*. What is implied in Prov. 10: 5; 14: 35; 17: 2; 19: 26 is that judged pragmatically, wisdom leads to a successful and significant life, while the lack of it results in an empty and pointless existence. In this frame of meaning, *bwš* is associated with *ḥpr*, as in Prov. 13: 5 and 19: 26. In short, what is at stake is not the subjective feeling of meaninglessness of life apart from wisdom, but the objective fact that life without it is a wasted effort. But then we are moving along on our continuum of meaning toward *bwš* as an expression of impotence as contrasted with the fulfillment of the divine will.

(3) VINDICATION/DEFEAT

In the Psalms where the theme is that of "waiting for the Lord", or a related experience, *bwš* is used (often in the *hiphil*) to describe either the vindication of those who wait for the Lord, or the defeat of those who fail to do so. The classic statement of this is in Ps. 25: 3:

Yea, let none that wait for thee be put to shame:
let them be ashamed who are wantonly treacherous.

The inadequacy of "shame" as a translation is apparent here: what is meant is that those who trust in Yahweh will be vindicated by him, and those who do not trust will be deflated or "let down" by his judgment. Even more forceful is Ps. 119: 116:

Uphold me according to thy promise, that I may live,
and let me not be put to shame in my hope!

Now clearly it would be inappropriate to attach eschatological significance to these passages; rather, they are dealing with the question of how and why to live a life of obedience to Yahweh. What is promised is that life will be given, a life sustained by divine power and purpose, rather than one that falls into disobedience and hence under judgment (cf. verse 115).

In certain passages where *bwš* is parallel with *ḥpr*, even greater emphasis is placed on the element of defeat of the enemies, as in Ps. 71: 24:

... for they have been put to shame *(bwš)* and disgraced *(hapru)* who sought to do me hurt (RSV).

But the inadequacy of these subjective terms is evident; what is intended is that God has defeated the enemies of his faithful servant. This is evident in Ps. 70(= 40: 13ff.) where the call for divine aid (verse 1), "... deliver me... help me" is matched by the invocation of divine judgment on the enemies, "let them be put to shame... let them be turned back". The imprecations of Ps. 83 state this even more emphatically: the enemies are to be whirled like dust, scattered like chaff (83:13), consumed as by a raging forest fire, driven as by a storm, terrified as by a hurricane. What an inadequate climax to this poem to imply (verse 17) that the enemies will wind up in embarrassment! The subjective element is here *(Ḳalōn)*, although it is heightened to include ignominy and dishonor. But the force of the parallel verbs is that *bwš* means active destruction, not a feeling of humiliation.

As B.W. Anderson (1973: 56-58) and others have shown, all these psalms are in the formal category of the lament, where the pattern moves through Address, Complaint, Confession of Trust, Petition for Deliverance, Oracle of Assurance, Vow of Praise. In the Petition for Deliverance an essential is the defeat and the ensuing humiliation of the hostile powers; the corollary is the vindication of the faithful, who are "not put to shame". This is true for both what Anderson has called the Community Laments (Pss. 12, 44, 58, 60, 74, 79, 80, 83, 85, 90) and the Individual Laments (of which the following are typical: Pss. 22, 35, 40, 69, 70). The term *bwš* is common in these, although it is obviously not found in all of these contexts. In the prayer for vindication, it is God Himself who is the vindicator of the righteous, as Ps. 70: 4-5 (esp. 5b) shows.

The same theme is present in other passages where *bwš* and *ḥpr* are joined by *klm*: 35: 4; 35: 26; 40: 14; 70: 3.[2] Here the context makes explicit the theme of vindication (Ps. 35: 23-24):

[2] Ps. 69:7 in MT, although even here *bwš* and *klm* in parallel may be terms for divine vindication.

Bestir thyself, and awake for my right,
for my cause, my God and my Lord!
Vindicate me, O Lord, my God,
according to thy righteousness;
and let them not rejoice over me!

Then in clear parallel to these petitions (and confirmed in verse 27 with its rejoicing in vindication) we read in verse 26:

Let them be put to shame *(yēbōšu)* and confusion *(yaḥpᵉru)* altogether
who rejoice at my calamity!
Let them be clothed with shame *(bōšet)* and dishonor *(kᵉlimah)*
who magnify themselves against me.

Although the subjective element of humiliation is probably still present in these passages, as for example Ps. 69: 7 shows (see Gunkel 1967), what is operative here is the conviction that faith in God will not go unvindicated. In the midst of opposition and seeming defeat, the Psalmist expects God to intervene in his behalf at an unspecified time in the future and to uphold him in the face of his mockers and his enemies. As in the case of the lament, we are here dealing with more than lexical matters, since these passages from the prophets all fall within the category of what has been called the *Heilsorakel* (See Gunkel 1967), although the appropriateness of the title and the presumed Sitz-im-Leben of the form (in the cultus, as an oracular response to a lament) have been called into question.[3] In the prophets, however, the expectation of vindication comes to be cast in more eschatological terms, which brings us to the fourth and final segment of our continuum.

(4) ESCHATOLOGICAL VINDICATION/
OVERCOMING THE EVIL POWERS

As early as Isaiah of Jerusalem, *bwš* is used in contexts depicting the judgment on the nations and the triumph of God in behalf of His people. The other side of the redemption of Zion (Isa. 1: 27) will be the "shame" of the idolaters, when they are destroyed by the fire of divine judgment (1: 29-31). Egypt will be in despair *(ubešu)* as a result of God's

---

[3] B. W. Anderson has reported orally that the appropriateness of this title and its presumed Sitz-im-Leben (in the cultus, as an oracular response to a lament) are doubtful; he would prefer the term "Vocational Exhortation", as a vehicle for arousing the nation to war or otherwise to fulfill its divine call. The call begins with an encouragement ("fear not") and moves to an assurance of the fulfillment of the divine promise ("I will be with you"). The eschatological orientation is to be seen, for example, in Isa. 41: 8-13.

judging that nation by drying up the Nile and thus the fertility of the land (Isa. 19: 9). The term appears in the prophetic predictions of the humiliation of the nations (Mic. 7: 16-17), the confounding of the hopes of the Philistines (Zech. 9: 5), as well as in the defeat of Israel by Egypt and Assyria (Jer. 2: 36). *bwš* is bracketed with *ḥpr* in the context of divine judgment on Jerusalem (Jer. 15: 9) and Babylon (Jer. 50: 12), as it is in the announcement of the consequence of false reliance on Egypt (Isa. 30: 5). *ḥpr* alone is used in Isa. 33: 9, where judgment precedes God's redemption of his people (verses 10 ff.). Where *klm* is linked with *bwš* is in Jer. 8: 12; 14: 3-4; 31: 19, and in the oracle against Jehoiakim (Jer. 22: 22), as well as in Ezekiel's predictions of the defeat of the enemies of the nation (16: 27, 54, 61; 43: 10-11).

In the second half of Isaiah, where the themes are clearly raised to the eschatological level, the terminology is the same, as when the defeat of the enemies and the restoration of the nation is promised (Isa. 41: 11-13). Perhaps the clearest statement of God's vindication of his people is in Isa. 54: 4, where the three roots appear – *bwš, ḥpr, klm* – and God's triumph, which is epitomized in the phrase of 54: 17, "vindication", offers assurance that Israel will be delivered from "shame". Conversely, the worshippers of the star spirits in Isa. 24: 23 are "put to shame" when Yahweh reigns on Mt. Zion in Jerusalem. The active results of being "put to shame" are evident in such texts as Jer. 46: 24, where the term *(hobyšah)* is parallel with "she shall be delivered into the hand of a people from the north".

Still more emphatic are those texts where *bwš* is associated with *ḥtt*, usually rendered, "to be dismayed". Like *bwš*, *ḥtt* has its subjective and objective aspects, as Jer. 1: 17 makes clear:

Do not be dismayed by them (niphal)
lest I dismay them (hiphil) before you.

These two terms are in parallel in Jeremiah's predictions of the defeat of the enemies (17: 18), of Egypt (46: 24), of Moab (48: 1, 20), and of Babylon (50: 2), where the destruction of the gods of Babylon is depicted in illuminating parallel form:

Babylon is taken,
Bel is put to shame,
Merodach is dismayed.
Her images are put to shame,
her idols are dismayed.

The text then goes on to announce that the city is to be destroyed and made uninhabitable (50: 3).

Finally, the eschatological connotations of *bwš* are most clearly expressed in those contexts where the verb or one of its synonyms is in parallel with some form of *yš*̄. In Pss. 14: 6; 53: 5, 6 (6, 7 in MT), there is a contrast between God's act of deliverance and the defeat or shaming of the enemies. The point is most graphically illustrated in the three-membered poetic promise of Jer. 30: 10 and 46: 27:

Fear not.
Be not dismayed.
I will save you.

The same cluster of meanings is evident in Isa. 41: 10, and has a rough parallel in I QM 15: 8. Thus the terms usually translated inadequately as "shame" or "humiliation" are in fact understated promises of eschatological vindication in the prophetic tradition. Experience of shame is the destiny of the enemies; deliverance from shame is the vindication of the faithful. The appropriateness of the use of a term that, in its basic use, connotes shame is confirmed by the fact that the people awaiting vindication have undergone or will undergo suffering and even defeat. Yet the net meaning is not a feeling of humiliation but the experience of deliverance, or in the case of the enemies, of defeat.

II

The New Testament terms based on the root, αἰσχ—, may also be classified under four headings, although these are not precisely equivalent to those we have been examining in the Old Testament.

(1) HUMILIATION, EMBARRASSMENT

There is a range of uses of the terms with this connotation, from the everyday world of being ashamed to beg (Luke 16: 3) or of being demoted to last place at a banquet (Luke 14: 9) to the statements in Hebrews that neither Jesus (2: 11) nor God (11: 16) is "ashamed" to be identified with the church. In addition, "Paul" asks Timothy to overcome any embarrassment he may have as a result of his being associated with the imprisoned apostle (2 Tim. 1: 8, 16).

(2) SHAMEFUL BEHAVIOR

Predominantly in Paul's writings, various forms of the root are used to describe disgraceful acts, such as women failing to cover heads, or men covering theirs (1 Cor. 11: 4), or women speaking in the congregation (1 Cor. 14: 35). Shameful practices in the ministry are to be renounced (2 Cor. 4: 2), as are shameful deeds (Rom. 6: 21). In Phil. 3: 19, where Paul is bitterly satirical of those who pride themselves on circumcision, αἰσχύνη is a euphemism for the genitals. In the later developments of the Pauline tradition, the root appears to describe the evil deeds of the sons of darkness (Eph. 5: 12) and the shameful teachings of the heretics (Titus 1: 11).

(3) DISAPPOINTMENT/CONFIDENCE, OR EFFICACY

In 2 Corinthians Paul expresses confidence that the Corinthians will not disappoint him, but that they will give generously toward the collection for the church in Jerusalem (9: 4). Similarly, he is confident in the effectiveness of his own apostolic ministry, so that he can work with no fear of shame, i.e. failure (10: 8). The Spirit produces efficaciously the transformation of the lives of believers, so that there is no place for disappointment (Rom. 5: 5).

Paul's confidence in the purpose of God in his own life is expressed in similar language in Phil. 1: 20:

It is my eager expectation and hope that I shall not be ashamed, but that with full courage now as always Christ will be honored in my body, whether by life or by death.

What Paul is anticipating here is that his martyrdom, which now lies before him as a present possibility could be interpreted by his opponents as a sign of divine disfavor. Against such a charge Paul asserts that he is fully persuaded – not ashamed – that God's design will be worked out, whether it includes his survival or his witness by a martyr's death. Similarly, in Rom. 1: 16 Paul expresses confidence in the gospel as the expression of the divine purpose to achieve redemption. To say that he is "not ashamed" of it is not to imply that it is socially or intellectually embarrassing, but is rather to declare that what he has staked his life and his apostolic work on will indeed deliver. Or rather that God will deliver on his promise, and accomplish his work of setting aright the creation (Rom. 1: 17). But this eschatological dimension leads us into the fourth and last of our categories.

(4) ESCHATOLOGICAL VINDICATION/
OVERCOMING THE EVIL POWERS

The quotations from Isa. 28: 16 (LXX) in Rom. 9: 33 and in abbreviated form in Rom. 10: 11 bring us into the context of meaning of the prophetic terminology for "shame". The New Zion is for Paul and the new people of God; whoever trusts in this enterprise which God is accomplishing through the ministry of the apostles can have confidence in its successful outcome: "he will not be put to shame". The same passage with the same implication appears in 1 Pet. 2: 6, as well.

As Bultmann noted, in 1 Cor. 1: 27 καταισχύνῃ is parallel to καταργήσῃ, implying that to "put to shame" means to "put out of commission", not merely to embarrass. But Bultmann did not draw attention to related passages which depict the evil powers as in process of defeat (1 Cor. 2: 6) and as doomed to be totally defeated in the New Age (1 Cor. 15: 24). The force of 1 Cor. 1: 17 ff. is thus that of eschatological victory, not merely of timeless triumph of the gospel.

The motif of eschatological vindication as linked with freedom from "shame" is apparent in the later New Testament tradition, as when "Paul" declares his confidence – "I am not ashamed, for I know whom I have believed, and I am sure..." (2 Tim. 1: 12) – that the gospel will continue to achieve the purpose of God until "that Day" of consummation. Similar confidence is expressed by the author of 1 John: "And now little children, abide in him, so that when he appears we may have confidence and not be disappointed by him at his *parousia*."[4] To escape disappointment is no more than the negative way of expressing confidence in the vindication that will occur at the *parousia*.[5]

Thus it is clear that in Paul and in the later writings of the New Testament the theme of eschatological vindication, so fully documented in the prophetic tradition, lives on in the connotations of terms |related to the root αἰσχύνω. The question yet remains, is this significance represented in the tradition of Jesus as well?

III

Here, of course the crucial text is Mark 8: 38 (with the approximate

[4] Not "Shrink from him in shame" as in RSV or "hide in shame" as in TEV. The usage here is parallel to that of LXX in Isa. 1:29 and Jer. 12:13, as Arndt and Gingrich note, though they fail to draw the proper conclusion from this, preferring rather to invent a special category for 1 John 1:28.

[5] Bultmann's puzzlement with this passage is evident in his indecisive treatment of it in Kittel (1964:169ff., 189ff.).

parallel in Luke 9: 26). Does ἐπαισχυνθῇ in this context fit any of our categories of meaning for the term?

(1) HUMILIATION

This meaning would not be impossible for the first occurrence of ἐπαισχυνθῇ. In that case the reference would be to the social, or intellectual, or religious opprobrium attached to being identified with Jesus. But a text which is climactic for Mark – concluding the section dealing with the confession of Peter and bridging to the Transfiguration Story – must mean more than "Whoever is embarrassed by Jesus and His words will be an embarrassment to the Son of Man in the *eschaton*." There seems to be an analogy between present response/future evaluation in this text and the contrast between confession now and denial in the *eschaton* as described in the Q saying Matt. 11: 6; Luke 7: 23. And the fact that the verbs in the Q saying are strong and quite unambiguous warns against treating "ashamed" as a subjective term in Mark 8: 38.

(2) DISGRACEFUL BEHAVIOR

This possibility makes no sense at all in Mark 8: 38.

(3) DISAPPOINTMENT; FAILURE TO MEASURE UP TO EXPECTATIONS

This fits well with the first occurrence of ἐπαισχύνθη in Mark 8: 38. It implies that there are those who, in the face of persecution or harrassment as a result of their identification with Jesus and His message ("my words"), become disheartened and dissociate themselves from the circle of the followers of Jesus. Or if this verse is to be interpreted in the setting of the community for which Mark is writing, it is likely that the hostility encountered by the community is being interpreted as the eschatological woes (cf. Mark 13: esp. verses 9-13, where trial and execution are anticipated) which must be endured if one is to share in the final vindication. The latter detail we shall consider in a moment under category (4), but here it is enough to note that what is called for is fidelity, not merely freedom from embarrassment. The concern expressed in 8: 38 is similar to that stated in more tentative form in Mark 10: 38,

"Are you able...?", and in more extreme form in 14:27: "You will all fall away...." The seriousness of the potential lapse is highlighted by the foolish boast of Peter, "Even though they all fall away, I will not" (14:29).

What is at issue in Mark 8:38a, therefore, must include disillusionment or dismay as a reaction to the time of difficulty and suffering that is the lot of both Jesus and his followers, according to Mark. Peter's rebuke of the notion of suffering and death (8:33) is rightly denounced as satanic, since it is in flat contradiction to Jesus' word about self-denial, acceptance of the cross, and forfeiting one's life (Mark 8:34-36) which is the only path to true life. Once more, Mark 13 is illuminating at this point. The hostility that is to be undergone is not general human conflict or a recurrent social-political struggle. What threatens fidelity to the witness, and what therefore may lead to becoming "ashamed" of Jesus and His word is that "... You will be hated by all men for my sake..." (Mark 13:13a). But this leads directly into the promise of vindication by God at the end of the age: "But he who endures to the end will be saved" (13:13b).

(4) ESCHATOLOGICAL VINDICATION/JUDGMENT

Those who have lost or who have never had confidence in Jesus as God's agent for bringing in the New Age will be "put to shame" in the day of eschatological judgment. The positive aspects of the vindication of those who maintain their confidence in Jesus and His words is not expressed in this context, though it is directly stated in Mark 13:13 and in non-Markan texts, such as Luke 22:28-30, where those who "continue with (Jesus) in (His) trials" are given not only a share in the kingdom but a role in the judgment by which they exercise authority in the New Age. The juxtaposition of 8:38 and 9:1 shows that the coming of the Son of Man and the Kingdom of God's manifestation "with power" are closely interrelated, at least so far as Mark understands them. The predictions of the passion (8:31; 9:31; 10:33-34, in addition to the less direct prediction in 9:11-12) all show that identification with Jesus means involvement in suffering. To reject this understanding of the necessity of suffering as antecedent to the New Age, or to reject one's need to participate in this suffering is, as 8:38a shows, to "be ashamed" of Jesus. But to fall into that evaluation is to invite judgment at the hand of the Son of Man, who will "be ashamed" of them (verse 38b).

It may seem that to interpret 8:38 in terms of related but contrasting meanings of the single word, ἐπαισχύνεσθαι is to perform *eisegesis*. But there is a close parallel for the two-fold meaning of "shame" in the prophetic tradition:

Let those be put to shame who persecute me,
    but let me not be put to shame;
Let them be dismayed,
    but let me not be dismayed. (Jer. 17:18)

The enemies are to be judged, but the man of faith asks that his own trust in God might be maintained. In Mark 8:38 only the negative side of the situation is explicitly mentioned, and unlike the Jeremiah passage, the verbs are middle rather than passive. Yet the shift in specific implication between the two occurrences of the word for "shame" is really analogous: if you are now ashamed, the Son of Man will put you to shame in the *eschaton*. The causative force of ἐπαισχύνω and its synonyms is well attested in the Old Testament, as we have seen. Isa. 24:23 (LXX, according to some manuscripts)[6] reports the moon as "put to shame", which can scarcely be taken in the subjective sense: it is rather the vivid picture of cosmic judgment. Often in LXX and in the New Testament, when (κατ)αισχύνεσθαι means "to be ashamed *of*", the occasion for the shame is stated in a prepositional phrase: Mic. 7:16 (ἐκ); Jer. 12:13 (ἀπό); 22:22 (ἀπό); Sir. 41:17-27 (ἀπό, sixteen times!); Phil. 1:20 (ἐν); I John 2:28 (ἀπό), although elsewhere "being ashamed" is expressed by the verb governing the accusative directly, as in 2 Tim. 1:8, 16; Heb. 11:16, and probably Rom. 1:16. The possibility cannot be ruled out categorically that the traditional translations of Mark 8:38 are correct, therefore: "Of him will the Son of Man be ashamed." But in light of the import of the term in prophetic tradition, and especially in the eschatological tradition, a more plausible interpretation is that Mark 8:38 is predicting that those who have abandoned faith in the person and words of Jesus will be visited with judgment by the Son of Man in the *eschaton*. The passage might then be paraphrased:

Whoever becomes disillusioned with Jesus and his words or defects from them by reason of persecution or the rigor of the demands of discipleship will find himself "put to shame" under divine judgment through the agency of the eschatological judge, the Son of Man, in the end time.

---

[6]   We are not here concerned with whether Luke has omitted "in this adulterous... generation" from his Markan source, or whether Mark has added them to a pre-Markan source; it is true, however, that their presence in Mark heightens the eschatological contrast between this age and the time of the *parousia*.

The corollary is implied, but not stated, that those who remain faithful will be vindicated by the Son of Man in the end time. What we see in Mark 8: 38 is yet another wordplay on the Old Testament eschatological terms which promise vindication to the faithful and judgment to the unfaithful. This interpretation of the text fits well the larger context in which it is found in the gospel of Mark, which at every crucial point evidences the perspectives and terminology of Jewish apocalypticism in the process of translation into the thought world of Hellenistic culture (see Kee 1972: (in Enslin Festschrift).

REFERENCES

Anderson, B. W.
    1973   *Out of the Depths: Studies into the Meaning of the Psalms* (Philadelphia: Westminster Press).
Bauer, W-Arndt-Gingrich,
    1957   *A Greek Lexicon of the New Testament* (Chicago & Cambridge).
Bultmann, R.
    1951   *Theology of the New Testament*, trans. by K. Grobel, 2 vols. (New York: Scribners).
Gunkel, Herman
    1967   *The Psalms: a Form-Critical Introduction*, trans. and introduced by James Muilenburg (Philadelphia: Facet Books, Fortress Press).
Kittel, G. (ed.), art. by R. Bultmann on αἰσχύνω, *etc.*
    1964   *Theological Dictionary of the New Testament* 1, trans. by G. W. Bromiley (Grand Rapids: Eerdmans).
Perrin, N.
    1967   *Rediscovering the Teaching of Jesus* (New York: Harper).
Reumann, John (ed.), H. C. Kee, The Transfiguration in Mark: Epiphany or Apocalyptic Vision?
    1972   *Understanding the Sacred Text, Festschrift in Honor of Morton S. Enslin* (Valley Forge: Judson Press).

ECLECTICISM AND ATTICISM IN THE TEXTUAL CRITICISM OF THE GREEK NEW TESTAMENT

CARLO M. MARTINI

Eugene A. Nida has consecrated his indefatigable energies not only to the field of translation, but also to the promotion of studies in the original texts of the Bible.

One of the results of this activity is The Greek New Testament (United Bible Societies 1969). In this critical text the external evidence has been given an important weight in the evaluation of the merits of each variant. The present paper will examine some problems connected with the use of this external evidence in the textual criticism of the Greek New Testament.

In the preface to Tasker (1964), The Greek text underlying the translation of the New English Bible (1961), we read the following:

> The task of the present translators would have been considerably expedited had they been able either to use an "established" Greek text, as did the makers of King James's Version in 1611, or to base their work on the consensus of a few ancient manuscripts, as did the Revisers in 1881.... But, as it is pointed out in the Introduction to The New English Bible, there is not at the present time any critical text which could command the same degree of general acceptance as the Revisers' text in their day or, we may add, as the Textus Receptus in 1611 (Tasker 1964: VII).

In fact a "textus receptus", as was the text of the sixteenth century, was the result of a uniform linguistic tradition and of liturgical standardization. Everything today is moving in an opposite direction. And as for the text of the Revisers of 1881, although it seems not completely appropriate to describe it as the result of "the consensus of a few ancient manuscripts",[1] it is nevertheless true that the situation of research in the field of textual criticism is today different from that of 1881, and that

---

Carlo M. Martini, S. J., is Professor at the Pontifical Biblical Institute, Rome, Italy.

[1] It is true that Westcott and Hort (1882) often choose for their final text many readings of such old witnesses as Vaticanus and Sinaiticus. But this was not due to a blind preference for a few ancient manuscripts, but to a careful evaluation of the entire textual tradition, as far as it was available to them.

the use and accurate evaluation of external evidence have become more complex than at the time of Westcott and Hort.

The present situation is summarized by Bruce M. Metzger (1968: 175) in this way:

Dissatisfied with the results achieved by weighing the external evidence for variant readings in terms of support from individual manuscripts or families of manuscripts and local texts, several scholars have directed primary attention to the individual variants themselves in an effort to find which will account best for the rise of the others. This process has been given various names. It has been called eclecticism, because in its application the textual critic pays less attention to questions of date and families of manuscripts than to internal or contextual consideration.

Two points are mentioned here as constitutive of what is called "eclecticism":

(1) *Dissatisfaction with external evidence.* Neither individual manuscripts (as B ℵ D), nor families (as Fam. 13 or Fam. 1) nor local texts (as Alexandrian or Caesarean) can give sufficient support to establish at least the probability of a reading against another. Therefore all the principles accepted so far are seen as no longer valid. Westcott and Hort (1882) gave great value to the concordance of B and ℵ; von Soden generally preferred the reading of H and I against K, except when there was a Tatian reading or a harmonization. All these kinds of procedures are abandoned as unsatisfactory.

2. *The primary attention given to internal or contextual consideration.* What is especially characteristic of this attitude can be better understood if we think of one of the main principles of Westcott and Hort: knowledge of documents should precede final judgment on the readings (Westcott and Hort 1882: 31). This principle did inspire most of the scholars who produced a critical edition of the New Testament in the last seventy years. The principle of eclecticism, on the other hand, seems to consist of the making of the judgment on a single variant in itself the main concern of the textual critic.[2]

---

[2] We should carefully distinguish from this kind of eclecticism an attitude which sometimes bears the same name, but which should be called more exactly an eclectic procedure in the constitution of a critical text. B. M. Metzger (1971: 272-273) describes it when speaking of the activity of the Committee for the preparation for The Greek New Testament of the United Bible Societies, in regard to the book of Acts: "Since no hypothesis thus far proposed to explain the relation of the Western and the Alexandrian texts of Acts has gained anything like general assent, in its work on that book the Bible Societies' Committee proceeded in an eclectic fashion, holding that neither the Alexandrian nor the Western group of witnesses always preserves the original text, but that in order to attain the earliest text one must compare the two divergent

The distinctive features of this attitude are well described in Kilpatrick's article (1964):

We do not concern ourselves that the Egyptian text or the Western text as a whole is right but we try to decide each variant by itself (Kilpatrick 1964: 64).

And further:

Let us look at the way in which such a procedure will operate. The readings considered will be accepted or rejected each and all, on their merits (Kilpatrick 1964: 65).

On the basis of this procedure there is, among many other grounds, an especially important historical motivation. This is discussed at length in Kilpatrick (1963). It is a highly stimulating article which has not received up to now due consideration, perhaps because it was published in a *Festschrift* which was not widely known.

The following facts are brought forth by Kilpatrick:

(1) The majority of the variants of the New Testament text have an origin before the year 200.

If we take together the readings of which we may assume on explicit or inferential evidence that they existed before A.D. 200, we find that they form probably the largest part of the deliberate changes in the apparatus (Kilpatrick 1963: 129).

(2) All the great textual types that are known to us are later than this date. The only exception could be the "Western Text", which in fact it is not a homogeneous text, but a mass of variations of different kinds and origins. Therefore a knowledge of text types and of text history (which is largely a history of text types) seems to be of no use in order to judge the value of a variant.

(3) In the absence of these historico-genealogical aids to determine the value of a variant, there is nevertheless an historical fact which is important in judging the nature of a variant prior to 200 A. D. This is the *atticistic tendency*, which was operating in the second century A. D., and brought scribes and correctors of the NT to substitute classical attic expressions for popular koine forms.

This atticistic tendency seems to have been at work especially in Alexandria. Therefore the so-called "Alexandrian Text" was, according

---

traditions point by point and in each case select the reading which commends itself in the light of transcriptional and intrinsic probabilities." This eclectic procedure acknowledges the importance of historical text types for the decision on variants. But it maintains that the original text cannot be found exclusively in one single historical text type, because both unconscious and conscious changes could and in fact did occur in all of them. In case of doubt, then, transcriptional and intrinsic probabilities control the decision.

to this theory, the most exposed to this type of change. It follows that the preference of Westcott and Hort and of modern editors in general for the text of B ℵ, and now for P⁷².⁷⁵, is basically wrong.

Let us quote some of the concluding words of the article mentioned above:

> The evidence suggests that none from our earliest Papyri onward have escaped... (the) influence of Atticism.... Westcott and Hort may have owed some of their partiality for ℵ B to the fact that these manuscripts often display a brevity and an idiom which is akin to the classical Greek on which they were brought up.... Detailed examination may well reveal that at number of places ℵ B and their allies present a text which is a stylistic rewriting of a text which has survived in the Western witnesses (Kilpatrick 1963: 136).

The importance of the three facts mentioned above is evident. The two first centuries were certainly decisive for the formation of the textual tradition of the New Testament. If we could know exactly what happened to the text in that period, and in what external conditions and with what mentality it was transcribed in the different Churches, our textual decisions on the original text would become much more certain.

It is expecially important to recognize and to evaluate exactly the role of the atticistic tendency in the transcription of the text in the period from the second to the fourth century. It is generally assumed that atticism was at work in the Byzantine tradition, and that it produced in it a good number of stylistic corrections.[3] The influence of atticism in the manuscripts written before A. D. 400 is, in my opinion, much more difficult to assess, especially in the Egyptian tradition. In order to show how complex the question is, I shall examine two of the examples which were proposed to show the atticistic contamination of Egyptian manuscripts.

Act 17: 15 ―   εν ταχει   D g co syp
      ―   ως ταχιστα   B rel

This is the only occurrence in the NT of ως with a superlative adverb. In fact in three other instances Acts has εν ταχει (12: 7; 22: 18; 25: 4) without variation; the same in Luke 18: 8.

---

[3] In the introductions to the volumes of the Göttingen critical edition of the Septuagint one can find an interesting collection of atticistic emendations in the manuscripts of the Greek Bible. See, for instance, Ziegler (1939:87) for the change of ειπα to ειπον in the manuscripts of the Lucianic recension. See also Ziegler (1943:88; 1952: 55ff.). For the Greek manuscripts of Luke see the evidence of stylistic emendation in Byzantine manuscripts in my study on Codex B and P⁷⁵ (Martini 1966: 119-122). Further reflections and bibliography on atticism can be found in Kilpatrick (1967).

In Mayser (1926: 51b), there are several examples of the idiom ως ταχιστα in the third century B. C. and a few from the second century B. C. It seems to have disappeared by the first century A. D. This disappearance is explained as a part of the general phenomenon of the superlative becoming rare in this time. Therefore, the conclusion proposed is the following: ως ταχιστα in Act 17: 15 is an atticistic reintroduction by the scribes of B ℵ, and the other manuscripts after them, of an attic expression, which was not in use in New Testament times. The original text has survived in D and in some few other witnesses (Kilpatrick 1963: 135).

All this is impressive, and it sounds like an accurate conclusion, but there are still many questions open.

(1) εν ταχει is not a popular expression, or typical of the κοινή. It is classical, too. We find it in Pindar (1953: 138), Aeschylus (1910: 30), etc. It is then not explained why an atticistic corrector should have substituted another expression for εν ταχει.

(2) It is not explained how this substitution reached all the representatives of the tradition, except D. It could be understandable that a substitution in favor of a classical expression takes place, for instance, in some Alexandrian manuscripts. But how could it be so strong to influence all the tradition?

(3) If there was really an atticistic corrector, why did he not correct also the other three passages in Acts (12: 7; 22: 18; 25: 4)?

4. But the decisive question is the following: is it really true that ως ταχιστα is not found in the colloquial language after the second century B. C.?

We saw that Mayser does not quote any example of ως ταχιστα after the second century B. C. We can add that Blass and Debrunner (1961: § 60,2, § 453,4, § 244,1) maintain (maybe on the basis of Mayser) that ως ταχιστα belongs to the literary language. But since the first publication of these works other papyri have been discovered. By looking into them we can find at least two examples of this usage in a period later than the time mentioned by Mayser:

P.S.I. (1925), VII, n. 792, line 10 (notice about collection of taxes): και ως[τ]αχιστα μοι δηλωσατε. This notice is part of a register of a public official (not probably a supporter of the atticistic revival) and is dated the seventeenth of May of the year 136 A. D.

Zenon Papyri (1928) III, n. 59427, 4-5: Letter from Epichares to Apollonius, of the year 28 or 29 A. D.: ως αν ταχιστα αποβ[ω εις K]αριαν.

The hypothesis of an atticistic corrections from the reading of D to the reading of the majority becomes then improbable.[4]

Let us now take a second example. There is often variation in the manuscripts of the New Testament between ζήσω and ζήσομαι, especially in the fourth Gospel.

John uses the future of ζῆν six times: 5: 25; 6: 51, 57, 58; 11: 25; 14: 19. The active form is preferred by:

— P[75] in all cases, except 11: 25 (in 6: 51 there is a lacuna);

— B ℵ in all cases, except 6: 51 and 11: 25

The middle form is the most common in many manuscripts. Δ, for instance, has always the middle, except in 6,58. In 5: 25 οἱ ἀκούσαντες ζήσουσι, we find the following division: ζησουσι P[66].[75] B (ℵ) D L W fam 1) ζησονται A Δ fam 13 rel pler.

Now it is claimed that the future active is used by Attic writers and the Atticisers; the middle is the koine form, current among non-Attic and later writers.

This view is based especially on a sentence of the *Anti-atticista*, which says ζήσει: Πλάτων, Πολιτείας ἕκτῳ, οὐ ζήσεται which is interpreted as follows. ζήσει is the correct attic form, supported by Plato in the Republic, and ζήσεται is condemned as non-Attic. The conclusion is that the evangelist wrote more probably the non-Attic middle form which was corrected later, in P[75] B ℵ, to the Attic ζήσει (Kilpatrick 1963: 132).[5]

To this conclusion I would like to make the following observations.

(1) Why should the atticistic reviser have corrected the text of John only partially (6: 51 B and 11: 25 P[75]B have ζήσεται)?

(2) Is it really certain that the active form is more classical?

According to Blass and Debrunner (1961: § 77) "while many active verbs form a future middle in Attic, Koine prefers the active for the most part". And in the special case of ζῆν they maintain (1961: § 77) that both futures are Attic[6]. Liddel, Scott, and Jones (1961) give examples of a classical usage for ζήσω as well as for ζήσομαι. What is certain is that the middle did prevail in later texts.

(3) How then is the sentence of the *Anti-atticista* to be interpreted?

---

[4]   D seems to have a certain preference for εν ταχει because it adds the word in Act 10:33.

[5]   Kieffer (1968: 160-161) examines the case in John 6:57.58 and thinks that the opinion of Kilpatrick is plausible. Gordon D. Fee (1968:49) studies this case from the viewpoint of P66, and his conclusion is in favor of an original active form.

[6]   This conclusion is preferable to that of Bauer (1958: 663), that the middle represents a later form.

I venture to suggest the following explanation. The *Anti-atticista* writes against the false linguistical purism of his time, which held that the only acceptable form was ζήσομαι, thus assimilating the case of ζήσομαι to that of verbs as γνώσομαι, λήψομαι, πεσοῦμαι, βοήσομαι, ῥυήσομαι, etc., for which there was only the middle form. Against this tendency, the *Anti-atticista* recalls that ζήσω is classical, too, because it is found in Plato, and therefore is not to be rejected. But this shows that ζήσω was still used, and therefore may well have been written by John in 5: 25 and in other instances.

We could go on with these examples, but from what we have seen it follows that the claim of atticistic influence on Egyptian manuscripts should be carefully examined case by case before we could arrive at a general conclusion.

Some kind of atticistic rewriting has been certainly at work in the textual tradition of the New Testament. But it is not certain that it was already at work in the second and third century in the manuscripts at Alexandria. This means that "eclecticism" should be always connected with a careful study and evaluation of the manuscript tradition. This study may reveal that there is a certain favorable presumption on the trustworthiness of certain manuscripts because they were transmitted in a situation which was not influenced by the trend of stylistic emendation which was felt in other places and times. It may be that after all the basic intuition of Westcott and Hort of the value of the old Alexandrian tradition has much to commend itself even today.

REFERENCES

Aeschylus
1910 *Prometheus Vinctus* 747, ed. by H. Weil (Leipzig).
Bauer, W.
1958 *Griechisch-Deutsches Wörterbuch zu den Schriften des Neuen Testaments und der übrigen urchristlichen Literatur*, Fünfte Auflage (Berlin: Töpelmann).
Blass, F. and A. Debrunner
1961 *A Greek Grammar of the New Testament and Other Early Christian Literature. A Translation and Revision of the Ninth-Tenth German Edition Incorporating Supplementary Notes of A. Debrunner*, by Robert W. Funk (Cambridge: University Press).
Fee, Gordon D.
1968 *Papyrus Bodmer II (P [66])*: *Its Textual Relationships and Scribal Characteristics* (= *Studies and Documents* 34), edited by J. Geerlings (Salt Lake City: University of Utah Press).
Kieffer, R.
1968 *Au delà des recensions? L'évolution de la critique textuelle dans Jean VI, 52-71* (= *Coniectanea Biblica. New Testament Series* 3) (Lund: Gleerup).

Kilpatrick, G. D.
1963 "Atticism and the Text of the Greek New Testament", in J. Blinzler, O. Kuss, and F. Mussner (eds.), *Neutestamentliche Aufsätze. Festschrift für Prof. Josef Schmid* (Regensburg: Pustet), 125-137.
1964 "An Eclectic Study of the Text of Acts", in J. Neville Birdsall and Robert W. Thomson (eds.), *Biblical and Patristic Studies in Memory of Robert Pierce Casey* (Freiburg, Basel, Barcelona; Herder), 64-77.
1967 "Style and Text in the Greek New Testament", in B. L. Daniels and M. J. Suggs (eds.), *Studies in the History and Text of the New Testament in Honor of Kenneth Willis Clark* (Salt Lake City: University of Utah Press), 153-160.
Liddel, H. G., R. Scott, and H. S. Jones
1961 *A Greek English Lexicon* (Oxford).
Martini, C. M.
1966 *Il problema della recensionalitá del codice B alla luce del papiro Bodmer XIV* (Roma: Pontificio Istituto Biblico).
Mayser, Edwin
1926 *Grammatik der griechischen Papyri aus der Ptolomäerzeit* 2:1 (Berlin: Walter de Gruyter).
Metzger, Bruce M.
1968 *The Text of the New Testament. Its Transmission, Corruption, and Restoration*, 2nd ed. (Oxford: Clarendon Press).
1971 *A Textual Commentary on the Greek New Testament* (London New York: United Bible Societies).
P. S. I.
1925 *Pubblicazioni della Societá Italiana: Papiri Greci e Latini* 7 (Firenze: Ariani).
Pindar
1953 Nemeah 5:35, ed. by B. Snell (Leipzig).
Soden, Herrman von
1902-1910 *Die Schriften des Neuen Testaments in ihrer ältesten erreichbaren Textgestalt* 1:1-3 (Berlin).
1913 *Die Schriften des Neuen Testaments in ihrer ältesten erreichbaren Textgestalt* 2 (Göttingen).
Tasker, R. V. G.
1964 *The Greek New Testament Being the Text Translated in the New English Bible 1961 Edited with Introduction, Textual Notes, and Appendix* (Oxford and Cambridge: Oxford University Press and Cambridge University Press).
United Bible Societies (eds.)
1969 The Greek New Testament, 2nd. ed.
Westcott, B. F., and F. J. A. Hort
1882 *The New Testament in the Original Greek. Introduction. Appendix* (Cambridge and London: Macmillan).

EARLY ARABIC VERSIONS OF THE NEW TESTAMENT

BRUCE M. METZGER

In the second edition of *The Book of a Thousand Tongues* (United Bible Societies, 1972), prepared under the general supervision of the versatile Eugene A. Nida, information is provided concerning the several modern translations of the Scriptures into various dialects of the Arabic language. These include, besides classical Arabic, those forms of the language currently used in Algeria, Chad, Egypt, Morocco, Palestine, Sudan, Tunisia, as well as the vernacular of Malta. The widespread usage of Arabic today (it is spoken by an estimated ninety million persons from North Africa to Iraq) makes it all the more interesting to investigate the earliest stages in the production of Arabic renderings of the New Testament. In what follows information is provided concerning the origin and variety of early Arabic versions, the most important Arabic manuscripts of the New Testament, the earliest printed editions, and aspects of the textual affinities of early Arabic versions.

1. THE ORIGIN OF THE ARABIC VERSIONS

In antiquity Arabia as a geographical term comprised the territory west of Mesopotamia, east and south of Syria and Palestine, extending to the Isthmus of Suez. This area, about one-fourth that of Europe and one-third that of the United States, was divided by the geographer Ptolemy into three regions: Arabia Felix, the Happy or Fertile; Arabia Petraea, the Stony; and Arabia Deserta, the Desert. When and how and by whom the Gospel was brought to these diverse areas is not known, for the data are scattered and inconclusive. According to Harnack (1924: 699 ff; 153 ff. in English 1908 version) by the middle of the third century there were numerous bishoprics in towns lying south of the Hauran and the

Bruce M. Metzger is Professor of New Testament at Princeton Theological Seminary.

Dead Sea, all of which were grouped together in a single synod.[1] On at least two occasions Origen was invited to Arabia in order to participate in doctrinal discussions that were convened because of certain heretical tendencies on the part of Beryllus (see Eusebius 1903 vi. 33; Kretschmer 1953: 258-279) and Heraclides (Eusebius 1903 vi. 37; Origen 1949). At a later date efforts were made to introduce Christianity among the nomad tribes. According to Socrates, during the fourth century Mavia the Queen of the Ishmaelites (the Saracens) arranged that Moses, a pious monk, should be consecrated bishop over her nation (Eusebius 1903 iv. 36; Theodoret 1954 iv.20; Duchesne 1896 :112-118). It also appears that during the same century Christian missions penetrated the southern part of the Arabian peninsula from Ethiopia. According to Philostorgius, through the efforts of one Theophilus, an Abyssinian of Arian faith, churches were built in Zafar, the capital of Himyaric Arabia, in Aden, and along the Persian Gulf (Philostorgius 1913 III. 6).

Who was responsible for making the first translation of the Scriptures into Arabic is not known. Various traditions have assigned the honor to different persons. According to a story reported by Michael the Syrian (died 1199) in his *Chronicle* (Chabot 1901: 431 ff.), in the seventh century ʿAmr bar Saʿd bar abī Waqqās, the Emir of the Arabs, requested John, the Jacobite Patriarch at Antioch (631-648), to make a translation of the Gospels from Syriac into Arabic, but to eliminate all references to the divinity of Jesus as well as mention of the cross and baptism. After the Patriarch had vigorously remonstrated against the restrictions, he proceeded to gather a group of bishops who prepared the translation, but without making the specified deletions. Although Baumstark (1938: 382) thought there might be some kernel of truth in the account, Graf (1944: 35), with more caution, raised serious questions concerning the general plausibility of the story. In any case, nothing further is known of such a translation, nor have any traces of it been discovered in extant manuscripts.

Another tradition concerning the translator of the Arabic version of the Bible is preserved in the encyclopedic work known as *al-Fihrist* (Dodge 1970). The author of this tenth-century survey of Muslim culture states that during the califate of Maʾmūn (813-833) a Muslim by the name of Aḥmad ibn-ʿAbdullāh ibn-Salām made a translation, from the Hebrew and Greek, of "the Torah, the Gospels, and the books of the prophets

---

[1] For a list of the chief churchmen in the several bishoprics see Devreesse (1942: 110-146); for a rich bibliography on pre-Islamic Christianity in Arabia see Henninger (1948: 222-224).

and disciples" (Dodge 1970: 42). The passage has been studied by Krachkovskiĭ (1918: 189-196), who suggests the possibility that the encyclopedist confused the translator with a Jew who converted to Islam, named ʿAbd Allāh ibn Salām (died 663).[2] Still another tradition, which for several centuries gained widespread currency,[3] has it that during the early part of the eighth century a Spanish bishop, John of Seville, translated the Gospels from the Latin Vulgate into Arabic. The story, however, was shown by de Lagarde (1864: xi-xvi; cf. also Renouf 1863: 241-259) to rest upon a misunderstanding; though manuscripts are known to contain an Arabic rendering made from the Latin, they have nothing to do with John of Seville.

2. THE VARIETY OF ARABIC VERSIONS

The variety of Arabic versions of the New Testament is almost bewildering. De Lagarde (1864: iii), with characteristic piquancy, commented to the effect that there are more Arabic versions of the Gospels than can be welcome to theologians, pressed as they are with other urgent tasks. According to the pioneering survey of more than seventy-five Arabic manuscripts made by Ignazio Guidi (1888: 5-76) the Arabic versions of the Gospels existing in manuscripts fall into five main groups: (1) those made directly from the Greek; (2) those made directly from or corrected from the Syriac Peshitta; (3) those made directly from or corrected from the Coptic; (4) manuscripts of two distinct eclectic recensions produced by the Alexandrian Patriarchate during the thirteenth century; and (5) miscellaneous manuscripts, some of which are characterized by being cast into the form of rhymed prose made classic by the Koran. Furthermore, more than one Arabic version has been corrected from others derived from a different *Vorlage*. The situation is complicated still further, for example, in a fifteenth century manuscript containing the Pauline epistles, some of which were translated from Syriac, others from Sahidic, and still others from Bohairic (Baumstark 1911: 15).

In addition to the classes of Arabic versions enumerated above, translations were also made from Latin into Arabic. The first to do so, it

---

[2] For an Arabic manuscript of the Pentateuch dated A.D. 820, translated for "ʿAbdallāh al-Maʾmūn", see Graf (1944: 88ff., note 2).
[3] The tradition is mentioned in the "Preface" to the 1611 version of the English Bible on the authority of a certain Vas[s]eus, who dates the translation A.D. 717; see Goodspeed (1935:24). In the nineteenth century J. L. Hug (1836: § 100) still repeated the same tradition.

seems, was Isḥāq ibn Balašk, or Isaac, son of Velasquez, a Spanish Christian of Cordova, who in 946 prepared a rather free translation of the Gospels. His *Vorlage* was a manuscript with an Old Latin text, strongly influenced by the Vulgate (Baumstark 1934a: 224-239; 1935: 107-109, cf. also Peters 1939: 175-177). Whether Isaac also translated other parts of the New Testament is not definitely known. In any case, a fragment of an Arabic-Latin manuscript of Galatians has been discovered which, on palaeographical grounds, is dated in the ninth or tenth century (see section 3, manuscript no. 5 below).

Subsequent to Guidi's preliminary survey two other monographs were published that provide the researcher in this field with an exceptionally broad range of codicological, textual, and bibliographical information: they are Graf's extensive research (Graf 1905: 138-185) based on Guidi's categories, and Henninger's briefer account of Arabic translations made for Melchites, Maronites, Nestorians, Jacobites, and Copts (Henninger 1961: 210-223).

3. EARLY ARABIC MANUSCRIPTS

Among the earliest known Arabic manuscripts of the Gospels and Praxapostolos the following may be mentioned as particularly noteworthy.

(1) What Burkitt (1898b: 136) considered to be "perhaps the oldest monument of Arabic Christianity" is a manuscript formerly belonging to the Monastery of Mār Sābā near Jerusalem, now cod. Vaticanus arabicus 13, called by Tischendorf ar[vat] (Greg. cod. 101), and assigned by Cardinal Mai to the eighth century, but by Graf and Vööbus to the ninth century. Written in Kufic letters, originally it contained the Psalter, the Gospels, Acts, and all the Epistles; of these only the Pauline Epistles, along with limited portion of the Synoptic Gospels, now remain on 178 folios. The Arabic text, which was translated freely from the Syriac, occasionally preserves Old Syriac readings (Peters 1939: 56 ff.).

(2) What appears to be the oldest dated copy of the Arabic Praxapostolos, containing on 269 folios the Epistles of Paul, the Acts of the Apostles, and the Catholic Epistles, is cod. Sinai arab. 151. Written A. D. 867 in a "rubricated transitional hand between Naskh and Kufic" (Atiya 1955: 6), the codex contains many annotations in the margin that provide exegetical comments on the Scripture text. The Arabic text of four of the Pauline Epistles (Romans, 1 and 2 Corinthians and Philippians) and of the comments, along with an English translation, was edited by Harvey Staal (1969).

(3) MS. Borg. arab. 95 of the ninth century (according to Vööbus it was copied before about A. D. 885) contains on 173 folios the four Gospels, translated from the Greek presumably at the Monastery of Mār Sābā. For a specimen of the script, see Tisserant (1914: pl. 55).

(4) A codex of 226 folios and dated A. D. 892, brought by Tischendorf to the Imperial Library in St. Petersburg, contains the Pauline Epistles in a version that appears to have been made from a Nestorian copy of the Peshitta.[4] Its text, which Tischendorf quotes as ar^{pet}, was studied by Stenij (1901).

(5) The library of the Chapter of Següenza has a parchment leaf, containing some portions of Galatians in Latin and Arabic, which is dated by its editors (De Bruyne and Tisserant 1910) on palaeographical grounds at the close of the ninth or the beginning of the tenth century.

(6) MS. Sinai arab. 155, dating from the ninth or tenth century, contains on 216 folios the Arabic version of the Wisdom of Sirach and several of the Pauline Epistles. The text of the latter was published by Gibson (1894).[5]

(7) MS. Sinai arab. 154, dating from the ninth century, contains a translation from Syriac of Acts (beginning with 7: 37) and all seven Catholic Epistles in the Greek order (Gibson 1899). The disputed Catholic Epistles (2 Peter, 2 and 3 John, and Jude) appear to have been rendered from the Philoxenian Syriac version; Acts and the rest of the Epistles, from the Syriac Peshitta. Another transcription of the text of the disputed Catholic Epistles is given in Burkitt (1897-1898).

(8) Two fragmentary leaves, one at Sinai and the other at Leningrad, of a bilingual manuscript of the Gospels in Greek and Arabic, dating from the ninth century, preserve portions of Matthew 13, 14, and 25-26. The two leaves are identified today as Gregory-Aland 0136 and 0137; the Arabic text of the latter was edited by Lewis (1894: 105 ff.).

Other early Arabic manuscripts at Sinai, which, like those already mentioned, are available in microfilm copies at the Library of Congress in Washington, are the following (the comments are those provided by Atiya 1955):

---

[4] One of the extraordinary readings of the manuscript is in Heb. 2:9, "And so he without God, who had united Himself with him as a temple, tasted death for all men." According to Burkitt (1898: 137, note §), who calls attention to this reading, the variant χωρὶς θεοῦ is not found in the Syriac Vulgate except in Nestorian copies. For other noteworthy readings in the manuscript, see Delitzsch (1857: 764-769).

[5] The text of I Corinthians in this manuscript was made the subject of a Ph. D. dissertation by Robert H. Boyd (Princeton University 1942).

(9) MS. Sinai arab. 70, the four Gospels, about the ninth century, "in excellent simple Kufic divided according to the readings of the Greek calendar".

(10) MS. Sinai arab. 72, the four Gospels, dated A. D. 897, "complete and excellent dated copy in neat Kufic, divided according to the readings of the Greek calendar".

(11) MS. Sinai arab. 73, Epistles of Paul, about the ninth century, incomplete text, beginning Rom. 6: 20, ending 2 Tim. 3: 8; "divided according to the Greek calendar".

(12) MS. Sinai arab. 74, the four Gospels, about the ninth century, written in "old Kufic; divided according to readings of the Greek calendar".

When the several Arabic versions represented in the extant manuscripts originated is not known. Most scholars have thought it improbable that any of them antedate Mohammed (e.g. de Goeje 1897; Schreiner 1897; Burkitt 1898b: 136; Graf 1905: 60; Vööbus 1954: 293; Henninger 1961: 206-310). On the other hand Baumstark (1931; 1934b; 1938) and Peters (1939: 48-62; 1939-1940; 1942-1943) contended for a pre-Islamic date (of as much as a century), basing their argument partly on certain liturgical data but chiefly on the consideration that missions to Arabia would require vernacular renderings of the Scriptures for the work of evangelization.

In any case, by the beginning of the thirteenth century amid the multiplicity of independent translations a need was felt for a more fixed type, and one which took account of all the three great national Vulgates of the East – the Greek, the Syriac, and the Coptic. Consequently, about A. D. 1250 a scholar at Alexandria named Hibat Allâh ibn al-'Assâl prepared a revised text of the Gospels with variant readings from the Greek, the Syriac, and the Coptic (see Giudi 1888: 22-24; Macdonald 1893: 163-176, 252). The edition, however, was found to be too complicated for popular use, and towards the end of the thirteenth century it was superseded by a less cumbersome recension. According to Guidi, this appears to have been translated from a Coptic (Bohairic) text much like that preserved in cod. Vatican Coptic 9, dated A. D. 1204/1205, filled out by inserting from the Syriac or the Greek various passages present in the later forms of those texts but absent from the ancient Coptic version (Guida 1888: 22-24),[6] In many manuscripts these additions are indicated by marginal notes.

[6] According to Vööbus (1954:289) the same type of type is also found in a codex at the University of Beyrouth, dated A.D. 1048.

During the succeeding centuries this recension, called the "Alexandrian Vulgate", became widely influential. Its text was not only the source of corruptions in other classes of Arabic versions, as well as most manuscripts of the Ethiopic version, but up to the twentieth century it also formed the basis of all printed editions of the Arabic Gospels since the *editio princeps* of 1591 (Burkitt 1898b: 137; Darlow and Moule 1911: 63). It should also be mentioned that all of the four Arabic versions of the book of Revelation, which was not regarded as canonical in the East, are of Coptic origin (Graf 1929).

4. EARLY PRINTED EDITIONS

As was mentioned above, all printed editions of the Arabic Gospels down to the present century represent varieties of the eclectic "Alexandrian Vulgate" prepared at the close of the thirteenth century. They have, therefore, little value for critical purposes.

(1) The *editio princeps* of the Gospels in Arabic (*al-Inğīl al-muqaddas. Evangelium sanctum* ...) was printed at Rome in 1590 and 1591 in the Medicean printing house; 1590 stands on the title page, 1591 in the subscription. It was edited by Giovanni Battista Raimundi (Raymund), superintendent of the printing office established by Cardinal Ferdinando de'Medici. A second printing in 1591 has an interlinear Latin translation made by Antonius Sionita. The edition was reissued with a new title page in 1619 and 1774. The manuscript base of the edition is unknown.

(2) The *editio princeps* of the New Testament in Arabic was prepared by Thomas Erpenius (Erpe; 1584-1624) and published at Leiden in 1616. The text of the Gospels was based on a manuscript bequeathed to the Leiden Library by Joseph Scaliger (ms. or. 2369), said to have been written in the monastery of St. John in the Thebaid, in the year of the Martyrs 1059 (A. D. 1342-1343). Two other manuscripts also employed by Erpenius for the Gospels are now in the Cambridge University Library (G. 5. 33 and G. 5. 27, written A. D. 1285). The Acts, Pauline Epistles, James, I Peter, and I John in this edition are translated from the Peshitta; in the remaining Catholic Epistles the version seems to have been made directly from the Greek. In the book of Revelation the text, according to Burkitt, is perhaps a combination of translations from the Greek and the Coptic.

In 1752 a Latin rendering of Erpenius's Arabic text of the Gospel of Mark was published at Lemgo by C. A. Bode.

(3) The Arabic version of the entire New Testament was included in the fifth volume (in two parts, 1630 and 1633) of the Paris Polyglot Bible. Two Maronites from Lebanon, Johannes Hesronita and Gabriel Sionita, were placed in charge of the work on the Arabic text and its vocalization, as well as the Latin translation.[7] The recension of the Gospels, contrary to de Lagarde's opinion (1864: xi), was not an interpolated reprint of Raimundi's Roman edition, but appears to be based on a manuscript from Aleppo similar to Paris Anc. f. 27 (of A. D. 1619) and Coisl. 239 (new Suppl. Ar. 27) (Gildemeister 1865).

(4) The Arabic version of the Paris Polyglot was reprinted, with minor alterations in text and Latin translation, in Walton's London Polyglot (1657). In the work on the Arabic text the editor was assisted by Edward Pococke, who also revised the Latin translation of the Arabic.

(5) The *editio princeps* of the complete Bible in Arabic, apart from the text given in the Paris and London Polyglots, was edited, under the direction of the Congregatio de Propaganda Fide, by Sergius Risius (Sarkīs ar-Ruzzī), Maronite Archbishop of Damascus, who had come to Rome in 1624, bringing with him many manuscripts of the Arabic Scriptures. After Risius's death in 1638 the work was carried on by others; the completed work, with the Arabic text and the Latin Vulgate printed side by side, was finally published at Rome in three volumes in 1671. Inasmuch as the Arabic has been brought into conformity with the Vulgate, the version possesses no independent critical value.

(6) In 1703 Faustus Naironus edited at Rome the Arabic New Testament in Karshunic characters, for the use of the Maronites, from a manuscript brought from Cyprus. It was reprinted at Paris in 1827. The Acts, Epistles, and Apocalypse represent the same version as that of Erpenius, but in a different recension.

(7) In 1708 the Gospels in Arabic were published at Aleppo by the Melchite Patriarch Athanasius IV of Antioch, with the financial assistance of a Russian Cossack hetman, Ivan Masepa.[8]

5. TEXTUAL AFFINITIES OF EARLY ARABIC VERSIONS

Many problems remain unsolved in the study of the earliest Arabic translations of the New Testament. For example, no more than a begin-

---

[7] For information about the basic texts and quality of translation of the Arabic version of the Paris and London Polyglots see Thompson (1955: 1-12, 51-55, 98-106, 146-150).
[8] For a description of the edition see *Zeitschrift der Deutschen morgenländischen Gesellschaft* 8 (1854), 386-389.

ning has been made in analyzing the textual affinities of individual Arabic manuscripts (see Guidi 1888; Vaccari 1925: 79-104; Euringer 1929: 259-273; Padwick 1939: 130-140). Curt Peters, who tested sample passages from all four Gospels in a group which Guidi found to be translated from Greek, concluded that not a few Tatianisms have found their way into this Arabic version (Peters 1936: 188-211; 1939: 54-62). In a thorough analysis of the entire text of Matthew and Mark in two Arabic manuscripts which were translated from the Greek, Bernhard Levin (1938: 67-69) found that in addition to Tatianisms many readings characteristic of the Caesarean text are also present. The version preserves an interesting agraphon as an expansion of Matt. 6: 34: "Sufficient unto the day is the evil thereof, and unto the hour the pain thereof."[9]

On the basis of a detailed analysis of sixty-three variant readings in the text of 1 Corinthians contained in codex Sinai arab. 155 (manuscript no. 6 above), Robert Boyd (1942: 153) concluded that the underlying Greek text "was of a predominantly Neutral or Alexandrian type which shows little effect of the assimilation toward the late Byzantine type of text". In view of the relative freedom from influence by the Byzantine recension, Boyd thought that the Arabic translation was made prior to the seventh century – a conclusion that is, however, not necessary if the translator had utilized a relatively old copy of the Greek text, antedating the emergence and spread of the Byzantine recension.

Following a lead partly pursued by Baumstark, Vööbus has discovered abundant traces of the Old Syriac type of text reflected in the Scripture quotations made by Christian Arabic writers.[10] It is also significant that Ibn Isḥāq, a Muslim whose treatise *Sīrat Rasūl Allāh* (the earliest prose work in the Arabic language to come down to us) was written about A. D. 725 at Medina, seems to have derived his knowledge of the Gospels from the Palestinian Syriac version, with which some of his quotations and allusions agree.[11]

The limitations of Arabic version(s) in representing the underlying Greek text involve the following types of testimony:

---

[9]   The same reading occurs in manuscripts B and C of the Palestinian Syriac Lectionary (manuscript A deest).

[10]   Vööbus, *Early Versions*, pp. 276ff.

[11]   Cf. A. Baumstark, "Eine altarabische Evangelienübersetzung aus dem Christlich-Palästinenischen", *Zeitschrift für Semitistik und verwandte Gebiete*, viii (1930-32), pp. 201-209; Alfred Guillaume, "The Version of the Gospels Used in Medina circa A. D. 700", *Al-Andalus*, xv (1950), pp. 289-96; and J. Schlacht, "Une citation de l'Évangile de St. Jean dans la *Sira* d'Ibn Isḥāq", ibid., xvi (1951), pp. 489-90.

(a) Variations in the number of the noun;

(b) Variations in the aspect, mood, or voice of the verb;

(c) Addition, omission, and variation in the use of conjunctions;

(d) Addition or omission of possessive pronouns and objective pronouns, indicating the specific person of reference;

(e) Unique variations in the use of certain personal pronouns; and

(f) Addition or omission of demonstrative pronoun.[12]

REFERENCES

Atiya, Azis S.
1955   The Arabic Manuscripts of Mount Sinai (Baltimore).
Baumstark, Anton
1911   Die christlichen Literatur des Orients 2 (Leipzig).
1931   "Das Problem eines vorislamischen christlichen-kirchlichen Schrifttums in arabischer Sprache", Islamica 4, 562-575.
1934a   "Markus, Kap. 2 in der arabischen Übersetzung des Isaak Valasquez", Oriens Christianus 3. Ser. 10.
1934b   "Arabische Übersetzung eines altsyrischen Evangelientextes", Oriens Christianus 3te Serie 10, 165-188, with an addendum on 278ff.
1935   "Neue orientalistische Probleme biblischer Textgeschichte", Zeitschrift der deutschen morgenländischen Gesellschaft 89, 107-109.
1938   "Eine frühislamische und eine vorislamische arabische Evangeliumübersetzung aus dem Syrischen", Atti del XIX congresso international degli orientalisti, Roma, 23-29. Settembre 1935 (Rome), 682-684.
Boyd, Robert H.
1942   "The Arabic Text of I Corinthians in Studia Sinaitica, No. II; a Comparative, Linguistic and Critical Study" (Princeton University Library).
Bruyne, Donatien De, and Eugène Tisserant
1910   "Une feuille arabo-latine de l'Épître aux Galates", Revue Biblique, N. S. 7, 321-343, with a plate.
Burkitt, (Mrs.) A. P.
1897-   "Die in der Peschito fehlenden Briefe des Neuen Testamentes in arabischer
1898   der Philoxeniana entstammender Übersetzung", edited by Adalbert Merx, in Zeitschrift für Assyriologie 12, 240-252, 348-381; 13, 1-28.
Burkitt, F.C.
1898   "Arabic Versions", in Hastings' Dictionary of the Bible 1 (Edinburgh and New York).
Chabot, J. B. (ed.)
1901   Chronique de Michel le Syrien 2 (Paris). Reprinted in 1963 (Brussels).
Darlow, T. H., and H. F. Moule
1911   Historical Catalogue of the Printed Editions of Holy Scripture 2 (London).
Delitzsch, F.
1857   Commentar zum Briefe an die Hebräer (Leipzig).
Devreesse, R.
1942   "Le Christianisme dans la province d'Arabie", Vivre et Penser 2 (= Revue Biblique 51).

---

[12] For examples from the Arabic version of I Corinthians illustrating each of these categories, see Boyd, op. cit. (footnote 5 above), pp. 138-42.

Dodge, Bayard (trans.)
1970 *The Fihrist of al-Nadīm* 1 (New York).
Duchesne, L.
1896 "Les missions chrétiennes au sud de l'empire romain", *Mélanges d'archéologie et d'histoire* 16.
Euringer, Sebastian
1929 "Zum Stammbaum der arabischen Bibelhandschriften Vat. ar. 468 and 467", *Zeitschrift für Semitistik und verwandte Gebiete* 7.
Eusebius
1903 *Ecclesiastical History*, ed. by E. Schwartz (= *Griechische Christliche Schriftsteller* 9) (Leipzig: J. C. Hinrichs'sche Buchhandlung).
Gibson, Margaret Dunlop
1894 *An Arabic Version of the Epistles of St. Paul to the Romans, Corinthians, Galatians, with Part of the Epistle to the Ephesians* (= *Studia Sinaitica* 2) (London).
1899 *An Arabic Version of the Acts of the Apostles and the Seven Catholic Epistles* (= *Studia Sinaitica* 7) (London).
Gildemeister, J.
1865 *De evangeliis in Arabicum e simplici Syriaco translatis* (Bonn).
Goeje, M. J. de
1897 "Quotations from the Bible in the Qoran and the Tradition", in *Semitic Studies in Memory of Alexander Kohut* (Berlin), 179-185.
Goodspeed, Edgar J.
1935 *The Translators to the Reader; Preface to the King James Version* 1611 (Chicago).
Graf, Georg
1905 *Die christliche-arabische Literatur bis zur Fränkischen Zeit* (Freiburg im B.).
1929 "Arabische Übersetzungen der Apokalypse", *Biblica* 10, 170-194.
1944 *Geschichte der christlichen arabischen Literatur* 1 (= *Studi e testi* 118) (Città del Vaticano).
Guidi, I.
1888 "Le traduzioni degli Evangelii in arabo e in etiopico", *Atti della R. Accademia dei Lincei, Memorie* anno 275, serie quanta, classe di scienze morali, storiche e filologiche 4, Partie 1ª (Rome).
Harnack, Adolf von
1924 *Die Mission und Ausbreitung des Christentums in den ersten drei Jahrhunderten* 2, 4te Aufl. (Leipzig). Translated into English as *The Mission and Expansion of Christianity in the First Three Centuries* 2, 2nd ed. (London, 1908).
Henninger, Joseph
1948 "Christenthum im vorislamischen Arabien", *Neue Zeitschrift für Missionswissenschaft* 4.
1961 "Arabische Bibelübersetzungen vom Frühmittelalter bis zum 19. Jahrhundert", *Neue Zeitschrift für Missionswissenschaft* 17.
Hug, J. L.
1836 *Introduction to the New Testament*, trans. by David Fosdick, Jr. (Andover).
Krachkovskiĭ, Ignaz
1918 "O perevode Bibliĭ na arabskiĭ yazik pri Khalife al-Ma'mūne", *Kristianskiĭ Vostok* 6.
Kretschmer, Georg
1953 "Origenes und die Araber", *Zeitschrift für Theologie und Kirche* 50.
Lagarde, Paul de
1864 *Die vier Evangelien arabisch* (Leipzig).

Levin, B.
  1938 "Die griechisch-arabische Evangelien-Übersetzung, Vat. Borg. ar. 95 und
       Ber. orient, oct. 1108", dissertation (Uppsala).
Lewis, Agnes Smith
  1894 *Catalogue of the Syriac MSS, in the Convent of S. Catherine on Mt. Sinai*
       (= *Studia siniatica* 1) (London).
Macdonald, D. B.
  1893 "The Gospels in Arabic", *Hartford Seminary Record* 3.
Origen
  1949 *Discussion with Heraclides*, edited by J. Scherer (Cairo).
Padwick, Constance E.
  1939 "Al-Ghazali and the Arabic Versions of the Gospels, an Unsolved Problem",
       Moslem World 29.
Peters, Curt
  1936 "Proben eines bedeutsamen arabischen Evangelientextes", *Oriens Christianus*,
       3te Serie, 11.
  1939 *Das Diatessaron Tatians* (= *Orientalia christiana analecta* 123) (Rome).
  1939- "Von arabischen Evangelientexten in Handschriften der Universitäts-
  1940 Bibliothek Leiden", *Acta Orientalia* 18, 124-137.
  1942 "Grundsätzliche Bemerkungen zur Frage der arabischen Bibeltexte", *Rivista*
  1943 *degli studi orientali* 20, 129-143.
Philostorgius
  1913 *Ecclesiastical History*, ed. by J. Bidez (= *Griechische Christliche Schrift-
       steller* 21) (Leipzig: J.C. Hinrichs'sche Buchhandlung).
Renouf, Peter le Page
  1863 "On the Supposed Latin Origin of the Arabic Version of the Gospels",
       *The Atlantis; or Register of Literature and Science of the Catholic University
       of Ireland* 4.
Schreiner, Martin
  1897 "Beiträge zur Geschichte der Bibel in der arabischen Literatur", *Semitic
       Studies in Memory of Alexander Kohut* (Berlin), 495-513.
Staal, Harvey
  1969 *Codex Sinai; Arabic* 151, *Pauline Epistles*, Part 1 (Romans, I and II Corin-
       thians, Philippians) (= *Studies and Documents* 2) (Salt Lake City).
Stenij, E.
  1901 *Die altarabische Übersetzung der Briefe an die Hebräer, an die Römer und
       an die Korinther* (Helsinki).
Theodoret
  1954 *Ecclesiastical History*, ed. by L. Parmentier and F. Scheidweiter (= *Griechishe
       Christliche Schriftsteller* 19, 2nd ed.) (Leipzig).
Thompson, John A.
  1955 "The Major Arabic Bibles", *The Bible Translator* 6. Reprinted in pamphlet
       form (New York, 1956).
Tisserant, Eugene
  1914 *Specimina codicum orientalium* (Bonn).
Vaccari, Alberto
  1925 "Una Bibbia araba per il primo Gesuita venuto al Libano", *Mélanges de
       l'Université saint-Joseph* 10 (Beyrouth).
Vööbus, A.
  1954 *Early Versions of the New Testament, Manuscript Studies* (Stockholm).

THE INTERPRETATION OF ROMANS 12:8:
ὁ μεταδιδοὺς ἐν ἁπλότητι

W. C. VAN UNNIK

Many Christians all over the world, now and in the future, owe an enormous debt of gratitude to Dr. Nida. They will not know it, because his name is not on the title page or in the colophon of the Bible translation they have in hand. But his spirit has helped and guided the minds and hands of those who labored to make the Bible available to each man in his own tongue in the present generation. By his many seminars, lectures, and books Dr. Nida has put his great learning in linguistics at the disposal of others; he has made his gifts a source of inspiration in many parts of the globe. His T(E)APOT[1] is a classic for all those who are struggling on the long and often rough path between the original text and the expression of its meaning in the vernacular.

Dr. Nida's name is closely associated with that method of translation called "dynamic equivalence". Hence, it seemed appropriate to discuss in his honor a little problem by which some of the difficulties encountered by a translator may be demonstrated. Has the last word been said when we have given a dynamic equivalence translation?

Sometime ago in reading a report of a conference devoted to this method of translating I came across a sentence that made me wonder. In November 1972 a meeting was held in Argenteuil, Belgium, under the guidance of some men who have good names in Bible work, viz. Dr. H. R. Weber, Rev. Kassühlke, and Rev. Fueter. The report said:

The Principles of Dynamic Equivalence translation were studied, and *their bearing on the interpretation of the Bible discussed.*[2]

The latter half of the sentence puzzled me. My troubles may result from the brevity of this report, but I am not sure of that. At any rate in my understanding dynamic equivalence translation is a *method* of re-

[1] E. A. Nida and C. R. Taber, *The Theory and Practice of Translation* (Leiden, 1969).
[2] *United Bible Societies, Bulletin* 93 (1973), 44 (italics are mine).

producing the understanding of the Hebrew or Greek original of the Bible in another language, not by word-for-word translation, but by the expression in the idiom of the receiving language. The translation, any translation, is based on exegesis; it is "exegesis in a nutshell", as was already discovered more than a century ago.[3] Our interpretation, even if we have only a translation in hand, does not depend on the principles of translation, but on the basic exegesis Now it may be that what the report quoted wanted to say was that a dynamic equivalence translation is a much better way to bring out the basic meaning of the original text than a so-called literal translation. But that is not clearly stated. However that may be, without sound exegesis, dynamic equivalence translation would be less than "a noisy gong or a clanging bell" (I Cor. 13:1, TEV). Nevertheless, it may be that even an excellent translation made according to this principle must remain unclear, since the original text is ambiguous. In that case footnotes are indispensible. This too, however, can only be decided on the basis of the exegesis of the original text in Hebrew or Greek.

In this paper we will discuss a little problem of this sort because it offers a good specimen of the difficulties one may encounter.

The text that is offered here for translation consists of only four words, Rom. 12:8 ὁ μεταδιδοὺς ἐν ἁπλότητι. At first sight it does seem rather simple and without great puzzles.

A representative though incomplete conspectus of English translations may be helpful:

A. V.: "he that giveth, *let him do it* with simplicity"
Rev. V.: "he that giveth, *let him do it* with liberality"
Weymouth: "he who gives should be liberal"
Moffatt: "the contributors must be liberal"
R. S. V.: "he who contributes, in liberality"
Barrett: "the man who practises charity, let him do it whole-heartedly"
N. E. B.: "if you give to charity, give with all your heart"
TEV: "Whoever shares what he has with others, must do it generously"

Similar lists of translations in other languages could be made[4] but

---

[3] W. C. van Maanen, *Het Nieuwe Testament sedert* 1859 (Groningen, 1886), 36, wrote about the Dutch translation of G. Vissering (2nd ed., 1859): "The extremely modest form... in which the result of profound exegetical research has been embodied ...a peculiar and yet complete exegetical-critical commentary on the New Testament" (my translation).

[4] As far as I can see, all *suggest* by their phraseology that Paul enjoins the distribution of material gifts, though the Dutch translation of the Bible Society with the word "wie mededeelt" is equivocal, for it may be "who distributes" or "who informs".

would be of little help in this paper. It is evident that there are two vital points in this part of the verse, namely the exact meanings of μεταδιδούς and ἀπλότης. The decision on the first point seems to be quite simple, for with the exception of Moffatt and RSV all translators seem to have based themselves on the same interpretation of μεταδιδούς though their reproduction in English may be somewhat different.

Moffatt and R. S. V. let Paul have a man in view who contributes to the church[5] and quickens his generosity. In itself this is a useful exhortation; it may have been as appropriate in the beginnings of the church as it is at present. But I wonder if this is the proper meaning of μεταδιδόναι. Up until now I have not found any Greek texts, where the word is used for contributions made to clubs, etc., which would substantiate this explanation.

The interpretation that is practically unanimously accepted,[6] goes in quite another direction: "it refers to a rich man who liberally gave his wealth in alms",[7] or, to quote Fitzmeyer, this "gift is that of philanthropy and differs from the second [sc. the *diakonia*, verse 7] because he is moved to dispense his private wealth".[8] In former times some commentators had thought of sharing spiritual gifts, but Bernhard Weiss, who mentions it, flatly rejects this opinion because it does not fit the context.[9] In the present century it was, as far as I know, only the great Theodor Zahn who held the view that Paul had both spiritual gifts and material goods in mind; a limitation to the latter category was not justified.[10] Nevertheless, the overwhelming majority of commentators did not follow this line. Lagrange, while admitting that the verb may have both meanings, chooses for the latter because the spiritual sharing is already mentioned by teaching and exhortation; "il s'agit donc de l'aumône".[11] If the need is felt to define the verb μεταδιδόναι somewhat more explicitly, it is explained in the way of Sanday-Headlam: "the man who gives alms of his own substance" (μεταδιδούς = who

---

[5] J. Knox, "Romans", in *The Interpreter's Bible* 9 (Nashville, New York, 1954), 585.
[6] See e.g. Severianus of Gabala in K. Staab, *Pauluskommentare aus der griechischen Kirche* (Münster, 1933), 223, who sees here a consequence of Jesus' saying Luke 6:30.
[7] A. E. Garvie, "Romans", in *The Century Bible* (Edinburgh, n.d.), 262.
[8] J. A. Fitzmeyer, "Romans", in *The Jerome Biblical Commentary* 2 (London, 1968), 325.
[9] B. Weiss, *Brief des Paulus an die Römer*, 7th ed. (Göttingen, 1886), 581.
[10] T. Zahn, *Der Brief des Paulus an die Römer*, 3rd ed. (Leipzig, Erlangen, 1925), 547; H. W. Schmidt, *Den Brief des Paulus an die Römer* (Berlin, 1962), 212, mentions the view of Zahn, but prefers the view of almsgiving.
[11] M. J. Lagrange, *Saint Paul, Épître aux Romains* (Paris, 1950), 300.

gives of his own, in contrast with διαδιδούς = who distributes other persons' gifts).[12] It would be a waste of paper to draw up a long list of exegetes, because in all present-day commentaries the same opinion, expressed in a variety of wordings, is found: Paul speaks of almsgiving or giving to the poor.[13] The added annotation of Hugo Grotius who took it as an injunction to the rich is interesting: "Est quidem opulentia bonum temporale, sed cum in usus pauperum confertur, fit spirituale."

For the explanation in the sense of almsgiving the following parallel texts are given by Lietzmann:[14]

(a) Luke 3: 11 in the speech of John the Baptist: ὁ ἔχων δύο χιτῶνας μεταδότω τῷ μὴ ἔχοντι.

(b) Eph 4: 18 the thief should not steal anymore, but work with his own hands, ἵνα ἔχη μεταδιδόναι τῷ χρείαν ἔχοντι.

(c) Hermas, Vis. III 9, 2.4 καὶ μὴ μόνοι τὰ κτίσματα τοῦ θεοῦ μεταλαμβάνετε ἐκ καταχύματος,[15] ἀλλὰ μεταδίδοτε καὶ τοῖς ὑστερουμένοις... αὕτη οὖν ἡ ἀσυνκρασία βλαβερὰ ὑμῖν τοῖς ἔχουσιν καὶ μὴ μεταδιδοῦσιν τοῖς ὑστερουμένοις.

Sometimes references to LXX are added:

(1) Job 31: 17 εἰ δὲ καὶ τὸν ψωμόν μου ἔφαγον μόνος καὶ οὐχὶ ὀρφανῷ μετέδωκα.

(2) Prov. 11: 26 ὁ συνέχων σῖτον ὑπολίποιτο αὐτὸν τοῖς ἔθνεσιν εὐλογία δὲ εἰς κεφαλὴν τοῦ μεταδιδόντος.

(3) Epist. Jeremiae 27: οὔτε πτωχῷ οὔτε ἀδυνάτῳ μεταδιδόασιν.

See also in Test. XII Patr.

Issaschar 7: 5 πτωχῷ μετέδωκα ἄρτον μου.

Zebulon 6: 4 ἐκ τῆς θήρας μου παντὶ ἀνθρώπῳ ξένῳ σπλαγχνιζόμενος μετεδίδουν.

The second question is concerned with the meaning of ἁπλότης.[16]

---

[12] W. Sanday and A. C. Headlam, *The Epistle to the Romans*, 5th ed. (Edinburgh, 1902), 357. Calvin had held the other view: "Per μεταδιδοῦντας... non eos intelligit qui largiuntur de suo; sed Diaconos, qui publicis Ecclesiae facultatibus dispensendis praesunt".

[13] A special interpretation was given by Martin Luther, *Vorlesung über den Römerbrief* 1515-1516, 4th ed., edited by E. Ellwein (München, 1957), 384-386; he mentions the giving of the subjects to their superiors and vice versa, and continues: "Aber diese Auslegung empfiehlt sich nicht. Der Apostel redet vielmehr von jenem Geben, das den Lehrern des Wortes und den Leitern zugute kommt", referring to Galatians 6:6.

[14] H. Lietzmann, *An die Römer*, 3rd ed. (Tübingen, 1928), 109.

[15] W. Bauer, *Griechisch-deutsches Wörterbuch zu den Schriften des Neuen Testaments und der übrigen urchristlichen Literatur*, 5th ed. (Berlin, 1958), Sp. 832, s.v.: "*aus d. Brühe fischen* d. h. alles für sich ergattern".

[16] O. Bauernfeind, in G. Kittel, *Theologisches Wörterbuch zum Neuen Testament* 1

It is usual to refer to other Pauline texts:

(1) 2 Cor. 8: 2 ὅτι ἐν πολλῇ δοκιμῇ θλίψεως ἡ περισσεία τῆς χαρᾶς αὐτῶν καὶ ἡ κατὰ βάθους πτωχεία αὐτῶν ἐπερίσσευσεν εἰς τὸ πλοῦτος τῆς ἁπλότητος αὐτῶν.

(2) 2 Cor. 9: 11 ἐν παντὶ πλουτιζόμενοι εἰς πᾶσαν ἁπλότητα, ἥτις κατεργάζεται δι'ἡμῶν εὐχαριστίαν τῷ θεῷ.

(3) 2 Cor. 9: 13 διὰ τῆς δοκιμῆς τῆς διακονίας ταύτης δοξάζοντες τὸν θεὸν ἐπὶ τῇ ... ἁπλότητι τῆς κοινωνίας εἰς αὐτοὺς καὶ εἰς πάντας.

(4) 2 Cor. 11: 3 φοβοῦμαι δὲ μὴ πῶς, ὡς ὁ ὄφις ἐξηπάτησεν Εὕαν ἐν τῇ πανουργίᾳ αὐτοῦ, φθαρῇ τὰ νοήματα ὑμῶν ἀπὸ τῆς ἁπλότητος καὶ τῆς ἁγνότητος τῆς εἰς Χριστόν.

It is often taken in the sense of "singleness of purpose and not with mixed motives, with the thought of ostentation or reward";[17] "wholeheartedly ... being without arrière-pensée in one's gifts".[18] Others translate it with reference to the above New Testament texts as "liberality" or "generosity".[19] Sanday and Headlam draw special attention to the Test. XII Patr. Issascher in which this patriarch is painted as an example of the virtue.[20]

Of course this interpretation gives a perfectly good sense if, and only if, the verb μεταδιδόναι has the implicit and unequivocal meaning of "to give to the poor". But is that so? Or have we in following this line more or less fallen victim to a certain exegetical tradition?

It is quite clear that the verb in question is used in connection with helping the poor in the texts cited before. But that idea is mentioned expressis verbis and does not seem to be implied in the verb itself.

Modern linguistics has taught us, insofar as we did not know it before, that words do not "have" meanings, but that they derive their meanings from their contexts. We translate not words but sentences and wider contexts. The trouble with the present text is that it is so extremely brief and lends itself to many interpretations, because the

---

(Stuttgart, 1933), 385-386 and J. Amstutz, ΑΠΛΟΤΗΣ, eine begriffsgeschichtliche Studie zum jüdisch - christlichen Griechisch, Bonn 1960, who follows 108 f., the common explanation of "almsgiving"; ἁπλότης = "in spontaner Freiheit und ohne bekümmertes Sorgen".

17 Sanday and Headlam, The Epistle to the Romans, 357.
18 C. K. Barrett, A Commentary on the Epistle to the Romans (London, 1957), 238-239.
19 J. B. Mayor, The Epistle of St. James, 3rd ed. (London, 1910), 39; and J. H. Ropes, Epistle of St. James (Edinburg, 1916), 139-140 ad Jac. 1:5 παρὰ τοῦ διδόντος θεοῦ πᾶσιν ἁπλῶς.
20 See the notes of R. H. Charles, The Testaments of the Twelve Patriarchs, Translated from the Editor's Greek text, (London, 1908), 103-105.

verb in question is used in a wide variety of "contexts", as we shall see presently.

This fact is made clear by Paul himself, for there are two more texts in his letters that may not pass unnoticed if we want to discuss our text without prejudice. The first is Rom. 1: 11

ἐπιποθῶ γὰρ ἰδεῖν ὑμᾶς, ἵνα τι μεταδῶ χάρισμα ὑμῖν πνευματικὸν εἰς τὸ στηριχθῆναι ὑμᾶς, 12 τοῦτο δέ ἐστιν συμπαρακληθῆναι ἐν ὑμῖν διὰ τῆς ἐν ἀλλήλοις πίστεως ὑμῶν τε καὶ ἐμοῦ.

This text, though it is hardly mentioned in connection with Rom. 12: 8, is, I think, extremely relevant because the object here is χάρισμα πνευματικόν and in Rom. 12: 6 Paul is also speaking of the different, charismata, one of which shows itself in ὁ μεταδιδούς. From this activity will result the strenghthening of the Roman Christians or better, as Paul corrects himself, a mutual comfort through that faith which they and he have in common. This μεταδιδόναι does not only help the faithful in Rome, but also the apostle.

The second text stands in a missionary context, viz. 1 Thess. 2: 8 οὕτως ὁμειρόμενοι ὑμῶν ηὐδοκοῦμεν μεταδοῦναι ὑμῖν οὐ μόνον τὸ εὐαγγέλιον τοῦ θεοῦ, ἀλλὰ καὶ τὰς ἑαυτῶν ψυχάς.[21] Paul has reminded the Thessalonians in what spirit he has preached the Gospel among them without error, guile, flattering, or greed, without seeking glory from men.[22] Then he argues that he has not made demands, but was gentle as a nurse.[23] Μεταδοῦναι τὸ εὐαγγέλιον is paralleled in this passage by λαλῆσαι τὸ εὐαγγέλιον (verse 2) and ἐκηρύξαμεν ... τὸ εὐαγγέλιον (verse 9). But Paul did not only talk about the Gospel: this μεταδοῦναι is more, not an outward message, but his own person.[24] This is shown by his labor with his own hands,[25] wherewith he demonstrates his independence, and, even more important, was able not to make demands on them.

Of course, in the line of thinking that used to speak of the "poor

---

[21] B. Rigaux, Saint Paul, Les Épîtres aux Thessaloniciens (Paris, Gembloux, 1956), 422, was correct in pointing out the difference with δοῦναι or τιθέναι τὴν ψύχην in John 10:11; 1 John 3:16, Mark 10:45 = to offer one's life = to die.

[22] For these negative qualifications cf. M. Dibelius, An die Thessalonicher I II, An die Philipper, 2nd ed. (Tübingen, 1925), 7-8, criticism of traveling preachers ("Wandellehrer der Zeit").

[23] See A. J. Malherbe, "Gentle as a Nurse", in Novum Testamentum XII (1970), 203-217.

[24] ψυχή as a reflexive noun, cf. Bauer, Griechisch-deutsches Wörterbuch, Sp. 1767, s.v. f.

[25] This is an often recurring theme in Paul's letters, cf. also 2 Thess. 3:8; I Cor. 4:12; 9:15; and in his "testament" according to Acts 20:34.

heathen", it might be possible to give the verb μεταδοῦναι the notion of "giving to the poor" in a spiritual sense. But that interpretation would run counter to the rest of the sentence, where Paul is not thinking of people who are in need, but of those on whom he could have make demands as an apostle. Besides that, as will appear presently, the combination of μεταδιδόναι with the Gospel is not so strange in Greek ears as it would appear at first sight.

We see from these texts that the verb has a much wider meaning for Paul than in the first set of texts (p. 172), that it can be used to express an essential element in his relation to his fellow believers, and that it is even wider than "to preach" but could also comprise the giving of oneself in it.

It may also be worthwhile to have a look at the Septuagint. The concordance of Hatch and Redpath shows that μεταδιδόναι does not have a prominent place in the vocabulary of the Greek Old Testament. Besides the texts already cited (p. 172), where the context gives a mark of aiding the poor to the verb, note four more:

(1) 2 Macc. 1: 35 καὶ οἷς ἐχαρίζετο ὁ βασιλεύς (sc. of the Persians) πολλὰ διαφορὰ ἐλάμβανεν καὶ μετεδίδου. Tedesche translated it this way: "the king then exchanged all kinds of gifts with those whom he wished to favor" and gave this correct explanation: "an oriental custom expressing satisfaction and pleasure".[26]

(2) 2 Macc. 8: 12 the Jewish leader Judas hears the news of the advances of his enemy καὶ μεταδόντος τοῖς σὺν αὐτῷ τὴν παρουσίαν τοῦ στρατοπέδου, the cowards fled. Here it means "to pass on, to intimate the news".

(3) Tob. 7: 10 (text of the manuscripts B.A., not in S) μετέδωκεν τὸν λόγον τῷ Ῥαγουηλ· this is the answer to Tobias' question: λάλησον ὑπὲρ ὦν ἔλεγες ἐν τῇ πορείᾳ.[27]

(4) Wisd. of Sol. 7: 13 in a hymn on Wisdom ἀδόλως τε ἔμαθον ἀφθόνως τε μεταδίδωμι. τὸν πλοῦτον αὐτῆς οὐκ ἀποκρύπτομαι. Though the verb is used here without additions, the context makes it clear that the object here is Wisdom. The use of μεταδιδόναι in this context is not peculiar to the unknown author of the "Book of Wisdom", but it reflects current usage. The text and other relevant material has been

---

[26] It is impossible to go into the investigation of this custom in this paper.
[27] See also Test. XII Patr., Dan. 6:9 καὶ ἃ ἠκούσατε παρὰ τοῦ πατρὸς ὑμῶν, μετάδοτε καὶ ὑμεῖς τοῖς τέκνοις ὑμῶν. Letter of Aristeas 43 in a letter of the Jewish High Priest to the Egyptian King about the ambassadors the king has sent οἱ καὶ μετέδωκαν ἡμῖν τὰ παρά σου, viz. message and presents. Testamentum Job 4:1 ὑποδείκνυμί σοι πάντα ἅπερ ἐνετείλατό μοι κύριος μεταδιδόναι σοι.

discussed in a special study, to which the interested readers may be referred.[28] By way of illustration some of the most telling parallels may be quoted:

(1) an inscription of Samos ($\pm$ 200 B.C.) in honor of a teacher μεταδιδοὺς ἀφθόνως τῆς καθ'αὐτὸν παιδείας τοῖς βουλομένοις μετέχειν.

(2) ps. Aristoteles, De Mundo 391a, where it is said about the philosophical soul πᾶσιν ἀφθόνως μεταδοῦναι βουληθεῖσα τῶν παρ'αὐτῇ τιμίων.[29]

(3) Dio Chrysostomus, Or. 41,9, Rome has been more superior than other men ἐπιεικείᾳ καὶ φιλανθρωπίᾳ. τοῦτο μὲν ἀφθόνως μεταδιδοῦσα καὶ πολιτείας καὶ νόμων καὶ ἀρχῶν ... τοῦτο δὲ ὁμοίως ἅπασι φυλάττουσα τὸ δίκαιον.

(4) Hippolytus, De Antichristo 29, after an explanation of the statue in Daniel 2: ταῦτά σοι, ἀγαπητέ, μετὰ φόβου μεταδίδομεν ἀφθόνως.

It would surpass the limits set to this paper if we were to reproduce the whole collection of texts using the verb μεταδιδόναι that I have brought together. But from this material it appears that μεταδιδόναι is seldomly connected with giving to people in need; even where it is used of presents, it may also be said of giving to the rich.[30] The verb has a much wider radius of action than just giving to the poor.

This negative statement may be supplemented by a positive observation: the giving always involves something important which enriches life in this world such as the fruits of the earth,[31] land, honor, citizen-

---

[28] W. C. van Unnik, "ΑΦΘΩΝΩΣ ΜΕΤΑΔΙΔΩΜΙ", in Mededelingen van de Koninklijke Vlaamse Academie van Wetenschappen, Letteren en Schone Kunsten van België (= Klasse der Letteren 23:4) (Brussel, 1971), quoted in this paper as "Aphthonoos".

[29] Cf. van Unnik, "Aphthonoos", 14-17, for a discussion of these texts.

[30] Xenophon, Anab. IV 5,6, some soldiers have lighted fires, but do not admit fellow soldiers εἰ μὴ μεταδοῖεν αὐτοῖς πυροὺς ἢ ἄλλο, εἴ τι ἔχοιεν βρωτόν. ἔνθα δὴ μεταδίδοσαν ἀλλήλοις, ὧν εἶχον ἕκαστοι. Josephus, Ant. Jud. VIII 175, of the Queen of Sheba τυχοῦσα καὶ μεταδοῦσα πάλιν τῷ βασιλεῖ τῶν παρ'αὐτῆς. Ant. Jud. IX 59, Elisha συνεβούλευσε δὲ ξενίων αὐτοῖς (sc. the soldiers of the enemy) μεταδόντα καὶ τραπέζης ἀπολύειν ἀβλαβεῖς. Even the poor can do it, see Dio Chrysostomus, Orat. VII 82, the poor πολλάκις δὲ καὶ μεταδιδόντας ὧν ἔχουσιν ἑτοιμέτερον than the rich, which is illustrated in § 83 with an example from Homer. In a definition of Chrysippus (ap. J. ab Arnim, Stoicorum Veterum Fragmenta [Lipsiae, 1903], 169-170) of the ἄγροικος: εἶναι δὲ καὶ ἀχάριστον, οὔτε πρὸς ἀνταπόδοσιν χάριτος οἰκείως ἔχοντα οὔτε πρὸς μετάδοσιν διὰ τὸ μήτε κοινῶς τι ποιεῖν μήτε φιλικῶς μήτε ἀμελετήτως. Here it means to share with others spontaneously. In Stoic ethics it has no special place.

[31] Cf. Diodorus Sic., Hist. Gen. IV 1, 7, on the benefit given by Dionysius καὶ τὰ περὶ τὴν φυτείαν τῆς ἀμπέλου φιλοτεχνήσαντα μεταδοῦναι τῆς τοῦ οἴνου χρήσεως τοῖς κατὰ τὴν οἰκουμένην ἀνθρώποις. V 67,2 of Demeter who commanded Triptolemos πᾶσιν ἀνθρώποις μεταδοῦναι τῆς τε δωρεᾶς καὶ τὰ περὶ τὴν ἐργασίαν τοῦ

ship,[32] or is something necessary for future salvation. With regard to this latter aspect it may be said that it is almost a *terminus technicus* for the communication of the teaching of salvation which is hidden from the masses, but in the possession of special initiated teachers.[33] Some special "treasure" is involved; hence in many texts a contrast is found μεταδιδόναι - οὐ φθονεῖν, that is to say the possessor should not guard it grudgingly, but put it freely at the disposition of others.[34]

If we look for an English expression that covers all these various occurrences of the Greek verb, I would suggest: "to let another man share in something very precious one possesses". It is not just giving,

---

σπόρου διδάξαι. In Philo's works many texts are found where God is the subject who gives man congeniality with Him, His nature, etc.; in a separate paper I hope to return to the use of μεταδιδόναι in the works of Philo.

[32]   Land: Herodotus, *Hist.* IV 145; rule: Herodotus, *Hist.* VII 150; Plato, *Leg.* 715 a; honor: Josephus, *Ant. Jud.* X 249; citizenship: Lysias, *Or.* 25,3, Diodorus Sic., *Hist. Gen.* XIV 8,3, XIX 2,8; Dionysius Hal., *Ant. Rom.* IV 23, 2-4. Dio Chrysostomus, *Or.* 38,4, defends himself against various objections made by his audience which is unwilling to listen to him; one point they make is this: τί δὲ σεαυτῷ λόγον μεταδίδως οὐ σοι μὴ μετέδομεν ἡμεῖς; to which the orator answers, as follows in 38,5, τί τοῦτο δυσκόλόν ἐστιν, ἀνδρὶ φίλῳ λόγου μεταδοῦναι βουλομένῳ ματὴν εἰπεῖν; here it has the meaning of "to give somebody the liberty to address the congregation"; this is clearly considered a privilege.

The verb is twice found in the writings of the Christian Apologists: Athenagoras, *Legatio* 30:2, "their subjects honoured them as gods" (τιμῆς μετεδίδοσαν); Justin Martyr, *Apologia* 66:3, about the Eucharist: the Apostles have handed down in the Gospels the command and the story of the institution καὶ μόνοις αὐτοῖς μεταδοῦναι (sc. bread and wine); cf. 66:1 the food, called *eucharistia* ἧς οὐδενὶ ἄλλῳ μετασχεῖν ἐξόν ἐστιν ἢ τῷ πιστεύοντι. This case in Justin Martyr is significant to demonstrate that something precious is involved. Except for the texts mentioned on p. 172 and in note 33 below the verb does not occur in the Apostolic Fathers (I Clemens 20:9 μεταπαραδιδόασιν ἀλλήλοις of the seasons "to give place to each other" is quite different).

[33]   An interesting series of texts will be found in O. Casel, *De Philosophorum graecorum silentio mystico* (Giessen, 1919), 5, 11, 31, 53, 56, 82, 94, 101, 103, 105-106, 113. It is often found in Magical Papyri for passing on the information in these books to other people. In van Unnik, "Aphthonoos", *passim* I have also collected and discussed a good many texts which show the use of μεταδιδόναι with regard to religious teachings. For teaching see also Isocrates, *Or.* XIII, against teachers of political rhetoric ταύτης τῆς δυνάμεως οὐδὲν οὔτε ταῖς ἐμπειρίαις οὔτε τῇ φύσει τῇ τοῦ μαθητοῦ μεταδιδόσιν .We may also add here two important Christian texts: Barnabas 1:5 on his purpose ὅτι ἐὰν μελήσῃ μοι περὶ ὑμῶν τοῦ μέρος τι μεταδοῦναι ἀφ'οὗ ἔλαβον... he was diligent to send something in order that they should have together with their faith perfect knowledge. Hippolytus, *De Antichristo* 1, there is great danger that this teaching is entrusted to unbelievers and blasphemers; μετάδος δὲ αὐτὰ εὐλαβέσι καὶ πιστοῖς ἀνθρώποις, referring to Paul's words in I Tim. 6:20 ff., 2 Tim. 2:1 ff.; if the apostle was so careful, how greater risk shall we run εἰ ἁπλῶς καὶ ὡς ἔτυχε τὰ θεοῦ λόγια μεταδώσομεν βεβήλοις καὶ ἀναξίοις ἀνδράσιν;

[34]   See van Unnik, "Aphthonoos", for the evidence.

but sharing. In this way the status of the other man either for this world or for life eternal is raised.

In practically all texts, this precious thing (gift, status, knowledge) is fully expressed. Usually it is expressed in the genitive, sometimes in the accusative. The beneficiary is mentioned in the dative. There are some cases in which μεταδιδόναι is used in an absolute sense, but then the object is implied in the context; so in Polybius XXIX 27,4 after the king had read the letter ἔφη βούλεσθαι μεταδοῦναι τοῖς φίλοις περὶ τῶν προσπεπτωκότων and XXXVIII 8,1 τοῦ δὲ Γολόσσου μεταδόντος τῷ στρατηγῷ περὶ τῶν εἰρημένων,[35] it is to share information which is important for future events.

As was said before, the difficulty, almost unsurmountable in Rom. 12:8, is the fact that μεταδιδούς is used here without appositions in an absolute sense, and the context in this case does not offer any help, not even in an implicit way.

In the light of the material both in Paul and in Greek texts nothing compels us to think that μεταδιδόναι refers here particularly to almsgiving. Since in 1 Thess. 2:8 it stands parallel with λαλῆσαι (verse 2) and κηρύσσειν (verse 9) and the verb is frequently used by the Greeks for communication of revelations, it can also be taken in that sense. The argument of B. Weiss and Lagrange, viz. that "das geistliches Mittheilen bereits vorher in seinen besonderen Formen erledigt ist",[36] does not carry weight. It should be noticed that μεταδιδόναι as an indication for communicating religious knowledge is something different from "teaching" and "comforting" and "prophecy". In the Pauline epistles the Christian instruction has a great variety of forms, as may be easily seen from the apostle's vocabulary (cf. e.g. the combination and difference of λόγος σοφίας and λόγος γνώσεως in 1 Cor. 12:8). And finally much depends on the way in which we construct Rom. 12: 7-8 (see below).

It may be remarked that the word ἁπλότης agrees well with this conception of μεταδιδόναι = to communicate or share religious knowl-

---

[35] Cf. H. G. Liddell, R. Scott and H. Stuart Jones, A Greek-English Lexicon, 9th ed. (Oxford, 1940), 1111, s.v.
[36] B. Weiss, Brief des Paulus an die Römer (see p. 171). But given this interpretation, it is not self-evident why later ὁ ἐλεῶν is mentioned, because this word is usually taken in the sense of a man who practises the "deeds of love" mentioned in rabbinical literature, see Barrett, A Commentary, 239. 2 Cor. 9:7 has the combination of cheerfulness with giving: ἱλαρὸν γὰρ δότην ἀγαπᾷ ὁ θεός, which is a reminiscence of Prov. 22:8 LXX, a passage in which also sowing and reaping are mentioned; this verse is followed in verse 9 ὁ ἐλεῶν πτωχόν (this expression also in Prov. 14:21, 19:17, 28:8).

edge. The astrologue Vettius Valens, who has declared ἄφθονον τὴν μετάδοσιν ποιησόμεθα (IV 11, 172 Kroll), says in one of his autobiographical passages: ἂν πλειστάκις περὶ τῆς ἐμῆς ἀφθονίας καὶ ἁπλότητος ὑπομιμνήσκω (VII 5, 301).[37] The same combination is found in Ode of Solomon 7: 3 (the Lord) "has shown Himself to me without grudging in His simplicity".[38] Two texts in Barnabas are important. Barnabas 8: 2 νοεῖτε πῶς ἐν ἁπλότητι λέγει ὑμῖν, then follows the explanation of the Red Heifer (Num. 19: 2 ff.). Cf. the note of Windisch:

will wohl sagen, dass es ein überaus einleuchtendes und leicht verständliches Mittel ist, an der Hand einer solchen Zeremonie die Geheimnisse der Erlösung darzustellen....[39]

Barnabas 17: 1 ἐφ'ὅσον ἦν ἐν δυνατῷ καὶ ἁπλότητι δηλῶσαι ὑμῖν things that refer to salvation. The "simplicity" is the manner in which God's mysteries are made plain to the believers.[40] In this way the *metadosis* of which the author has spoken in the beginning (1: 5, cf. p. 177, n. 33) is given to the readers in simple terms. In this connection it is also interesting to read the following description of the apostolic preaching in Ps. Clem. Hom. I 11,4 οὐ γραμματικὴν ἐπαγγελλόμενοι τέχνην, ἀλλὰ ἁπλοῖς καὶ ἀπανούργοις[41] λόγοις τὴν αὐτοῦ (of God) βούλησιν ἐκφαίνοντες, ὡς πανθ' ὀντιναοῦν ἀκούσαντα νοεῖν τὰ λεγόμενα.[42] Here the word ἁπλοῦς is used in a significant way in

---

[37]   See the evidence in van Unnik "Aphthonoos", 39-46.

[38]   Translation of J. Rendel Harris and A. Mingana, *The Odes and Psalms of Solomon* 2 (Manchester, 1920), 240, and my discussion of this text in W. C. van Unnik, "De ἀφθονία van God in de oudchristelijke literatuur", in *Mededelingen der Koninklijke Nederlandse Akademie van Wetenschappen*, afd. Letterkunde, Nieuwe Reeks, deel 36, nr. 2 (Amsterdam, 1973), 7-8.

[39]   H. Windisch, *Der Barnabasbrief* (Tübingen, 1920), 348.

[40]   See also 6:5 ἁπλούστερον ὑμῖν γράφω ἵνα συνιῆτε. In the text of Hippolytus, *De Antichristo* 1, quoted before p. 177, n. 33, ἁπλῶς is used in an unfavorable sense' but that depends there on the context. With the meaning of "without further ado" it is often found in Greek literature.

[41]   Cf. Paul in 1 Thessalonians 2 for his preaching which is in sharp contrast with that of others; 2 Cor. 4:2 μὴ περιπατοῦντες ἐν πανουργίᾳ μηδὲ δολοῦντες τὸν λόγον τοῦ θεοῦ and Eph. 4:14 ἐν πανουργίᾳ πρὸς τὴν μεθοδείαν τῆς πλάνης. Philo, *De Opif. mundi* 156, has an interesting combination though ἁπλότης is used here of simplicity of human character: after eating the fruit in Paradise τοῦτ'ἐξαπιναίως ἀμφοτέρους ἐξ ἀκακίας καὶ ἁπλότητος ἠθῶν εἰς πανουργίαν μετέβαλεν. Cf also 2 Cor. 1:12 Paul's boat is the witness of his conscience ὅτι ἐν ἁπλότητι (var. ἁγιότητι) καὶ εἰλικρινείᾳ τοῦ θεοῦ, οὐκ ἐν σοφίᾳ σαρκικῇ, ἀλλ' ἐν χάριτι θεοῦ ἀνεστράφημεν ἐν τῷ κόσμῳ.

[42]   See also Hermes Trismegistos XVI, where Hermes says of the Egyptian books in their original language δόξει τοῖς ἐντυγχάνουσί μου τοῖς βιβλίοις ἁπλουστάτη εἶναι ἡ σύνταξις καὶ σαφής, but through translation in Greek they have been spoilt and become unclear.

contrast with the rhetorical trics which deceived men with words, which made the simple truth complicated and unintelligible; the gospel is preached in plain words, so that every man can understand it.

As is well known, the Christian mission had to find its way in a world in which there were many competing preachers of salvation, philosophers, sorcerers, adherents of mystery religions, astrologers, etc.; many gods and many ways to blessedness were revealed. The secrets were wrapped in darkness to be opened only to the initiated. When in this context the word ἁπλότης is used, it means the end of all veiled, secret truth; the preacher of the gospel should bring his message in plain words, so that all can understand it. So the word fits well the verb μεταδιδόναι in the sense of communicating the riches of the gospel.

This aspect of ἁπλότης is of course not the only one. The others that have been mentioned before (see p. 173) also make a good sense in this connection. Many of these preachers of religious knowledge enviously guarded their secrets; they were proud of their powerful possession that opened the doors to heavenly and earthly happiness. Had not Paul given the warning to the Corinthians that "knowledge puffs up" (I Cor. 8: 1)? The apostle had good reasons to start the pericope of our text with the admonition (phrased in Greek with a rhetorical wordplay!): μὴ ὑπερφρονεῖν παρ' ὃ δεῖ φρονεῖν, ἀλλὰ φρονεῖν εἰς τὸ σωρονεῖν (Rom. 12: 3).[43]

This brings us back to our starting point, Romans 12: 8, and the whole passage of which it is a part.

In practically all editions and commentaries a new sentence starts at verse 6 ἔχοντες δέ.[44] I have often wondered why that is done; Lietzmann, for example, even had to supplement it with a fairly long addition[45] or ἔχοντες has to be taken as ἔχομεν. In my view the parallelism in verses 4 ff. points in another direction. Paul here applies to the

---

[43] See ἁπλῶς in a long series of virtues Marcus Aurelius, *Eis Heauton* VI 30 τήρησον οὖν σεαυτὸν ἁπλοῦν, ἀγαθὸν, ἀκέραιον, σεμνόν,ἄκομψον, τοῦ δικαίου φίλον, θεοσεβῆ, εὐμενῆ, φιλόστοργον, ἐρρωμένον πρὸς τὰ πρέποντα ἔργα. Cf. A. Bonhöffer, *Epiktet und das Neue Testament* (Giessen, 1911), 108.

[44] *The Greek New Testament*, edited by K. Aland, M. Black, B. M. Metzger, A. Wikgren, has no annotation *in loco*, though it is always careful in registering all differences in punctuation. But Tischendorf in his *Novum Testamentum Graece* 2, ed. octava critica maior (Lipsiae, 1872), 430, and J. M. S. Baljon, *Novum Testamentum Graece* (Groningae, 1898), 493, have a comma.

[45] Lietzmann, *An die Römer*, 109: "Statt hinter διάφορα erst den allgemeinen Gedanken zu Ende zu führen ('so lasst sie uns auch dementsprechend benutzen'...) bringt Pls sofort Beispiele und fällt dabei aus der Konstruktion."

church the famous image of the body with its different members[46] (cf. also 1 Corinthians 12). In verse 4 he makes three points: (a) the body is one, (b) the body has many members, and (c) not all members have the same function. How are these three points matched in the sequel? Verse 5 has: one body in Christ (a); individually members one of another (b); therefore point (c) would be left over, if it did not find its complete conterpart in verse 6a ἔχοντες δὲ χαρίσματα κατὰ τὴν χάριν τὴν δοθεῖσαν ἡμῖν διάφορα. It is this last point that the apostle wishes to stress here: unity in Christ is not uniformity, but variety in the gifts of the Spirit (cf. 1 Cor. 12: 11 πάντα δὲ ταῦτα ἐνεργεῖ τὸ ἕν καὶ τὸ αὐτὸ πνεῦμα, διαιροῦν ἰδίᾳ ἑκάστῳ καθὼς βούλεται). So the image and its parallelism demands that not a full stop be put behind verse 5, but a comma.

In verses 6b-8 Paul examplifies these differences. Though there are agreements in terminology with other lists of charismata (1 Cor. 12: 8-11; 1 Cor. 12: 28; Eph. 4: 11), the catalogues cannot be squared with each other in all details. The enumeration here in Romans distinctively has four items connected with polysyndeton, followed by three with asyndeton. According to Blass, Debrunner, and Funk

polysyndeton produces the impression of the extensiveness and abundance by means of an exhausting summary; asyndeton, by breaking up the series and introducing the items staccato fashion produces a vivid and impassioned effect.[47]

Even more important, I would say, is the shift in emphasis, because in the last three items the apostle does not speak of the *activity* in which the charisma will manifest itself, but of the *spirit*, the *ethical attitude* of the Christian in which he does certain activities and in which the charisma presents itself.[48] In these last three examples Paul stresses the fact that prophecy, service, teaching, and exhortation are not in them-

---

[46] See the notes of H. Conzelmann, *Der erste Brief an die Korinther* (Göttingen, 1969), 248-249, n. 7 and 8.

[47] F. Blass, A. Debrunner, and R. W. Funk, *A Greek Grammar of the New Testament and other early Christian Literature* (Cambridge, 1961), § 460; see also § 454,3 with a reference to Rom. 2:17; with regard to εἴτε ... εἴτε cf. § 446: not disjunctive, but practically καί.

[48] H. Ridderbos, *Romeinen* (Kampen, 1959), 280, says: "*mededelen*, nl. van zijn bezit"; though these words might be taken in a spiritual sense, the whole sequence of thought and the Dutch idiom show that it is meant of material possessions. Then Ridderbos continues: "Who has received the possibility to do so (viz. to distribute) – *this is also a gift of God!* – shall do it", etc. (my translation and italics). I wonder how these italicized words can be substantiated by parallels from early Christian literature.

selves a charisma, but that the gift of grace must also show its grace in the relation to others as simplicity, zeal, and cheerfulness.[49]

We have investigated the usage of μεταδιδόναι in the Greek language. It goes without saying that my material is far from complete, but I am convinced that it is fairly representative, and at least much fuller than that of previous commentators of this text in Rom. 12: 8.

The result is that only in a few texts of Jewish and Christian origin has the verb to do with giving to the poor; even in these cases this connection is clearly expressed by indicating to whom the gift is made. On the other hand other Jewish and Christian texts employ the word in a quite different setting, so that the linguistic evidence makes it impossible to treat this verb μεταδιδόναι in itself as a *terminus technicus* for "almsgiving". Up till now I have not come across a single instance in pagan Greek literature where it has this meaning.[50] In marshalling all data at our disposal for the present moment we see that the verb describes this action: to let another person participate in precious goods one possesses. These "precious goods" may consist in material matters, but in most cases they are immaterial – status, information, education, special knowledge. We often meet the word in a context of religious knowledge which is secret and may be communicated to all man, to some special group, or to nobody.

In the light of this evidence there is no compelling reason why the word μεταδιδούς should be explained here as "almsgiving". On the contrary a different interpretation lies more at hand. I know that it is extremely difficult to abandon an exegesis that has been adopted by all modern commentators. But we are forced by Greek usage to do so. If in the future somebody wishes to maintain the – what I think – false explanation, he must present arguments derived from Greek texts and

---

[49] It is impossible to discuss here the meaning of προϊστάμενος, which is also explained in different ways, either as "the leader" or "he who gives aid", see W. Bauer, *Griechisch-deutsches Wörterbuch*, Sp. 1402, and B. Rigaux, *Saint Paul, les Épîtres*, 576-578. I mention this question here, because there is the trap of a *circulus vitiosus* here, exemplified by M. Dibelius in his explanation of 1 Thess. 5:12: "Charakteristisch ist auch, das Rom. 12:8 die Stellung von προϊστάμενος zwischen μεταδιδούς and ἐλεῶν auf Liebestätigheit weist" (also Bauer, *Griechisch-deutsches Wörterbuch*, Sp. 1402). And along the same line it may be argued that in Rom. 12:8 μεταδιδούς should be taken as "almsgiving", because it is followed by προϊστάμενος and ἐλεῶν. But that is sheer prejudice. If μεταδιδούς should be explained differently, as is argued in this paper, the whole argument is worthless.

[50] In the careful and thorough investigation of the Greek vocabulary for benevolence made by H. Bolkestein, *Wohltätigheit und Armenpflege in vorchristlichen Altertum*, (Utrecht, 1939), the verb μεταδιδόναι is missing. This is the more significant, since the Greeks had many synonyms for this activity.

not from a *communis opinio* of commentators.[51] Because the verb is used here without appositions, it is difficult to find an English equivalent that covers all shades of meaning. Since, however, this absolute use stands in a religious context, it in all probability points in the direction of participation in the riches of the Gospel.

We have tried to discover the "atmosphere" that surrounds this verb μεταδιδόναι, to lay bare the associations it has in the Greek language of Paul's days. On the strenght of our findings I would recommend as a translation:

Let he who communicates (the riches of the gospel) show his charisma in simplicity – without self-exaltation, because the riches of the gospel itself is grace.

We cannot evade here some expansion either in the translation or in notes, because the weight carried by μεταδιδόναι and ἁπλότης in the world of Paul's days is unknown to our contemporaries.

May this exercise in exegesis and translation of one little phrase in the New Testament be a small *antidoron* of this author for Nida's *metadosis*!

---

[51]　This request may seem to force a door open, but is inspired by some bad experience.

Part Two

STUDIES IN LANGUAGE AND CULTURE

MEN, GRAMMARS, AND MACHINES,
A NEW DIRECTION FOR THE STUDY OF MAN

BENJAMIN N. COLBY AND RODGER KNAUS

What do anthropology, linguistics, and artificial intelligence have in common?[1] Until recently the answer would have been, "Very little". Anthropology had been caught up in a "structuralist" phase where native terminologies and mythic symbols were described in terms of static components. Though meaning and symbol was seen as having paramount importance, anthropological structuralists were singularly oblivious to the idea of culture and communication as processes. Many linguists, on the other hand, were so involved in transformational generative processes that syntax was described as an autonomous phenomenon relatively independent of meaning structures and symbolism. Finally, early workers in the computer field were unaware of relevant developments in either anthropology or linguistics.

Now, however, the importance of process rules that can model semantic and conceptual structures is being appreciated in all three disciplines, and of the three, artificial intelligence – at least that branch which is concerned with comprehension – has cast the widest net. The search for a theory of comprehension that will result in useful computer programs is forcing us to consider important aspects of human thought we might otherwise overlook. These aspects would seem best handled by "grammars" that extend well beyond the usual notion typically held in linguistics.

We normally think of a grammar as a set of rules which, when combined appropriately, generate or analyze sentences. Using parsing and generation algorithms with a set of separately formulated rules allows a linguist to build up, experiment with, and change his description of a language in a series of successive approximations to some stable gram-

Benjamin N. Colby is Professor of Anthropology at the School of Social Sciences, University of California, Irvine, California. Rodger Knaus is Research Assistant at the School of Social Sciences, University of California, Irvine. California.
[1] Work on the Ixil divination analysis reported here was supported by National Science Foundation grant number GS-2306.

matical description that adequately accounts for a large percentage of discourse examples, and to describe processes such as parsing and generation in language-independent ways. These desirable features of a grammar have stimulated some work on similar approaches to non-linguistic cultural processes, as well as work on linguistic processes in semantics and pragmatics phenomena, which transformational generative grammar has been unable to account for.[2]

The first example of this extended application of a grammar in anthro-pology is a simple description of narrative actions called EIDOCHRONIC ELEMENTS or EIDONS. The eidochronic phenomenon has to do with the organization of plot structure into cognitive "chunks". These chunks, or eidons, represent a class of event varieties that typically occur in a sequence determined by the employment of special rules. So far our most developed analysis of eidochronic phenomena has been done for Eskimo folk tales.

The actions in Eskimo folk tales can be described as a series of re-sponses to a single motivating event. These responses can be subdivided into actions which constitute an engagement between the protagonist and an adversary (usually) and a series of actions which provide a resolution to the problem originally created in the motivating event of the story. Thus a simple Eskimo story (Move) contains one eidon in a Motivation category (M) and various combinations of eidons in Engagement (E) and Resolution (R) categories:

$$1. \text{ Move} \longrightarrow \widehat{M \ \text{Resp}^n}$$

$$2. \text{ Resp} \longrightarrow \widehat{E^m \ R}$$

With these two rules we can generate such sequences as, $\widehat{M \ E \ R}$, $\widehat{M \ E \ E \ E \ R}$, $\widehat{M \ E \ R \ E \ R}$, but not $*\widehat{M \ E \ R \ R}$ or $*\widehat{M \ R \ E}$. Additional rules for lower-level elements of Eskimo stories are described elsewhere (Colby 1973a; 1973b).

As an example of lower-level events, one of the Engagement eidons in Eskimo folk tales is characterized as "challenge" because it involves some action on the part of the protagonist which is designed to bring the antagonist into an engagement or struggle; or, conversely, it involves

[2]   Among the more interesting recent critiques of transformational generative theory is one by Watt (1972) who contrasts the objectives of transformational generative grammars with mental (psycholinguistic) grammars. The issue of competence vs. performance models is shown by Watt to be a cover for a fatal inadequacy of trans-formational theory.

an action on the part of the adversary to engage the protagonist. For instance, the hero might be challenged to a game, contest, or fight. Or the protagonist might ridicule or otherwise provoke the adversary into a fight. The conventional "narrative logic" we carry in our heads would expect this action to take place before, rather than after, a struggle and would expect a victory to occur after, rather than before, a struggle. Thus if we characterize part of an Eskimo story as involving a challenge followed by a struggle and then by a victory, we are probably talking about a typical pattern which, in different details, is universal.

More specialized actions, such as possession (where the protagonist gains permanent possession of game, fish, or other food, succeeds in persuading a woman to marry him, or takes possession of a house and/or wives of another), present a more unique syntactic relationship. It is hard for someone not familiar with Eskimo stories to predict where the action we have labeled as possession might take place with respect to the challenge – struggle – victory sequence. Yet the location of the possession eidon follows a specific rule.

At this stage of understanding, it looks as though we are dealing with a set of rules that are similar to a syntactic grammar. The eidochronic rules transcend the sentence and represent the narrative action at a higher level and in a different system than what is accounted for by a language grammar. In the Eskimo stories there appear to be six intermediate categories of eidons; value motivation, immediate motivation (only one motivation category can appear per story unit or move), preliminary action, main action, immediate resolution, and value resolution.[3]

We are currently at the beginning of our studies of Ixil Maya narrative collected in the Guatemalan highlands. In the Ixil data it looks as though the eidochronic grammar has four, rather than three, basic categories of eidons: motivation – consequences – appeal – answer. At this stage we see no intermediate level. These basic, but tentative categories are illustrated in the diagram below:

THE MOUNTAIN GOD (an Ixil folktale)
1. Move   ———→Injury + Restitution
2. Injury   ———→ Motivation + Consequences
3. Restitution ——→ Appeal + Answer
4. Motivation   ——→ Wrongdoing

---

[3]   The empirical basis for determining the boundaries of these categories is given in Colby (1973b).

5. Consequences → Transport + Interrogation + Hospitality +
   Explanation
6. Appeal ⎯⎯⎯→ Appeal
7. Answer ⎯⎯⎯→ Instruction + Release

The basic plot of Ixil, Eskimo, or any other narrative, being concerned with the sequencing of narrative events and actions, constitutes the eidochronic component of what we would thus call a narrative grammar. There are other components of a narrative grammar as well. The poetic component, for instance, concerns the choice of words, their rhythm, and similar matters connected to the language of the narration. This component is a separate system in itself and, unlike some of the other components, obviously must be analyzed in the original language. Another component is the dramatic or highlighting component. This is the part of narrative which deals with various highlighting processes that heighten interest in the narrative and focus the attention of listeners or readers on particular aspects of a narrative. Such devices as repetition of events, contrast, and limitations on the number of characters in a scene are among the kinds of highlighting that occur in the dramatic component. There is also the linguistic component itself which includes the phonetic, syntactic, and semantic aspects of the language in which the story is told, and finally there is the symbolic component which includes metaphoric, metonymical, and synecdochic relations which are concerned with the symbolic significance of objects, characters, and less frequently, some of the actions of the story.

While the eidochronic component of traditional narratives is most easily discerned in folk tales, the symbolic component predominates in myths. Unlike folk tales which have more of a cognitive or "cerebral" quality (in that their actions follow rationally out of each other in the "narrative logic" we spoke about earlier), the myths tend toward the "irrational". The symbolism of myth is highly saturated; the symbolic objects carry a maximum of meaning, not all of which is coherent or synonymous. Body parts, artifacts, and common natural and cultural elements of the environment are all so much a part of an individual's world from his earliest memory that they are bound to be imbued with a rich variety of deep-seated meanings. These meanings are drawn upon during fresh metaphorical and mythical usage and probably during the dream process as well. The symbolic component, consisting of these more nebulous qualities, is difficult to analyze. Attempts at describing this component are still in the prescientific stage, and it may be necessary to develop our knowledge of how the eidochronic component operates in a wide variety of genres and cultures before we can discover how best to work with the symbolic component which interdigitates with it.

It is important to recognize that these five narrative components are not merely levels of a single hierarchical system but instead represent entirely separate systems. Each component requires its own theoretical framework and analytical approaches. If grammars can be developed for these other components of an overall narrative grammar they may be very different in character from the eidochronic rules that were developed for the Eskimo stories.

In the quest for narrative regularities one must consider that just as a linguist cannot construct a grammar after hearing only two or three sentences of a new language, an analyst who seeks to work out an eido-chronic grammar must look at many more than two or three stories from the particular group he is studying. Nor can one select stories from all over the world or even from continents any more than one can write a single grammar of the different languages of a continent. To be sure, there are interesting linguistic universals being discussed and tested now; but to do any meaningful work with universal elements, one must first have worked out replicable analyses of particular narrative cultures.

The extension of grammar to include narrative and many other kinds of cultural processes can be thought of in terms of problem solving. The rules of a problem-solving grammar, when used by a parsing-like algorithm, decompose the original problem into a series of subproblems and simple solution elements. The rules also indicate how these parts of a solution are to be combined to solve the given problem. This viewpoint can be illustrated with a problem domain familiar to linguists and language-oriented artificial intelligence scientists – automated parsing.

In parsing, when a terminal symbol is encountered in constructing a derivation, the parser tries matching the terminal against the appropriate symbol in the string being parsed. The terminal symbol represents a problem of finding a string symbol at some specified point in the string which matches the terminal. This problem is elementary in the sense that the parser can immediately decide whether the terminal and string symbols match.

A nonterminal corresponds to a nonelementary problem. The parser cannot use a simple test to decide if there is a derivation corresponding to the nonterminal. Instead, it must use a rewriting rule to decompose the problem of finding the derivation into finding derivations for each of the symbols on the right side of the rule. If these subproblems are solved, the solutions can be combined into a derivation for the nonterminal. However, if one of the subproblems fails, the particular decomposition into subproblems which the rule represents fails to solve the problem represented by the nonterminal. If all the rules fail to solve the problem, the problem itself has no solution.

The following problem-solving procedure, called PROBLEM REDUCTION, corresponds to a simple top-down parser:

Solve (problem) =

    If the problem is elementary, then if it has solutions, return them, or else return failure. Or else apply Solve 1 to the list of problem expansions obtained by applying rules to the problem. If any solutions are found, return them, or else return failure.

where

Solve 1 (expansion) =

    Apply solve to each problem in expansion. If any fail, return the empty list. Or else return the list of all solutions obtained from solutions to problems in expansion.

Figure 1 shows the result of parsing *The cat is on the mat* using problem reduction with the grammar.

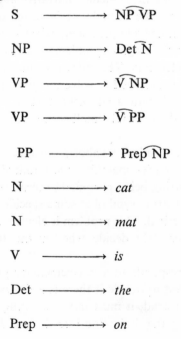

S	$\longrightarrow$	NP͡ VP
NP	$\longrightarrow$	Det͡ N
VP	$\longrightarrow$	V͡ NP
VP	$\longrightarrow$	V͡ PP
PP	$\longrightarrow$	Prep͡ NP
N	$\longrightarrow$	*cat*
N	$\longrightarrow$	*mat*
V	$\longrightarrow$	*is*
Det	$\longrightarrow$	*the*
Prep	$\longrightarrow$	*on*

Descending line segments connect a problem with subproblems generated from it. Groups of subproblems which must all be solved to solve the parent problem are joined with an arc. Groups of subproblems not joined by an arc represent alternative solutions for the parent problem. Problems which failed to be solved are indicated by cross-hatching the segment leading to them.

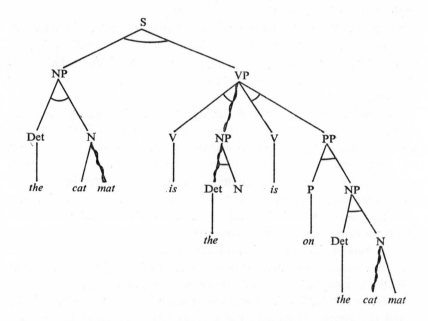

Computer programs based on problem reduction have been written for a number of problem domains, including symbolic logic (Newell, Shaw, and Simon 1963; Siklossky, Rich, and Marinov 1973), Euclidean plane geometry (Gelernter 1963; Goldstein 1973), and integration (Slagle 1963).

In linguistics, the rules of a grammar can rewrite strings. But in problem-solving programs, the rules transform data structures, such as nested property lists or logical formulas. Corresponding to the left side of a grammar rule is a predicate which tests problem states for rule applicability. If the rule applies, a procedure corresponding to the right side of a linguistic rule transforms the state. A program built out of such predicate-transformation rules under the control of an algorithm such as problem reduction is called a production rule program. Recently, several such programs have been written to explore models of human behavior. T. Moran (1973) has written a program to analyze line drawings and store the resulting information in a high level data structure. From this data structure, the program simulates a verbal protocol which a subject might give while analyzing the drawing. The purpose of the program is to show that a hierarchical semantic structure, rather than a photo-like image, contains enough information for constructing the protocol. The main processes required by the program are each implemented with a set of production rules.

Newell and Waterman have used a set of rule-implemented procedures to analyze verbal protocols from subjects solving cryptoarithmetic problems. The program attempts to analyze the protocol as the verbalization of a problem reduction procedure used by the subject in solving the problem.

An application of a problem-solving approach in anthropology was developed by the authors in a program that generates Ixil-Mayan sickness divinations. Using Mayan astrological data, personal data about the client, and simulated data from a divination ritual, the program uses a set of around sixty divination construction rules in a simple problem-solving program to construct possible divinations. Another set of rules selects a final divination from the set of generated possibilities. Examples of divination-constructing rules are:

"A human victim of a sin may avenge the sin"

"If a particular relative or dead ancestor of the victim is suggested by the astrological data, that relative may be the avenger"

"If the god having dominion over the sin is suggested astrologically and the avenger is human, the avenger has appealed to the god for justice and the god has punished the client"

In the computer, each rule is represented as a small program. The purpose of the program is to study the principles of divination which the Ixil-Maya use. While the Ixil priests feel that their divinations are deterministic, they are unable to state rules to produce them. The output of the program, however, can be compared to actual divinations; if necessary, the divination rules can be modified to bring about closer agreement between program and priest. After repeating this process as necessary, one would obtain a set of rules adequate for the limited range of divination being studied.

The present rules used by the program represent an early stage in this process of approximation. Below is an actual divination followed by the program's divination:

Client Property list: The client is a sick adult female with a dead father and grand-father.

Active calendar days and day names:

11 Thunder

2 Snake

11 Tooth

Priest's divination: Female client once angered a man. The man is performing witchcraft against her.

Program's divination:

Sin:	Envy
Victim:	Man
Punishment:	Witchcraft
Outcome:	Recovery

The example programs described above illustrate the usefulness of the computer in developing problem solvers using problem-solving "grammars". The computer allows detailed study of a particular rule set impossible by hand. Using a program guarantees that the problem solver has been correctly and objectively applied to its problems. The relative ease of changing the rules in a problem solver encourages the social scientist to experiment with variations of his developing problem solver.

In addition to the tasks already mentioned, computer programs have proved simple mathematical theorems, played above-novice chess, done simple computer programming, carried on dialogs in nearly natural language on restricted subjects, and simulated paranoia. Programs have drawn analogies and taken advice from nonprogrammer chess experts. Such programs show that symbol manipulation and problem solving can be done by a machine, within limits imposed by its speed, size, and complexity.

An artificial intelligence program is useful as a possible theory about how a subject performs some action. For example, the Ixil divination program uses a rule that examines all possible divinations that can be generated by a particular choice of day names and then chooses that divination which is most serious. Viewing the program as a theory about divination, one might predict and attempt to verify or disprove this hypothesis about the priest's divination. Obviously, the mere coincidence of result is no implication that the generator rules for the two are the same, but the program at least gains credibility as a theory. It also will have performed the useful purpose of insuring that key input variables are not overlooked.

A computer program, like a geometrical figure, is a precisely defined mathematical object. Writing a program to represent a theory forces the social scientist to state his theory precisely. Questions about the implications of a theory stated as a program may be answered either empirically by running the program, or theoretically by proving a theorem about the program. Furthermore, although such studies are not yet common, the above examples suggest that symbolic computer programming is an ideal formalism for expressing cognitive operations for certain cultural processes.

The development of grammars for nonlinguistic cultural processes will often require attention to that aspect of symbolic behavior described as pragmatics. By pragmatics we mean the assumptions, inferences, and beliefs that accompany our communicative behavior. Anaphoric references and other processes which have received increasing attention in linguistics of late (Watt 1973) will require the modeling of thought processes and problem-solving behavior in ways that may be similar to what we have discussed.

As we think more of human behavior in terms of grammars that can be clearly described in a set of rules or that can be represented as computer programs, we run up against a crucial question that is likely to have increasing importance in the future. Although no computer program written or imagined in reasonably concrete form can exhibit anything at all that resembles human intelligence, the range of problem-solving activities that have previously been thought unique to the human mind but which now have become "mechanical" is increasing steadily. In their different ways, the computer and the chimpanzee show that the symbol manipulator must join the tool maker as not necessarily human. In the past anthropology has concerned itself with many interesting questions about the relations between modern and primitive man and between man and animal. We must now address ourselves equally to questions about man and machine. One such question would be: to what extent is the activation of a grammar a merely mechanical process? Questions such as this one will be crucial for any theory of cultural processes or cognitive behavior that may be offered in the coming years.

REFERENCES

Colby, Benjamin N.
   1973a "A Partial Grammar of Eskimo Folktales", *American Anthropologist* 75, 645-662.
   1973b "Analytical Procedures in Eidochronic Study", *American Journal of Folklore* 86, 14-24.
Colby, Kenneth M., Franklin Hilf, Sylvia Weber, and Helena Kraemer
   1972 "Turing-Like Indistinguishability Tests for the Validation of a Computer Simulation of Paranoid Processes", *Artificial Intelligence* 3: 3.
Feigenbaum, Edward A., and Julian Feldman (eds.)
   1963 *Computers and Thought* (New York: McGraw-Hill).
Gelernter, H.
   1963 "Realization of a Geometry Proving Machine", in Feigenbaum and Feldman (eds.), *Computers and Thought* (New York: McGraw-Hill), 134-152.
Goldstein, Ira
   1973 "Elementary Geometry Theorem Proving", manuscript.
Koffman, Elliot B., and Sumner E. Blount
   1973 "Artificial Intelligence and Automatic Programming in CAI", *Third International Joint Conference on Artificial Intelligence* (Stanford, California), 86.
Moran, Thomas
   1973 "The Symbolic Nature of Visual Imagery", *Third International Joint Conference on Artificial Intelligence* (Stanford, California), 472-478.
Newell, Alan, J. C. Shaw, and H. A. Simon
   1963 "Empirical Explorations with the Logic Theory Machine: A Case Study in Heuristics", in Feigenbaum and Feldman (eds.), *Computers and Thought* (New York: McGraw-Hill), 109-133.
Siklossky, L., A. Rich, and V. Marinov
   1973 "Breath-First Search: Some Surprising Results", *Artificial Intelligence* 4:1, 1-28.
Slagle, James R.
   1963 "A Heuristic Program that Solves Symbolic Integration Problems in Freshman Calculus", in Feigenbaum and Feldman (eds.), *Computers and Thought* (New York: McGraw-Hill), 191-206.
Waterman, D. A., and Alan Newell
   1973 "Pas-ii: An Interactive Task-Free Version of an Automatic Protocol Analysis System", *Third International Joint Conference on Artificial Intelligence* (Stanford, California), 431-445.
Watt, William
   1972 *Competing Economy Criteria* (= *Social Science Working Papers* 5) (Irvine, Ca.: School of Social Sciences, University of California, Irvine).
   1973 *The Indiscreteness with which Impenetrables are Penetrated* (= *Social Science Working Papers* 20) (Irvine, Ca.: School of Social Sciences, University of California, Irvine).
Zobrist, Albert L., and Frederic R. Carlson, Jr.
   1973 "An Advice-Taking Chess Computer", *Scientific American* 228:6, 92-105.

LINGUISTICS AND PHILOLOGY

H. A. GLEASON, JR.

Unhappily, neither major term in this title is understood in the same way by everyone. Few scholars would give a second thought to the popular notion of a linguist as a speaker of many languages. But beyond that negative consensus, I dare say we would find somewhat less than overwhelming agreement as to the exact limits of linguistics. But this is of little consequence, as I shall restrict my attention, apart from a few moot points I want to discuss, to one endeavor which I trust we all agree has some central place: the analysis and description of specific languages, the yield of which is grammars. This is central, not only because it is the major research effort of the majority of linguists, but also because, as most of us recognize, it is a prerequisite for most, if not all, of the other activities which any one of us might wish to include within linguistics.

"Philology" presents as great a problem. Some linguists hardly use the term at all, and seem not to miss it. Some use it as a near synonym for "linguistics". For many it is simply an unknown alien territory just outside the bounds of their interest. For most, perhaps, it is a somewhat broader and less sharply focused discipline which overlaps linguistics to some extent.

As before, I am focusing on only one component, one which I believe to be central: the description of texts. It is, again, centrality that I advance as justification for using the term philology for this fragment, in some ways the counterpart of the portion of linguistics that concerns me in this article.

One way of putting the difference and the relation is the following:

H. A. Gleason, Jr., is Professor of Linguistics at the Centre for Linguistic Studies, University of Toronto, Toronto, Ontario. This paper was delivered at the annual meeting of the Canadian Linguistics Association (June 1969).

Linguistics, at least potentially, deals with those things which are common to all texts in a given language, whereas philology deals with those things which are peculiar to specific texts.

Such a distinction is old, probably as old as the separation of the two disciplines. But it has been clouded over recently by a peculiarly unfortunate bit of folklore popular among linguists – the notion that the description of languages was forsaken during the "Bloomfieldian interlude" in favour of description of corpora, that is, of collections of texts and other materials. If this were true, it would make Bloomfieldian linguistics a most vacuous aberration, for the true philologist selects the texts he studies for their assumed intrinsic worth, whereas the Bloomfieldian spurned any such consideration and seemed to prefer materials of negligible significance per se.

It would seem, on the face of it, improbable that intelligent men would behave so irrationally. And of course they did not. The Bloomfieldians as linguists had no interest in descriptions of corpora, and well understood that a grammar could not be anything of the sort.

The folklore is rooted in an error of historical interpretation. Bloomfieldians did use collocations like "describe a corpus", but always, as close examination will show, elliptically for "describe the language exemplified in a corpus". That this was their intention is abundantly clear from their continual wrestling with the problem of discriminating systematic gaps from accidental gaps, a question totally meaningless in the context of describing a corpus.

More troubling to me is the fact that the accusation should carry so much weight among so many linguists. The way it is often stated suggests that many see the close study of a corpus as somehow an inferior intellectual activity, perhaps not a worthwhile task at all. It indicates that the uncharitable attitude toward text that arose among some later Bloomfieldians as they reacted against ethnography and literary studies has not died, but has flourished among their heirs, to the point where it is now a serious encumberance to the profession.

I have been on a digression, though a necessary one, leading off from the notion that linguistics studies the shared features of texts (and this is what makes intrinsic valuation of little consequence in selecting a corpus), while philology studies the unique features of texts. Without some modification and further elaboration, this distinction is inadequate or untenable. We must look at it from three directions:

First, "unique" and "shared" are complementary terms, meaningful primarily by their contrast. The unique features can only be characterized, described, or given significance against a background of shared features, and vice versa.

An important implication follows: the linguist and the philologist, at a fundamental level in their work, share the central task of separating the unique from the general in a corpus. Only after they have made the separation do the two react in opposing ways. Each puts out of central consideration that which the other focuses upon. Hence, at some stage of their operations, linguistics and philology might profitably share much of the same methods. Perhaps, indeed, they should share the actual operation of the methods, that is, they might pursue part of their tasks jointly.

Second, there are features in texts not shared by all the texts in that language, even potentially, and yet not unique to individual texts. Prominent here are matters that are commonly mentioned under the ill-defined rubrics "genre" and "style". It is unclear whether these are properly assigned to linguistics, to philology, to a third discipline distinct from both, to a hyphenated joint enterprise, or should be divided between the two in some way yet to be found. Certainly they fall outside linguistics as it has traditionally been practiced, since linguists have tended to act as if genre and style did not exist, "at least not in my texts". Philologists have given them more attention, but seldom have gone much beyond the specific manifestations, in which form they are certainly within their jurisdiction.

Third, we should look more closely at the material the linguist uses in his analysis. He has three major kinds of data for the description of a language, and, as long as he stays with that central activity of linguistics, hardly more than these three, plus some intergrades and mixtures. These are: elicited material, text, and what is misleadingly called "intuition about language".

The latter should certainly be given no more than subordinate status, though in recent times it has been popular to give it pride of place, at least in statements of procedure. There is a great deal to be said for the notion that a language is in fact identical with the native speaker's intuition about his language, though I myself would prefer a somewhat different formulation. The fallacy is in confusing intuition about language with perception of that intuition. Our most fundamental convictions about the psychology of speech should warn us against this. Language is operated out of awareness, and it is important that it should be so. Whatever may be the nature of our language mechanism, it is presumably organized precisely in such a way as to keep its own operation far in the background. Or, putting it another way, language is designed for the convenience of the average user, not that of the linguist; their demands are often directly opposed. Therefore, introspection should be highly misleading, as I think empiric evidence confirms.

Notice that a distinction must be maintained between intuition about language competence, *langue* if you prefer, and intuition about bits of language performance, *parole*. With regard to the latter the native speaker should be able to say something worthy of close attention. But this is not so much another working basis for linguistic analysis as a commentary on the corpus, though it is valuable marginalia.

The Bloomfieldian, in his programmatic statements, dismissed ALL intuition. In practice, of course, he did quite otherwise. The Chomskyan, in his programmatic statements, accepts only native speaker intuition. In practice, inevitably, he does quite otherwise. It has been repeatedly pointed out that Chomsky rests most of his published argumentation on corpus.

Elicited material and text are commonly lumped together as "corpus" in contradistinction from introspection. That is one of several reasons why the distinction between the two has not been examined as closely as it might.

The common distinction between elicitation and text rests on the control which the linguist exercises over the form and content of the material. When this is zero, as in fortuitously overheard utterances, or minimal, when he asks merely "Tell me a tale", or "Tell me how you plant rice", the material is called "text". When it is collected by requests comparable to: "Translate for me 'My aunt's pen is on the table'", it is "elicited".

We traditionally assume that there is a certain artificiality in elicited material, and a contrasting spontaneity and naturalness in text. And so, we say that text is the preferable basis for a grammar, but our actual practice is not always thus. Most linguists make much less extensive and effective use of their text materials than they do of their elicited words, phrases, and sentences.

Why? Simply because it is easier that way. And it is easier for several reasons, not all of which are universally recognized, though several are worth examining for what they can tell us about language and about linguists.

It is a commonplace, now, that the features of language vary in frequency in a way that Zipf first brought forcibly to our attention. It is doubtful that this fact has much theoretical significance, but it does have immense practical implications. The least frequent features are infrequent indeed, while the most frequent ones are bothersomely plentiful. That means that we have to handle a large mass of text material of minimal value to get an adequate exemplification of some of the rarer constructions. But because of the intermeshed systematic nature of language, some of these rarer items are crucial. Handling text, then, becomes exceedingly laborious at the paper-doll-cutting level.

A major objective in any carefully designed elicitation programme is to decrease the frequency of the commonest items and to increase the frequency of the rarer ones with minimal distortion of all linguistically interesting features, that is, to change Zipf's parameters in a controlled, purposeful way. A skilled field worker is able to do just this – to produce a corpus much easier to handle and more productive in a reasonable size than any body of less planned material.

Second, even when adequately represented in text, grammatical features may be hard to find, demanding filing systems of considerable sophistication. (Computers have not yet fulfilled their promise as replacements for filing, largely because our computer programmes are by no means sophisticated enough!) But we can plan elicitation programmes to by-pass much of this, turning out material already arranged, or partially arranged. And when we fail in this prefiling, it is usually easier, if the informant is available, to go and elicit what we need than it is to find it in our existing corpus, even if abundantly attested there.

These things are familiar enough to anyone who has either observed the usual kind of professional field work or introspected into his own strategy and procedures. You will notice that all these advantages to elicitation are pragmatic on the lowest level of the physical handling of corpus material.

The commonly mentioned advantage of text is hardly any more fundamental. Features are likely to be overlooked in elicitation. Perhaps it never occurs to the linguist to ask for them. Perhaps the contact language does not provide a ready mechanism to obtain them. But they do appear in text. And so the linguist is put on the trail. Then he can go and elicit, perhaps with some more elaborate procedure, the additional examples he will need. If this is all, text is not so much a source for language data as for direction in elicitation. It is deeply subordinated.

There is, I maintain, a great deal more to the matter than that. The difference between elicitation and text is much more fundamental. It does not lie in the control of content, which linguistically may be of little consequence. It does not lie in the control of frequency, which has only practical significance. It does lie in the matter of genre and style, and hence in communicative effectiveness.

A typical competent informant replies to our elicitation in a flat uniform way that can be called "neutral" in the sense that it is out of gear, idling, doing no communicative work. But it is not simply that no communication is going on (other than the abnormal matter of transmitting linguistic information which the informant does not really understand), but the fact that the material often has little if any communicational usefulness and that what it has is not apprehended by the informant. We do not ordinarily see communicational possibilities out of communicational contexts.

Only when he gives a text is the informant likely to slip out of this neutral, nonfunctional mind-set, and communicate. To do so, he must bring into play a great deal more of the language mechanism. Among other things, good texts vary along dimensions of genre and style, seldom achieving the colorless my-aunt's-pen genre or the poker-faced style normal in elicited material. And this variation in genre and style exploits language resources not used in neutral.

This imposes an extra task on the linguist. If he wishes to use his texts fully, the linguist must first identify some of the manifestations of genre and style, that is, he must bring into play a whole new set of techniques which are more familiar to the philologist. Of course he cannot do a full philological analysis as preliminary to his own work, because such an undertaking would necessarily be in part dependent on his grammatical results. But he must delineate some broad outlines in an etic way, and he must be continually alert to pick up and use additional scraps of information about genre and style as he proceeds. That is to say, an additional dimension of analysis must be carried along concurrently through all serious work on text.

Without that, texts become of limited usefulness. Commonly they are mere mines from which the linguist can extract an occasional fragment which seems compatible with his elicited material, and which can accordingly be used as if it were elicited. For it is characteristic of genre and style that they are not manifested in a text at every point, so that judicious excision can avoid their complexities and give, as it were, neutral excerpts.

But if this is so, the excerpts from text contribute little or nothing that the elicited material cannot do just as well, and with much less effort for the linguist. So really, why bother? The use of texts is often just *pro forma*. We have been told that linguists gather them, and we bow politely to the convention.

And as a consequence, most of the texts brought back from field work lie only partially exploited in the files, with a little sample published as an appendix to that doctoral dissertation. The peculiar contribution that texts might make, as texts, never sees the light of publication.

That is the pragmatic aspect of the problem. But that is not all. Seldom do texts have that uniformity of nature which is demanded by our currently most popular ideas of language and our current methods of language analysis. Elicited words, phrases, and sentences approach it – usually closely enough to maintain the fiction. Texts – real texts – do not, and so present a theoretical challenge – I mean a challenge to our theories. This challenge we have not generally been prepared to face, or even to recognize.

Real life communicational needs call on a far wider spectrum of language features than the elicitation procedures ordinarily call forth. We all know how hard it is to get the full range of intonational patterns by the most ingenious elicitation programmes. There are syntactic patterns too which are nearly inaccessible to elicitation; they are too genre-bound or too style-bound to arise in that neutral form of language. As a result I find myself possessed of suspicions of serious deficiencies in our schemata of language organization, based, as they are, largely on the kind of language emerging from elicitation and on the mental set that has controlled elicitation.

Take for example the stratificational model as I have, myself, described it. It envisions a series of strata linking substance of content with substance of expression, cognitive perceptions of the world and human activities to vocal noises. It has at one end semology, in effect a mapping of linguistically relevant dimensions of cognitive perception not only in inventory but also in tactic. But the important thing to notice is that it is wholly or largely restricted to cognitive matters. Other dimensions of communication are not, as described, specifically provided for.

I like this model better than its competitors for several reasons, not the least because I surmise that provision for some of these other dimensions of communication can more easily be attached to it – I wish I could honestly say, be integrated into it. Indeed in the last half dozen years some rough ideas have begun to emerge as to how this can be done. Yet I must say in all honesty that this model shares, pretty largely, the common failing of all the models.

What I am in effect saying is that we are, I think, approaching the time when no linguist ought to be satisfied with any scheme of language organization which does not either provide within itself a place for certain aspects of genre and style, or provide a workable interface with some other mechanism which does. Which of these solutions turns out to be the better is a matter of indifference to me, but one or the other we must have.

This section of the discussion started from a discrimination between three kinds of linguistic data – elicitation, text, and introspection. I hope that no one will align it with the familiar controversy and construe it as an argument against the transformational-generativist's appeal to introspection in favour of a Bloomfieldian reliance on corpus. It is nothing of the kind. I am rather arguing for the primacy of text before elicited material, an issue that is immediately obscured once the word "corpus" enters. I am saying that elicitation can ordinarily give nothing more than an emaciated kind of language, a limited language in the special sense that creoles or pidgins have been called that, but without the established social basis that makes language limitation in pidgins and creoles such an interesting problem.

I am saying that linguistics should be basically a kind of text analysis. Elicitation and introspection are only secondary and tertiary techniques, of limited pragmatic usefulness, by themselves dangerous, though in two quite disparate ways.

I must pause to be sure I have forestalled a misunderstanding. I am not advocating a new kind of corpus description, but corpus-based language description. Its subject matter is the potentialities of text formation. With this in mind the fundamental distinction from which we started remains. Linguistics concerns itself with those things potentially common to all texts in a given language, whereas philology concerns itself with those things unique to particular texts, including the particularities of exploitation of language potentialities.

Because linguistics is a special kind of text analysis, it cannot neglect philology, another and complementary kind of text analysis with different but interrelated aims. At the minimum, philology must be an ancillary art; ideally, it should be a partner throughout the work.

At this point I might balance my presentation by turning and examining a question complementary to that I have been examining: how might philology make use of linguistics, and how does actual practice match the potential? This would be ungracious of me, a nonphilologist, and not much to the point in a paper directed primarily at linguists. But I will ask a related question, one more pertinent to linguists: what do the unfilled needs of philologists tell us about shortcomings in our own work? The close relationship between the two disciplines guarantees at least some relevance to such an examination. And in any case it does provide a platform from which we can view ourselves from a partially new perspective.

The first thing that I think we would see would be distressing evidence of a kind of intellectual McCarthyism, a tendency to overreact against the assumed enemy, for us not radicalism but popular folklore and traditional (that is, philological in another of its senses) approaches to language study.

From the philologist's perspective, certainly, the clearest example of this is the typical linguist's attitude toward written language. We hide behind the dogma that "only speech is language". But if a purely non-oral document is not in language, what is it in? In our more open moments we concede that writing is an "imperfect reflection of speech", but we resolutely turn our backs on the evidence whenever any bit of speech might seem to be anything like a reflection of written language.

Thus we have missed not only an important diachronic force in a language like English, but equally a whole spectrum of synchronic patterns, many of them of fundamental practical importance to us as speakers of English if not to us as linguists.

The philologist is justifiably impatient with our narrowness, not only because he finds the supporting attitudes repelling, but also because he needs, just as we need, precisely controlled information on the relation of speech and writing in all its multidimensional complexity. If this is not the linguist's responsibility, whose is it?

Language, spoken or written, is used to communicate. That means that a hearer somehow decodes the complex rope of twisted messages – cognitive meaning is only one strand – so that he may react immediately, store them for the future, or whatever. How he does this presents two fundamental challenges to two different disciplines. Psycholinguistics must face the problem as to how the human system processes the language cues in the speech form that it somehow abstracts from the substance of expression. But prerequisite to this is another task, that of specifying those cues and their modes of interaction. This must fall to linguistics.

Bloomfieldians paid lip service, at least, to this task. If they had little success, perhaps it was because there were extenuating circumstances in the limitation of data and research personnel. The Friesian subsect made this question central in their stated concern, but preferred to talk glibly, to rely on gimmickry – remember all those telegrams, headlines, and jabberwocky? – and to avoid the real issues.

The latter-day heirs of the Bloomfieldians have preferred to dismiss the problem as insoluble in principle, and hence necessarily excluded from linguistic investigation. If they are right in this, then clearly their principle must be wrong. For, in the long run, which is the more important human fact about, say, a sentence – its abstract representation, or the mechanism by which it discharges its communicative function? (If indeed the two are to be distinguished!)

There is no question but that the delineation of the signals in a sample of language and the disentangling of their communication functions is a difficult task, and one that we little understand as yet. Still, we can be quite sure that there are few simple one-to-one relations between the signals and the matters signalled. Instead there is interlocking in both directions. Single overt language features are related to several message points, and single message features are related to several signals.

This is, indeed, one reason that it is necessary to consider genre and style along with the cognitive functions of language. This interlocking extends across these lines. There are few if any items that exclusively signal genre, or style, or any of the other dimensions, and perhaps many that participate in signalling on all these dimensions. Abstracting one from the remainder is a difficult task, except when the problem can be largely avoided by restricting attention to the limited neutral language that issues from elicitation sessions.

The philologist then would like to see us produce something like interpretive grammars, aids in decoding, or descriptions of the linguistic aspects of the decoding process. His need, I feel, points to our need also.

The philologist finds our grammars inadequate to his needs in several ways. The easiest way for me to indicate what one of these may be is to hark back to my own more philological past, when I was learning Hebrew with an immediate philological objective and an ultimate theological goal. My initiation was through Davidson's venerable grammar, forty-nine dreary lessons, the first ten dealing with all the minutiae of morphographemics, and at the end a brief four chapters that contained some syntax.

Most of you, if you do not know Davidson, know its congeners. The thoroughness of treatment is roughly in inverse proportion to the philologic significance. No linguist is responsible in this particular case: Davidson was a philologist and exegete. Yet his book represents what the philologists might reasonably hope the linguists would rescue them from. The hopes have been little rewarded, and the linguists have produced more in the same mould.

To be sure, we are working on syntax more than we used to, though we are carefully keeping our results from profane eyes. More of that in a moment.

At this point I must mention our almost complete neglect of what, after all, is the real crux of the matter for the philologist, and I think, too, for us – the structure of discourse. Davidson is in the tradition; he says absolutely nothing.

Two things are responsible for our neglect. The first is the acceptance of the sentence as the upper bound of linguistic concern. For a few, this has been a matter of principle. But if I judge aright, this generation of linguists is unique in the extent to which this notion is held as dogma. It seems to me particularly difficult to defend, since I find the sentence one of the most difficult units to identify or characterize. (Many of the better efforts have defined the clause instead, a much more significant unit.)

More often in a longer sweep of linguistic history, the sentence has been looked on as a boundary of convenience. It was the goal to shoot for at the time, and it seemed to be a line that would require for its crossing some redeployment and retooling.

In a sense this is right, and this retooling has been the second factor responsible for our neglect of discourse structure.

It is in this vicinity, as you go up the ladder, that it becomes imperative to employ what I have been discussing under the rubric of philological techniques, to add to the work the parallel analysis of genre and style. It is exceedingly difficult to elicit convincing discourse samples longer than short sentences, or certainly, to elicit them with the close control that we would like. And so the corpus here must be text with all the attendant complexity.

Moreover, it is in this vicinity that syntactic methods of Bloomfieldian or various post-Bloomfieldian approaches seem to me to begin to face insurmountable difficulties. That is a moot point, but one on which some pertinent experience will soon become available. There are two approaches which until recently have been doing the greater part of this work. Tagmemics projects upwards the same methods to ever higher levels of structure. Stratificationalism sees the unity of discourse in a different sort of structure. As between the two, I have laid my bets on stratificationalism, and expect that when something better comes along, as it must, it will inherit this general notion of discourse structure in some measure.

This break in technique does not confirm the sentence as a natural unit. For in my experience, once methods have been found for working with larger units, they turn out to be superior to our older methods for working with sentence-like units. The more significant bound is the clause. Or putting it another way, I suspect that the sentence is better looked on as a small piece of discourse rather than a large syntactic construction.

I mentioned above that, though we are doing more with syntax, we are keeping much of it to ourselves. This is the consequence of the latest stages of a half-century long trend, gradually accelerating toward generative grammar. I mean toward quasi-mathematical statement with a goal of high explicitness. A generative grammar need not, you remember, be transformational, though today most are. And there is an accompanying, probably related, movement toward a totally different kind of prose when prose appears. Both of these have made grammars increasingly difficult for linguists to read, and far more so for interested scholars outside our profession.

In short, we have taken increasingly to talking to ourselves, to a kind of unilingualism which says to the outsider, "If you want to talk with us, learn our language." In the scholarly community, that is the height of irresponsibility. Linguists have emerged from the defensiveness of a distrusted minority to the arrogance of new power in the academic world. We have not yet learned either good manners or good citizenship.

Of course we must talk to ourselves, but we must also talk to others. If our scholarly neighbors and logical allies, the philologists, cannot understand us, we are failing.

So one need is to learn again to write grammars that are readable, that convey grammatical information to would-be nonlinguist users. This does not demand that we abandon the generative way of working, but that we learn to package our product in two ways for two markets.

This is for the philologist only a practical matter. For us linguists, however, it is a great deal more. We have become scornful of less formal statement, and largely oblivious of its place in the economy of scholarship. We have been hypnotized by the "scientific rigour" of formal statement, and forgotten the cost. And that is appreciable.

Every abstract formalistic model brings with it artifacts of the model, things that seem to be statements about language, but which arise wholly or largely in the requirements of the model and of the notation. And these artifacts generate pseudo-problems of various kinds. This is inevitable. We cannot even take effective steps to minimize the impact if we operate exclusively from within the model. Nonformal, simplistically data-oriented work is only partially an antedote, of course, but it can, to some extent, buffer some of the more serious side effects.

The time has come when we must cease the single-minded building of our "scientific" tower toward the heavens of full formal explicitness, lest all that result be the confusion of our metalanguages.

Almost of a piece with this over-commitment to formalism, and similar in its effects both to the profession itself and on the accessibility and usefulness of our product to philologists and others, is the elaborate series of barriers we have erected to insulate our models from the empirical base in language data. These barriers are producing a sort of schizophrenia as we move ever more toward a purely speculative discipline while making stronger and stronger pretensions of being scientific. The key to this system began innocently enough in de Saussure's distinction between *langage*, *langue*, and *parole*, was nurtured by Bloomfield's positivism, and has blossomed in the mystique of competence and performance, whose chief function is to by-pass the established conviction that no physical system can be well-defined, so that linguistics can be simultaneously generative and an explication of something within the native speaker. But the cost is high. It has become increasingly difficult to falsify theory except from an a priori commitment to an opposing theory.

And so, only an aphorism can argue the point: the only competence which is linguistically significant is the competence to process performance.

Some of these questions that I have thrown out so recklessly deserve much longer discussion, and there are some others that deserve mention in a more thorough presentation. But I make no pretence of having established my case. My intent has been rather to raise some issues, to identify a few areas where I think redirection or development is needed.

Linguists must move a little farther away from the linguistics-centered view of the universe of scholarship most succinctly formulated by the scheme that classifies our neighbouring disciplines into prelinguistics, those we need before we can start on our work, and meta-linguistics, those that need us before they can get on with theirs. I have tried to show that interdisciplinary cooperation is not something restricted to the fringes, to the hyphenated linguisticses, but an ongoing continual necessity in our central activities. I have used the example of textual philology, but the same claim could be made and defended with regard to some others also.

And especially, I would plead for a broader linguistics which can attack the increased intricacy of language as it is used in real communicative situations, by urging that our analyses be based largely on materials taken from language in use, that is, on text.

BAREFOOT IN AN ASCENDING ELEVATOR: A MEDITATION

CULTURE AND RELIGION AT THE MEETING POINT BETWEEN THE CURVE-MIND AND THE STRAIGHT-MIND

KOSUKE KOYAMA

I

Introducing the "curve-mind" (liturgical spirit) and the "straight-mind" (technological spirit).

The Kuching museum in Sarawak is one of the best museums in South East Asia. As you enter, a large glass showcase of colourful tropical birds with unusally thick and long curved beaks greets you. The second floor is full of bamboo art crafts in which bamboo has been woven into many varieties of curved shapes. There is a model display of animal, fish and bird traps made of bamboo and wood sticks. No metal is used! Traps constructed of bamboo do not give a cruel impression at all. An animal may walk into one taking a lazy afternoon stroll. Curvi-form animistic patterns of the Sarawak art are painted on the museum ceilings. The beautifully curved shape of a canoe is no doubt harmonious with Sarawak's curved streams. As you look at all these curves, you remember the mighty curves of the Sarawak rivers that fascinated your imagination as you flew overhead. You also remember the impressive curved roofs of the Buddhist temples in Bangkok, and the curved contour of the great Shwedagon Pagoda in Rangoon.

Graceful curves of all varieties invited me to begin a spiritual journey back, as it were, to the elemental structure of human psyche itself. They relaxed me. They comforted me. They whispered to me. They embraced me.

There is one room in this museum (on the ground floor to your right as you enter) which plays completely different psychological music. This room is called the Oil Room. The Oil Room demonstrates several kinds of off shore and inland oil drilling models. "Developing Sarawak!"

Kosuke Koyama is Senior Lecturer in Phenomenology of Religion at the University of Otago, New Zealand.

the signboard proclaims. I was suddenly surrounded by highly technological equipment; drills, shafts, gears, and diesel engines. I regretted
walking innocently into this room after such a lovely spiritual embrace
and dialogue in the Bamboo Room. My mental tranquility was disrupted.
Looking at these drilling models – still completely at a loss as to how the
mind of the Bamboo Room can be related to the Oil Room – I could hear
thunderous noise, smell polluted air, and see the smiling technological
men whose bank accounts are steadily increasing.

I took a deep breath as I came out of the museum. It was a "schizophrenic deep breath". A beautiful blue sky and tall coconut trees outside
the building urged me to digest what I had seen – the disconcerting and
confusing contrast between the two rooms. Am I over reacting? The
two rooms sparked off once again the irritating question with which I
have had to live for some time. Let me try to describe the psychological
impacts of these two "culture" rooms. The Oil Room expresses the
human mind which is (1) STRAIGHT (look at the straight and strong long
steel shaft), (2) FAST (look at the power of the fast engine that rotates the
enormous iron mechanism) and (3) SELF-ASSERTIVE (look at the sharp
aggressive head of the drill needles). The Bamboo Room represents
an almost exact opposite type of human mind which is (1) CURVED (look
at the graceful curves of the bamboo bird traps), (2) SLOW (look at the
model canoes and paddles) and (3) DIALOGICAL (look at all these bamboo
works harmoniously blending with surrounding nature). I must not
take this "contrast" too strictly, yet I did perceive the presence of such a
contrast. It may be said that the former represents the male outlook,
while the latter that of the female. This may be a useful observation but
I have no background for developing it.

The curved, slow, and dialogical spirit is the indigenous spirit of
Sarawak. Sarawak's mother nature is curved, slow, and dialogical.
Her self-understanding is curved, slow, and dialogical. Her history is
curved, slow, and dialogical. The Sarawak man, in his appreciation of
the relationship between his spirit and the outside world, does not travel
in the direction of a straight, fast, and self-assertive mentality. He goes,
on the contrary, towards animism (curve), symbolism (slow) and integration (dialogue). First, the animistic mind does not behave in a straight
action-reaction with man, nature, and gods. It works through the curve
made up of a variety of mediums. It travels by making an indirect approach. Souls, both human and others, are contacted personally (curve)
and not mechanically (straight). True, the Sarawak spears are sharp and
straight, but they are controlled by the curve-mind.

Second, the "Bamboo" animistic mind sees the world (mountains, trees, stones, water, birds, fish, and so on) as a living reality with various active personal souls. This mind makes the world a fascinating spiritual and dialogical environment by giving, renewing, and maintaining the imaginative mythologies and symbols. Mythologies and symbols are products of careful reflection towards the understanding of self-identity engaged over a long course of time in the life of the community. Symbols once created by man's mental and spiritual insight demand man to become mentally receptive in order to reunderstand, reintuit, and re-appreciate them. The fast mind often fails to touch the depth of symbolic messages. Symbols demand man to take time (go slow) to appreciate them. No symbols can be appreciated instantly.

Third, the mind represented in the Bamboo Room is constantly engaged in communication with the spirits of the world. Lively dialogue is ceremoniously going on always. This mind is not lonely. It has a variety of companions twenty-four hours a day. It is a community mind and community minded. It finds its meaning and structure basically in an empirical appropriation of togetherness with man, world, and gods. It is afraid of any possibility which brings forth fragmentation or partial experience of life. It desires to see man as a one integral totality against the background of the totality of the cosmos. The *adats* of Indonesia are elaborate expressions of the one decisive value of the whole in which parts find themselves. Happiness of the whole is the prerequisite for the happiness of the individual. Dr. John S. Mbiti (1973) summarizes the African spirituality in this fascinating formula: "I am because we are, and since we are therefore I am." One cannot enjoy his private happiness apart from total cosmic happiness. Totality is a DIALOGICAL community concept. Dialogue is a totality community concept.

The Bamboo Room briefly conveyed these messages to me. As I was strongly impressed by the visual lines of various curves and their psychological implications, I decided to refer to the spirituality behind the displays of the Bamboo Room as curve-spirituality. Curve-spirit-uality gives life to the curve-animistic, slow-symbolic, and dialogical-total mind. This spirituality is not a monopoly of the animistic Sarawak. On the contrary, I feel, it belongs to the deep stratum of the human spir-ituality. I am using the loaded word "spirituality" according to the tradition of the Hebrews who held that the image of "wind blowing" ("current of air" – *rûaḥ*) expresses the basic nature of spirituality. There is such a (curve, slow, dialogical) wind blowing within man's soul.

My observation of the curve-spirituality was in fact stimulated by the

strong impression of the Oil Room imprinted on my mind. I felt the
Oil Room was a threat directed at me personally. Was it because at that
time I had just finished my engrossed reading of *Only One Earth, The
Care and Maintenance of a Small Planet* by Barbara Ward and Rene
Dubos? The Oil Room does not present the best image of technology
available today. A 747 Jumbo Jet Room with shining model aircraft
would have been much more attractive. Yet, even in the context of the
ugly image of the technological drill, there is something which can be
said generally about technology. May I do so by explaining a little further
these three points.

The spirit of technology is (1) straight. Since there are so few straight
objects in the natural world, something straight to our minds is artificial.
Straight signifies efficiency. Man flying at 600 miles an hour at the altitude
of 33,000 feet is both artificial and efficient. The unartificial and inefficient
man is destined to walk on land three miles an hour. When man's kidney
deteriorates, technology comes (dialysis machine) and artificially and
efficiently cleanses the blood. Technological B52s can destroy people
and land artificially and efficiently by the enormous amount of bombs
they are capable of carrying. Artificiality and efficiency are the two major
expressions of the technological mind. It is the mind that engages constantly in the rearrangement of the "natural" and "inefficient" human
surroundings to produce "artificial" and "efficient" human surroundings.
It is, thus, a highly creative spirit.

The technological spirit is (2) fast. It is fast in the sense that it neither
tries to deal with, nor tries to express, the comprehensive truth about
man. It is not concerned with the concept of human totality. Technological mind is thus not an *adat*-istic mind. It works in specific areas with
specific subjects which carry specific meanings to human life. A washing
machine is a technological comfort to housewives. It takes care of laun-
dering. Its contribution is specific. An automobile serves in the specific
area of transportation. A printing press works in the specific area of
printing. Since these technological devices work in specifically assigned
areas they can work fast. The recently opened new Hong Kong-Kowloon
submarine tunnel is a magnificent technological achievement. Its contribution is in the specific area of transportation in Hong Kong. It enables
vehicles literally to travel fast. The 38th parallel that divides South
Korea from North Korea is a straight fast line, in the sense it is an
artificial and technological (politico-technological) line. There are a
number of politico-technological lines in Africa and Asia drawn by the
colonial masters.

No one expects the technology of a washing machine, an automobile, a printing press and a tunnel to solve the totality of human problems. These products solve only specific problems. Technological achievement is a compartmentalized (partial and fragmented) one. Technology can continually create new products but it is unable to come to the point of creative integration to produce human meaning. A washing machine plus an automobile plus a printing press plus a tunnel plus other innumerable technological products and "lines" do not and cannot cover a total and profound human need and meaning. "Behold, heaven and the highest heaven cannot contain thee" says King Solomon in his prayer at the dedication of the temple (2 Chron. 6:18). May I say, "Behold, technology and the highest technology cannot contain human spirit and meaning!" The technological mind finds itself unfamiliar with and incompetent to tackle this kind of task.

The technological mind is (3) self-assertive. Since it is free from the concern of how its creation would affect the total inner quality of human life, it can behave distinctively self-assertively. Let me illustrate this from Rangoon, Burma.

Shwedagon Pagoda stands on Rangoon's Singuttara Hill. It was built, tradition says, to enshrine the Eight Sacred Hairs of the Buddha which were given personally to the faithful visitors from Rangoon. The gold gilded pagoda is a marvel to view from nearby as well as from a distance. The visitors are required to remove shoes and socks at the foot of the hill ("... put off your shoes from your feet, for the place on which you are standing is holy ground" – Exod. 3:5). The approach itself is already in the sacred territory of the Sacred Eight Hairs. Every barefoot step prepares man to come to the presence of the holy. Every step is a liturgical step. The time spent as one walks up hill is liturgical time. Sweat you feel on your forehead is liturgical sweat. These liturgical steps, liturgical time, and liturgical sweat – curved, slow, and dialogical – are there, from older times, as the best possible arrangement for man to approach the holy. I am using the word "liturgical" meaning human community's spiritual and mental attitudes in which it carefully approaches the anticipated presence of the holy and celebrates the efficacy of the holy in relation to the community life. Man has approached the holy with the Bamboo Room mind. There is an inner congruity between liturgical mind and the Bamboo Room mind.

Recently, however, a vertical elevator was built to lift the visitors to the top of the hill, in a matter of less than a minute, to where the pagoda stands. The visitors find themselves in a "square box" which goes

up straight, fast, and self-assertively. The only liturgical element
persisting even in this case is bare feet since visitors are asked to
remove shoes and socks before entering the elevator. Bare feet in the fast
ascending elevator arouses a queer feeling. This feeling is an eloquent
psychological symbol for the presence of liturgy in the technological
way of life. The technological (Oil Room) mind asserts itself challenging
directly the historic meaning of liturgical approach (Bamboo Room)
to Shwedagon Pagoda. It does so even at the expense of destroying the
time honoured sacred view of the great pagoda.[1]

II

*Technologically prepared possibility of "the new mobile burning bush
which does not consume" and its relationship to "the old stationary burning
bush which does not consume"* (cultural dimension).

The spiritual disturbance which I felt in the Kuching museum re-
asserted itself again in a striking way within me when I found myself
in the fast ascending elevator barefoot. It was simply an unusual experience for me to ride in an elevator barefoot. A queer feeling! I was neither
completely a pilgrim nor a tourist.[2] Had I worn socks and shoes, I
would have been a happy (fast) tourist. Had I walked up the hill under
the strong Rangoon afternoon sun, I would have been a faithful (slow)
pilgrim. I was momentarily suspended between the two possibilities.
I suffered abruptly but quite consciously from the loss of my personal
identity.

[1]   The experience Dr. W. A. Visser't Hooft (1973:270) described here points to the
same issue: "In 1963 the monastic community of Mount Athos celebrated its thou-
sandth annivery. Mount Athos is a conspicuous promontory in Northern Greece
with beautiful scenery where monks of different Orthodox nations live in twenty
large monasteries and very many small communities or hermitages and form a self-
governing republic. No women are allowed to enter this self-contained world. The
Orthodox call Mount Athos 'the Holy Moutain'. I had always wanted to visit this
unique place where history has stood still and where one can get a glimpse of the
Eastern Christian world as it lived and prayed centuries ago. Now to visit this monastic
world, known as a place of total seclusion, with a large company of pilgrims from
many churches and countries, was certainly not the best way to discover its real
significance. How deeply our visit disturbed the quiet life of the monks came out
especially in the fact that we were the first visitors in the history of Mount Athos
to be transported in motor cars. At one point I saw a poorly clad monk jump away
into the bush, as if he had met with the devil himself."
[2]   This observation was made to me by Dr. William Smalley as we discussed "queer
feeling" in Bangkok.

I have never before held my own shoes with such a strange sense of clumsiness. I heard the shoes shouting at me, saying that they belonged on my feet not in my hands! Yet my bare feet kept reminding me that temporarily the shoes must be in my hands since I was on the way to the presence of the holy. With the feeling of confused indecision – somewhat similar to the unpleasant sensation of stomach indigestion – I arrived at the top of the hill. Suddenly I found myself artificially and efficiently in front of the holy. I was psychologically and philosophically prepared AND unprepared to appreciate the pagoda and its message. A beautiful blue sky and tall coconut trees outside the Kuching museum urged me to understand what I had seen there. In Rangoon my own personal identity was challenged. I had personally become a problem to myself. The disturbance was not outside me. It was now located within me.

May I say in the language of symbolism that all Burma is in this strange ("Bamboo-Oil", "pilgrim-tourist", "liturgical-technological") elevator? May I say that today all Thailand, and perhaps all South East Asia, Asia, and even the whole world is riding in this elevator and experiencing the queer feeling and indigestion within themselves, within the very texture of their culture and spirituality, even though it may not be self-evident to all of us?

The "queer feeling" took place because of the turbulent convergence of the two powerful winds (liturgical and technological) which is producing an atmospheric low pressure in which we are living. When I say that the whole world is in the elevator I am not thinking of the whole world geographically. What I wish to make clear is that the queer feeling can become a useful ("tangible") symbol through which perhaps the universal spiritual and psychological uneasiness of our world today can be expressed.

I perceived that there were two winds (the Bamboo Room curve, slow, and dialogical wind and the Oil Room straight, fast, and self-assertive wind) blowing around us in the ascending elevator. They were blowing around us yet they originated within us, the human spirit (*rûaḥ* wind). The human spirit is deeply liturgical and technological. Even the simplest and most unsophisticated liturgy does require technology in the fundamental sense. One must walk up to the top of the hill where the pagoda stands. In this case one needs a path, or a way, or steps. The concept of making a path is already a highly technological concept. The liturgical mind travels the way prepared by the technological mind. Whatever the tools used in the animistic context of sacrifice making, technology is proudly there.

Unmistakably one can see the joint operation of the liturgical mind and technological mind in the Biblical narrative of the Tower of Babel which elucidates so profoundly the spiritual and cultural climate of our own day:

Come, let us build ourselves a city, and a tower with its top in the heavens, and let us make a name for ourselves, lest we be scattered abroad upon the face of the whole earth (Gen. 11: 4).

The Ark of God was placed on the cart (I Samuel 6). Whenever and wherever man's spirit moves – the human spirit never ceases blowing (the origin and possibility of culture and civilization) – it expresses itself liturgically and technologically. Both the liturgical mind (Bamboo Room spirituality) and the technological mind (Oil Room spirituality) are as old as self-awareness of man as man. So I do not think there is such a thing as a purely technological mind or a purely liturgical mind. The human mind expresses itself mysteriously in both ways creating the "convergence".

It is important at this point for us to understand realistically that the historical performance of these two minds are poignantly ambiguous as they become at one time agents of creation, and at another agents of destruction. There are damaging superstitions, inhuman practices, and unenlightened methods of producing the necessities for life suggested in the Bamboo Room. Yet the Bamboo Room indicates profoundly and creatively to mankind that it will find its historical destiny far more satisfying and peaceful to its own well-being if it approaches nature with a curved, slow, and dialogical mind. The Oil Room suggests that its destructive power can upset even the ecological balance of this planet by making possible gigantic and fast exploitation. Yet, this exploitative straight, fast, and self-assertive technological mind has contributed to and is participating in the process of liberation of man from inhuman toils and impoverished living conditions.

The observation that man's spirit is deeply liturgical AND technological is a basic one which points to the possibility of effecting that "queer feeling". The question we are to tackle is, however, found in the area of ambiguity as it expresses itself in today's turbulent encounter between these two minds. The queer feeling is one of the symptomatic manifestations of this ambiguity. What concerns us is not a combination of a path (tool) and a pagoda (the holy), but it is a combination of an elevator (fast technological tool) and a pagoda (the slow liturgical holy). Here obviously the liturgical mind is disturbed and disrupted by the technological mind. This unsettled situation derives from the unprecedented outburst of the technological mind resulting in the massive impact of technological devices upon the liturgical human mind.

The liturgical mind works in anticipation of the sacred moment of encounter with the holy. Where there is no such anticipation man is deprived of the opportunity to become a pilgrim. The sense of the holy stimulates the liturgical mind and vice versa. The Eight Sacred Hairs are the sacred object of veneration (as is the Sacred Tooth of the Buddha enshrined in the Sacred Tooth Temple in Kandy, Sri Lanka). No amount of hair from a Hong Kong Chinese barber shop will inspire the Rangoon Buddhists to construct a pagoda. Why not? It is simply because it is not from the head of the Buddha. The Buddha's hair is a remarkable symbol which can inspire the people to come to meditate upon the life and doctrine of the Buddha. The hairs contain both magical and symbolic potentiality. For some, it signifies the way to the final deliverance; for others magical efficacy of one kind or another. It is up to the man who comes to venerate it. Whatever the perception of the people – those with a magical understanding would far outnumber those with a symbolic one – there is some sense of the presence of the holy.

In the famed Zagorsk monastery outside Moscow, the continuous stream of old Russian women carrying candles in their hands, making the sign of the cross in a slow and careful motion, approach the innumerable icons, venerate them, and kiss them. There is a sense of the presence of the holy there. They see clearly the difference between paintings and icons. The former is an art which must not receive veneration, while the latter is sacred and must be approached liturgically.

In Singapore every year on *Thaipusam*, which is a sacred day for Hindu devotees, a large number of devotees proceed slowly under the unbearable hot tropical sun, each carrying a heavy *kavadi* supported by countless spokes pierced into the flesh, towards the temple. Each painful step signifies a liturgical self-mortification to meet the holy at the end of the long march. The holy must not be met on the basis of easy, fast convenience.

Tenrikyo centre in Nara, Japan, the residence built for the ever-living, though invisible, foundress Miki Nakayama (who passed away in 1887), is sacred and the faithful approach liturgically with great reverence.

Such a listing has no end. One simple fact is that the DISTINCTION – between barber-shop hair and the Buddha's hair, paintings and icons, carrying furniture and carrying a *kavadi*, the ordinary house and the holy house, – is maintained. One is able to locate innumerable such

instances in the widest range of human experiences. The concept of
distinction makes itself known to us as we observe our life in all
possible contexts. The concept of human culture contains such a
sense of distinction in the varieties of human context. The health of
culture depends on what kind of distinctions dominates the given
culture. The human spirit is active, ever producing new distinctions and
ever challenging accepted distinctions. And a matter of critical importance
for culture is that every moment of awareness of distinction is a moment
of both inspiration and anxiety.

I notice that in broad general terms that which is separated (the
holy) has been traditionally approached with the liturgical curved,
slow, and dialogical mind. Therefore it is always possible for an elevator
arrangement to cause queer feelings within the varieties of experience of
the holy. When the perception of the holy as the slow holy is stronger,
due to the sense of having a fast tool, a correspondingly stronger queer
feeling is felt.

The technological mind does not have such an inner link with the sense
of the holy. It can place an elevator, without any mental trouble, either
in one of many Singapore shopping complexes or in the sacred Singuttara
Hill. In the shopping centre, a person stepping out of an elevator may
find himself in the kitchen utensil section. In Singuttara Hill a person
finds himself in front of the holy pagoda. The bullet train in Japan can
take both pilgrims and tourists from Tokyo to Osaka in four hours. The
technological mind provides man with the fast convenience. It will not
ask the question of human meaning in approaching and encountering
the holy. It does not observe the principle of separation. There is no
problem for a woman to step out of an elevator and find herself at once
in the kitchen utensil section. But what happens when she suddenly finds
herself in front of the "burning bush which does not consume"? (See
Exod. 3:1-6.)

Technology can bring man suddenly in front of the "burning bush
which does not consume". Does it really? When a fatal kidney ailment is
controlled by the remarkable performance of the dialysis machine, when
the hopeless heart patient is given a new lease of life by receiving a
transplanted heart by the most sophisticated medical technology, when
man flies in the stratosphere at 600 miles an hour perceiving the curvity
of the earth in the light of the glorious setting sun (positive), when the
nuclear bombs exploded upon cities and instantly killed thousands of
people (Hiroshima and Nagasaki), when the planet's ecological balance
is threatened, when the streets of Singapore and Bangkok are completely

saturated with motor vehicles with their deafening din and unbearable fumes (negative) – granted some of these experiences are not everyday experiences, yet they have a persuasive influence upon our everyday life – does not technology bring man, though unintentionally, in front of the "burning bush which does not consume", a pointer to the presence of the holy?

Technology may produce occasions in which man asks the questions regarding human totality. Does it not do this, as indicated above, positively AND negatively through its pervasive ambiguity? And does it not bring this situation to us straight, fast, and self-assertively, that is to say, at times by eliminating the significant traditional religious liturgical process of approach to "the presence of the holy"? Does it not do so by abolishing the stationary concept of the holy (the holy is located in some definite places) and instead giving us a concept of the holy as we encounter it in the context of our life? Does not elimination of the slow approach suggest that? Is it not true that technology, in the act of providing an elevator to the Shwedagon Pagoda, challenges the Shwedagon Pagoda with its stationary concept of the holy? Is it not suggesting that the places of the holy must become movements of the holy, not a stationary encounter with the holy, but the mobile encounter with the mobile holy? Does not today's technology force us in this direction by introducing and cultivating within our minds the mobile image of the mobile holy, the perception of the holy in the movement? In this sense is not pervasive technological influence "sacralizing" our world?

May we say that technology grants us a new possibility of being encountered by the new types of the "burning bush which does not consume" since it widens the possibility of human experience? The Roman Emperor Hadrian never travelled by air! True, the technological mind desacralizes the "burning bush which does not consume" by analyzing the phenomenon by its own methodology. Yet at the same time it brings man, paradoxically, the new possibilities of encountering with the new "burning bush which does not consume" hitherto unknown. Is it not true that this sense of paradox was perceived and is at work at the depth of our civilization today? And can we not characterize the difference between the old burning bush and the new burning bush in terms of the former being the stationary burning bush (having an approach to the holy places) and the latter the mobile burning bush (a fast approach, or "suddenly in front of a moving burning bush" or even elimination of approach)? Has not the technological mind (one of the powerful winds blowing today) in its own paradoxical way brought out the far widening experience of encountering the holy in the profane (*pro-fanum* meaning "outside the temple") contexts?

We are living today in a world of interaction between the two kinds of concept of the holy – the holy in the old stationary burning bush and the holy in the new mobile burning bush. It is often vigorously pointed out, as I mentioned, that our world today is secular and the spirit that negates the idea of the holy in human experience is becoming more dominant. Science-technology is said to be one of the outstanding agents by which this suffocation of the idea of the holy is taking place. This particular observation, in my mind, requires from us much careful examination. I assume that this observation is generally made with the holy in the old stationary bush.

At this moment I would like to point out that there has emerged the new mobile idea of the holy because of the tremendous sophistication and massive influence upon human life by the technological advances. I notice also the increasing communication (dialogue within the human mind) between the holy in the old stationary bush AND the holy in the new mobile bush. This is being conducted in two ways, positively and negatively.

Take for instance a Thai farmer, whose traditional sense of the holy is nurtured by the Buddhist temples, Buddhist monks, and the image of the Buddha in a certain definite locality, and who is instructed that he should live in a liturgical relationship to these sacred objects and persons (stationary), who one day may experience the saving efficacy of the dialysis machine (mobile) which encounters him. How will he look at the image of the Buddha AND the dialysis machine from that time on? Such medical experience will surely initiate some kind of communication within his mind between the holy in the image of the Buddha (old, stationary, liturgical) and the holy in the dialysis machine (new, mobile, technological) even though he may not employ such an expression (positive).

The same farmer might walk through traffic congested streets in Bangkok. The heat and smell of motor exhaust will surely make him unhappy and even irritated. He may long for his small village outside Bangkok where the air is clearer and the croaking of frogs replaces the traffic din. In this case the technology-packed (heavy traffic) streets are asking the man the question: are not the Bangkok streets demonic? Arousing such a question which is to do with demons ("unclean spirit"), technology may provide occasion for the man to compare this new mobile unclean spirit with the old stationary unclean spirit (animistic localised doctrine of the unclean spirit). Thus, arousing the question of the demons on the streets as he walks, technology forces man to ask questions about angels ("clean spirit"), the idea of holy (negative).

Is this far fetched? I don't think so. It is simply the description of anxiety the farmer felt caught in the demonic traffic of Bangkok. Isn't it true that technological situations have given man numerous new possibilities in which he becomes both inspired and anxious? And if one does not become inspired by a dialysis machine and if one does not become uneasy in Bangkok's demonic traffic isn't there some terrible spiritual insensitivity within him? Could such a man of insensitivity appreciate satisfactorily to his benefit the presence of the holy in the traditional stationary arrangement?

Take a boatman working in the Hong Kong harbour. He knows through his stomach and his muscles what a hard job it is to get around in the harbour (slow, liturgical mobility). One day suppose he finds himself by chance sitting in a car (Mercedes Benz!) and speeding (fast, technological mobility) through the magnificently lit submarine tunnel from Kowloon to Hong Kong at fifty miles per hour (positive), will he not talk about it as something of a new experience in his life? How smooth it was, how efficient it was and how uncanny and fascinating it was to drive under the water on which he has worked for many years? Will not this something new occasion the question of the holy even though he may not use such an expression? Was not the submarine tunnel something of the mobile "burning bush which does not consume" for him, since it is a fascinating "wonderful sight" (Exod. 3:3) which may arouse the sense of the new possibility of style of life within his mind? May not such an experience – rather an ordinary one – become a pointer to that which is extraordinary?

The same boatman by some chance sees on television the huge B52s bombing Vietnam. Even as his tired eyes see the tremendous aircraft one after another flying in the sky like magic giant silver birds, will he not at least feel anxiety? Will he not ask why are the great planes used for the purpose of destruction (negative)? This kind of destruction is far greater (mobile) than the destruction in the traditional scale (stationary). Will not the question of destruction which provokes the question of creation bring man face to face with the holy even though he may not realise it?

Again, is it too far fetched? No, I don't think so. I am again speaking of the new possibility of inspiration and anxiety that technology provokes. And what else points to the presence of the holy more persistently than inspiration and anxiety one experiences in his soul? Earlier I said that a woman who steps out of an elevator only to find herself in the kitchen utensil section has no problem, but actually she does feel the (ever acute) problem of going through inspiration and anxiety by the overwhelming presence of the technological kitchen conveniences.

These two people, one in Bangkok and one in Hong Kong, were not on the way to a pagoda, the place where the presence of the holy is stationary, anticipated. They were neither going to a Hindu temple nor sitting in a Buddhist temple where the holy images are stationary housed. They were neither liturgically walking nor liturgically sitting nor liturgically speaking. They were, on the contrary, in the context of mobile everyday life. In the context of everyday life one experienced the medical saving power of the dialysis machine, the other sped through the submarine tunnel. One walked on the Bangkok streets and another watched an evening newsreel on the television. The holy was not anticipated. The awareness of the holy loomed in their mind "outside the temple" through technologically prepared inspiration and anxiety.

These are similar to the situation of Moses who was leading his flock in the field of Midian. The presence of the holy confronted him without his anticipation. He was puzzled. "I must go across and see this wonderful sight. Why does not the bush burn away?" "I must go across to see how this machine saves my life." "I must go across to see how the car can drive so comfortably under the sea." "I must go across to see what harm is done by motor exhaust." "I must go to see what immeasurable damage has been done by the giant bombers." They are the great moments of inspiration and anxiety.

Are the experiences of these two men, however, really similar to that of Moses in the field of Midian? Am I not watering down or even distorting the idea of the holy? How can I speak of the awareness of the holy in relation to a dialysis machine, a Bangkok street, the submarine tunnel, and B52s? In the language of culture I do not think I have either watered down or distorted the human awareness of the holy. Today's culture, which is destined to live under the dominant influence of technology, demands man to have eyes to see some pointers to the presence of the holy within the technological environment. I see the possibility of this as we go through the ambiguous experience of inspiration and anxiety. Perhaps the day has come when technological mobile pointers are much more meaningful to man's search of the holy than the stationary pointers. I am not suggesting a watered-down concept of the holy. I am speaking of a new possibility, a new approach to the presence of the holy. Do we see in such incidents the quality of ineffable *numinous* and *mysterium tremendum*?

Is the holy stationary *numinous* and *mysterium tremendum*? Or is it mobile *numinous* and *mysterium tremendum*? Both. What I wish to say at this point is that varieties of technological situations, from the nondramatic to the dramatic, can become a mobile (without liturgical approaches – liturgical steps, liturgical sweat, liturgical time) "burning bush", the signs indicating the direction to the presence of the holy. What paradoxical creativity of technological situations we live in today! There are only signs and symbols possible with regard to the holy. The holy, by its very nature, cannot be directly grasped. The holy which is grasped is the unholy. "... Come no nearer; take off your sandals..." (Exod. 3:5).

In Rangoon I suddenly found myself barefoot in a fast ascending elevator. I was neither a pilgrim nor a tourist. I was suspended. The liturgical experience of approach was taken away from me, yet liturgical feet (bare feet) were with me in the square ascending box. Though I had a queer feeling of indigestion I did not feel hostile to what the technological straight, fast, self-assertive arrangement did to me. It was a pregnant moment of inspiration and anxiety. Instead, there I glimpsed the new possibility of coming to the awareness of the holy through the mobile burning bush which the technology of ours could provide us.

III

How does the "convergence of the two strong winds" challenge the great religious truths to be interpreted and communicated (religious dimension)?

I would like to discuss the implication of the foregoing presentation on the contents and mode of the truths expressed in the Thai Buddhism and the Judaeo-Christian traditions. How should we appropriate such great religious truths and live meaningfully with them within the context suggested by "an elevator arrangement" to the presence of the holy?

A. THAI BUDDHISM

Remarkable flexibility of juxtaposition of the liturgical approach and the technological approach to the Buddhist truth by means of a paradox of achieving a-historical bliss by historical self-discipline.

I understand that in Thai Buddhism, the Fourfold Noble Truth occupies a comparable place to the Apostles' Creed in Christianity.

(1) What now, O monks, is the noble truth of Suffering? Birth is suffering, old age is suffering, death is suffering, sorrow, lamentations, pain, grief and despair are suffering.
(2) But what, O monks, is the noble truth of the Origin of suffering? It is that Craving which gives rise to fresh rebirth and, bound up with pleasure and lust, now here now there, finds ever fresh delight.
(3) But what, O monks, is the noble truth of the Extinction of suffering? It is the complete fading away and extinction of this craving, its forsaking and giving up, liberation and detachment from it.
(4) But what, O monks, is the noble truth of the path leading to the extinction of suffering? It is the noble Eightfold Path, namely, right understanding, right thought, right speech, right bodily action, right livelihood, right effort, right mindfulness, and right concentration.

Gotama Siddartha obtained the Enlightenment after much meditation and self-mortification. It was one of the most moving stories of the human spirit in search of the ultimate truth about man's existence. His physical, intellectual, and spiritual journey to the Enlightenment was curved, slow, and dialogical. This remark can be visually and emotionally confirmed if one spends an afternoon in the inner yard of the famed Marble Temple in Bangkok where numerous images of Buddha are displayed. Among them one will be surely impressed by the one sitting statue of the starved Gotama.

"Birth is suffering" is neither a pessimistic nor optimistic observation. It is an integral part of the Enlightenment he achieved. It is obviously not a technological truth, a compartmentalized truth. The technological mind which can freely place "elevator" in any context, is neither concerned with nor makes an observation such as "birth is suffering". "Birth is suffering" speaks to the foundation of human existence. It is a fundamental totality observation. It reminds me of the New Testament expression: "... a man with an unclean spirit" (Mark 5:2) which indicates the totality truth beyond medical truth about man. It is not an observation made by the straight, fast, self-assertive mind. The Fourfold Noble Truth is, it seems to me, more the product of the curve, slow, dialogical mind than of the straight, fast, self-assertive mind. That which has been arrived at by the curve, slow, dialogical process – for instance, "birth is suffering" – must be approached liturgically.

There is definitely the quality of slowness attached to The Fourfold Noble Truth. I am not, of course, referring to the mental slowness. I am speaking of the special kind of slowness in relation to man's quest after the truth about man and the process of the propagation of that truth among men. This slowness derives from its concern in the totality of human meaning. "Birth is suffering", "craving gives rise to fresh re-birth", and "the extinction of this craving" are pronounced to illuminate and to grasp the total meaning of human life. Such a totality observation points to the moment of the holy insight and holy discernment. Man must slow down in deep reflection (to expel ignorance, *avijja*, by the curve-dialogical circumspective mind) and meditate upon the truth addressed at the root of human existence: "birth is suffering...."

When something is said of the root of human existence, it has a comprehensive and "ontological" meaning. Whoever man is, wherever he is, whether he is walking three miles an hour on land or flying 600 miles an hour at 33,000 feet, or even exploring the mysterious terrain on the moon, this is the Buddhist truth in the light of which a Buddhist must understand his life. It is a mobile truth *par excellence* in the sense that it does not require any physical approach such as a path leading up to the temple at the top of a hill. "Birth is suffering" is, in this sense, a fast doctrine, but its incomparable mobility becomes clear when we notice the fact that once formulated by the Buddha, it is free from him who formulated it. It is, as it were, a "strong truth" which can travel and work by itself apart from the historical Buddha. It is, in this sense, a history-gravity-free truth. And perhaps as far as the mode of truth is concerned it displays an interesting congruity with the mode of tech-nological truth – a fast truth. Once invented, the telephone system is free from the inventor Alexander Graham Bell. The history-gravity-free truth has "technological" mobility. It is a super-mobile burning bush.

But "birth is suffering" is a stationary truth, too. Man is fastened to this worldly existence. Failing to achieve elimination of self (*anatta*), man is drowned in the world of transitoriness (*anicca*) and therefore lives a life of devastating unsatisfactoriness (*dukkha*). As I see it, no matter how one proposes to explain it, the primary truth about man is that "man is born". If man is not born then "birth is suffering" is a useless truth. Man is not a "beyond-birth-(history)-man". He does have cravings. He desires to own all possible technological conveniences, for instance. Craving is an historical concept if it has any meaning at all. I cannot imagine a-historical or trans-historical craving. "The extinction of this craving" means a hard historical struggle on the part of man. It means historical resistance against the historical power of craving. True, the ultimate goal of this struggle is trans-historical bliss. The goal, however, cannot be conceived and formulated outside of this historical experience.

Only history enables man to speak about a-history and trans-history. In this historical struggle against one's historical craving, I see the history-concerned character of Thai Buddhism.

We must understand that we do not take food because it tastes good, but in order to cure pain and satisfy hunger. When we take food to satisfy hunger, even though the food is not good, it will satisfy the hunger. Suppose we take food for the sake of its flavour, without further consideration, if it is not good, then aversion will occur. On the other hand, if it is good, then greed will occur. This would mean that we are taking the food to encourage defilements. When food is good, greed, which is a craving or attachment will occur. When it is not good, dissatisfaction or dislike will occur. We shall be unable to prevent defilements if we have this attitude. To eat without consideration, is to create more cycles of birth and death, which is the endless continuation of suffering. Therefore, when we are applying the application of mindfulness as we are going to take food, we must understand the reason at each mouthful; so that when we are eating, it will be solely for the purpose of being free from suffering. (Buddhist University 1965: 88ff.).

In this historical struggle to achieve deliverance from history ("eat but do not taste it!") – what a comprehensive and ontological struggle! – man needs all kinds of liturgical – curve, slow, dialogical – approaches to the presence of the holy. Man's spirituality needs experiences of liturgical process. The fight against craving is enlightened and strengthened by walking liturgical steps, sweating liturgical sweat, and spending liturgical time. The spiritual attachment to the paths in contrast to the elevator will not be easily eradicated.

Thai Buddhism presents us with this paradox of a-historically oriented historical struggle. I see in the spiritual tradition of the Thai Buddhism two strands existing: possibility of fast mobile encounter with the super-mobile truth "birth is suffering" (without approach, technologically), and the possibility of coming to the truth "birth is suffering" slowly through the approach (liturgically). With Thai Buddhism the queer feeling cannot become really disturbing since there is a basic juxtaposition between "with approach" and "without approach" which is made possible by the Buddhist paradox of an a-historically oriented historical struggle. This basic juxtaposition is the specific freedom and indigenous adaptability for the technological age.

I have noticed from time to time that Thai Buddhism has the advantage of strong truth in its practice of the devotional life of the truth. I personally know a Thai bank manager who in his most up-to-date well appointed office suddenly engages in meditation on "birth is suffering" (without any liturgical approach – as he would pick up a telephone) and yet he tells me how important it is for his personal devotional life to go to the temple liturgically and participate in it, and how the temple, the monks, and the Buddha's images help his fight against his cravings. Here I become aware of the work of the strong truth. "Birth is suffering" after all can be either technologically (straight, fast, self-assertively) or liturgically (curve, slow, dialogically) approached! Either way man can be a pilgrim as long as he is coming to the truth: "birth is suffering".

B. THE JUDAEO-CHRISTIAN BIBLICAL TRADITION

Intensely paradoxical character of the "slow God" because of His history-involvement.

The history of the people of Israel, their complex strange God-led history – or their awareness of their own meaning of history (what a different world from that of the Buddha!) – seems to me more in character with the curve, slow, dialogical mind (the Bamboo Room curve-spirituality) than the straight, fast, self-assertive mind (the Oil Room straight-spirituality). The Biblical God, the God of the Judaeo-Christian tradition, is, in the language of the Rabbi Abraham Heschel, "God in search of man". In the Jahwist epic which was written about 950 B.C., we hear the divine search of man expressed simply yet powerfully "... the Lord God called to the man, and said to him, 'Where are you?'" (Gen. 3:9). When God comes to man, the forgiving grace of God intends to save man instead of destroying him. His forgiving grace is his forgiving mind which makes divine theological curves towards man because of his love. Hosea, the eighth century B.C. prophet from the northern kingdom of Israel which was at that time under the severe threat from Assyria, describes the mind of God, as it were, going through the painful curve, slow, and dialogical process in its dealing with his disobedient and rebelling people. Gottfried Quell (1964:32) writes on Hosea:

When he acts in love, God demonstrates no less than His proper character as the holy God. Hence He suffers under the lovelessness of His people, whose covenant faithfulness is only like the morning dew which quickly dispels (6: 4). In face of its sin He is overcome by a kind of helplessness: "O Ephraim, what shall I do unto thee? O Judah, what shall I do unto thee?"[3]

Is not this "helplessness" in the mind of God the poignant expression of the mind of the history-involved God? Is not God's manner of history involvement curved, slow, and dialogical? In the face of faithlessness in His people why did not the God of Hosea act straight, fast, and self-assertively? At the time of historical crisis Hosea glimpsed the helplessness of God! Was it not the love of God that created the sense of helplessness within the mind of God?

Forty years of national migration through the wilderness, three generations of the united monarchy (Saul, David, Solomon) and twenty kings of Judah (up to B.C. 587) and nineteen kings of Israel (up to B.C. 722), the hosts of the prophets and priests, the experience of exiles and restorations – isn't this rather a slow way for God to let His people know the substance of the covenant relationship (God-man and man-man)? Isn't this too history-involved, therefore too slow? Isn't this too dialogical? Too dialogical, therefore too inefficient? Isn't this too much love, therefore too many curves?

The truth in this tradition is not history-gravity-free, but history-gravity-full truth. We have noticed the similarity in the mode of truth between "birth is suffering" and the Buddha, and technological telephone and Mr. Bell. Both are "strong truths", the truths which can work apart from the ones who gave birth to them. The Judaeo-Christian tradition, in sharp contrast, presents a different concept of the truth. In this tradition, God who comes to man – in His coming to man, in His dealing with man, in His relationship to man – He is the truth. The truth here is then, in its very structure, decisively the "Personal Truth". It cannot be separated from the "Person of God".

Hosea speaks of the personal truth of God – how God profoundly suffers because of the unfaithfulness of His people – through the tragic image of his own personal experience with his unfaithful wife. The truth is presented in the image of personal marriage relationship. Amos, another eighth century prophet from Judah, speaks of the personal truth of God as the social truth of God.

Seek good, and not evil, that you may live; and so the Lord, the God of hosts, will be with you, as you have said. Hate evil, and love good, and establish justice in the gate; it may be that the Lord, the God of hosts, will be gracious to the remnant of Joseph (Amos 5: 14, 15).

God's personal truth is God's social ethics. The truth which is personal therefore historical-ethical, historical-ethical therefore personal, is the outstanding characteristic of the truth in the Judaeo-Christian tradition. Elaboration of this theme will demand work which is far beyond the scope of this paper.

When we come to the Christian tradition this basic character of the truth is intensified as the Christian sees it. In the sending of His Son to the world at a definite time in this history of ours ("... suffered under Pontius Pilate..."), God reveals Himself as the emphatically history-committed God. The Son of God walks around in the first century Palestine, meets the people, speaks to them and lives with them. He comes to a "full stop" (death) as though the history-gravity effects its maximum power upon him. Even a slow movement could not be continued. He came to our history so deeply that he reached the point of greatest history-gravity. He lost his mobility. He was nailed down. Crucifixion implies, if anything, cruel immobility.

The fifth-century theologians expressed through the thought form of their days the history-gravity-full Christian truth as they spoke about the person of the Redeemer.

... we all with one accord teach the profession of faith in the one identical Son, our Lord Jesus Christ. We declare that he is perfect both in his divinity and in his humanity, truly God and truly man composed of body and rational soul, that he is consubstantial with the Father in his divinity, consubstantial with us in his humanity... (The Council of Chalcedon A.D.451).

How decisively is God involved in history in the person of Jesus Christ? "Consubstantially" God comes to a "full stop" at the crucifixion of Jesus. What I am trying to say is that the truth in the Judaeo-Christian Biblical tradition ("O Ephraim, what shall I do unto thee?", or a summary of Christian truth given by the Apostle Paul, "For you know the grace of our Lord Jesus Christ, that though he was rich, yet for your sake he became poor, so that by his poverty you might become rich" – 2 Cor. 8:9) is "weak" truth in the sense that this poverty and the Person of Jesus Christ cannot be separated. In this tradition the truth and the person are one. One cannot speak of the truth apart from the person and the person apart from the truth.

The God who is history-involved, the God who is faithful to the historical covenant relationship, as the Judaeo-Christian tradition holds, reveals himself more in the image of curve, slow, dialogical than in that of straight, fast, self-assertive. If I say this I must at once say that I do not understand what is precisely meant when I say God's mind is more like curve, slow, dialogical than straight, fast, self-assertive. I am perhaps only pointing to the truth I can see only "dimly" (1 Cor. 13:12) and trying to live in the realm of meaning where my theology breathes. For my part, I feel more at home with the "slow God" than with the "fast God". The Judaeo-Christian affirmation that "God is love" means to me God is personal-historical, and since He is personal-historical He is a personally "slow God".

Does this mean that the Judaeo-Christian truth works much more freely and congenially within the liturgical "current of air" than within the technological "current of air"? Putting it in a more abrupt way, does the Judaeo-Christian truth work more efficiently in the Bamboo Room than in the Oil Room since it would feel essentially more at home in the former than in the latter? More message for the people of Sarawak than for the people of Singapore? Is this the situation? If so, is there a possibility of the "slow God" being meaningful in the technological "fast world"? Thai Buddhism can enjoy, as we have seen, freedom within the context of the convergence of the two strong winds because its truth is "strong". How does the "weak" truth find itself in the same convergence of the two strong winds?

The Judaeo-Christian truth is history-involved. It comes to man historically. It comes to man through God's experience of history – His helplessness and His "full stop" in His Son! At this very point, the "slow God" claims paradoxical sovereignty over all "speeds" – liturgical and technological. An intensive paradox! But how?

What do I mean by the image of "slowness" with regard to God? It certainly means something more than the measurable speed in relation to motion, such as the concept of three miles an hour or 600 miles an hour. It is true that, judged in terms of today's available technological speed, the image of walking in the desert for forty years is an extremely slow movement. The concept of slowness, however, when applied to the Biblical God points beyond this obvious physical slowness in motion. The "slowness" of God cannot be measured by the technological mind, as the mind of God that asks "where are you?" is, at the beginning of the slow process of salvation, a foreign subject to the technological mind. Technology may unintentionally bring man to hear the divine search "where are you?" But it does not intend to do so. The slowness of God is a qualitative, not quantitative concept. It points to the quality of speed. It tries to point out the dimension of meaning to the man who walks three miles an hour and who flies 600 miles an hour. The "slowness" of God is the "slowness" which can contain all possible physical, mental, and spiritual speeds since it is to do with quality of mind of God which is able to give meaning to all possible speed arrangements in human experiences from babies crawling to rocket travel, from walking up a path to a fast elevator, from rowboat to hydrofoil hovercraft. The "slowness" of God mysteriously challenges all human physical, mental, and spiritual speeds and asks the basic "totality question": "what do we do with these speeds?"

The history-gravity-full truth enlightens both the liturgical and technological minds. The "slow God" does not suggest the same quality of "slowness" suggested in the Bamboo Room. It is not liturgical slowness symbolized by the careful slow approach to the presence of the holy. It is not to do with man who goes "slow". It is primarily to do with God. And He experiences history slowly. This is the language of theologically constructed symbolism. How can we speak of God's experience in history?! God experiences history "slowly" because of His love for history. This is a special "slowness" of theological quality. He experiences history most slowly and carefully to the point of reaching a "full stop" (what a history-gravity-full truth!). God claims His sovereignty over all technological speeds ("elevator") and technological helpfulness (planes, tunnels, dialysis machines, and so on) by going most slowly through history; thus God reveals Himself to be the meaning of history. "For the foolishness of God is wiser than men, and the weakness of God is stronger than men" (1 Cor. 1:23). "For he was crucified in weakness, but lives by the power of God" (2 Cor. 13:4).

Then by feeling "helplessness" within Himself and coming to the "full stop", the history-gravity-full truth in the Judaeo-Christian tradition becomes a mobile truth. All possible movements and speeds are within the radius of this mobility of meaning that paradoxically derives from the truth of the "slow God". The mobility of this truth must not be interpreted in the similar vein to the mobility of the Great Monkey in the Ramayana Epic which flies gravity-free around in the great sky with supersonic speed. The meaning of the history-gravity-full truth comes to us through the image of the nomadic tent. "The Word became flesh and tented among us ..." (John 1:14). God does not experience our history with supersonic speed. He tents among us. In doing so (deus absconditus!) He gives meaning to the world in the convergence of the two great liturgical and technological winds. The Judaeo-Christian Biblical tradition presents the paradox of sovereignty of "slow God" over all "speeds". In this paradox we see the Christian insight against any spiritual drive towards deification of technology. Technology itself must not become "the holy", though it may occasion man's spirit to see the holy.

The Biblical God stands over all liturgical and technological possibilities since He is the one who has experienced our history most carefully, slowly, and costly in the manner of greatest involvement.

Often we find ourselves walking from the Bamboo Room to the Oil Room, and from the Oil Room to the Bamboo Room. At times we find ourselves in an elevator barefoot. Our culture today has surrounded us by the far increased occasions of causing inspiration and anxiety in our souls because of technological advancement. Within our minds we realize the dialogue between the old stationary burning bush and the new mobile burning bush is taking place. The great religious truths are inescapably placed in the context of the two great "currents of air", liturgical and technological. Buddhism demonstrates its peculiar freedom of juxtaposition of the old burning bush and the new burning bush by its "strong" truth, while the Judaeo-Christian Biblical tradition reveals the intensely paradoxical historical dimension of the concept of the "slow God". God is love, therefore God experiences history slowly. Experiencing history thus, divinely slowly, He claims His sovereignty over all liturgical (the Bamboo Room) and technological (the Oil Room) possibilities, today and tomorrow.

REFERENCES

Buddhist University
    1965   *Development of Insight,* published on the occasion of the Royal Ceremony at the cremation of His Holiness the late Patriarch, Somdech Phra Ariyavam-sagatanana Nanodayamahathera (Bangkok: Buddhist University).
Kittel, G. (ed.)
    1964   *Theological Dictionary of the New Testament* 1 (Grand Rapids: Eerdmans). Translated from the German 1933 edition.
Mbiti, John S.
    1973   "Harmony, Happiness and Morality in African Religion", *Drew Gateway* 43:2 (Winter), 108.
Quell, Gottfried
    1964   "Love in the OT" in Kittel (ed.), *Theological Dictionary of the New Testament* 1 (*Grand Rapids: Eerdmans*), 32.
Visser't Hooft, W. A.
    1973   *Memoirs* (London: S. C. M. Press).

SPEAK AND TALK:
A VINDICATION OF SYNTACTIC DEEP STRUCTURE

D. TERENCE LANGENDOEN

In this paper I show the following. The English verbs *speak* and *talk* are synonymous. They differ, however, in their selection restrictions. Therefore the claim that all selection restrictions are semantically based is false. At least some selection restrictions must be represented in the syntactic component of a grammar.

For two expressions (lexical items, phrases, sentences) to be synonymous, they must express the same sense. Both *speak* and *talk*, I claim, express the sense given in (1).

(1) "emit linguistic sounds"

That is, *speak* and *talk* are both semantically more specific than *utter*, the sense of which is given in (2).[1]

(2) "emit sounds using the vocal tract"

And they are less specific semantically than such verbs as *say*, *tell*, and *communicate*, all of whose senses include mention of what is communicated by the emitted linguistic sounds. Neither *speak* nor *talk* expresses the notion that any thought, idea, or feeling is communicated by the emitted linguistic sounds.[2]

Speak and *talk* do, of course, differ in usage, just like any other pair of synonymous expressions. The synonymy note under *speak* in *Webster's Third New International Dictionary* states this usage difference nicely.

SPEAK is a general term of wide application. It may on occasion differ from

---

D. Terence Langendoen is Executive Officer of the Ph. D. Program in Linguistics at the City University of New York Graduate Center, New York City, New York.

[1]   To see this difference, compare *Gene uttered a low growl* with the semantically anomalous **Gene spoke/talked a low growl.*

[2]   This fact is somewhat less obvious, but is borne out by the fact that sentences like *Gene spoke/talked for ten minutes without saying anything* are not anomalous, and the fact that one can *speak/talk gibberish*. Of course, there are specialized senses for both *speak* and *talk* in which communication of specific ideas is expressed, but as I point out in the text below, this fact does not bear on the question of what the verbs mean in their nonspecialized sense.

TALK in suggesting a weighty formality. TALK in general may suggest less formality and is likely to implicate auditors and interlocutors.

As the double use of "may" indicates, the difference pointed out in this note are rhetorical rather than semantic in nature. That is, the use of *speak* does not entail formality (the locution *speak informally* is not contradictory), and the use of *talk* entails neither formality nor the presence of auditors or interlocutors (the locutions *talk formally* and *talk without talking to/with anyone* are not contradictory). Therefore, none of these differences has anything to do with what the verbs mean.

Speak and *talk* also each have specialized meanings which they do not share. Thus, for *speak*, we have "give a rebuke or reprimand" (*I'll speak to him about that*) and "communicate by being interesting or attractive" (*That painting really speaks to me*); while for *talk*, there is "persuade, influence, or affect by talking" (*We talked him out of it*) and "reveal secret or confidential information" (*Unless he talks, we're safe*).[3] But these differences in specialized meaning are irrelevant to the question of the synonymy of the two verbs in their nonspecialized sense.

The fact that *speak* and *talk* are synonymous has a consequence for linguistic theory. McCawley (1968: 134-136) has argued that all selection restrictions are semantically based. In reply, Katz (1972: 396) pointed out several counterexamples, any one of which is sufficient to refute McCawley's hypothesis. However, none of Katz's examples involved a verb, the part of speech *par excellence* that carries selection restrictions. But now we have such an example, since *speak* and *talk* are synonymous verbs but differ in their selection restrictions.[4] To see this, consider sentences (3) and (4).

(3) *Gene spoke six words.*
(4) **Gene talked six words.*

Substituting for the word *words* in (3) and (4) other expressions that denote linguistic elements, for example *syllables, phrases, sentences,* etc., the pattern is the same. The verb *talk* is anomalously used with direct objects that denote linguistic elements, *speak* is not.[5] In the formalism

---

[3] Several more specialized meanings could be given for each verb. Moreover, both *speak* and *talk* enter into idiomatic combinations with particles, such as *up* and *out,* with quite different senses (compare the meanings of *speak up* and *talk up,* for example), and the derived agentive nominals *speaker* and *talker* are also distinct semantically. How to explain such states of affairs as this is a crucial problem in lexicology.

[4] This example, with discussion, does appear in Katz (1973:567).

[5] Incredibly, *The American Heritage Dictionary* gives, under *talk,* the example *Those are real words the baby is talking.* Everyone I have asked concerning this example

(roughly) of Chomsky (1965), *speak* is positively specified for the selection restriction [___[Linguistic Element]], *talk* is negatively specified for that restriction.[6]

The only way in which one could save McCawley's hypothesis against this crushing counterexample would be to show that the grammaticality difference between (3) and (4) is due to some other device in the grammar besides selection.[7] There is, as far as I can determine, exactly one possible alternative of this sort. Suppose we say that (4) is well-formed at the level of deep structure (or semantic structure, if one is a generative semanticist), and does not contain a violation of a selection restriction. Then, there might just be a syntactic transformation that deletes direct objects of certain verbs (call it Object Deletion), and this rule might just apply obligatorily to direct objects of the verb *talk* when those objects are specified as linguistic elements. Certainly there is a rule of Object Deletion in English; it applies, for example, in the derivation of sentences like (5) from structures like those that underlie (6).

(5) *Gene writes elegantly.*
(6) *Gene writes letters/articles/books/poetry/ ... elegantly.*

Indeed, to avoid the embarrassment of having to say that sentences like (5) are potentially infinitely ambiguous, depending upon which direct object in (6) is deleted, one would have to say that what is deleted is specified simply as [Specimen of Writing], a feature much like [Linguistic Element].

Unfortunately for this line of argument, the parallelism just established between *talk* and *write* breaks down. Object Deletion applies, in the case of *write*, when its direct object is specified only as [Specimen of Writing]; if it is further specified, the rule is inapplicable. Thus, given the structure underlying (7), we cannot obtain (8), or anything else for that matter, by Object Deletion.

---

has found it anomalous, some even spontaneously suggesting that *talking* should be replaced by *speaking* in the example.

[6]   This observation appears also to falsify the claim in McCawley (1971:290) that "a selection restriction imposed by an item... is a presupposition about what an item in semantic representation purports to denote", since clearly it would be absurd to say that *talk* presupposes that its direct object in semantic representation cannot denote a linguistic element. The sense of *talk* in fact dictates that its semantic direct object must denote a linguistic element.

[7]   In desperation, one could try to argue that (4) is grammatical, and only unacceptable. But on what independent basis one could substantiate such a claim, I have no idea.

(7) *Gene wrote six words.*

(8) *Gene wrote.*

Furthermore, it is a general fact about Object Deletion that semantically specific direct objects cannot be deleted; it is simply not a fact about the application of that rule in sentences whose main verb is *write*. This matter becomes particularly clear if one considers the deletion of "cognate objects" in English by Object Deletion. Thus, while (9) is obligatorily transformed into (10) by Object Deletion, (11) is, and must be, unaffected by that rule.

(9) **Gene dreamed a dream.*

(10) *Gene dreamed.*

(11) *Gene dreamed a particularly striking dream.*

From this property of Object Deletion, we conclude that (4) cannot be ungrammatical by virtue of the failure to apply Object Deletion. Object Deletion, even were it to be applicable to direct objects of the verb *talk*, could not be applicable in (4) because of the specificity of the direct object in that sentence. We conclude that the sentence must be ungrammatical because of some deformity in it at the level of syntactic deep structure. That deformity is nothing other than a violation of a syntactic selection restriction.

REFERENCES

Chomsky, Noam
  1965 *Aspects of the Theory of Syntax* (Cambridge, Mass.: M. I. T. Press).
Katz, Jerrold J.
  1972 *Semantic Theory* (New York: Harper and Row).
  1973 "Interpretive Semantics Meets the Zombies", *Foundations of Language* 9, 549-596.
McCawley, James D.
  1968 "The Role of Semantics in a Grammar", in E. Bach and R. Harms (eds.), *Universals in Linguistic Theory* (New York: Holt, Rinehart, and Winston), 124-169.
  1971 "Interpretive Semantics meets Frankenstein", *Foundations of Language* 7, 285-296.

NO MAN, HAVING PUT HIS HAND TO THE PLOW...

PAUL LESER

I

For two decades, as long as I had the good fortune of teaching at The Hartford Seminary Foundation, I have tried to persuade students to investigate how Luke 9: 62 has been translated into different languages. While the English translation is correct, many other translations mistranslate ἄροτρον, the key word. For the research I wished to have done, a student at The Hartford Seminary Foundation would have been in an ideal position since the school has a library in which translations of Luke in several hundred different languages are available and since it offered (until recently) a combination of New Testament studies, Greek, Semitic languages, linguistics, and anthropology. However, since no one ever took up my suggestion I now should do what I had hoped someone else would.

But I cannot do it. Not being a New Testament scholar, nor a linguist, I am not qualified to do the work that ought to be done. My only, but insufficient, qualification is that I happen to know something about the plow, or rather – and this leads me to the main question I intend to ask – about the plow as well as about the ἄροτρον. Thus, all I can do is to ask the questions which Luke 9: 62 poses and which seem not to have troubled commentators and translators. But I am in no position to give any answers to the questions.

II

The English translation, as I have said, is correct. In English there is just one word, "plow". Only a small band of specialists has felt the need for an additional term, and for that reason has introduced into English

Paul Leser is Professor Emeritus of Anthropology at the Hartford Seminary Foundation, Hartford, Connecticut.

the term "ard" which, however, no outsider is able to understand. To describe the difference between the plow proper and the ard, I shall quote from E. Cecil Curwen (1946: 56):

We shall ... reserve the term "plough" for the heavy implement normally possessing wheels, coulter, share and mould-board – such as could have been seen at work a generation or two ago in England. The primitive light implement possessing none of these features we shall, for lack of an English word, distinguish by the convenient Scandinavian term *ard*.

Curwen, however, is not entirely right. Many (actually, almost all) ards do possess a share. "True" plows have a one-sided share while ards have a symmetrical share. Many languages distinguish between the two kinds of plows, and where the distinction exists the average person is fully aware of and acutely sensitive to the difference between the two implements. To quote from Bratanić (1952: 51):

... there are ... several kinds of old ploughing implements, the chief ones being the *plough* and the *ard*.... It is ... necessary to make a distinction between them. The plough is an asymmetrical implement with a short beam. It breaks up the soil by cutting and inverting it in slices (furrows). In order to make slices the plough has a *coulter* for cutting off the soil ... vertically, a *share* for cutting the bottom of the furrow slice, and a single *mouldboard* for turning it to o n e (generally to the right) side only. The complete plough ... has also a two-wheeled forecarriage, an a s y m m e t r i c a l share (usually widened to the right side only), and t w o separate *stilts (plough-tails, handles)*. On the contrary, the normal ard is a symmetrical implement in general, with a symmetrical share, without a proper mouldboard (but sometimes with two symmetrically fixed mouldboards or mouldstrokers), as a rule with one handle only, and with a long beam (prolonged to the yoke), being usually without coulter and forecarriage. ... This difference is not only felt vividly in all Slavic languages *(plug – ralo)*, but there are traces of such linguistic distinction among many European peoples (cf. e.g. French *charrue – araire*, Danish *plov – ard*, Swedish *plog – årder*, Lithuanian *pliugas – arklas*, German *pflug – haken* or *arl*, Italian *pio[ve] – aratro* etc.).

(See also Bratanić 1954: 302.)

In the Holy Land, as in most of the Mediterranean area prior to the modern era, there never were "plows" but only "ards" (Avitsur 1965). Thus in Luke 9: 62 the reference is to an "ard" and not to a "plow". Yet, since in English the word "ard" is not intelligible to anyone outside the extremely limited group of specialists, the English translation "plow" is entirely correct; as a matter of fact, is the only permissible translation.

Not so, however, in those languages where words comparable to "ard" are alive, and where the average person is conscious of the difference between the plow and the ard.

Therefore, the following (Swedish, Slovakian, French) translations are wrong:

Ingen, som ser sig tillbaka, sedan han har satt sin hand till plogen, är skickad för Guds rike. (Bibeln eller den Heliga Skrift n.d.: 96)

Žádni sïahnúce ruku swogu k pluhu, a ohledagíce sa naspátki, neňi sposobní ku králowstwi Božému. (Swaté Písmo nowého Zákona 1893: 115)

Celui qui met la main à la charrue, et regarde derrière lui, n'est point propre pour le royaume de Dieu. (La Sainte Bible 1924: 853)

'Άροτρον in Swedish is *årder*, not *plog*. To a Swede the difference is basic, and distinguishing between the two comes naturally to him. Not only is the distinction clear in Swedish but even more important is the fact that there are areas in Sweden where only the *årder* (on this Swedish implement, see Erixon 1948) was used and never any *plog* (Jirlow 1970: 19). Thus the only correct translation into Swedish would be: "no man who puts his hand to the *årder* and looks back ..."

Similarly, in Slavic languages the word *ralo* should have been used in the translations of Luke 9: 62 and not *plug*.

French dictionaries (e.g. Larousse 1912: 54) explain the word *araire* (which, of course, is derived from Latin *aratrum*) as a *charrue sans avant-train*. Since there never was a forecarriage in the Holy Land the use of the word *charrue* instead of *araire* again gives a wrong impression.

III

But does it matter? Yes, it does, because the implement without a one-sided moldboard is handled differently than the plow equipped with a one-sided moldboard, and the use of the plow WITH a forecarriage likewise results in a different plowing technique. The plow proper requires the undivided attention of the plowman. HE MAY NOT LOOK BACK. If he would his furrow would not be straight; the field would not be plowed properly. Even a short lack of attention may result in some annoying damage. The ard, however, does not require such constant attention and anyone looking back after having put his hand to the *årder* or *ralo* or *araire*, may very well do so without running into trouble.[1]

[1] Farrar (1889:198) in his commentary to Luke 9:62 claims that "the light ploughs of the East, easily overturned, require constant attention" (see also *The Union Bible Dictionary* 1842:504 "constant and close attention"). Having myself used both the heavy central European "plow" and "the light ploughs of the East", I must emphasize

Thus, to a reader who is conscious of the difference between the *plog* and the *árder* (or *ralo* or *araire*) the meaning of Luke 9: 62 becomes distorted. To him, if one of the cognates of plow is used, the verse no longer means what it means to a reader in whose language there is only one term (be it ἄροτρον or *aratrum* or Spanish *arado* or English *plow*). Instead of being understood as a spiritual maxim it will be interpreted as a special technical instruction: as long as you use the ard it is of course quite all right to look back, but if you look back while using the plow, that's different – the results will be terrible.

That, of course, was not the meaning for the simple reason that in the Holy Land there existed only one of the two main types of plow and therefore the verse could not possibly have been construed as making a distinction between two different kinds. To make my point (addressing myself to an audience that may not know much about plowing) I should like to use a modern metaphor: "No one who uses an electric typewriter without plugging it in is fit for the kingdom of God." Such a sentence would not make sense: if you have an electric typewriter you want to plug it in, and if you have an ordinary typewriter you cannot plug it in anyhow.

In plowing with the plow proper, a straight furrow must be plowed.[2] With the kind of implement that has been in use in the Holy Land it is

---

that it is only the heavy plow that requires constant attention and that "the light ploughs of the East" do not. Furthermore, if an ard should overturn, it is not at all difficult to put it back into proper position, while if the heavy European plow overturns, there will be real trouble.

[2] Not so in using the ard. *The Interpreter's Bible* (1952:183), commenting on Luke 9:62, says: "No one who has ever tried to plow a straight furrow can miss the point: the task requires a man's uninterrupted attention." (Similar comments in Grundmann 1961:206; *A Catholic Commentary* 1953:953; Manson n.d: 121ff.) Correct. But in the Holy Land the plowman had no need to focus his attention on plowing a straight furrow because in using the ard it is immaterial whether the furrow is straight or not, see e.g. Leser (1931:266ff. and the literature named there, and generally 646 "Kreuz- und querpflügen").

It should be added that the disparaging remarks about the ard made by several commentators (e.g. *The Union Bible Dictionary* 1842:504, col. b: "it is probable that the best of ancient ploughs was inferior to the worst we have ever seen"; Bruce 1897:537: "a very inferior article to that used in this country") are false. Such remarks may be due to a lack of acquaintance with the soil and climate conditions of the area. In Israel, the ard is superior to the European (and American) plow: "... from 1878 onwards ... efforts were made to introduce the European mould-board plough [which] ... however ... did not give the desired results; easily damaged by stones, it required endless repairs; was unfit for hillside ploughing, had to be laid up every so often in the rainy season; compacted the soil and so created an impermeable layer or [hard-] pan ...; and above all, so far from contributing to the raising of yields as hoped for, it generally caused them to be below those of the neighbouring fields of the fellahin.

rather immaterial whether the plowman plows straight ahead because if, by looking back or by some other lack of attention he occasionally leaves some of the soil unplowed, it is easy to correct his error when he comes back. He plows boustrophedon anyhow, thus returning at the very next turn to the same spot, while the moldboard plow does not plow boustrophedon, but is forced to use a different system (see figures 1 and 2).

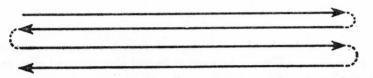

Figure 1.   Boustrophedon Plowing with the Ard (after Vakarelski 1970: 351)

Figure 2.   Plowing with the Moldboard Plow (after Vakarelski 1970: 351)

In most instances, the man plowing boustrophedon will not be satisfied merely with that, but, after having given his field the once-over, will

---

Moreover, where it was used the summer crops failed completely. The reason for all this was simple enough: the mould-board ... plough was adapted to the soils and the climate of Europe with its summer rains and the need to provide for the drainage of rainwater. However, in a semi-arid country it is needful to conserve the water from the winter rains, and above all, to make the best use of every drop of the late rains in early spring. Turning the sod, as was done by the mould-board plough caused the soil to lose its moisture" (Avitsur 1965: vii).

The ard "was admirably suited for ploughing the sometimes quite steep hillsides of our country, without causing erosion. ... All these important advantages were missing from ... the European plough" (Avitsur 1965: x).

"... the disappointing experience with the European turning plough ..." (Avitsur 1965: xi, see also ix).

zigzag or cross-plow the entire area right away. Therefore he may very well look back while plowing. Hence the Greek version of Luke 9: 62 does not mean what the sentence "if you use an electric typewriter plug it in" would mean to us, but rather "if you begin working and you are thinking of what lies behind you, you are not fit for the kingdom of God".

IV

Then, why did the Swedish, Slavic, and French translators who were conscious of the difference between *årder* and *plog, ralo* and *plug, araire* and *charrue* use the wrong term, thus misleading the reader (and, probably, misleading themselves)? I cannot answer the question because the research that I had hoped someone would do has not been done, and I am not qualified to do it. It would be necessary first to examine the oldest Swedish, French, Croatian, Ukrainian, etc., translations and to see whether in the oldest translations the wrong term does appear. If it should, then it would be necessary to find out how these translators did their work; did they have dictionaries at their disposal where perhaps ἄροτρον or *aratrum* was translated into *plog, plug, charrue* instead of *årder, ralo, araire*? Or did they use an English or German translation of Luke and were misled by the German *Pflug* or the English *plow*? DID Luther write *Pflug*?[3] In his time and in his area, was the word *Haken* or the word *Arl* used as well as the word *Pflug*? There are, I understand (Brockhaus 1929: 684, column b; British Museum 1965: columns 272-274), versions of the Bible in "Plattdeutsch" dating back to 1534 (see also Darlow and Moule 1911: 481 ff.), which I have not been able to obtain. How do they translate Luke 9: 62? In Plattdeutsch the word *Haken* (for the ard type) is quite common to this day, as is the word *Arl* in Styria (Koren 1950).

Also, there are translations into Provençal (Brockhaus 1929: 684, column a), which I also have been unable to obtain. Both the word *araire* and the plow type it denotes are particularly common in southern France. Do the Provençal versions of the Bible use *araire* or *charrue*?

Did the oldest Swedish translations really use the word *plog* as do the

---

[3] Stier and Theile (1863:277) do not mention any other word but *Pflug*. According to von Bahder (1925:138) the word *pflügen*, not yet in existence in Middle High German, came into use principally through Luther who uses it as well as the word *ackern*.

recent translations? Or did they by any chance write *årder*? If that should be the case, when was the change from *årder* to *plog* made?

The early translators probably all wrote Latin and spoke Latin and knew it well. Could it be that while studying Latin in school they had learned to translate *aratum* into *plog*, *plug*, *charrue* and then simply applied this mistranslation when they had to translate Luke 9: 62 either from the Greek or perhaps from the Vulgate? Probably the answers to all of these questions are known to the Biblical scholar and I am only revealing my ignorance by raising them.

V

Raising additional questions which must be asked, I must continue to reveal my ignorance.

Most of the French translations which I have consulted actually are not truly "French", nor are they the oldest French translations. The Bibles of 1567 and 1568 were printed in Geneva. The translation published in 1669 was prepared in Geneva and printed in Amsterdam. The translation of 1683, although printed in Paris with the permission of the king and the approval of the authorities, had been translated in Louvain.

The Paris edition of 1805, on which the editions of 1820 and 1832 are based, was not available to me. It seems to be rare: the catalog of the Library of the British Museum lists two Geneva translations of 1805 (British Museum 1946: column 185; 1965: column 242) and refers to London editions of 1814, 1817, and 1819 based on the Paris edition of 1805 (British Museum 1946: column 186; 1965: column 242), but does not list a copy of the Paris edition of 1805 itself. However, that edition, in turn, seems to be "based on the text of the Bible of Geneva" of 1693 (British Museum 1946: column 186; 1965: column 242). Since the edition of 1820 was printed in New York at the expense of the American Bible Society, it will be necessary to admit, for any later edition, the possibility of its having been influenced by the inability of the English language to distinguish between the two kinds of plows.

Thus, the only edition of those which I have seen that could be truly French would be the edition of 1816, printed with the approval of the cardinal-archbishop of Paris and based on the edition of 1771, having also consulted the editions of 1759, 1776, and 1785, none of which I have been able to obtain. Only a student of the history of French Bible translations will be able to trace to its origin the use of the word *charrue,* instead of *araire.*

I know even less about the history of Swedish translations. The oldest Swedish translation at my disposal is not older than 1774. According to the catalog of the library of the British Museum, the "first Swedish Bible", published in Upsala in 1541, was "translated from the German version of M. Luther" (British Museum 1946: column 235). This is the reason why I am inclined to assume that the use of *plog* instead of *årder* in Swedish Bibles is due to dependence on Luther's German. But is my assumption correct? And if so, why did Swedish translators let themselves be swayed by Luther's German and did not use the term *årder,* which they must have known to be the only accurate one?

Parts of the oldest Danish translation also seem to be "little else than a verbal transmutation of the version of Luther" (Henderson 1813: 19). Other parts, however, and in particular the four Gospels, follow Erasmus' Latin translation (Henderson 1813: 16-18). Furthermore, the problem must be considered during which period the word *ard* in Danish went out of use.[4]

While I do not happen to know any French or Swedish edition which gives a correct translation of ἄροτρον, I do know translations into Slavonic (1816), Bulgarian (1874 and 1882), and Ukrainian (1893) which use the proper term *(ralo).* Thus, there are translations into Slavic languages which I would consider correct.

Those Polish editions (1832, 1891, 1943) which I have seen use the word *plug;* however, the 1943 edition was printed in Philadelphia, the 1891 edition, while printed in Warsaw, derives from the British and Foreign Bible Society, and the 1832 edition was published in Leipzig by the publisher Karl Tauchnitz.

The Slovakian (1883), Slovenian (1883, 1884), and Croatian (1874) translations which I happen to have seen all are connected with the British and Foreign Bible Society, and therefore the hypothesis is tempting that their use of the cognates of *plow* is due to that connection and to an English prototype. Although no such connection is expressly stated in the Czech translation (1870) which I have before me, and which writes *pluh,* I suspect that it, too, is of British origin: in the lower left

---

[4] Hvarfner (1968-1969:192) states expressly that the distinction between *ard* and *plov* has disappeared in Denmark. His claim is supported by the fact that Sophus Müller (1900) uses the term *plov* exclusively although he states that there had been two "old" terms for the "plowing implement" – "Arl og Plov" (1900:222: "to gamle Betegnelser for Pløieredskabet").

corner of the title page there appears in small print the word "Bohemian".
Thus I would be inclined to assume that the use of the wrong term in
Slavic translations is due to the influence of the English word *plow*.
Yet the Ukrainian translation which, as stated above, uses the word
ralo, probably is as British as the Czech translation of 1870: on the left
page facing the table of contents, the words "Ruthen. New Test."
appear in small print. I am lost.

VI

Once again I must state that the English translation is correct, and so are
the translations into those other languages where there is only one word
for ἄροτρον, whether it is cognate with *plow* (e.g. Danish *plov*, see above
fn. 4) or with *aratrum* (e.g. Spanish *arado*). Where a language has two
different words, thus distinguishing the two different kinds, and where,
therefore, until now, I have claimed that *araire, ralo, årder* (and not
charrue, plug, plog) should have been used in the translation of Luke
9: 62, I now am forced to retract that claim. To explain the straits
in which I now find myself I again will use a metaphor from modern
life. Today we have different makes of automobiles. The warning "If
you drive a Pontiac and you don't fasten your seat belt you might get
into trouble" could lead to a misunderstanding. Such a warning would
seem to imply that if you drive any other make, a Ford or a Buick
(or, perhaps, to make the misunderstanding more evident: if you drive
a Cadillac or a Rolls Royce), it might not be necessary to fasten your seat
belt. Where there are two or more possibilities, the selection of only
one puts the emphasis in the wrong place. Where people are aware of two
different kinds of plowing implements (as we are aware of different
makes of cars), selecting one and not mentioning the other automatically
leads to the conclusion that the other one is not implied. "No one who
puts his hand to the *årder* ..." thus will be understood in the sense that the
årder alone is meant and that the *plog* is not implied.

Thus I am afraid that the translation which I asked for in Slavic
languages or in Swedish or French would be quite wrong. In languages
in which there are two words for ἄροτρον, Luke 9: 62 cannot be translated
at all or only in a ludicrously involved way: "No one who puts his
hand to the plow or to the ard and looks back ...."

But ignoring the translation problem, what does the Greek verse mean?
It could not have had a meaning comparable to what I heard over the

radio while writing this article: "He who looks back at the stock market dies of remorse." But could it be that the Bible verse does not refer to any specific behavior but was a household phrase, a kind of a proverb? I read in my Swedish-German dictionary (the Auerbach *Ordbok*, 1932, an outstanding and admirable work which I love): "lägga handen vid plogen *bildl.* die Hand an den Pflug legen" (Auerbach 1932: 917). Thus in Swedish to put the hand to the plow is used only as a figure of speech meaning: to get going. Is this an old Swedish metaphor or is the phrase the result of the influence of Luke 9: 62 on Swedish thinking? In many languages all kinds of popular, often mocking sayings are associated with the plow.[5] Were they also in Aramaic?

VII

However, the problems arising from translating ἄροτρον into French, Swedish, and Slavic languages seem small compared with the difficulties connected with the translating of Luke 9: 62 into the language of a people who do not know any plowing implement. The usual way to solve this problem, I understand, is to substitute the word for some other agricultural implement. As an example I take the Nyakyusa New Testament (1960: 130 f.) where *ikumbulu*, the word for hoe, is used.

Here again a strange difficulty arises. The Nyakyusa, in tilling the soil, build carefully constructed ridges, an excellent method of preventing erosion. There are broad furrows between the ridges, and in the following year the ridge is built up in the furrow of the previous year, the new furrow now occupying the area of the previous year's ridge (Leser 1960: 373-378). As long as you alternate between furrow and ridge it does not make a difference whether while working you look back or ahead, but what you must do is to look sideways, from ridge to furrow, and vice versa (see figures 3 and 4). However, when you begin to take a new area into cultivation and begin to build the first ridges on ground where there were neither ridges nor furrows, then you MUST intermittently look back while hoeing because otherwise your ridge will not be straight, and will run in a wrong direction.

[5] For striking examples, see Vilkuna 1971:83. See also Plummer 1901:268. I am greatly indebted to the Reverend Dr. Paul Brennan for having drawn my attention to this passage as well as to the comments by Reiling and Swellengrebel. Furthermore, see Meyer 1878:402f.; Meyer 1880:108; Bruce 1897:537; Gressmann and Klostermann 1919:475; Strack and Billerbeck 1924:165f.; Creed 1930:143. As to textual variants see Cerfaux 1954:498-501.

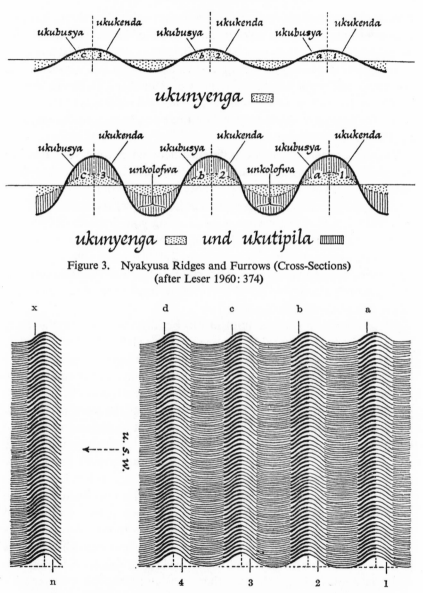

Figure 3. Nyakyusa Ridges and Furrows (Cross-Sections)
(after Leser 1960: 374)

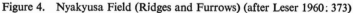

Figure 4. Nyakyusa Field (Ridges and Furrows) (after Leser 1960: 373)

In many areas the use of the hoe poses an additional difficulty for the translator. Hoeing, among the Nyakyusa, is man's work as is plowing everywhere. But among most people where the hoe (or the digging stick) is the standard agricultural implement it is the woman who uses it, and never the man. So here we are faced with the problem not just of gender but even of sex roles in the division of labor. The Greek text uses the male gender both in οὐδείς and in εὔθετος. The Revised Standard Version, avoiding the gender in the translation of both, nevertheless commits itself by saying "no one who puts *his* hand to the plow ..." The King James version translated "no *man*, having put *his* hand to the plow ..." Is it permissible to translate Luke 9: 62 into: "no *woman* who puts *her* hand to the *hoe* ..."?

Woman or man, there is a difference between putting your hand to the plow and putting it to the hoe. Putting your hand to the hoe does not imply that you are beginning to hoe. If you put your hand to the hoe you are picking it up, and this you do at home, carry the hoe to the field, and there you may begin your work. Putting your hand to the plow is different. It means putting your hand to the plow handle and thus implies the beginning of plowing. Bauer (1958: 215) expressly quotes Hesiod: ἀρχόμενος ἀρότρον ἄκρον ἐχέτλης χειρὶ λαβών. Thus, in Greek, the meaning of "putting your hand to the plow" really was: beginning your work. But was it also in Aramaic?

There were many other implements besides the plow in the Holy Land. Christ could have said: "No one who puts his hand to the sickle ...", but he did not say that. May one agricultural implement be substituted for any other? The direction in which the spade most often and the hoe frequently is worked is sideways, sometimes by stepping back; if so, you *must* look back. Even where the direction of the work is the same as the direction in which the plow is used, would it be permissible to make Christ say in a translation: "No one who puts his hand to the harrow and looks back ..."? Today the farmer does not put his hand to the plow at all but the plow is drawn by the tractor to which it is attached; would it be permissible to translate: "No one who puts his hand to the tractor ..."? Today, at least in this country, few people have ever touched a plow. What the plow was in everyday life two thousand years ago is today the automobile. If we were to translate: "No one who puts his hand to the steering wheel and looks back", wouldn't we change the entire meaning? Shouldn't we rather translate: "No one who puts his hand to the wheel and his foot on the accelerator and does *not* look into the rear mirror ..."? It cannot be the meaning of Luke 9: 62 that we should work recklessly. Yet, depending on the way in which hoeing is done, an admonition against looking back while hoeing would mean to suggest careless instead of conscientious work.

Would it be permissible to translate: "No one who goes to the field to work and looks back ..." (Reiling and Swellengrebel 1971: 400; Strack and Billerbeck 1924: 166)? But even such a translation would not be intelligible in a culture in which agriculture is unknown. The Enga translation (although written for a New Guinea people who practice agriculture with the digging stick) avoids even that difficulty: "Whoever determines to do a piece of work, and then has a change of mind about doing it, is not capable of having God as his boss" (Brennan 1973).

VIII

Nothing that I have said so far will help anyone to understand Luke 9: 62 better. Quite to the contrary, the problems over which I have stumbled, will, perhaps, become burdensome to others. Is it fair to raise questions when one is not able to offer any answers? The specialist in an extremely narrow field (the ethnology of the plow) who has no knowledge of the pertinent disciplines – New Testament, Bible Translating, Greek – should have remained silent. Yet, I cannot resist the temptation to raise even one more question. Not being able to understand Luke 9: 62, I wonder whether my difficulties just possibly could be due to a wrong translation from Aramaic into Greek? A few years ago I was fascinated by Jakob Hausheer's brilliant conjecture[6] (utterly convincing to this uninitiated layman) concerning the other Bible verse with which I happen to have a particular relationship, Matthew 5: 48.[7] Hausheer succeeded in perfectly fitting the verse into the context (Bruppacher 1965: 243 f.) and making understandable what otherwise to this day would be to me one of the most difficult passages in the Bible. Could perhaps a similarly plausible conjecture be found for Luke 9: 62 which suddenly would disperse all the problems which I have raised?

---

[6] Bruppacher (1965:243) calls it "einen glänzenden Fund". The *Kirchenblatt für die reformierte Schweiz* (where Bruppacher's article was published) is not easily available in the United States; insofar as I know the only complete set is in the possession of the Library of Princeton Theological Seminary. An abstract of three lines was published in *New Testament Abstracts* 10 (1965-1966), 188, #511. A more detailed summary of Bruppacher's article appeared several years ago in an English language periodical but at present I am unable to trace it.

[7] It was my "confirmation verse". In my hometown in Germany, after confirmation, you visit your minister who then writes a Bible verse into your hymnal which you have brought with you for that very purpose.

REFERENCES

I Bible Translations

(a) French Translations

1567 La Bible, qui est toute la Saincte Escriture: contenant le Vieil & le Nouveau Testament, Autrement, La Vieille & Nouvelle Alliance. Avec argumens sur chacun livre ... (Geneva: Imprimerie de François Estienne).

1568 Biblia Latinogallica. La Bible Françoiselatine, qui est toute la saincte Escriture, contenant Le Vieil & Nouveau Testament, ou Alliance (Geneva: Imprimerie de Iaques Bourgeois. Pour Estienne Anastase).

1669 Le nouveau testament qui contient tous les livres de la Nouvelle Alliance de nôtre Seigneur Jesus Christ, traduit sur le Grec, reveu & corrigé, par les Ministres & Professeurs de Geneve ... (Amsterdam: Louys & Daniel Elzevier).

1683 La Saincte Bible, contenant le vieil et nouveau testament. Traduite en François par les Theologiens de l'Université de Louvain. ... Fidelement reveuë, corrigée, & enrichie de Figures en Taille-Douce. Avec Privilege du Roy, & Approbation des Docteurs. (Paris: Antoine Dezallier).

1684 Le Nouveau Testament, c'est a dire, la Nouvelle Alliance de nostre Seigneur Jesus Christ (Amsterdam: Zander Wybrants).

1700 La Sainte Bible, traduite en François sur la Vulgate; ... Tome troisième. Avec Approbation (Liege: Jean François Bronckart).

1816 Le Nouveau Testament de notre Seigneur Jésus-Christ, traduit sur la Vulgate par Le Maistre de Sacy. Edition stéréotype, publiée par les soins de M. Frédéric Léo (Paris: Firmin Didot, Imprimeur du Roi et de l'Institut de France). (Pour l'exécution de la présente édition stéréotype, on s'est principalement servi de celle de 1771, imprimée, avec permission de son Éminence Monseigneur le Cardinal de Noailles, archevêque de Paris, et avec approbation et privilége du Roi, chez Desprez, imprimeur ordinaire du Roi, et du Clergé de France. On a aussi consulté les éditions de 1759 et de 1776, et la Vulgate sortie des presses de Fr. Amb. Didot, aîné, en 1785, dédiée au Clergé de France. Note de l'Éditeur, Fr. Léo.)

1820 La Sainte Bible, qui contient le Vieux et le Nouveau Testament. Imprimée sur l'edition de Paris, de l'année 1805. Edition stéréotype, revue et corrigée avec soin d'après les textes Hebreu et Grec. Aux frais de la Société Biblique Americaine (New York: Daniel Fanshaw).

1831 La Sainte Bible, contenant l'Ancien et le Nouveau Testament, traduite sur la Vulgate Par le Maistre de Sacy (Paris: J. Smith).

1832 La Sainte Bible, qui contient le vieux et le nouveau testament: Imprimée sur l'edition de Paris, de l'année 1805. Edition stéréotype, revue et corrigée avec soin d'après les textes Hebreu et Grec (New York: Daniel Fanshaw).

1924 La Sainte Bible ou l'Ancien et le Nouveau Testament, Version d'Ostervald (Paris: 58 rue de Clichy).

(b) Swedish Translations

1774 Prof-Öfwersattning Af then Heliga Skrift, på Hans Kongl. Maj:ts Nådigste Befallning, af Then till Swenska Bibeltolkningens öfwerseende i Nåder förordnade särskilde Commission (Stockholm: Johan Pfeiffer).

1796 Wår Herres och Frälsares Jesu Christi Nya Testamente (Linköping: D. G. Björn).

1845   Nya Testamentet. På föranstaltande af Swenska Bibel Sällskapet. 34th edition (Stockholm: Samuel Rumstedt).
1891   Bibeln eller Den Helige Skrift I. Gamla Testamentet, enligt gällande äldre öfwersättningen, II. Nya Testamentet enligt Normalupplagan af Kong. Maj:t godkända Nya öfwersättningen (Stockholm: Evang. Fosterlands-Stiftelsens Förlags-Expedition).
n.d.   Bibeln eller Den Heliga Skrift. ... Översättningen Gillad och Stadfast av Konungen den 2 Oktober 1917.

(c) Danish Translations

1777   Biblia, Det er Den Gandske Hell. Skriftes Bøger, Efter den 1699 udgangne Huus- og Reyse-Bibel (Copenhagen, Kongel: Waysenhuses Bogtrykkerie).
1849   Vor Herres og Frelsers Jesu Christi Nya Testamente (New York: American Bible Society). (Danish and English in parallel columns.)
1889   Bibelen eller Den Hellige Skrift, indeholdende det Gamle og det Nye Testamentes Kanoniske Bøger (Copenhagen: British and Foreign Bible Society).

(d) Slavic Translations

Slavonic

1816(?) Novyy Zavĕtĭ Gospoda Našego Iisusa Xrista (St. Petersburg [?]).

Bulgarian

1874   Bibliya sireychi Svyashchenno-to Pisaniye na Vetkhyy i Novyy Zaveytu. Veyrno i tochno preyvedeno otu pirvoobrazno-to (Constantinople: Vu Knigopechatnitsya-tya na A. Kh. Boyadzhiyana).
1882   Novyy Zaveytu na gospoda nashego Iisusa Khrista (Vienna: Adolf Holzhausen).

Croatian

1874   Sveto Pisma Staroga i Novoga Zavjeta, Preveo stari zavjet G. J. Daničić (Budapest: British and Foreign Bible Society).

Slovenian

1884   Novi Testament Gospoda in zveličarja našega Jezusa Kristusa. Polog Grškega Izvirnika (British and Foreign Bible Society).

Czech

1870   Biblia Sacra, To gest: Biblj Swatá, aneb wssecka Swatá Pjsma Starého. i Nowého Zákona (Prague: A. Reichard and Company).

Slovakian

1893   Swaté Písmo nowéjo Zákona pedla ebecného latinského od sw. rimskekatolickég církwi potwrđeného preložené. With imprimatur by Cardinal Archbishop Alexander Rudna (Vienna: British and Foreign Bible Society).

Polish

1832   Nowy pana naszego Jezusa Chrystusa Testament przez X. Jakuba Wuyka, Societatis Jesu, Na Polski Jezyk Przełeżony (Leipzig: Karl Tauchnitz).

256 PAUL LESER

1891 Biblija Świeta to jest Wszystko Pismo Świete Starego i Nowego Testamentu
(British and Foreign Bible Society, and Warsaw: Adolf Kanter).
1943 Biblija Świeta to jest Wszystko Pismo Świete Starego i Nowego Testamentu
(Philadelphia: The Judson Press).

Ukrainian
1893 Svyate Pysïmo Novoho Zavitu Movoyu Rysïko-Ukrainïskoyu pereklali
vkupi P. A. Kulish i dr. Pulyui (Vienna: Adolf Holzhausen).

(e) Nyakyusa Translation

1960 Tesitamenti umpya gwa malafyale gwiṭi Jesu Kilisiti umpokụ gwa kịsụ
(London: British and Foreign Bible Society).

II Other References

Auerbach, Carl
1932 Svensk-Tysk Ordbok, 3rd stereotyped ed., 5th printing (Stockholm: P. A.
Norstedt).
Avitsur, Shmuel
1965 The Native Ard of Eretz-Israel: Its History and Development (= Aveshalom
Institute for Homeland Studies. Man and His Works Series for the Study of
the History of Technology in the Land of Israel 5) (Tel-Aviv: Sifriath Hassadeh
Publishing House).
Bahder, Karl von
1925 Zur Wortwahl in der frühneuhochdeutschen Schriftsprache (Heidelberg:
Carl Winter's Universitätsbuchhandlung).
Bauer, Walter
1958 Griechisch-Deutsches Wörterbuch zu den Schriften des Neuen Testamentes
und der übrigen urchristlichen Literatur, 5th ed. (Berlin: Alfred Töpelmann).
Bratanić, Branimir
1952 "On the Antiquity of the One-Sided Plough in Europe, Especially among
the Slavic Peoples", Laos 2, 51-61.
1954 "Nešto o starosti pluga kod Slavena. Upsomeni Lubora Niederlea", Sveu-
čilište u Zagrebu, Filozofski fakultet, Zbornik radova 2, 277-306.
Brennan, Paul
1973 Letter of October 5.
British Museum
1946 The British Museum Catalogue of Printed Books 1881-1900 6 (Ann Arbor:
J. W. Edwards).
1965 The British Museum Catalogue of Printed Books 17 (London: The Trustees of
the British Museum).
Brockhaus
1929 Der Grosse Brockhaus 2, 15th edition (Leipzig: F. A. Brockhaus).
Bruce, Alexander Balmain
1897 The Synoptic Gospels 1, edited by Nicoll.
Bruppacher, H.
1965 "Ein neues Jesuswort", Kirchenblatt für die reformierte Schweiz 121, 242-244.
Catholic Commentary on Holy Scripture, A
1953 (London: Thomas Nelson).
Cerfaux, Lucien
1954 Recueil Lucien Cerfaux 1 (Gembloux: J. Duculot). Réimpression anastatique
1962.

Creed, John Martin
1930   *The Gospel According to St. Luke: The Greek Text with Introduction, Notes, and Indices* (London: Macmillan).
Curwen, E. Cecil
1946   *Plough and Pasture* (London: Cobbett).
Darlow, T. H., and H. F. Moule
1911   *Historical Catalogue of the Printed Editions of Holy Scripture in the Library of the British and Foreign Bible Society. Vol. II. Polyglots and Languages other than English* (London: Bible House).
Erixon, Sigurd
1948   "Svenska årder", *Liv och Folkkultur* 1, 129-157.
Farrar, F. W.
1889   *The Gospel According to St Luke, with Maps, Notes and Introduction*, in *The Cambridge Bible for Schools and Colleges* (Cambridge: University Press).
Gressmann, Hugo, and Klostermann, Erich
1919   *Handbuch zum Neuen Testament*, herausgegeben von Hans Lietzmann, 2nd vol., *Die Evangelien. Die Synoptiker* (Tübingen: J. C. B. Mohr [Paul Siebeck]).
Grundmann, Walter
1961   *Das Evangelium nach Lukas*, 2nd ed., *Theologischer Handkommentar zum Neuen Testament* 3 (Berlin: Evangelische Verlagsanstalt).
Hvarfner, Harald
1968-   "Die Verbreitung und Stabilität der Arbeitsmethoden", *Ethnologia Europaea*
1969   2-3, 191-196.
Henderson, Ebenezer
1813   *A Dissertation on Hans Mikkelsen's (or, the first Danish) Translation of the New Testament: In which, besides historical notices respecting the circumstances connected with its publication, it is shown to have been made, not from the Vulgate, as has hitherto been believed, but from the Latin version of Erasmus, and the earlier editions of Luther's Testament* (Copenhagen: Thorstein E. Rangel).
The Interpreter's Bible. The Holy Scriptures ... in Twelve Volumes
1952   Vol. 8 (New York and Nashville: Abingdon).
Jirlow, Ragnar
1970   *Die Geschichte des schwedischen Pfluges* (= *Nordiska museets handlingar* 72) (Stockholm: Boktryckeri Thule).
Koren, Hanns
1950   *Pflug und Arl. Ein Beitrag zur Volkskunde der Ackergeräte* (Salzburg: Otto Müller).
Larousse
1912   *Petit Larousse Illustré*, 79th ed. (Paris: Librairie Larousse).
Leser, Paul
1931   *Entstehung und Verbreitung des Pfluges* (Münster: Aschendorff).
1960   "Felder und Bodenbaugeräte der Nyakyusa", *Ethnologica*, new series, 2, 363-383.
Manson, William
n.d.   *The Gospel of Luke*, in *The Moffatt New Testament Commentary* (New York, London: Harper).
Meyer, Heinrich August Wilhelm
1878   *Kritisch exegetischer Kommentar über das Neue Testament. Erste Abteilung, zweite Hälfte. Kritisch exegetisches Handbuch über die Evangelien des Markus und Lukas*, 6th edition, edited by Bernhard Weiss (Göttingen: Vandenhoeck and Ruprecht).

258   PAUL LESER

1880   *Critical and Exegetical Commentary on the New Testament*, the translation revised and edited by William P. Dickson and William Stewart. Part I, Second Division, *The Gospels of Mark and Luke* 2 (Edingburgh: T. and T. Clark).

Müller, Sophus
   1900   "Oldtidens Plov", *Aarbøger for Nordisk Oldkyndighed og Historie*, 2 Raekke, 15 Bind. (Copenhagen: Gyldendalske Boghandel).

Nicoll, W. Robertson (ed.)
   1897   *The Expositor's Greek Testament* (New York: Dodd, Mead).

Plummer, Alfred
   1901   *A Critical and Exegetical Commentary on the Gospel According to St. Luke*, 4th ed., *The International Critical Commentary* (New York: Charles Scribner's Sons).

Reiling, J., and J. L. Swellengrebel
   1971   *A Translator's Handbook on the Gospel of Luke* (= *Helps for Translators* 10) (Leiden: E. J. Brill).

Stier, N., and K. G. W. Theile
   1863   *Das Neue Testament unsres Herrn und Heilandes Jesu Christi. In übersichtlicher Nebeneinanderstellung des Urtextes, der Vulgata und Luther-Uebersetzung, sowie der wichtigsten Varianten der vornehmsten deutschen Uebersetzungen* (Bielefeld : Velhagen and Klasing).

Strack, Hermann L., und Paul Billerbeck
   1924   *Das Evangelium nach Markus, Lukas und Johannes und die Apostelgeschichte erläutert aus Talmud und Midrasch* (Munich: C. H. Becksche Verlagsbuchhandlung Oskar Beck).

The Union Bible Dictionary
   1842   (Philadelphia: American Sunday School Union).

Vakarelski, Christo
   1970   "Traditionelle landwirtschaftliche Geräte der Bulgaren", in Iván Balassa (ed.), *Getreidebau in Ost- und Mitteleuropa* (Budapest: Akadémiai Kiadó).

Vilkuna, Kustaa
   1971   "Die Pfluggeräte Finnlands", *Studia Fennica* 16, 5-173.

THE SUBJECTIVITY OF ANACHRONISM

NORM MUNDHENK

After several years of debating the issues, a certain amount of suspecting and accusing each other of belonging to stereotyped extremes, and a good deal of personal wrestling with troublesome implications, those of us in Bible translation circles seem finally to be working out basically agreeable central principles about how to handle cultural adaptation in translation. Important concepts like the difference between historical material and illustrative material, the difference between frequently repeated and specific events, the significance of certain Biblical images, and others, have helped to clarify our thinking, and in general to know better what we are doing.

The first draft of a book by Nida and Reyburn dealing with this subject came out at the height of the debate. The book has not yet been put into its final form, but when it is it will doubtless be considerably revised. It seems safe to say that it will contain a good summary of all of these basic concepts, as well as a number of other important insights. But it also seems safe to say that it will leave many of us still unsatisfied, still conscious of many points of uncertainty and disagreement. This whole question of the limits of adaptation seems to resist being made scientific in the sense that we can establish principles that will always produce the same answer for a given problem, no matter who applies them. On any given matter it is still likely that even the small group of United Bible Societies translation consultants will come up with two or more different, and often conflicting, opinions.

Sometimes the disagreement will be about what the principles themselves encourage or exclude in a particular case. More often we will agree that "yes, that's what the principles suggest", but will remain personally unconvinced that it really is the right solution, or troubled by whether the "right" answer is really the best one.

Norm Mundhenk is Translation Consultant for the United Bible Societies.

It seems to me that it is impossible to do full justice to this question of cultural adaptation without taking into consideration the person you are translating for. In the final analysis, a translation is good or bad, right or wrong, in terms of how the reader understands and reacts. Reactions to and understandings of cultural adaptation vary considerably from reader to reader, and what hits the nail on the head for one person can cause considerable offense to the next.

I think of this problem as a result of the SUBJECTIVITY OF ANACHRONISM. Like the cultural adaptations I am discussing, this term may be valid only for me, and may offend others. By ANACHRONISM, for instance, I mean any kind of cultural adaptation which doesn't fit the context. I know that etymologically the word is supposed to be limited to things which don't fit because the time is wrong. But I have always understood it in terms of things which are out of place for any reason. Let us look at two non-Biblical examples. The legend of King Arthur of England and the wizard Merlin seems particularly to lend itself to the use of conscious, time-oriented anachronism on the part of modern novelists. Mark Twain in *A Connecticut Yankee in King Arthur's Court*, T. H. White in *The Once and Future King*, and C. S. Lewis in *That Hideous Strength* all use the device of taking someone from the time of the author and placing him in King Arthur's day, or vice versa.

The second example, however, is not time-oriented, nor was the author conscious of the anachronism. It shows more clearly how it is possible for something to seem out of place to one reader where a different reader might not notice it at all. I am interested in English dialects, and had noticed one particular grammatical usage common in England, but not used at all in America.[1] Several years ago, shortly after I had noticed this, I read a short story in an American magazine about a rustic New England family. The characters were occasionally made to speak using this construction, as well as a word or two which sounded suspiciously British to me. Puzzled, I wrote the author, who admitted that she had spent a great deal of time in England, and that even though she was American her speech might well have become more British. I cannot help but wonder if I was the only reader of that story to be struck by these particular anachronisms – anachronisms of dialect, they might be called.

For anyone who finds this wider meaning of the word "anachronism" annoying, I am perfectly happy to have them substitute ana-something-

---

[1] Putting the verb *do* after an anaphoric auxiliary, as in "Bake her a cake?"/"Yes, I think I could do", or "I don't think she's finished it yet, but she might have done."

else-ism, if they prefer to put in the proper Greek root there. Or just call it an "unacceptable adaptation".

By SUBJECTIVITY I mean that in the final analysis what is acceptable or not will probably vary with every individual reader of the translation. I was annoyed to find the supposedly pure New Englanders in the short story speaking with a British grammatical structure which they might well never even have heard used. How many of those reading this article of mine feel you would have been bothered by this? I have collected a few examples of anachronisms in Bible translation which have bothered either me myself or some other UBS translation consultant. I will not identify the sources, but most of those which are not my own examples I do not object to. Some I feel would be most acceptable translation. Note your own reactions to the items in this list, and I think you will see clearly enough how subjective some of these reactions can be.

Gen. 1: 1 Some argue that the Hebrews themselves never thought about creation in the philosophical way that we do, and in particular that they never worked out the doctrine of creation *ex nihilo*, creation of something from nothing. Therefore, to translate this verse so as to suggest that this is the thought behind it is anachronistic – attributing modern ideas to ancient man. The identical argument has been used against translating "heaven and earth" in this verse as "the universe".

Matt. 5: 25 in Today's English Version mentions the "police"; in the New English Bible "the constable". Both of these may suggest only the modern uniformed officer of the law with his gun or nightstick.

Matt. 15: 17 in the Jerusalem Bible refers to the "sewer", which may seem unduly modern.

Matt. 25: 1 in Phillips and the New American Bible has ten "brides-maids", a word which for certain people inevitably conjures up girls in matching modern dresses, with bouquets in their hands.

Matt. 25: 27 in the TEV and Phillips talks about putting money in the "bank", which may suggest stately buildings with Greek columns in front, and well-dressed tellers behind the counter.

Mark 1: 7 in the King James Version talks about undoing the latchet of Jesus' shoes, which if understood at all today may cause one to imagine Jesus in his flowing garment, with stout Elizabethan shoes on his feet.

2 Cor. 13: 12, and in other similar places, Phillips has Paul urging "a handshake all round" in place of the literal "holy kiss". Some feel this would misrepresent the actual Biblical custom.

1 Tim. 6: 19 in Phillips uses a metaphor which might sound as though it comes straight from a modern business executive: "their security should be invested in the life to come, so that they may be sure of holding a share in the life which is permanent".

Examples like this could be multiplied – is it right to translate Alpha and Omega as A and Z? Can an Indian translator feel free to use an idiom describing sorrowful weeping as "the Ganges and Jumna flowed from her eyes"?

Before continuing with the discussion, it might be well to point out that it is both virtually impossible and translationally undesirable to totally avoid cultural adaptation. Theoretically it might seem easy enough to produce a translation completely true to the historical context of the original book. But in practice this is extremely difficult. First, we do not always know enough about cultural or biological details to be sure what exactly the original writer was referring to. Second, even when we are fairly sure, we do not necessarily have any word in our language that unambiguously means exactly what the ancient Greeks or Hebrews meant.

The very fact that we have a word in our own language usually means that it refers primarily to some modern thing. Even with words like *table*, *bread*, *bed*, *basket*, *well*, or *sandal*, all unquestionably correct words to use in a translation, the reader will often be picturing to himself item after item which would have looked decidedly queer to the Biblical characters. This applies equally to words for plants or animals. Again, if we have a word in our language, then in most cases the primary meaning will be the particular species which flourish in our area of the world, or at least the ones which are usually seen in pictures. To the trained zoologist or botanist, if not to the layman, these may be quite different from the Biblical species. In other areas of vocabulary, too, concepts familiar to the reader will subtly replace the true Biblical concepts, until a fair amount of cultural adaptation has crept into the translation. This will be true even when the translator has tried to scrupulously avoid any adaptation.

Of course it IS possible to be precise with language. Historians, archaeologists, botanists, zoologists, and scientists of various other descriptions all have their own specialized vocabulary. If we were willing to borrow this, then no doubt whenever the experts know exactly which species of bird or jackal, or what type of pot or jar is referred to in a particular case, we could put it down unambiguously for what it was. The very thought of such a "translation" should be enough to convince us that the solution is worse than the problem. But for those who want a good reason to reject this approach, it is enough to point out that it itself is anachronistic in a serious way. Not only were such scientific systems completely unknown in Bible times, but even if they had been known, in almost no case was a Biblical writer trying to write anything approaching a scientific treatise. Such a work might be of some value as a reference book for translators. It would have little connection with the purpose of the original author, and it would be unintelligible to almost any modern reader. In short, it would not be a translation at all.

We are translating into modern language, using modern words, as we must and should. Linguists use the concept of "idiolect" to recognize the fact that no two people speak exactly identical languages. Some words that you know and use I may never have heard of. Other words which we both know well may in fact mean quite different things to each of us. Perhaps the word "anachronism" is a good example. Because this is so, each of us will have certain words with broad meanings, words which we will have no difficulty applying to similar items from other cultures or times. And each of us will also probably have words with narrow meanings which refer for us quite specifically to the item in our own culture. Even if other cultures have similar things with similar functions, we will feel better to call them by a different name rather than by a narrow word of ours. Which words are broad and which narrow is apparently a matter of a certain amount of idiolectal variation. Hence the disagreement on such words as *police, bank,* and *bridesmaid.*

An interesting example of this frequently comes up over the translation of "synagogue". For some, "Jewish church" or "Jewish mosque" is a natural and effective translation. For others, a "church" can only be Christian, a "mosque" can only be Muslim. Whenever an individual has a narrow meaning for a particular word and is troubled by the use of this word in a Bible translation, we have an example of subjective anachronism.

If we accept, then, that there is such a phenomenon as the subjectivity of anachronism, what is its significance for Bible translators? Does it simply tell us that no translation will be perfect for every reader, a fact which may be true enough, but about which there is little we can do? To the extent that this subjectivity is an individual matter, I think this is where the matter does end. But to a certain extent I think this subjectivity can be objectified. That is, it is possible to predict the general reaction which will be typical of a group of readers, and to make the translation as appropriate as possible for this group.

It is well known that people with differing cultural and Biblical sophistication react to translations in different ways. Unfortunately, this important fact is often used mainly as an argument against cultural adaptation. The information should rather be used to show us when cultural adaptation will be more acceptable and when it will cause misunderstanding.

If we think of the peoples of the world as Bible readers, I think it is helpful to divide them into five different groups on a scale of their general knowledge about other cultures, and particularly about the Bible culture. First, peoples with no formal education, and hence little awareness of cultures they do not know from firsthand experience. Although I myself have little personal experience with cultures of this sort, from a theoretical point of view it seems possible that they should be divided into two categories: those who have little contact with cultures other than their own, and those who are aware of considerable cultural diversity in their world, even if it seems small to us. Counting these as two groups, the third is then made up of both types of cultures once they are beginning to be exposed to the modern world. Through education or other means, they are beginning to learn about cultural diversity from secondhand sources. The fourth group consists of the majority of people from societies with modern educational systems. Such people will have had varying amounts of exposure to the sort of information these systems provide, but they will not usually have mastered it. In particular, they may know little or nothing about the Bible and the cultures underlying it. Finally, on the fifth level of sophistication, are the people who know the Bible and/or Biblical culture quite well.

Cultural adaptation, like other techniques used in translation, must be judged on the basis of whether it adds to or detracts from the main goal of giving the reader the closest possible understanding to what the original readers had. One of the most obvious dangers of cultural adaptation is that it can seem to deny or make little of the historical and temporal setting of the Biblical events, when in fact these are a most important part of the Bible message. By making the Bible sound as though it happened ten years ago ten miles away, a translator can quite easily lead his readers to reject his work. Some may react that if in fact such a thing had happened, they would certainly have known about it, and therefore it must be the purely fanciful invention of some story teller. Those who know better may feel that the translator is either lying to them or talking down to them in a patronizing way, as though they were not capable of grasping the real facts.

People who react in these ways may of course fall into any of the five groups mentioned above. But as a matter of probability I think we can rank the groups as follows, starting with those who will be most disturbed or misled by cultural adaptation: group three, group four, group two, group one, group five. In other words, I think we will have to be particularly careful in using any cultural adaptations with groups three and four, and that we can use cultural adaptation with much more freedom when translating for groups one and five. Let us look at these groups one by one.

Group Three: Cultures Beginning to be Introduced to the Modern World

This group is probably the most difficult to translate for from the point of view of cultural adaptation. Their experience is limited and on many points totally lacking. On the one hand we want to keep them from being completely lost by a cultural point. On the other hand we want to keep them from thinking that something is identical to their culture when it is not. This can be like walking a tightrope. Over and over a translator will feel that only a cultural adaptation will convey the right image or produce the right emotional reaction. He may make an excellent adaptation, well within rules anyone would accept as permissible. But when the people discover that it is not the literal truth, they may be seriously offended.

I should emphasize that my personal experience of cultures which would be examples for these five groups is quite limited. Those who have known people who fit any of these categories may be able to make important additions or corrections to this summary. However, I have noticed a fascinating two-way division of cultures which cuts across these categories, and which could be of considerable importance for this discussion. Cultures seem to react in two opposing ways when they become Christian. Some peoples feel that with the new faith must come a completely new way of life. Anything obviously connected with their old religion they want to suppress, and even other cultural items may be dropped, one by one (religion is more intimately involved with the other cultural areas in many of these cultures than it would be in modern Western culture, anyway).

Other peoples seem to feel that it is quite natural to simply "baptize" their old culture in almost all its details, keeping it, but giving it a new, Christian, basis and meaning. Obviously this is something that a missionary may have strong feelings about one way or the other, and doubtless many societies have responded to conversion in a way different from their own natural bent because of the force of the missionary personality. But I am convinced that this difference is there in the cultures themselves, and is not simply the result of differing missionary theologies. Some missionaries, armed with a sound anthropological training and a deep understanding of Christian potentials in the cultural tradition, have nevertheless not been able to convince the new Christians not to throw out certain of their old customs the missionary felt innocent or even good. Other missionaries, horrified at some of the stories related in the cultural mythology about "God", have naturally assumed that they must find a new name for God, only to be told by the people that they now realize what God is really like. The old stories were simply lies, and there is no reason to think that God is less God because people tell lies about him!

If the particular group-three culture being dealt with happens also to be one of those which is rejecting its own traditions as part of its non-Christian past, then obviously the anti-adaptation tendencies of this group will just be reinforced. But if it is a culture quite ready to view its own traditions either neutrally or as Christianizable, then the people may be much more ready to see the value of cultural adaptation. Even if their suspicion of being patronized would at first lead them to reject adaptations, it seems quite possible that a serious attempt to teach them why adaptations are used might prove successful.

As already said, a translation without any adaptation is really impossible. But someone translating for cultures in group three may find that he has to keep adaptation at a minimum, at least when dealing with many areas of the culture.

Group Four: People with a Basic Education but Little More

There is no reason why a good basic education could not train people sufficiently in the underlying principles of translation so that they could learn to understand and appreciate cultural adaptation in translation. In fact, however, the more typical effect of a basic education seems to be quite the opposite. These people may react against cultural adaptation as strongly or more so as those in group three, but for a different reason. They are sufficiently aware of differences of culture and particularly of time that they can spot real or apparent anachronisms quite quickly. Their reaction seems to be to suspect that the translator was incompetent, sloppy, or possibly guided by questionable theology or motives. If some of the leaders of such a group become convinced that a translation is faulty, they will often find it quite easy to convince the people not to use it. Arguments against adaptation will be obvious, familiar arguments. Anything said in its favor will sound backwards and overly subtle.

Again, since some cultural adaptation is necessary and desirable, it is particularly important to try to prepare the leaders, the ones to whom people listen in forming their opinions and biases, whether these leaders are in the church, the press, or elsewhere. We should do what we can to help everyone to understand what is being done and why, but we will be particularly fortunate if someone who is respected and who can explain things clearly comes to realize the validity of the translation. Nevertheless, when translating for this group, too, it is probably best to keep adaptation to a minimum, and to stay well within the margins of error.

Groups One and Two: Cultures Isolated from the Modern World

No matter who we are translating for, the historical fact that God's Biblical revelation was made through a particular culture and a particular Man in that culture must not be lost sight of. A reader should certainly think that "God speaks his language". He should certainly realize that what God says can be applied over and over again to his own life and his own people. But he must not think that the Bible itself is talking about his people (except of course in cases where it is!).

The Bible itself has enough introductory information and background information scattered through it already to give the translator many opportunities to bring out this historical side without in any way being untrue to the authors. At other times, necessary historical and cultural background will have to be provided by other means – pictures, extra-Biblical teaching, and implicit details skillfully made explicit in the text itself without thereby making the Bible sound like an introduction to Bible culture. Other techniques are also useful in providing necessary background, but we need not discuss them here. In short, the reader must be aware throughout that he is reading about God's dealings with another tribe, though of course there will be many places where the Bible tells him of God's great interest in his own tribe as well.

Given, then, that the reader knows he is reading about another people, we must also emphasize that we want him to grasp as fully as possible, both intellectually and emotionally, what God was saying to these people. This can be accomplished much more effectively for any people by using familiar images and figures of speech, and by keeping to a minimum references to customs, objects, or animals which are strange, and which therefore detract from the intended impact of the account. People such as these we are now talking about, who have little or no knowledge of the Biblical culture, are not going to be put off by anachronisms. To refer, even in an image, to a kangaroo would considerably disturb many other people who happen to have the knowledge that kangaroos are known only in a limited part of the southern hemisphere. But a person from group one or two, living in the area where kangaroos are a common part of life, will see nothing anachronistic in mentioning them in the Bible. Since as a common animal they will probably have some important symbolic value, it may often be that the original author's purpose can be translated most effectively precisely by some mention of a kangaroo.[2]

Similarly, for such people, unaware of the slow historical development of the things they take for granted as part of the modern world, time gaps may not mean anything. Many translators would probably be willing to put a kangaroo in a translation long before they would put an airplane in it. But particularly if it is only some quality of the airplane which is being used to make a point, and the reader himself is not going to be disturbed by its use, I do not see that we are doing anything essentially different or wrong by treating it in the same way as any other cultural adaptation. It is only the translator's own subjective feelings which make one thing a less acceptable anachronism than another if the readers themselves see no difference.

I realize that some will object to this argument. Let me discuss briefly three of the more convincing objections I can foresee. First, some will say that this is taking undue liberties because whether the people are able to grasp the issues or not, the translator has a certain responsibility to maintain as much objective consistency as possible. There is a sense in which I accept this argument. For those working with a jungle tribe whose only known modes of transportation are canoes and planes, I would certainly agree that it is better to suggest that Paul went by canoe down a great river than by plane through the sky when making the journey from Jerusalem to Rome. Actually in a story as long as Paul's journey, a translator should make every effort to get across to his readers something of the concept of the sea, even if they have never known it.

---

[2] One interesting result of the subjectivity of anachronism is that we can sometimes be convinced that something is an anachronism when it is not. Elephants, for instance. They were not completely unknown in Israel, though many Bible experts might have trouble remembering where they occur. Look at 1 Macc. 6:34-46. Of course this is a specialized situation, and it would still be historically quite inaccurate to suggest they were in any way a part of daily life. But they were not unknown.

But when similar problems arise in passing, in a single verse, there may be no practical way to keep the readers from understanding it completely in terms of their own experience. We do want people to grasp the historical side of the Bible, and in matters of history we should try to come as close as we can to getting across the real facts. But the built-in strangeness of the Bible message will doubtless produce some bewilderment anyway, and whenever the subject matter permits we should try to say things as naturally as we possibly can. If a comparison to a plane or a kangaroo comes in that category, I see no reason to shrink back from using it.

One fact true of many languages may help to ease the translator's conscience, especially when he finds himself forced to make adaptations in the historical material itself. Perhaps he is concerned that the only grain his people know is rice – how can he substitute rice for the Biblical wheat? Or the only boat they know is a canoe. How can he use such a word to translate the sea-going ships of the Bible? Languages, like individuals, seem to understand some words in a broad sense, and other words in a narrow sense. I do not mean to suggest that such problems are always easily solved, but quite often I think the translator will find that he need not have worried. Even if only rice is now known, when wheat is seen or introduced everyone may quite naturally call it "rice". A special identifying word may distinguish it when necessary, but it may not always be used. The word didn't mean "rice" after all! It meant "grain", and the translator was misled because there was only one example. In the same way, people may quite naturally call a ship a kind of "canoe", and in some cases may even call a sheep a kind of pig. The translator, concerned that he is taking too great a liberty, may sometimes even find that he has not adapted at all in one sense. It is true, of course, that most people will continue to understand the most common, and therefore the wrong, thing when they read. But this would probably be true in any case for those who have only their own experience to help them.

The second objection which is often raised to cultural adaptation for groups like this is that BECAUSE the people do not know about Biblical culture, history, or in fact any of the important things we learn from our education, they need to have all these things clearly in the Bible so that it can be used as a textbook to open their eyes and broaden their horizons. If someone wants to use the Bible to teach from, a translator can have no objection. But this is certainly not the primary purpose of the Bible, and a translator will often have to subordinate this potential use to the far greater need to communicate accurately and effectively.

Finally, the most frequent argument (worded differently, of course) is that groups one and two do not remain groups one and two, but will quickly be changing into group three. Then, however much they may need the adaptation now, these very adaptations will become a stumbling block which may turn the people away from this translation, and maybe even from the church. I cannot argue with this point. If in fact the change is coming, or will come before a new translation could be done to meet it, then no doubt a translator must constantly try to imagine what his group will be like as group three readers, and limit his kangaroos and airplanes accordingly. It may even be that there are no groups left in the world which it is really practical to consider merely as groups one or two. But if there are such groups, and if it will be possible to prepare a new translation or at least a revision when the need really does arise, then I feel that a translator can be much less concerned about the problem of anachronism when making a translation for them than he might be with most other groups.

The discussion so far applies equally to both of the groups of isolated cultures. I have divided these cultures into two purely on the theoretical possibility that the people's reactions might be different depending on how many alternate cultures and traditions they are aware of. For those who know other cultures well, it seems quite possible that they would be much more conscious of the uniqueness of certain of their own cultural traits. When this is so there could be doubts and objections if the Biblical culture is made to share something which they know perfectly well no other culture has. Frequently there will be unexpected parallels between the Biblical culture and one's own, and there is of course no reason to avoid bringing these out. But it may be necessary to be careful when making adaptations that a FALSE impression of similarity is not created. On the other hand, for peoples of group one, conscious only of their own culture, even this type of rather backwards anachronism should not occur. It would be interesting to hear more on this subject from those who have actually done translation for such people.

Group Five: People Who Know the Bible and Biblical Culture Well

Clarence Jordan was a white Baptist preacher from the Southern part of the United States. Long before the civil rights movement became the widespread and even respected thing that it is today, he was involved in organizing an interracial community on a farm in Americus, Georgia. The community was subjected to the harrassment and terror that they knew would come. Struck by numerous convincing similarities between his situation (as a kind of Paul?) and the New Testament situation, Jordan started a translation which would really make the New Testament hit home to the people he worked with, both black and white. The language and imagery apparently came straight from the cotton patch, and that is what he called his work – the Cotton Patch Translation. He had not finished it before his death, but he had done several gospels, Acts, and all of Paul's letters.

The remarkable thing about this translation is not the language, which is so specific to the area and period in which he was working that even I as an American living at the same time (though of a different region and generation) do not always recognize his vocabulary and usage. The language is interesting, but I at least would not want to read too much of it. Instead, his great accomplishment was to translate in the way I stated above we should not translate – to make it sound as though it happened ten years ago, ten miles away. Yet I feel that for the group he was aiming at this was real translation; its faults may be more obvious, but I honestly doubt that they are any greater than those of any other translation.

Of course for someone who did not know the Bible story at all – and I suspect there are a good many such people in America even now – the Cotton Patch translation would be misleading. It might still be a good book for such a person to read, and might even give him an excellent understanding of the main Biblical truths, but it could definitely not be said to be giving him the original Bible message. It would be more like a sermon or commentary than a translation. But for those of us who know the historical events already, such a translation is not going to mislead us; there is no danger that we are going to start believing that the Good Samaritan drove a car or that the infant Jesus slept in an apple crate.

A Cotton Patch type of translation fails to convey the full message, it is true, but its failures are no problem for those of us who already know this message. Other translations, limited by the need to maintain the historical facts, simply cannot create in us the emotions which were stirred up in the original readers. Eating meat sacrificed to idols remains a serious issue today for Christians in certain parts of the world. But most Americans have trouble enough understanding why there should be objections in the first place – it's still meat, after all, whatever nonsense someone may have put it through. We agree too facilely with what Paul is saying. His readers either found his comments hard to take, or else they agreed only after a serious struggle over the issue in their own lives. It is simply impossible for most Americans, for instance, to read these passages with any real feeling for what he is saying. But these were emotional issues, and to fail to communicate the emotion is to fail in the translation.

The same can be said time and again throughout the Bible. The feelings aroused by the fact that Jesus associated with "sinners and tax collectors" and with Samaritans are an example. Many of us read this with a feeling of smug superiority over the spiritually shortsighted people who would have done otherwise. Surely at the least our reaction should be a sobering awareness of what it would mean for us socially to associate with people who are our society's social or religious outcasts. The cross itself is perhaps one of the most important New Testament symbols, packed with emotion for those of Jesus' time. Yet to us it is the proud symbol of our faith, and even non-Christians will readily wear it as a kind of fetish. Emotions of the cross as a stumbling block are simply lacking (unless we don't want our friends to know we are Christians), and it is difficult to see how such emotions can be brought out in any translation which has to emphasize the historical side of the account. But in all of these cases, there is usually an easy way to stir up the correct emotions in us – by mentioning the things from our own lives and surroundings that we would naturally react to in these ways.

Translation is fully successful only when the reader of the translation comes as close as possible to the experience of the reader of the original. Modern translations have made a vast improvement over the formal equivalence translations of the past, though they have not tried hard enough to carry the nonfactual aspects of the message. But even granted an excellent translation which does everything possible while still remaining true to the historical facts, the modern reader will surely find that his experience in reading it is widely different from that of the original reader in many places. "Cultural translations" will not be easy to do, and I doubt that many societies will find the convenient parallels that Jordan found for the southern United States of his time.[3] But when

---

[3] Even he was not able to maintain the transfer to modern times throughout. Since Paul's journeys in *Cotton Patch* are to various of the southern states, and the appeal to Rome is the appeal to Washington, a long sea-journey from Atlanta to Washington is impossible, and other ways of traveling could hardly present the same dangers. Jordan at this point simply gives up (with a note to the readers) and switches back to the first century for the duration of the voyage.

such translations are well done, I think we must accept them for what they are – real translations of great value for group-five people.

In certain cases, then, cultural adaptation can be quite acceptable. It must always be done carefully, following the basic principles, and with the purpose of furthering the correct understanding and emotive reaction. My own feeling is that the ideal translation must make use of cultural adaptation, at least in figurative language, to a fairly high extent. When adaptation must be done sparingly, as with groups three and four, it is for practical and psychological reasons, rather than for translational reasons per se. It is because of a subjective feeling on the part of these readers that such adaptation is unacceptable, anachronistic. However, it is only fair to admit that the vast majority of translations being done are aimed at people in these two categories. The vast majority of the world's population fits in these two categories.

As people concerned to have God's message accepted and read, we must of course be aware of these practical and psychological matters. But if in fact we feel that they prevent us from doing our work in the most effective way, there is no reason why we should let things go at that. Wherever these limiting factors seem to be absent, we should be ready to encourage translators to do the most effective work they can. In other areas, we can at least continue the long process of education. This matter of the judicious use of cultural adaptation is not the only point of widespread misunderstanding of what a good translation should be like. Much education is still needed to help people accept and appreciate the most basic ideas of dynamic equivalence translation.

It may well be that ideally every large language needs at least two translations. After all, people in group five who can benefit from a full "cultural translation" must have at least one "historical translation" on which the necessary prior understanding rests (unless of course they know the original languages). Good, clear, historical translation, going as far as possible in bringing out the full informative, emotive, and other aspects of the original, will certainly remain the priority for some time to come. Cultural translation being what it is and Bible Societies being what they are, it is difficult to imagine a Bible Society sponsoring a cultural translation in any case. But wherever someone has the ability, prophetic insight, and Christian love to do a translation of this kind, he is performing a great service to the Bible readers of his language.

AGREEMENT TYPES DISPERSED INTO A NINE-CELL SPECTRUM

KENNETH L. PIKE

1. THE NOTATION

We start with an array of nine cells (see Fig. 1) which leads to a kind of notation, or representation, which has proved useful in some recent tagmemic discussions.[1]

	Functional Slot, or Role	Category or Construction	Specific Item or Instance
Grammatical	1 e.g. subject	2 e.g. noun phrase	3 e.g. the boy
Sememic or Situational	4 e.g. actor	5 e.g. animate	6 e.g. Ted, son of Mr. Joe James of 420 Sixth Street
Phonological	7 e.g. ... ′ ...	8 e.g. CV CVV	9 e.g. / ðə boˡ /

Figure 1

Kenneth L. Pike is Professor of Linguistics at the University of Michigan, Ann Arbor, Michigan, and President of the Summer Institute of Linguistics. This paper was presented to the Linguistic Society of America, Atlanta, Georgia (December 29, 1972).

[1] For related notation, see Becker (1967), Wise (1971), Klammer (1971), Hale (1972; 1973), and Trail (1973). For a different kind of graphing of relation between elements of tagmemes, see Reszkiewicz (1963). By arrows under a formula he connects an element or one tagmeme with another which it presupposes (as *very* connotes – presupposes – *good*), while an arrow over the formula connects one tagmeme with another which it determines in some feature or features (as *these* is treated as determining that *books* will be plural).

The first row contains grammatical elements, the second row contains sememic elements related to the grammar, and the third row contains phonological elements.

Intersecting the rows are columns of which the first gives role (or function, or slot). In Cell 1, for example, grammatical function in the clause nucleus may be subject, object, predicate, indirect object, or other. (The choice of clause level for illustrative elements is incidental. Other levels of structure could have been used.) In Cell 4, sememic function of clause is often called case. For Cell 7, stressed position could illustrate a phonological slot.

The second column contains constructional categories (or distribution classes, or slot fillers). Cell 2, for example, may contain a noun phrase – a grammatical constructional category. Cell 5 might contain, related to a situational construction, an animate category of actors. Cell 8 could have a phonological CVC syllable pattern.

The third column contains specific instances or items for which a "derivation" or analysis is proposed. In the first row, Cell 3 contains (or cites) one specific lexical ("dictionary") entry, which may occur at any hierarchial level (from specific morpheme to specific discourse – or poem). Cell 6 has a specific encyclopedic ("referent") entry. Cell 9 carries a phonemic representation of some variant of the entry in Cell 3.

2. "SAMES" ACROSS TWO TAGMEMES

Now I give sample items in which two tagmemes in a construction are the SAME WITH REFERENCE TO SOME COMPARABLE CELL of the array. This sameness I shall call AGREEMENT. (I shall work backwards through the array.)

Cell 9 – e.g. rimes or alliteration. The riming pattern of a sonnet, or the alliteration pattern of some Old English verse, has phonological agreement describable in reference to this cell.

Cell 8 – e.g. vowel harmony. In many West African languages one may find a vowel triangle split into two sets: one set of vowels whose throat position is normal (or "relaxed") and another whose tongue-root position, independently variable, is front (or "tense") (Stewart 1967; Pike 1967). In general, the vowel of a stem has been arbitrarily chosen from one of these classes. Suffixes, however, have morphophonemic vowel alternates, and that alternate of the suffix must be chosen which will match the stem set (but not the particular member of that set, which would have been registered in Cell 9 instead of Cell 8).

Cell 7 – e.g. stress focus. In certain question-answer situations in English some word of the question may be under some degree of stress, and the normal focused reply stresses the elicited data.

Question: What do you wánt?
Answer: I want a pén.

But peripheral replies, inappropriate since not elicited, might include

Answer: Í want a pen.
Answer: I wánt a pen (but I don't expect one).

For a different kind of illustration of Cell 7, compare stress controls in poetic meter.

Cell 6 – e.g. referential identity. Here the referent must be the same, even though the lexicon may differ radically.

Question: Is John coming?
Answer: That rascal is coming, unfortunately.

Referential identity is encyclopedic, rather than lexical, since items homophonous in Cell 3 (*John* vs. *John*) must be distinguished in Cell 6 (*John-son-of-Bill,* vs. *John-son-of-Tom*) by reference to elements in a particular UNIVERSE OF DISCOURSE, whether it be one of history, literature (e.g. Hamlet), or science fiction.

Cell 5 – e.g. time vs. place. Categorization may seize on a wide variety of situational components; context singles these out for momentary reference.

Now is the TIME.
HERE is the PLACE.

Cell 4 – e.g. actor, at some hierarchical level.

THE BOY sings, but as a singER he is a flop.

Cell 3 – e.g. lexical identity.

So long as á BILL is coming, I don't care whát BILL it is – I just need him for my "alphabet soup" party.

Cell 2 – e.g. number.

THE BOY sings well.

Cell 1 – e.g. subject focus.

JOHN shot at the tiger, but THE TIGER was not hurt.

3. CONTROLLING ELEMENTS ACROSS TAGMEMES

In the preceding section I listed, in terms of a nine-cell array, various types of AGREEMENT across tagmemes. Now I wish to discuss, using the same frame of reference, some sources of CONTROL of these agreements. This task is much more complex, and also more interesting, because the sources of control may be multiple. (Perhaps, indeed, they always are multiple; if so, this should be fascinating to prove, and to explain in theoretical terms. We do not attempt that here.)

3.1. *Singular vs. Plural*

Let us begin with the control of singular vs. plural in Cell 2 of the predicate in the following clause (where preposed numerals label the cells and dotted lines connect from controlling elements to the controlled elements).

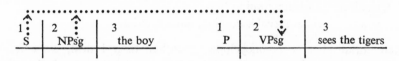

Here two (of the three) rows of the basic array are suggested by the lines. Cells 1 and 2 of the top ROW of the first tagmeme are involved in the control: both subject function and singular class are involved. One component of Cell 2 – singularity – of the predicate tagmeme is affected.

But the preceding active material contrasts with control of passive in

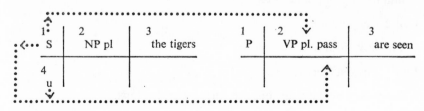

In this instance Cells 1 and 4 of the first COLUMN (where *u* means "undergoer") control the passive component of the predicate.

Both rules operate on the clause, as we can see in the following composite.

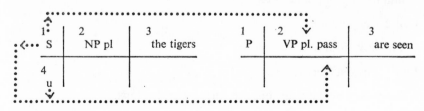

Cell 3 is not directly involved in the rule, since any member of the plural class has the same effect. (Note, however, that this implies that each cell has associated with it a CONTRASTIVE-FEATURE MATRIX – a point we are not developing here – to differentiate from one another the members of the slots which potentially fill that cell.)

Now, however, we ask the general question, what is the total set of kinds of cell combinations which work together to control other cells? I can give only a preliminary sample here. I do not yet have theoretical grounds for delineating the total set of possibilities. Empirical search will, I hope, eventually point the way to such constraints.

3.2. *Case Frame*

When one particular verb class (i.e. from Cell 2 of word level) in a predicate tagmeme slot controls the presence or absence of other tagmemes, the result may be a CASE FRAME (to use a Fillmore [1968: 26] label) characterized in part (not totally) by that verb.

For English, we have:

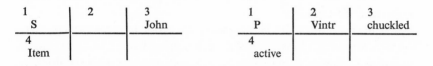

with *chuckle* as a verb which in part comprises an intransitive construction. For the subject tagmeme, in the situational row, we use the term *item* to refer to the general "thingness" of most members of the nominal class, or to the reification of nominalized elements.

3.3. *Different Subject*

Suppose, next, we look at Cashibo (Shell 1957) where the presence of a certain affix *x* (Cell 3) of a particular class *y* of verbs (Cell 2) in a clausal predicate slot *z* (Cell 1) of the marginal slot *w* (Cell 1) of a biclausal sentence will predicate that the specific filler (Cell 3) in the subject slot *j* (Cell 1) of the marginal clause *k* (Cell 3) will have the SAME referent *R* (Cell 6) as the referent *R* (Cell 6) of the specific filler *n* (Cell 3) of the subject slot *o* (Cell 1) of the clause *p* (Cell 3) in the nuclear slot *q* (Cell 1) of the including sentence. That is, the *x* verb affix of the marginal clause demands that the subjects of marginal and nuclear clauses have the same referent.

We give a partial formula for a sample sentence (the solid lines between cells represent branches in a constitutent tree diagram):

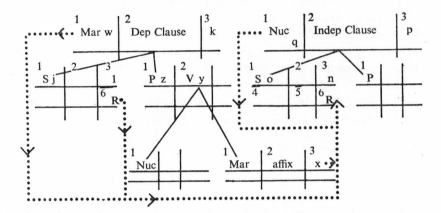

Here the triggering morpheme is two hierarchical levels below (Pike and Pike 1973) the level of the surface sequence of tagmemes of the clause in which it is embedded, and it affects a cell one level below the surface of the next clause.

Nothing prohibits us in this notation from crossing as many hierarchical levels as we wish, since the notation is adapted to represent an entire discourse by linear mapping in the six-cell notation (Schoettelndreyer and Pike 1973) with each node of its constituent tree dispersed into a spectrum of the six or nine elements.

4. SPECIAL PROBLEMS

I now move to some items where the nine cell notation illuminates old problems.

4.1. *Truth*

Two sentences which are equally grammatical, in terms of tagmemic and dictionary constraints may contrast in truth value. This shows up as encyclopedic differences of Cell 6.

For ordinary arithmetic, Cell 6 includes, as a component, the TRUTH or FALSITY of the item cited in Cell 3, RELATIVE TO A UNIVERSE OF DISCOURSE – here, that of ordinary arithmetic. (But $2 + 2 = 1$, truly, in the universe of discourse of "Modulus" 3.)

versus

1	2	3 $2+3=5$
4	5	6 true (for ordinary addition)

1	2	3 $2+3=7$
4	5	6 false

4.2. *Homonymy and Synonymy*

Two items may sound alike (Cell 9) but refer to different things (Cell 6).

versus

1	2	3 see
4	5	6 observe
7	8	9 /si/

1	2	3 sea
4	5	6 ocean
7	8	9 /si/

Or two items may have the same referent (Cell 6) but be represented by different morpheme strings (Cell 3).

versus

1	2	3 boy
4	5	6 male youth

1	2	3 young chap
4	5	6 male youth

4.3. *Class Membership*

Difference of implicit semantic class membership (included in Cell 5) may point to different referential interpretations (Cell 6) of a single morphemic sequence (Cell 3).

versus

1	2	3 the author of Waverly
4	5 class of persons seen as whole persons	6 Scott (as a whole person who wrote)

1	2	3 the author of Waverly
4	5 class of role types or role bearers	6 the author of Waverly seen abstractly as a composition role bearer

4.4. *Clash of Grammatical and Sememic Category*

A plural form may refer to a single item.

1	2 pl	3 scissors
4	5 sg	6 a cutting instrument with two opposed blades

Or a unit may have included plurality, such that focus may either be on the unit or on its inner multiplicity.

1	2 sg	3 This is my people	versus	1	2 pl	3 These are my people
4	5 pl	6		4	5 pl	6

4.5. *Clash of Grammatical and Sememic Gender*

1	2 fem/neuter	3 She/it (is a beautiful ship)
4	5 neuter	6

4.6. *Category Change via Universe of Discourse*

1	2	3 The trees walked
4	5 trees as animate	6 (in a science fiction novel)

4.7. *Specific versus Generic Relations behind some Tautology*

An apple is an apple

implies

1	2	3 an apple
4	5 is one particular but unspecified member of the class of fruit called "apple"	⟨··6

where the same morpheme sequence is used both for specific and for generic purposes.

4.8. *Naming Distinctions*

1	2	3 (the morpheme) *Paris*
4	5	6 (the capital of France) Paris
7	8	9 the pronunciation /pǽris/

4.9. *Tense vs. Time*

1	2 tense	3
4	5 time	6

5. CUMULATIVE CHANGE VERSUS RESISTANCE TO CHANGE IN PLOT REFERENCE

In the preceding sections reference has been treated from the point of view of a static sentence and static plot, as if there were no changes during the development of the plot. Such a view is unrealistic, since a plot is dynamic, with referents growing, moving, and changing, during its development. How, one must now ask, does this factor show up in the scheme utilized here? Note the problem: if during the development of a plot all continuity of identity of a changing hero is lost, the plot is lost, since it is no longer about the hero (who can no longer be identified). If, on the other hand, no change in him is recognizable, the plot is lost, if it is specifically about the changing man, or his changing environment, or the man changing in a changing environment; if this change cannot be accommodated, the plot is again lost.

As a partial solution, language sometimes retains identity by means of grammatical-lexical referents (Cell 3), but handles CUMULATIVE CHANGE through selectional restrictions related to the relevant encyclopedic elements (Cell 6). We illustrate this point by sentences from a recent article[2] by I. Warburton and H. S. Prabhu:

[2] Warburton and Prabhu (1972). I came across this paper after giving my own to the linguistic society, and was delighted to see its differentiation between selectional restrictions due to semantic features and those due to syntactic ones. I have now incorporated one or two of their examples.

For earlier discussion of referents changing according to rule during a discourse, see Padučeva (1970:695): "Rules can be suggested which, given the initial name of some object, yield all generally possible derived names of the same object. This does not mean, however, that all these derived names can be used in every context. A separate system of restrictions governs the choice of the appropriate derived name in the given context."

In the lexical component of a name, transformations may be purely syntactical (*Napoleon* to *he*; *a pretty girl with blue eyes* to [*the*] *girl*), or semantic with possibility of increasing information contained in the name, provided that "the allowed sources for this increase of information are only the preceding text and the information which can be supposed to be a part of the language competence of a language user" (e.g. *linguistics* to [*this*] *science*; or *Jane was the daughter of Peter. Jane adored her father.* Or, from *Mathematics studies not things but relations*, one can get: *This peculiarity of mathematics explains why...*).

After John had undergone a sex-change he became a nun.

but not simply

*He became a nun.

Here, in the first sentence, *he* (from Cell 3) is used to indicate the continuing identity of the individual *John*, but the characteristics describing John as a whole will be carried in a cumulative encyclopedic-historical sense (via Cell 6) and allow him to become a nun. In the second sentence, the central meaning of *he* as "male" has no plot context to force an encyclopedic change, and hence that sex factor clashes within the clause with a characteristic of the central meaning of *nun* as "female", forcing the sentence to be treated as ill-formed. In the nine-cell notation, our concept of the cumulative nature of the encyclopedic referent would show its controlling influence as follows:

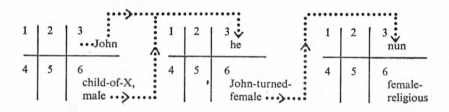

in which the arrows show the direction of the control, but with multilevel relations (Section 3.3) ignored.

Similarly, change is seen in:

When the baby grows up, it will become mayor of the city.

where the baby is referred to as *it*, but this pronoun would not normally refer to the mayor.

That relation to a current universe of discourse is an encyclopedic factor (just as a *unicorn* or a *cyclops* can be treated in an encyclopedia) rather than normal reality, is seen relative to the dream world in this further sentence from Warburton and Prabhu:

John dreamt that he was a woman and that he gave birth to twins.

where the actor (Cell 4) of the second clause is female giving birth relative to the dream world (Cell 6), but the antecedent *he* (Cell 3) holds the grammatical reference constant. Compare, also:

After the iceberg melted, it collided with the boat.

I would add, however, that when the universe of discourse – say a science fiction novel – holds to the new state long enough, the lexical-grammatical selection of pronouns may then shift, so that the pronoun chosen will contain as a central feature the gender which matches the new encyclopedic reference. That is, *he* may eventually be replaced by *she*. At the transition stage, however, considerable deliberately introduced oscillation from one to the other may occur, where the author suggests to the reader the problem faced by the persons in the story itself as they accommodate to the new stage of events.[3]

REFERENCES

Becker, Alton L.
  1967 *A Generative Description of the English Subject Tagmeme.* Dissertation (University of Michigan).
Fillmore, Charles J.
  1968 "The Case for Case", in Emmon Bach and R. T. Harms (eds.), *Universals in Linguistic Theory* (New York: Holt, Rinehart, and Winston), 1-88.
Hale, Austin
  1972 "Syntactic Matrices: An Approach to Descriptive Comparability", a paper presented to the XIth International Congress of Linguists, Bologna (August 1972).
  1973 *Clause, Sentence and Discourse in Selected Languages of Nepal and India* (= *Summer Institute of Linguistics Publications in Linguistics and Related Fields* 40).
Klammer, Thomas P.
  1971 *The Structure of Dialogue Paragraphs in Written English Dramatic and Narrative Discourse.* Dissertation (University of Michigan).
Padučeva, E. V.
  1970 "Anaphoric Relations and Their Manifestation in the Text", *Actes du Xe congrès international des linguistes* 2 (Bucarest: Editions de l'académie de la république socialiste de Roumanie), 693-698.
Pike, Kenneth L.
  1967 "Tongue-Root Position in Practical Phonetics", *Phonetica* 17, 129-140.
Pike, Kenneth L., and Evelyn G. Pike
  1974 "Rules as Components of Tagmemes in the English Verb Phrase", in Ruth Brend (ed.), *Advances in Tagmemics* (Amsterdam: North-Holland Linguistic Series), 175-204.
Reszkiewicz, Alfred
  1963 *Internal Structure of Clauses in English, an Introduction to Sentence Pattern Analysis* (Wrocław, Warszawa, Kraków: Załad Narodowy Imienia Ossolińskich Wydawnictwo Polskiej Akademii Nauk).
Schoettelndreyer, Burkhart, and Kenneth L. Pike
  1973 "Notation for Simultaneous Representation of Grammatical and Sememic Components in Connected Discourse," in Austin Hale, (ed.), *Clause, Sentence and Discourse Patterns in Selected Languages of Nepal (= Summer*

---

[3] I have seen such stories, but do not have the relevant bibliographical data.

Institute of Linguistics Publications in Linguistics and Related Fields 40), 321-360.

Shell, Olive A.
1957 "Cashibo II: Grammemic Analysis of Transitive and Intransitive Verb Patterns", *IJAL* 23, 203-208.

Stewart, J. M.
1967 "Tongue-Root Position in Akan Vowel Harmony", *Phonetica* 16, 185-204.

Trail, Ron
1973 *Clause, Sentence, and Discourse in Selected Languages of India* (= *Summer Institute of Linguistics Publications in Linguistics and Related Fields* 41).

Warburton, I., and H. S. Prabhu
1972 "Anaphoric Pronouns: Syntax vs. Semantics", *JOL* 8, 289-292.

Wise, Mary Ruth
1971 *Identification of Participants in Discourse, a Study of Aspects of Form and Meaning in Nomatsiguenga* (= *Summer Institute of Linguistics Publications in Linguistics and Related Fields* 28).

SECULAR CULTURE, MISSIONS, AND SPIRITUAL VALUES

WILLIAM D. REYBURN

Any view of secularism and religion today requires a consideration of two fundamental facts which are world-wide in scope and historically and paradoxically related. The first is the fact that Christianity has encircled the globe in the wake of western colonial expansion; the second is that western scientific technology and its offspring, the competitive world market economy, have become the life style across the earth. The spread of Christianity aimed to bring to the peoples of the world the spiritual values in the abundant life promised in fellowship with Jesus Christ. In this there was a clear-cut decision on the side of man and his humanity, a personal appeal to him to give himself in the service of others. People were important as individuals because of their relationship to one another and to God. This is true even if at times the carriers of the Christian message were crippled by national or ethnic prejudices. The expansion of scientific technique and the market economy, while bringing countless blessings, has nevertheless tended to be basically indifferent to man's spiritual concerns. The market economy appears to possess an ethos of its own which, when carried to extremes of production and consumption as it is today, is often dehumanizing. When discussing Christian missions today it is essential to hold these two factors in balance, for both have been agents of far-reaching cultural change which have set the world-wide stage which confronts us.

The aim of this paper is to show that there is a rapidly growing set of presuppositions which, while not universal, are increasingly found and are growing at an alarming rate in all areas of the world. Moreover, these presuppositions of life give rise to great satisfactions on the one hand and to subtle but fundamental spiritual losses on the other. Thankfully there is at the same time an ongoing effort in various forms to rediscover some

William D. Reyburn is Translation Consultant for the United Bible Societies, Beirut, Lebanon. This paper was read at the meeting of the International Association for Mission Studies held at Driebergen, The Netherlands (August 1972).

of the values which are being lost in the process of secularization. I shall deal only with a limited area of secularization and shall not attempt to relate this to specific religious systems, but will offer some observations and questions for Christian missions at the end.

Before looking into some of the growing cultural assumptions which men everywhere are coming to live by, it is essential to recall that Christianity has moved across the world carrying its own conflicts and contradictions with it. The Portuguese, for example, used every conceivable method to identify their missionary work with colonial administration. The history of Spanish colonization in Latin America is a similarly well-known example. The East India Company, on the other hand, did all it could to keep missionaries out of its territories. The British government in Nigeria encouraged missionary work among the Ibo and Yoruba but made it exceedingly difficult for missionaries to enter the Muslim areas of the north. The results of colonial attitudes have left their imprints. In many cases this has meant that one area of a country was exposed to western education with its emphasis upon scientific technology while other areas continued along traditional lines of development. Eastern and northern Nigeria, among others, reflect this conflicting pattern of development which contributed in no small way to the civil war there.

The multiplicity of missions, their national origins, and their range of outlooks confront people everywhere with a bewildering variety of claims. Today it is not uncommon to find within one mission, whether Catholic, Anglican, or Protestant, missionaries (frequently according to age and the institutions where they studied) holding views which range from political, economic, and social conservatism to extreme liberalism.

In short, it is hardly surprising that people who find themselves the targets of missionary efforts are not enthusiastic about identifying themselves with any other than national or often local structures.

In part, the resolution of the diversity of conflict has been the struggle leading in many cases to national independence. However, national independence or local autonomy are not in themselves able to escape the forces which are giving rise to world-wide secular culture with its unquestioned material gains and its ubiquitous spiritual losses.

TWO MAJOR ASPECTS OF WORLD-WIDE SECULAR CULTURE

The two dominating forces which would appear to contribute most to the dynamics of secular culture and which exist in some advanced form in every continent of the world today are scientific technology and the world market economy. It may appear far too limiting to assign such importance to these two factors. I believe, however, that these two are fundamental and that numerous other components stand in a dependent relation to them. I shall try here to outline some of the presuppositions which stem from these and which throw considerable light on our understanding of world-wide secular culture.

With particular reference to the acceptance of scientific technology the following presuppositions seem to hold:

1. The universe is regulated by mechanical laws and is theoretically within man's control.

2. Knowledge of the universe is gained not by experiencing it but through rational logical analysis.

3. Man and his environment can be dominated by technology.

4. Higher education is the necessary road to technology.

5. What is best is what is "scientifically best" and most efficient.

With reference to the world market economy we may note the following:

6. Nature must be exploited in order to produce and to consume.

7. Wealth grants power and status and can be obtained through control of the market.

8. True reality is what can be produced.

9. Production and consumption must be organized. Therefore, the institution takes precedence over the individual or even the group.

10. Every man in a producer-consumer society must be classified by role and status.

11. Competition is necessary for advancement and success in the market.

12. The machine has the right to make inhuman demands upon people.

While few of us would be anxious to exchange airplanes for dugout canoes, modern medicine for folk remedies, comfortable living quarters for mud huts, it should be recognized that scientific technology and the market economy, particularly in wealthier nations of the world, carry with them consequences which are already visible in the not-so-wealthy countries of the world. For example, there has proven to be precious little room for transcendental values. The growth of cities which have made so many advances in history possible demonstrate the loss of a sense of mystery, as when a family no longer plants and waters the soil or depends upon nature for its livelihood. Instead of knowing the stars and experiencing nature, the city man may not even be able to see the sun or the stars. When man no longer lives in a delicate harmony with nature he seems to become nature's enemy and declares open war on her. The Alaskan Eskimo danced in honor of the whale he killed and always returned its skull to the sea. He cooperated with the sea and had a respectful attitude toward the source of his livelihood. Today the Eskimo fires a harpoon gun and laughs at the idea of placing a moratorium on whale killing. He no longer dances in honor of the dead whale. Of course he has a good excuse: the missionaries were against dancing and tore down his dance houses.

VANISHING SOCIETIES

The world-wide spread of the market economy has given rise to the feeling that men are less important than raw materials and property. As a consequence many societies have been forced out of existence. At the time of the opening of the Portuguese colonization it is estimated there were three million Indians in Brazil. In 1964 there were 200,000, and by 1972 there were less than 100,000. Villages have been bombed and people infected with smallpox. The Indians are simply an obstacle to the market economy.

Another case is that of the Plains Indians of the western United States. To the Plains Indian a claim of land ownership was beyond belief. The land belonged to a force greater than man and it was man's only to use. White men claimed it, staked it out, owned it. The whites were willing to fight for it, kill for it; then having taken it they exploited its forests and polluted its rivers; any misuse was legitimate so long as it turned raw materials into consumer goods and made the wheels of business go round.

The market economy has cared little for men who would not compete for jobs and be driven by machines and work schedules. They become a forgotten people without dignity and without status. When Robert Kennedy visited the Indian school among the Blackfeet in Idaho, U.S.A., he asked the white teachers if Indian history was taught. "There is no history to his tribe", was the reply (Stoutenburg 1971: 55 and *passim*). When asked if there were any books on Indian life in the library, one was produced. It depicted on the cover a white child being scalped by an Indian. Little wonder Indians in the U.S.A. should cry for "Red Power" and join hands with the Black Power movement.

Where the market economy produces a callous disregard for humanity, the results of consumer goods are paid for at a high price. In the U.S.A.

the Indian population has doubled from 300,000 at the end of World War I to 600,000 today. However, visit any Indian reservation and talk with the youth. There you will find an atmosphere of hopelessness and apathy. In the U.S.A. the average life span for whites is sixty-eight years; for Indians it is only forty-two years. White young people average eleven years of school attendance. Indians manage only five. Lung tuberculosis is seven times higher among Indians than among whites and the highest suicide rate in the U.S.A. is found among Indian youth.

When Russian whalers and hunters came into contact with the Aleuts in 1800 they were the largest Alaskan ethnic group, numbering probably 25,000. By 1900 the Russians had reduced them to 2,500. During World War II the Japanese carried off the last remnants into forced labor.

The Eskimos of Alaska traded baleen for guns, ammunition, and liquor, which in turn caused them to throw over most of their spiritual values. The missionaries induced the Eskimos to give up their sod houses and build wooden frame houses. The wood had to be purchased from white importers. Then doors, glass windows, and iron stoves were required. The houses were drafty and cold compared to their snug sod houses, but the transition to the money economy had been made and there was no turning back. Today they require everything available on the market including snowmobiles, gasoline, spare parts, etc. Their whaling skills are gone, their boat building is a dying art, Eskimo dogs proliferate and are utterly useless and untrained. During World War II there was employment and money, now there is the state welfare. The discovery of oil at Prudhoe Bay has awakened the Eskimos to play the market game, too. Consequently, they are claiming rights to the oil. And why not? How else in the market economy does one get recognition and power except through the control of money?

The story of the degradation of humanity and even the complete loss of ethnic existence may be seen around the world. The British Parliament declared at one time that the Tasmanians were not human and could be shot like wild game. Today there are no Tasmanians. The African Bushmen were without metal spears and axes. The Bantu had these and as a result the Bushmen were forced to cling to a precarious existence by taking refuge in the inhospitable Kalahari desert. Yap Islanders, the original Hawaiians, the Australian aborigines, all have suffered from the relentless oppression of civilized people who believe fervently in scientific progress and whose value is measured in terms of the market economy.

It would appear that any small ethnic group in order to continue its traditional life must exist in the most forbidding and inhospitable areas of the world (e.g. the Bushmen and the Lapps). The Eskimos, at least in Alaska, have not been allowed to escape the disasters of the market economy in spite of the hostility of their natural environment. The same is true of many of the Indians of Amazonia. Even such a place as New Guinea, with its coming independence and its peoples' desire to share in the consumer goods of the manufacturing nations, will soon be brought fully into the market orbit. The cargo cults give evidence of this orientation. In 1965 when some of the people of New Guinea were told to vote for whomever they preferred as their chief, they voted for the man they believed most capable of delivering the most cargo to the tribe. They voted for President Lyndon B. Johnson (Stoutenburg 1971: 186).

The basic evil of the market economy system is that it is totalitarian in outlook. Those who operate within its monolithic system first tend to lose sight of people as people, and having done this they lose sight of spiritual values. There remains only economic man and all are expected to fit a common mold – the producer-consumer role. This was most aptly expressed by the Australian aborigine who said: "We want to share with the whites but we are not the whites. We are *yulngu* – ourselves" (Stoutenburg 1971: 158).

A DOUBLE SET OF VALUES REQUIRED

It would be wrong to assume that the presuppositions of scientific technology and the market economy produce people who are absolutely committed. The systems may be monolithic, but apparently people are not. In fact it has become abundantly evident that people in industrialized societies of the West operate with one set of work values in faithfulness to the job or organization and another set in an attempt to be faithful to something demanding from within. A man may be thoroughly clock-oriented, and role and status conscious at his work, but the moment he leaves the factory or office he may put on another frame of mind, one which allows him to forget the clock, forget his role and enter into a different world where he may simply and lovingly care for his tiny garden, or sit endlessly staring into a television screen, where unfortunately in many countries his role as consumer is hammered at him.

Modern industrialized man is a two-valued creature: one set of values is demanded by the machine and the organization, while the other (which he would like to think is his own) is often determined for him by the publicity people. They make certain he does not in his private life stray too far from the straight and narrow paths of the consumer society, for the education he has received has prepared him to function as a producer in the market economy and the advertisers feel it is their calling to educate him to do his part also as a consumer. The picture of the two-value system of modern man is not unlike the remark sometimes heard on mission stations: "When the natives leave the station they seem to go straight back into the ways of the world."

IDENTITY AND THE CULTURE OF YOUTH

The most pervasive loss in the technological era dominated by the values of the market economy is the surrender of self-awareness, for it would seem that if men allow themselves to be open to awareness and the experiencing of spiritual values they soon run afoul of the mindless machine. The soft voice of the inner life can hardly be heard in a life that is crowded, noisy, machine demanding, and organizationally directed. Yet this is the case in every industrial country in the world.

There are of course many who view life in the market economy as a new spiritual challenge, or even a new kind of spiritual awakening. This may be true, but the evidence for it is not found among those who are committed to its ethos but rather among the very people who reject it and who are forging a new way of life which is taking shape in nearly every industrialized country both East and West. I refer to the culture of young people, with their symbols of long hair, clothes which express the body, music which expresses the inner feelings, and drugs with which they reach out to a spirituality which their parents rejected as scientifically invalid. To the radical youth the technological way of life has been a betrayal. The life-denying ethos of the machine society has produced a dullness of conscience. For the sake of the market economy whole peoples have been exterminated, and as the machine rolled ahead it has deadened countless individuals to the existence of personal awareness. To the radical youth of today individuals have value, not merely as producers and consumers, but as people. They are sceptical of cold scientific analysis, the kind technology has depended upon. Their cry is for freedom, freedom for each person to build his own life style, to do his own thing.

In relation to the self there are today three basic groupings: primitive groups, folk societies, and industrial conglomerates. Primitive and folk societies are clearly tied to the in-group. Industrialized man's life is with the organization. Men in primitive groups and folk societies see themselves in terms of the face-to-face group, or the kin group. Men in industrial conglomerates confront the faceless organization.

Youth culture says no to all three. To them the individual self is the only true reality. It is therefore a crime to be used by the family, the clan, the organization, or the state. It is wrong to be alienated from oneself, to be schizophrenic, to live today for the future. However, being true to oneself and struggling to preserve self from alienation need not mean a selfish existence. On the contrary, youth culture is more concerned for the welfare of its community and recognizes by all its outward symbols the presence of that community. Technological life places a high value on excellence. Therefore a highly competitive spirit must be exercised in order to succeed. Not so among these youth. They refuse to classify, to pigeonhole. If a person is brilliant, that is his thing, but lack of brilliance does not make him less a person. Hierarchical arrangements so essential in the technocrats' world make little sense to youth. They are not impressed with you because you are professor, doctor, director, or general. Without having ever read Karl Marx they have a critical reading of society which has often escaped their elders.

How is it possible that in so short a time the technological world with its market economy could have produced a world-wide generation so much in contrast with the values of the older generation? The answer is that one needs only to deny the presuppositions listed earlier and a different style of life will take shape.

A failure to take seriously this world-wide youth phenomenon with its clothes, hair, drugs, sex, and music, would be as disastrous as the Australian aborigine who refused to believe in the existence of the world-wide market economy. It would be equally disastrous for the church or for missions to fail to see that underlying this youth revolution is a profound search for man's spiritual belonging in a secularized world. In a sense this is a search for identity and one can only wish it success.

IDENTITY AND NATIONAL LANGUAGES

There are many ways in which people are seeking identity within what often appears as the chaos of secularization and our ever shrinking world community. Nationalism is one of the means through which people attempt to identify themselves and their aspirations, be these political, economic, social, or linguistic. Because there is a strong tendency on the part of churchmen and many political leaders to misunderstand the function of language within the process of nationalism, I would like to deal with the matter briefly here, for it would appear that the national language question illustrates perhaps better than any other the dynamics of group identity, and this in the face of rising nationalism and internationalism and the world market economy.

There is a strong tendency on the part of many to believe that secularization means the loss of regionalisms and leads automatically to the greater facility of world language domination. The facts do not support these beliefs (Deutsch 1942, as reported in Nida 1972: 414). If the record in Europe is any indication of what may happen in other areas of the world, e.g. Africa and Asia, then it would be worthwhile to consider the development in Europe, for here more than anywhere there have been pressures for national development and international exchange, ever since the Protestant Reformation. Rather than experiencing a reduction of official languages with recognized literature, the past two centuries have witnessed a significant increase. In 1800 there were only sixteen languages in Europe which could be regarded as official and literary: Greek, Church Slavonic, German, French, Icelandic, Russian, Spanish, Portuguese, Italian, Swedish, Danish, English, Dutch, Polish, Hungarian, and Turkish. However, by 1900 there were thirty so-called literary languages: Old Church Slavonic had lost out but the following had been added: Welsh, Flemish, Norwegian, Finnish, Rumanian, Czech, Slovak, Serbo-Croatian, Slovenian, Bulgarian, Ukranian, Yiddish, Estonian, and Latvian. These additional languages represented a population of some eighty million speakers.

Furthermore, between 1900 and 1937 the number of languages having a significant literary development and used officially to some extent in education rose to fifty-three with the addition of: Lithuanian, Irish, Scottish-Gaelic, Basque, Breton, Catalan, Rheto-Romance, Lusatian-Serb, Albanian, Hebrew, Karelian, White Russian, Moldavian, Georgian, Ossete, Bashkir, Cheremis, Churash, Morovin-Saamoyede, Syryen (Komi), Tartar, and Vodiak. These represent a population of approximately thirty million. Such developments did not stop in 1937: Maltese, Frisian, Swiss German, and even Provençal have joined this development.

The processes are frequently similar: one dialect becomes dominant and other dialects give way at least for literary purposes. Dictionaries and grammars are written for schools and important literary productions are published. Often there is an intense struggle against outside influences: Ukranian fights against Polish borrowings, Slovenian purges itself of Serbo-Croatian forms, Slovak speakers rid their language of Czech influences, and Catalan writers avoid Spanish words like the plague.

What is taking place outside of Europe? First, there is the important pidginization of certain European languages which have served the market economy. New Guinea Pidgin, based on English, is becoming the mother language of an ever growing number of its million speakers. The same is true of Creole in Sierra Leone and of Papiamento in the islands of Curaçao and Aruba where elements of Portuguese, Spanish, and Dutch have formed a synthesis. In Haiti French has served as the base for Haitian Creole spoken by well over three and a half million. There are in addition to pidgins and creoles other new languages called koines, languages which have been greatly simplified for the sake of interlingual communication. Some examples are Swahili in East Africa and Zaïre, and Hausa in West Africa.

In addition to the so-called new languages (pidgins, creoles, and koines), there are the regional languages which are not simplifications but are national languages which are given official recognition in an attempt to bring people in a new country within a single national language, for example, Bahasa-Indonesian, Swahili in Tanzania, Pilipino (Tagalog) in the Philippines. In South India, where English was previously the language of universities, there is today an increased tendency to use the regional languages: Tamil, Malayalam, and Telegu.

While it would be convenient for the world market economy to have a single world language, or for a given country to have a single national language, it appears that multilingualism will be the norm for many peoples of the world. For example, in Africa one will go on speaking the language of one's in-group. A language will also be required for the out-group. This will normally be a national language, either a pidgin, koine, or a regional language. In addition, for the purposes of belonging to the technological society that serves the world market economy, a world language such as English, French, Portuguese, or Arabic will be required (Nida 1956; Nida and Wonderly 1971).

In spite of radio and television there is every reason to believe that most people will operate on a multilingual basis. The identification of a man with his face-to-face group is today as significant and functional as it ever was. However, as he is brought into the orbit of the technological society and the world market he requires more than one level of identification, in most cases a regional or national and, in many cases, an international language.

In terms of the individual this means that men in most areas of the world today exercise not only the language that is appropriate to the group but also in some sense the values he assumes are appropriate. Interestingly enough, the more intimate the group the more real are the values, a fact which places some question on the reality of international meetings, ecumenical gatherings, United Nations, etc.

The rise of a world-wide youth culture, as a reaction to the heartless demands of the technological society and the market economy, and the recognition of multilingual nationalism are both overpowering evidences that men seek a meaningful identity for themselves and that men express in one form or another the necessity to be true to the demands of a meaningful existence – that men should have life and have it more abundantly, and that they should communicate it.

SOME CONCLUDING QUESTIONS FOR CHRISTIAN MISSIONS

This article may not appear to be directly related to any concern for Christian missions. I believe, however, there are several important conclusions which we are forced to draw.

Missionaries from the West are normally fully committed to a scientific technology and the world market economy with all or most of its presuppositions. Witness the material living, the work program, the institutionalization of the mission program, the reports turned into the home office. The basic orientation is: "Do those things which are most effective in the most efficient manner and which will produce the greatest results." The attitude taken differs little from any manufacturing organization.

The result is the endless effort to produce everything from Christians to committees, including the loving care given to counting the pages of literature produced, the numbers of Bibles sold, the number of births, marriages, baptisms, church members, evangelization kilometers, and all this divided by the number of missionary hours to arrive at the number of dollars per unit soul saved. While this is an exaggeration (in some cases) it does reflect the basic premises of much of foreign missions where statistics are the only objective way of knowing if the investors are getting value for money. For after all, this is the same business exercise those who are providing the money carry out in order to remain competitive in the market economy.

Missions are today more and more operating on an institutionalized level. In most cases where national churches have been formed, the need

for foreign missionaries is in a specialized role, such as teacher, agricul-
turalist, medical doctor, or seminary professor. These roles are: (a)
often removed from the grass-roots life of the people, (b) given higher
status than local church personnel, (c) executed in somewhat impersonal
terms, (d) carried on through the medium of the out-group language,
(e) identified more with the foreign community than the national community, and (f) conducted on a limited term basis.

There is little doubt, wherever one goes throughout the world today,
that foreign missionaries are advancing the cause of the two factors I have
dealt with in this paper: technology and the market economy. There are
at the same time numerous genuine expressions of other values, such as
love, sacrifice, personal concern, dedication, and reconciliation, which
are at work and which refuse to be counted, measured, or turned into
statistics.

Missionaries have taken pains to establish the fact that they are not
attempting to impart their national backgrounds, be these British,
American, Belgian, etc. However, is it really relevant any longer?
If people everywhere are coming to live under the presuppositions of
the technological society and the world market economy, what difference
does it make if the brand is British, French, German, Japanese, Russian,
Chinese, or American? Is it realistic to think that missionaries from the
West could convince Hindus in India that they are in India to bring a
spiritual way of life? Not according to many Hindus. Where the life
of so-called "spiritual leaders" (including churchmen or missionaries) is a
life oriented to the demands of a hierarchical business organization, is it
not somehow in conflict with a genuine life of personal and spiritual
awareness? Is the spiritually concerned missionary in a secular society
able to live out his busy organizational role and still communicate spiritual
values to his colleagues? If it is difficult with his colleagues, it is still
more so with persons who share little of his cultural background.

Do most Christians concerned with the communication of God's
love in Christ whether in the West or the East share their faith with
non-Christian friends at the request of the latter? I doubt it. Do foreign
missionaries in Africa, Asia, or Latin America live in such a style of life
that nationals in those continents could gain from them only spiritual
advantages? I don't see much evidence for this. The advantages are
nearly always opportunities to join the technological society or to win
some products of the market economy. Are the young men in the seminaries being trained for church leadership because they are leaders or
because they are available? Too often it is the latter. Do the laymen in the

secular life in Asia, Africa, Latin America, or anywhere for that matter, want to be identified with the leadership in the national church? In some cases the answer is yes, but in a significant number of areas it is no. Is the church separating from the youth culture? In many areas it is. Do theological professors expect to go on talking about God to young people or does youth culture require a radically different approach? The answer in both cases appears to be yes. Radical youth – and they are increasing at a tremendous pace – is not satisfied to "talk about". They want nothing less than EXPERIENCE.

Finally, is there a hope that the youth in all areas of the world will respond to the gospel and revitalize the mission of the Christian church? One would like to be optimistic on this point. My own feeling is that they could give Christianity a new emphasis and this emphasis would challenge the presuppositions of the technological society and the world market economy – the secular structures of our lives – and would bring us much closer to a personalized Christianity and give us a greater estimation of the value of every person.

REFERENCES

Deutsch, Karl W.
   1942   "The Trend of European Nationalism", *American Political Science Review* 36, 533-541.
Nida, Eugene A.
   1956   "The Role of Language in Contemporary Africa", *Practical Anthropology* 3, 122-137.
   1972   "Why Translate the Bible into 'New Languages'?", *The Bible Translator* 23:4, 412-417.
Nida, Eugene A., and William L. Wonderly
   1971   "Communication Roles of Languages in Multilingual Societies", in W. H. Whiteley (ed.), *Language Use and Social Change*, published for the International African Institute (Oxford: The University Press), 57-74. Reprinted in *The Bible Translator* 22, 19-37.
Stoutenburg, Adrien
   1971   *People in Twilight* (*Vanishing and Changing Cultures*) (New York: Doubleday).

Mʀ NICOLAAS WITSEN,
Burgermeester en Raad van Amsterdam,
Extraordinaris Ambassadeur in
Groot-Britanje enz.

IS.TIRION Excudit.

1. Mr. Nicolaas Witsen after M. van Musscher by J. Houbraken.
   Engraving 164 × 104 mm.

2. Nicolaas Witsen Photograph of a reproduction in "Geschiedenis van Amsterdam" by H. Brugmans. Vol. 4 p. 539. Engraving by Blooteling.

THE SEVENTEENTH CENTURY CHEREMIS:
THE EVIDENCE FROM WITSEN

THOMAS A. SEBEOK

For Eugene Nida: "pour étendre les progrès de la lumière de l'Evangile" (Witsen to Leibniz, May 22, 1698)

... It appears to be the will of God that science should encompass the globe and should now come to Scythia, and that for this purpose its instrument should be Your Majesty; for you are so situated that you can take the best from Europe on the one side and fiom China on the other and, through good institutions, improve upon the achievements of both. Indeed, since in most parts of your empire all studies are as yet in a large measure new and resemble, so to speak, a *tabula rasa*, it is possible for you to avoid countless errors which have crept in gradually and imperceptibly in Europe. It is generally known that a palace built altogether anew comes out better than one that is rebuilt, improved upon, and much altered through many centuries (Vernadsky 1972: 366, after Ger'e 1873: 207).

This fragment of a memorandum addressed to Peter the Great, who reigned over Russia from 1689 to 1725, was drafted by Gottfried Wilhelm Leibniz on January 16, 1712 – one of the many letters he penned to the Czar from the time the two men met at Torgau, in October 1711, until Leibniz's death, in 1716. The correspondence bears witness to Leibniz's lively interest in the Czar's activities, and to the possibilities of scientific discovery in Russia. When Leibniz encountered Claudio Filippo Grimaldi in Rome, in 1689, and learned from that Jesuit Father of his plans to return to his missionary activities in China by land – specifically via Muscovy – his curiosity was much aroused by this as yet hardly encompassed, let alone explored, Eurasian land mass which he once characterized as *le pays... du Nord de l'Europe et de l'Asie... si importante de nostre globe*.

Thomas A. Sebeok is Distinguished Professor of Linguistics and Chairman of the Research Center for the Language Sciences at Indiana University, Bloomington, Indiana.

A year later, from a letter dated December 4, he therefore received with keen attention a piece of news, communicated to him by the librarian Henri Justel, that *une carte de Tartarie* had been printed in 1687 (it has not been ascertained whether Leibniz had been aware, since as far back as October 1684, of the earliest public announcement of this forthcoming project, placed by Gijsbert Cuper, in the *Nouvelles de la République des Lettres*). He promptly disseminated reports of this welcome publishing event to several of his professional acquaintances, as can be read from such letters of his (in part still unpublished, but preserved in the Archives of the Public Library of Lower Saxony, in Hannover) as the one he wrote to Father Grimaldi, on June 10, 1691. He did not, however, actually get a chance to see and examine this map until 1694, when a copy reached him in Hannover through the good offices of one Heinrich Hüneken, a resident of The Hague. Leibniz reciprocated by sending the author a copy of his *Codex juris gentium diplomaticus*, receipt of which was acknowledged in 1697.

The author of this famed map was Nicolaas Witsen (born in Amsterdam on May 8, 1641, died in Amsterdam on August 10, 1717), who, since his voyage to Moscow at the age of twenty-three, had gained great reputation as one of Europe's most knowledgeable experts on Russia. Upon receipt of his map, Leibniz resolved to profit as much as he could from Witsen's experiences, and to exploit his contacts. Accordingly, he initiated a correspondence in 1694, whereby Witsen's role eventually (after September 6, 1697) became that of a middleman, a sort of culture broker, for which he was exceptionally well-fitted, if only because of his situation as a prominent Netherlander. At the end of the seventeenth century, after all, the universities of his country were teeming with scholars and students from all parts of Europe. A hub of intellectual life, The Netherlands also became a place of refuge for French Huguenots and English academics alike. Amsterdam alone boasted of some four hundred printing establishments and bookshops; indeed, Witsen himself was heavily involved in publishing activities – he certainly had a hand in the publication of practically any work having to do with Russia.

After an initial exchange of politely formal letters between Leibniz and Witsen, three full years were to elapse before the resumption of their correspondence on a regular, full-scale basis. This renewal of contact was quite evidently triggered by a major event, namely, the arrival in Holland of Peter the Great in 1697. The following brief excerpt about Peter's studies and work in Amsterdam is taken from the preamble to the Naval Service Regulations of 1717 (of special interest is

the fact that the Czar inserted certain passages himself, which are reproduced in italics):

Thus he [Peter] *turned all his thoughts to building a fleet*; *and when, on account
of the Tatar attacks, Azov had been besieged, and later successfully taken,* he
could not bear to deliberate long over his unalterable desire but quickly set
about the work. A suitable place for shipbuilding was found…, skilled ship-
wrights were called in from England and Holland, and a new enterprise was
started in Russia in 1696 – the building of ships, galleys, and other boats – at
great expense. So that this work would be established in Russia forever, he
decided to introduce this art among his people. For this purpose he sent a
large number of noble-born persons to Holland and to other states to study
naval architecture and seamanship.

And what is even more remarkable, the monarch, as if ashamed to lag behind
his subjects in this art, himself undertook a journey to Holland, and in Amsterdam, *at the East India shipyard,* he devoted himself, together with his other
volunteers, to learning naval architecture; in a short time he perfected himself
in what a good ship's carpenter should know, and with his own labor and skill
he built and launched a new ship (Vernadsky 1972: 313, after Ustrialov, 2,
1858-1863: 400).

Witsen was Burgomaster of Amsterdam as well as Director of the
Netherlands East India Company at that time (Bodel Nijenhuis 1855).
Peter lived in his house during a portion of his sojourn, and the Russian
guests were, so to speak, under Witsen's patronage (cf. the remark of
H. Doerries referred to in Müller 1955: 7, fn. 1). Peter himself, incidentally, was adequately versed in the Dutch language, having studied it
with Andrew Winius, a man of Dutch origin who served as one of the
d'iaki, or clerks, of the Posol'skii Prikaz, his Foreign Office (Baxrušin
1955: 44).

Leibniz, who was fascinated by the Czar, now sought to establish
and maintain contact with him through Witsen. Their first face-to-face
encounter was not to take place until 1711, however, and his report
concerning that occasion was to constitute the subject of Leibniz's last
letter to Witsen. Leibniz endeavored to garner all available information
from him pertaining to the Czar's peoples and territories. Witsen was
evidently impressed by Leibniz's character and motivation for wanting
to secure Peter's good will and cooperation. Persuaded accordingly,
Witsen set in train his far-flung contacts, and proceeded to respond to
and satisfy, step by step, Leibniz's numerous demands until his final
known reply, dated November 29, 1712; after that, it seems, Leibniz
let their epistolary relationship lapse.

The Leibniz-Witsen correspondence as a whole (thoroughly and
illuminatingly discussed by Müller 1955) covers five main sets of topics,

including missionary activities, questions of mathematics, China and Japan, all interspersed with political and scientific news, as well as many details of an ethnographic character, the emphasis depending on the problem area that occupied Leibniz at the time of writing. But the persistent central theme, a small part of which concerns us here, remained Russia and Peter the Great. Leibniz asked Witsen to urge the Czar to order the collection of research materials, particularly for the purposes of comparing languages; this request was in good conformity with his philosophy of language, especially insofar as it related to his conception of etymology on the one hand, and his general philosophical system on the other (cf. Aarsleff 1969). He was, however, aware that his linguistic concerns might seem to conflict with his other interests. On July 25, 1697, that is about six weeks before he even commenced his exchanges with Witsen, he had written to another correspondent, Palmieri:

Quant à la diversité des nations je souhaiterois fort de pouvoir obtenir des échantillons des langues de ce pays là, sçavoir de celles, qui sont entièrement différentes de la Russienne par exemple de celle des Czircasses, Czeremisses, Kalmucs, Sibériens, etc., et peut estre qu'on apprendra par là de quel endroits de la Scythie les Huns et les Hongrois sont sortis. Et comme maintenant la jurisdiction du Czar va jusqu'aux frontières des Tartares de la Chine, cette information seivira à mieux connoistre und grande partie du globe terrestre. Les différentes races des nations ne se pouvant mieux discerner que par les langages et leur harmonie ou cognation. Je vous supplie d'insinuer tout cecy de bonne manière, et même (si cela se peut commodément) sans beaucoup de bruit. Car bien des gens ne se soucient pas de ces curiosités, qu'ils s'imagines estre inutiles. Vous n'est pas de leur sentiments et moy non plus (Ge're 1873: 10-11; Aarsleff 1969: fn. 11).

In this letter, he mentions explicitly, and, so far as I have been able to verify, for the first time, the Cheremis, who today constitute the fourth largest Finno-Ugric ethnic group in the Soviet Union, concentrated now, as they were then, mainly in the upper Volga Basin (Sebeok 1956a).

The youthful Witsen journeyed to Moscow as a member of Jacob Boreel's 1664-1665 trade delegation, whose objective was to improve commercial relationships between their country and Russia. Even though Witsen's family had been trading with the Russians since about the beginning of the seventeenth century, this circumstance did not smooth his way or make his stay any easier; it was, in fact, fraught with the familiar difficulties that have beset generations of travelers to that country. Witsen was assigned a "guide", who incidentally kept him under close observation, necessitating the use of subterfuge to realize certain meetings, for example, his clandestine rendezvous with the banished Patriarch Nikon. In view of the paucity of contemporary evidence (cf. Gebhard 2, 1881-1882), it must be assumed that, while in Russia, Witsen was already pursuing his life-long quadruple path: commercial, political-diplomatic, scientific, and missionary – the latter on behalf of the reformed church (or, as he wrote to Leibniz on May 22, 1698, "pour étendre les progrès de la lumière de l'Evangile" – Eckhardt 1717: 364).

Witsen knew better than anyone that his 1687 map was inaccurate: large regions beyond the Urals lay still unexplored, indeed, were rightly suspected to be awaiting discovery and exploration. Not surprisingly, his descriptive account of *Noord en Oost Tartarye*, first printed in Amsterdam in 1692, suffered from the same inevitable deficiencies, compelling its self-critical author to make constant revisions. In 1705, he permitted the publication (also in Amsterdam) of a second, improved edition, but this, too, failed to satisfy his scholarly standards. Although he continued the process of revision up to his last years, he could not bring himself to issue a third edition, because, being unable to collect firsthand the data that he felt he needed, he was forced to fall back upon the uncertain accounts of travelers who seldom possessed either the background knowledge or the means required to conduct proper field work (on Witsen's sources, see Trisman 1951). Both the first and the second editions were rapidly exhausted and became exceedingly rare. Nonetheless, for the purposes of what follows, the 1785 reprinting of the latter, in possession of the Houghton Library, has proved equally serviceable.

In the second edition of his *Noord en Oost Tartarye*, Witsen provided two sorts of information pertaining to the Cheremis: an ethnographic sketch, and a single linguistic text. According to Leibniz,

Die Erforschung des Landes, der geographischen und klimatischen Gegebenheiten muss ... durch die Erfassung und Beschreibung aller Volks- und Stammestypen ergänzt werden, also der Menschen, die diesen weiten, kaum bekannten Raum Nordeuropas und -asiens bewohnen (Müller 1955: 25).

His twin goals were to ascertain how the different races and ethnic groups fit together, and what linguistic criteria could be adduced to support their relationship. From such knowledge, he had hoped to be able to infer the provenance of all these populations, and perhaps ultimately the origin of man. Witsen became Leibniz's most tireless informant in this quest; the data he furnished fueled Leibniz's intuitive classification of the languages within his purview, in 1710 (cf. Richter 1946; Waterman 1963). In this scheme, as against his other major branch, "Aramaic", the Finno-Ugric languages and Samoyede fell into that subdivision of the "Japhetic" branch which he designated "Scythian", a term deriving from the name of the region that he had assumed to have been the homeland – or *vagina populorum*, as he once called it – of the inhabitants of vast reaches of contemporary Europe and northeast Asia. Of the four subdivisions of Scythian, the third constituted an accurate classification of what are now called the Uralic languages, that is, Finno-Ugric plus Samoyede, with Cheremis being presumably subsumed by Leibniz under *Finnisch*, a term he applies ambiguously to both an entire family of languages and to one subclass thereof.

A primary set of data upon which his linguistic classification was founded consisted of interlinear versions of the Lord's Prayer assembled from as many languages and dialects as possible. He importuned many of his Russian connections with such requests, for, as he explained in 1698,

Wenn man das *Vater Unser* in solchen Sprachen erhalten könnte, mit einer Uebersetzung zwischen den Zeilen in einer bekanntern Sprachen, würde es gut seyn, um solche Sprache besser gegen andere zu halten, deren *Vater Unser* man bereits hat.

According to Aarsleff (1969), he made at least a dozen similar requests, "apparently without much success, though the great compilation he had in mind was later made..." (this subsequent project, carried out during the reign of Catherine the Great [1762-1796], under the overall direction of Pallas, is discussed in Sebeok 1960). However, one respondent who did not let Leibniz down was Witsen, who, "Comme je vois, que vous désirez d'avoir le *Pater noster* en des Langues de Pais éloignez" (Eckhardt 1717: 361, dated October 16, 1697), had supplied him, by the turn of the century, with texts not only from over half a dozen Uralic and Altaic – or, as Leibniz termed them, *Türkisch* – languages, but also from Hottentot, including the *Symbolum Apostolicum* and the Ten Commandments in this African language (Eckhardt 1717: esp. 375-384). The Mongol text, which he obtained himself "avec beaucoup de peine" from a native slave at the Embassy of Muscovy, led him to remark, in a letter dated December 4, 1697, on his informant's limitations:

La stupidité de ce Moegal, qui est ici, est si grande, qu'on ne peut pres, que tirer de sa bouche aucune connoissance, ni de sa Patrie, ni de Mœurs du Pais (Eckhardt 1717: 361-362).

No wonder he mistrusted information that, by necessity, came to him secondhand (or worse) from his "amis de Mosco" (Eckhardt 1717: 367), whose identity and methods of data gathering have, on the whole, remained opaque (cf. Trisman 1951).

In his letter of July 21, 1698, he signals to Leibniz that more versions of the Lord's Prayer would be forthcoming, and, almost a year later (with a letter dated July 5, 1699), he encloses three such texts, one of them in Cheremis. This text, constituting the earliest coherent document in that language, with a Dutch interlinear translation, has been published twice: first, on page 622 of the 1705 edition of Witsen's *Noord en Oost Tartarye* (also reproduced in subsequent reprintings, and in Figure 1, below); second, as a part of the Witsen-Leibniz correspondence (Eckhardt 1717: 369-370). The two versions differ in some minor graphic details,

Het Vader Onze in de Ceremiffe *Tael.*

Onze Vader,	*Memnan uziu,*
die daer zyt	*ilimazet*
in de Hemelen,	*Kiufuilufte,*
Uwe Name worde	*tinin liumet*
geheiligt,	*volgufertes,*
Uwe Koninkryke	*Tinin Vurdufchu*
kome,	*tooles,*
Uwe wille gefchiede,	*Tinin jerek ilies,*
zoo als in de	*kufu i*
Hemelen,	*Kufiulufte,*
alzoo op der Aerden,	*i ijulniu,*
ons dagelijks Brood,	*memnon kedzin Kinde,*
geeft ons heden,	*puske malana ikelfet,*
ende vergeeft ons	*i kode malana*
onze fchulden,	*memnon fuiluk,*
als wy vergeven	*kufe me kondena*
onze fchuldenaren,	*malano tuirulifticzy,*
en leit ons niet	*i tzurty memnon*
in verzoekinge,	*i langoske,*
maer verloft ons	*i utura memnon*
van den Boozen.	*i Jalaez.*

Figure 1

e.g. as to the representation of some of the vowels: *memnon* (1705) *vs. memnan* (1717) "our", *Jalaez* (1705) *vs. jalaz* (1717) "evil", etc. Although it is difficult to be certain, internal evidence suggests that, of the dozen or so dialects spoken by the Cheremis, the text at hand corresponds to the pattern coded as *KK* (in Sebeok and Zeps 1961: 16), that is, the one spoken today in and around Koz'modem'jansk, and especially important as it had served as the basis for the Western literary standard of the Cheremis.

In *Noord en Oost Tartarye* (1705), the Lord's Prayer is embedded in a matrix of ethnographic observations about the Cheremis, running (double column) from page 619 through page 623, and mentioned again in the third paragraph of page 883. Witsen's account presents a unique source depicting important aspects of Cheremis life in the seventeenth century, which may be favorably compared with later, successively more scientific reports (e.g. those enumerated in Sebeok 1956a or Sebeok and Ingemann 1955). In conclusion, by way of a modest contribution to ethnohistory, I append a lightly edited and annotated English translation of the relevant passages; their full analysis and critical evaluation must, however, await a future occasion.

[619] The Cheremis.

The Cheremis are neither baptised, nor circumcised, and therefore pagans: they live around the city Nizhni Novgorod, in the woods, on both sides of the Volga river: they live in the area between Vjatka and Voločda, as far as the river Kama.

Near the little town of Vasiligorod, which is built entirely of wood, by Czar Ivan Basilevits, who occupied it with soldiers, to support the Crimean Tatars, lying on the Volga, there live also Cheremis Tatars, occupying an area well above Kazan. The river Sura flows past the aforementioned town, which was formerly the separation between the Russian and the Kazan areas.

These people are fast walkers, and they are good archers. They are also grouped with the Tatars: have a special tongue: were formerly in the power of the Kazan Czars.

There is little wheat in their land; but it [620] is brought there, and exchanged against skins. Some of the Cheremis live in houses; but most of them live in tents on the field. The men desert the women if they have not borne children within three years.

These peoples pay tributes to their Majesties the Czars — in fodder.

The Cheremis use no other weapon than bow and arrow. They are divided into Nagornoi, or Pogorski, and Loegowooi, or Lugowiki; have a special language, and consist of a little over 20,000 souls. They all work the land, or are hunters, and they have many children; although they are not always enthusiastic [about them], perhaps because they wed young; because they marry in their twelfth or thirteenth year, particularly the wealthy. They make their bows and arrows for the hunt, but they also use dogs. The men are dressed like the Russian peasants: they know nought of priest or church; much honey and cattle is found with them; most of them are pagans, but a few are Moslems; they use many carts and horses; they live quietly, and in peace, except that at the time of Stenko Rasin's defection they defected with him but when he was conquered and tried many of them perished.

They marry as close a relative as they desire, and they don't know incest.

They follow here the inhabitants of the island of Ceylon, because the present king of that island, son of Raja Singa, whom he sired by his eldest daughter, has again married his own sister, a pious man, according to their overpious law. They [i.e., the Cheremis] bury the mead in jars, and pots, under the soil, and when this becomes sour it intoxicates the more readily: they also have beer and brandy; they love as food cabbage and cucumbers: there are no whores among them, and the person guilty of fornication is killed; they are very much inclined to drink. They worship trees and idols, put animals on wooden sticks, which they then leave about and worship. They don't know how to write. [Cf. Sebeok 1956b.] They live around, and in the neighborhood of Kazan. They don't know wine. They burn their cadavers, or these are buried, and sometimes they are thrown in the water. They take two, three, or four wives, as many as they can feed.

If they take an oath, they take a piece of [620/2] bread on two points of two sabers, and the person who takes the oath has these stuck in his mouth: other people drink salt water when they take an oath.

The men shave their entire head, but not the beard.

The women go around in a strange clothing, with wide sleeves, as the Japanese do, and the seams have been sewn on the outside with blue silk; they wear wide trousers, which one can see — there are no skirts covering them; and shoes of tree bark, they take hold of a wooden spade, or wooden cap by the middle, which they fasten high up, and this is decorated with cowries, bells, clocks, and these dangle before their forehead and down towards the shoulders, have long strands at the back, which trail behind them, and sometimes they stick copper or silver coins on their forehead: just as the women in Vjatka, a city of their Majesties the Czars, wear wide wooden caps on their head.

It is peculiar that, although these Cheremis live in houses, they have no villages. Each has a dwelling in the woods, so far from the next person that one cannot reach another by shouting.

The following was related to me in writing from a neighboring place about the Cheremis.

The homes of the Cheremis peoples start at Vasiligorod, a city which existed before, called after the Czar by that name, and built by him: they live in the region on both sides of the Volga, to the city Kazan; they live for the most part in huts; their daily food is game-roast and fish; they are good archers, and they urge their children to practice archery. It is said that they are faithless, rapacious, and cruel people, but otherwise not malicious of character. One differentiates between Pogorski and Lugowiki, the former bear the names of mountains because they live on the mountainside, or the high side on the right side of the Volga; the latter, of the low country, because they live on the left side of the Volga, in the plains, which is a fat land, rich in woods and trees: the former, for lack of feed, have their cattle graze on the latters' pastures, or have them fatten up there. They use the same language.

These pagan Cheremis, have the following customs which do not [621] differ much from those of the Circassians: their children, when they are half a year old, are given a name, usually after their parents, on a day set aside for the purpose [cf. Sebeok 1950], no writings are found with them, nor is any religion propagated by teaching; nevertheless most of them recognize and worship only one immortal benevolent God, whom they sometimes invoke; but they also invoke the Sun and the Moon; particularly the Sun in the spring, because the soil, cattle, and men benefit from its force and benefaction; and if they dream of any animals during the night, then they worship these the following day. When one asked one of them about the beginning of the world once, he answered, *Čort snai*, i.e., ask the Devil about it; on which occasion, when he was interviewed further, whether they knew the devil, he said, the Cheremis knew him very well; the devil was a spirit, which could do men a lot of harm, and did do a lot of harm to the Cheremis if they did not propitiate him by appropriate offerings.

The most important part of their idol-worship seemed to consist of offerings, about which they report the following.

The offerings have to take place at certain places, viz., forty *verst* [about 2/3 mile] south of Kazan, near a marsh at the river Nemda, where, according to them, the devil is living, and anyone who appears there without offerings or gifts, dries up immediately, yes exhaustion overcomes him so quickly that he can hardly go home from there. Ten *verst* from there is another water well-known among them, called Schoksihem, lying between two mountains, this is only two Dutch ells deep, but it nevertheless never freezes, however cold the winter. Here, as they say, the devil is also living, and is much more powerful and strict than at the aforementioned place, and is therefore greatly feared by the Cheremis, and taken to be much holier than Nemda; but no offerings may more be made at Schoksihem, and any Cheremis who approaches this water too closely, or steps into it, will have to suddenly fall down and die, but strangers and Christians are not harmed by this.

Their offerings consists of oxen, cows, and sheep, they cook the meat over a fire, stretch against the same fire the skin on poles, and then hold the dish with the cooked meat in one hand and a bowl of mead in the other hand, [621/2] and pronounce the following words. "I offer this to God, he certainly will be willing to take this from me, and in return provide me with oxen, sheep (this, or something else they desire), go hither Thou offering, and take my request to God;" after which he throws both the meat and the mead against the stretched skin, into the fire. If a wealthy person dies among them, his best horse is consumed at the usual offering place by the relatives and friend, the deceased is lowered in the earth and his clothes are hung up there.

They take as many wives simultaneously as they desire, and as they can manage; although these wives, among others, were relatives and sisters, whom they buy, as many as they desire, and as many as they can support. The dress of the men consists of a long skirt and stockings: when they are married, they shave their head bare, but the unmarried ones leave a pluck of hair on their skull, some braid them together: the children who are most dear to the parents wear a ring through the nose. The women go about with uncovered face, hung with coarse cloth and linen, and wrapped; the wealthy ones are dressed in stockings and over-skirts, like the men, except that they often wrap their head in a white cloth: a bride wears an ornament over her head, an ell long, as a horn, at the end of which there hangs a silk tassle with many colors, and in the midst of this there hangs a little bell. So much for the report that was sent to me.

Many believe that after 1,000 years men come back to this life, and in this they appear to follow the old Pythagorists. If someone dies, they bury him according to his vocation: if he was a farmer, then they place farmer's gear over his head on the grave; if he supported himself with bees and honey, a beehive, etc. They give the deceased a flint stone in their grave, so that he can make a fire at the time of his resurrection; and also an axe, so he can build himself a hut. They have nothing in common with Christianity, nor with the *Alcoran*, except for a few who are Moslems, although a few of them have been converted to Christianity through the zeal of the Muscovites. They are all subject to their Majesties the Czars; and, it is said, they take the loyalty oath as follows: two swords are placed crosswise [622] on a table, and each one who has to take the oath sticks his head under the cross of the swords, and so receives, from the hands of the Russian Chancellor, a piece of bread, cut in a square; after which he withdraws his head again: the meaning is that they will remain loyal to the Czar until the sword, i.e., until death, the Czar who supports them and gives them bread.

Here follows the *Pater Noster* in the Cheremis language (see Figure 1, above).

These Cheremis are archenemies of the Kalmucks, as well as of the Crims [Tatars], to whom they are held, and if necessary are forced.
The describer of the land, Maginus, says of the Cheremis, and Mordvins, that they live in dense woods without houses; that they speak their own language, and that some of them are supposed to be Moslems; that both men and women walk fast, and both carry bows: they feed themselves (he says) with honey and game: they rarely eat bread; they dress in shaggy skins.... They sometimes offer animals to God, and they stretch the skins on sticks, and perform ceremonies before them, by throwing a bowl full of mead down before them, which they then throw on the fire near this stretched skin, praying for cattle, and all temporal abundance. They also worship Sun and Moon: sometimes they honor animals, and cattle of which they have dreamt during the night. They use a language which differs from that of the other Tatars. [622/2] If someone is buried, they hang his clothes from a tree, slaughter a horse, if he was a man of means, and consume it at the side of a river. The men there wear long linen skirts: they shave their head bare; but the unmarried ones wear a pluck of hair in the back, which is sometimes tied up. The women wear coarse white linen clothes: the head considerably wrapped up. So far Maginus. The princedom Cassinov, or Cusimut, is near here, on the Oka. The inhabitants there lean towards Tatar ways, both in language and otherwise. The women blacken the nails of their fingers, and go bareheaded.
The clothes of the Cheremis, according to a story told me by a Persian merchant who traveled there, are often of white cloth and Russian linen skirts, men and women almost the same way and the same shape, so that you cannot tell one from the other by their clothes, except that the women are bareheaded, and one sees a braid hanging down from the back, with a horse tail or a cow tail tied to the end; which is stuck in the belt which men and women wear around their waist. The virgins and young girls wear a thin little board, six or eight *duim* ["thumb", or centimeter] wide, of white polished wood, above

the forehead, standing up, about three span high, which bends forward a little: at the top of this little board there hang, made of wood and other material, half moons, which dangle against each other, and make a noise and a movement; and this serves them as ornament, and entertainment. They live in the woods, in a few houses. If a child is born, they plant a tree, and watch it grow and yearly increase a branch, by which they remember the age of the child, since they know nothing of reading or writing, and cannot count either; under the tree, particularly the ones planted for daughters, they are used to bury a kind of large earthenware pot, or *pottise*, near the root. This jar is filled with a beverage prepared in a special way, and closed off, the earth on top, and left thus closed until the child marries, when it is opened and drunk to make merry the mutual families and relatives; being that this beverage, which is then very fresh and strong, is intoxicating. [623] They do not know offices; they support themselves with shooting, fishing, hunting, and a little plowing of land.

They know nothing of God or Heaven, nor what the world is like, nor what goes on in it: they are naive and bad: their only religion consists of asking advice and help from certain priests who pretend they can practice witchcraft and can confer with the devil; these [priests] then beat on a little drum, mutter a few words under their breath, and then declare that this animal, or no animal, has to be slaughtered, either a sheep, a billy-goat, a cow or a horse, and that the skin has to be placed on a pole, and has to be worshipped, as the need requires, either for health, for the increase of cattle, for a good catch, or fishing, and good crop, because all their expectations are focused on temporal comfort, and well-being; and one sees therefore displayed at almost every house some kind of stretched skin, at the top of some pole, for which this poor people bows. These people reach a high age; and eye witnesses have told me that they have seen and spoken with people a hundred and thirty years old.

One doesn't hear of entertainment among them. There are not many of them, ant it seems that previously they have been either disposed of, or have moved, or have died out: one often doesn't see a house for ten miles in their region. All the houses look alike, and are bad. The most important household item is a kettle.

They hunt with dogs, but also shoot the game with arrows, and the fish with blunt darts, although they also have badly made nets for catching fish. They carry bow and arrow, but no rifle; they make their journeys from one place to another on foot.

They are not pretty, but ugly, but they don't have such flat faces as the Samoyedes; about in the middle between those and other people.

To transport wares or loads they also use deer before the sleighs in the winter, or little carts in the summer.

In these areas are found the heaviest pole trees that are found anywhere. So much for the report by the aforementioned Persian traveler.

Then, on page 883, there is the following additional and final reference to the Cheremis:

Neither are counted to the Tatar races the Cheremis, the Chuvash, Votjaks, and other peoples, who all have the same religion as the Mordvins. There are some people among the aforesaid peoples, particularly among the Cheremis, who adhere to the Tatarian faith (i.e., the Moslem faith). These peoples are not forced to participate in the Muscovite campaigns, although they recognize their Majesties the Czars and pay tribute to him: a similar subordination and service is true of the Samoyedes, and other peoples living near the Ice Sea, which are all differentiated by special language and religion: and these people extend as far as the very high mountains adjacent to Siberia.

REFERENCES

Aarsleff, Hans
 1969 "The Study and Use of Etymology in Leibniz", *Studia Leibnitiana, Supplementa* 3, (Wiesbaden: Franz Steiner), 173-189.
Baxrušin, S. V.
 1955 *Naučnye trudy* 3:1 (Moscow: Akademiia Nauk SSSR).
Benz, E.
 1947 *Leibniz und Peter der Grosse* (Berlin: W. de Gruyter).
Bodel Nijenhuis, Johannes T.
 1855 *Verspreide bijzonderheden over Mr. Nicolaas Cornz. Witsen, burgemeester van Amsterdam* (Arnhem: J. A. Nijhoff).
Braudo, A.
 1904 " 'Vitzen' [Witsen]", *Entsiklopedičeskij slovar' Brokgauza-Efrona* 6 (St. Petersburg), 568-569.
Eckhardt, Johan Georg (ed.)
 1717 *Illustris viri Godofr. Gvilielmi Leibnitii Collectanea etymologica, illustrationi lingvarum, veteris celticae, germanicae, gallicae, aliarvmque inserventia* (Hannover: Nicolai Foerster).
Gebhard, Johan F.
 1881- *Het leven van Mr. Nicolaas Cornelisz. Witsen* (1641-1717), 2 vols. (Utrecht:
 1882 J. W. Leeflang).
Ger'e, Vladimir
 1873 *Sbornik pisem i memorialov Leibnitsa otnoriaščixsia k Rossii i Petru Velikomu* (St. Petersburg: Akademiia Nauk).
Müller, Kurt
 1955 *Gottfried Wilhelm Leibniz und Nicolaas Witsen* (Berlin: Akademie Vlg.).
Richter, Liselotte
 1946 *Leibniz und sein Russlandbild* (Berlin: Akademie der Wissenschaften).
Sebeok, Thomas A.
 1950 "Concerning Cheremis Names", *Language* 26, 276-278.
 1956a *The Cheremis* (New Haven: Human Relations Area Files).
 1956b "Cow Swallows Book: An Instance of Cheremis Nativism", *Ural-Altaische Jahrbücher* 28, 215-219.
 1960 "Eighteenth Century Cheremis: The Evidence from Pallas", *American Studies in Uralic Linguistics* (Bloomington: Indiana University Publications), 289-345.
Sebeok, Thomas A., and Frances J. Ingemann
 1955 *The Supernatural* (= *Viking Fund Publications in Anthropology* 22) (New York).
Sebeok, Thomas A. and Valdis J. Zeps
 1961 *Concordance and Thesaurus of Cheremis Poetic Language* (The Hague: Mouton).

314 THOMAS A. SEBEOK

Trisman, V. G.
  1951 "Russkie istočniki v monografii N. Vitsena 'Severnaia i vostočnaia Tatariia'",
        Akademiia Nauk SSSR. Institut ethnografii. Kratkie soobščeniia 13, 15-19.
Ustrialov, Nikolai G.
  1858- *Istoriia tsarstvovaniia Petra Velikogo*, 5 vols. (St. Petersburg: Tip. N-go
  1863   otdeleniia Fobstv. Ego Imp. Vel. Kantseliarii).
Vernadsky, George, et al. (eds.)
  1972 *A Source Book for Russian History from Early Times to 1917*, Vol. 2: *Peter
        the Great to Nicholas I* (New Haven: Yale).
Waterman, John T.
  1963 "The Languages of the World: A Classification by G. W. Leibniz", *Studies
        in Germanic Languages and Literatures* (Seattle: Washington University),
        27-34.

LINGUISTIC DE-STIGMATIZATION ?

BERTHE SIERTSEMA

> ... and I will give him a white stone, with a new name
> written on the stone which no one knows except him
> who receives it.
>
> (Revelation 2:17)

EMOTIVE AND CONNOTATIVE "MEANINGS"

The idea of linguistic stigmatization and de-stigmatization has to do with
what Eugene A. Nida called EMOTIVE MEANINGS in one of his many
valuable contributions to the science of translating (Nida 1964: 70ff.).
First a few remarks about these kinds of "meanings", therefore.

"Emotive meanings", Nida says, "relate to the responses of the
participants in the communicative act"; and the appreciation of native
speakers for these emotive meanings is described as "a 'feeling' for the
appropriateness of words in certain types of linguistic and cultural
contexts". As examples of such emotive values of words Nida mentions
"vulgar", "obscene", "slang", "pedantic".

Nida and Taber (1969) use the term CONNOTATIVE MEANING when
dealing with the same phenomena. Connotative meaning is said to
"deal with our emotional reactions to words" (Nida and Taber 1969: 91).
Besides positive reactions they mention as examples of negative reactions
"feelings of revulsion, or disgust, against such words as the famous
four-letter words in English which refer to certain body organs and
functions".

In both cases the authors locate the cause of the hearer's negative
feelings in the speaker's use of the WORDS as such. Nida writes:

In describing emotive meanings... we either analyze the behavioral responses
of others to the use of certain words... or we try to diagnose our emotional
attitudes toward words of our mother tongue,

Berthe Siertsema is Professor of General Linguistics at the Free University, Amsterdam,
The Netherlands.

and in the next sentence mention is made of the "evaluation of words" (1964: 71). Similarly, Nida and Taber, after defining connotative meaning as "emotional reactions to words" (1969: 91) and illustrating their definition with the examples of taboo words mentioned above, state explicitly:

The fact that the taboo is against the word and not the referent[1] can be seen from the fact that there are quite innocent scientific terms which refer to the same things and which are perfectly acceptable. But the feeling against the words is such that even though everyone knows them, they are not used in polite society, and even many dictionaries refuse to print them. Such words are thought to defile the user (1969: 91).

Even noncivilized societies have their "vulgar language" as distinguished from ordinary popular language: "vulgar language is a universal phenomenon" (Nida and Taber 1969: 124).

SOCIAL VALUE (LOAD)

So far, there is no difficulty and the matter is quite clear: in all languages there are words that should not be used in polite society and the speaker who does use them there is frowned upon because he has not observed the society's rules of "appropriateness of words". Notice that in these cases it is the SPEAKER who is thought to be "defiled"; it is the speaker who is disapproved of, because he uses the "wrong word", a word belonging to a different social setting from the one he is speaking in. The different setting may be considered a "lower" one, as in the case mentioned by Nida and Taber of certain four-letter words used in polite society, or a "higher" one, as would occur if in four-letter-word circles a speaker should use the "innocent scientific terms" to refer to the body organs and functions meant. This would be equally inappropriate, he would equally be frowned upon – worse, he would probably be laughed at – by the company concerned. In this respect the evaluation of a speaker's (or writer's) vocabulary is not different from that of his grammar and pronunciation: these performance features are social class indicators *par excellence*.

Nancy Mitford (1956) has filled a whole book with examples of this

---

[1]   The term *referent* is used in this paper in an abstract sense of "thing meant usually", "type of thing meant", as well as in a more concrete sense of "thing meant *hic et nunc*". When the word occurs the context will leave no doubt in which of the two senses it is to be taken.

curious tendency of civilized man to distinguish himself in his speech, to demonstrate in it that he belongs to a different circle, that he knows what is "U" and what is "non-U", what belongs to the speech of the "Upper class" and what does not. The terms are Alan S. C. Ross' invention (1956), and his examples show that besides the cases mentioned the distinction is found in entirely haphazard sets of words. In Dutch, for instance, we have a comparable distinction but with different sets of words, equally selected at random, it seems. Thus the English distinction between U *jam, wireless,* and *table-napkin* vs. non-U *preserve, radio,* and *serviette,* respectively, has no parallel in Dutch; inversely, the Dutch distinction between U *pak* 'suit', *auto* 'car', and *onderwijzer* 'teacher' vs. non-U *kostuum, wagen,* and *schoolmeester* has no parallel in English for the first two sets of words (as far as I know), and the reverse distinction for the last one, for *teacher* is classed by Ross as "essentially non-U" (D. *onderwijzen* = E. *teach*) whereas the word with *-master* (D. *meester*), e.g. *maths-master,* is the English U equivalent (Ross 1956: 32). Ross also remarks on the "philologically trivial ... nature" of these linguistic class indicators and points out moreover how ephemeral they are. Indeed, the Dutch *wagen* for "car" started its life as a U understatement. These sorts of distinguishers can indeed be compared to badges, as Nida and Taber do when they write: "recognized differences in speech ... easily become badges of belonging, a mark of pride in one's group". The writers observe that at the same time there is an opposite tendency "especially among members of the more ambitious and socially insecure groups,... to imitate the speech of the more secure and privileged class to which the speaker aspires" (1969: 128).

Nida and Taber mention quite a few other sociological factors that affect linguistic variation besides social class, viz. age, sex, educational level, occupation, and religious affiliation (1969: 127), but I will not enter into these here.

It is for the capacity of certain words to bring about the kind of reactions just described that I would have liked to reserve the term CONNOTATIVE: these words "indicate" something "besides" their referents. Since this "something" is of a social nature, however, and since the terms connotative and connotation are already established as Nida and Taber use them, i.e. for the whole range of "feeling tones" (Osgood 1960) attached to a word used, the term SOCIAL seems to be a better label for the category that I have in mind here. Ullmann's term EVO-CATIVE (1962: 133), which he traces back to Bally, would also have been most appropriate if this category had not been put on a line in his book with several other "sources of emotive overtones" in which the distinction which I want to make here between the word as "source" and the referent as "source" is not explicitly made.

I would preferably not subsume the said capacity of certain words under their MEANING but would rather call it their SOCIAL VALUE or LOAD. The social value or social load of a word, then, is to be defined as its inherent indication of the social setting in which it belongs. This need not necessarily be a setting of social class or any of the other factors mentioned by Nida and Taber (1969: 127) but may widen into a setting of moods or styles in general, such as the "pedantic" kind in Nida's enumeration (1964: 70).

It is characteristic for words with such social values that the language usually has a parallel set of other words for the same things, such as the ones enumerated by Ross, or as the "innocent scientific terms" Nida and Taber refer to (1969: 91). The social value distinction may, as we saw, be attached to sets of words for unpleasant, but also for neutral or pleasant things, and as regards the last two sets, it may in less than a lifetime disappear altogether from the words indicating those things to settle on words indicating quite different things (Ross 1956: 34). The changes in this category seem to just happen, nobody knows how, and for no other reason than the unconscious general drive of human "birds of a feather" to "flock together". They want to be identifiable as members of "that flock" — a better flock, if possible, than the others.

EMOTIVE VALUE (LOAD)

Nida gives more examples, however, of words with "emotive meanings" and so do Nida and Taber of "connotative meanings", most of them words that tend to be replaced by euphemisms. Thus Nida and Taber mention the word *toilet* which is replaced by, i.a., *washroom, comfort station, lounge, powder room*; the word *garbage man*, replaced by *sanitary engineer*; and *undertaker*, replaced by *mortician* (1969: 91).

Now this looks to me like a different category from the kind of words they have dealt with first. For one thing, the words *toilet, garbage,* and *undertaker* are not "thought to defile the *user*" of these words – at most he may be considered to be somewhat behind the times; it is not the speaker that is disapproved of in these cases, it is the REFERENT, no matter by what word it is named. Hence the desire to camouflage this referent by a euphemism. When Nida and Taber state, for instance, that "the entire complex of euphemisms surrounding death and burial undoubtedly contains a strong ingredient of fear" (1969: 91), what they mean is fear of the referents, of death and burial, surely not fear of the euphemisms nor even fear of the non-euphemistic words by which these referents are named.

This camouflage function is absent in the former category of words, and this makes for two more differences between that group and the one dealt with here, namely that euphemisms are still more ephemeral on one hand, but that on the other hand there is a certain stability in their referents. Successive euphemisms tend to be used for the same sort of things all the time – things people fear or dislike. That is why euphemisms are so ephemeral, they may be replaced two or three times in one's lifetime; also, they are often consciously, intentionally, and explicitly replaced. For, as soon as their meaning becomes so well-known that the camouflage function is lost, a new camouflage is looked for in the form of a new euphemism to vaguely hint at the unpleasant referent; *undertaker* and *toilet* were also euphemisms once.

Nevertheless, and in contrast to the former category of words, it is not considered inappropriate when in certain contexts and situations, for instance in businesslike or other matter-of-fact discourse in which clarity is of first importance, the non-euphemistic word is used. This is a fifth point of difference as compared with the first group. A good illustration of this (and implicitly of the camouflage function of euphemisms) is to be found in the introduction to a recent collection of papers on *mental illness*, a term disapproved of and replaced by a euphemism by several psychiatrists nowadays, as we shall see. The term occurs in the very title of the collection, however, and the editors write:

Probably none of the thirty-five contributors is entirely satisfied with the connotations of "mental illness". Yet most authors, in this book and in others, continue to use the term, however hesitatingly, and we have used it in the title of this book. Our reason, developed after considerable debate and soul-searching, is that *no other term in common usage conveys a similar meaning* to most readers. "Mental illness"... holds *a widely understood* meaning for the general public (Edgerton and Plog 1969: 5, italics mine).

For the capacity of certain words to bring about these latter kinds of emotional reaction, i.e. reactions to their referents, I would like to reserve the term EMOTIVE. I would preferably not subsume this capacity under their MEANING, but would rather call it the EMOTIVE VALUE or LOAD of the words. Max Black names it emotive *influence* and rightly distinguishes it from emotive *meaning*, which is present, he says, when a word is "*interpreted*, as a *sign* of feelings and attitudes expressed by the speaker or intended to be aroused in the hearer", as in words like *hurrah*! (Black 1963: 219). Stevenson (1944: 72ff., 78ff.) tries to cover the various emotive sources and effects of words in a distinction between "independent", "dependent", and "quasi-dependent" emotive *meaning*, but he writes from a nonlinguistic point of view; hence his later discussion with Black on these distinctions (Stevenson 1963: 159ff) leaves an impression of talking somewhat at cross-purposes.

In contrast to the social value of a word, which causes its acceptability or unacceptability as a word in the social circle in which it is used, the emotive value of a word may endanger its use and cause it to be replaced by euphemisms in any circle. On the other hand, in the absence of euphemisms the emotive value of a word may vary per speaker, hearer, context, and situation. This is what Nida and Taber mean when they say in their terminology: "The connotations of words may be highly individual" (1969: 91).

These are two more points of difference between the two kinds of words under discussion. Still another difference is that emotive value is not restricted to certain specific words only. Although the referents of some words evoke predominantly positive feelings in the majority of people and those of other words predominantly negative ones (in which case they tend to be camouflaged by euphemisms), we can still safely say that in principle any word with a lexical content may in one context or another and with one speaker (hearer) or another have either positive or negative emotive value. Nida (1964: 114) and Nida and Taber (1969: 93) give several examples when they are dealing with the subject, and so does Ullmann (1962: 130-140). Even such a "neutral" word as *sandy* – to add one of my own – has positive emotive value in *sandy beaches* and negative in *sandy vegetables*. An "unfavorable" word like *steal* is emotionally positive if its object is a *heart* or a *show*, and a "favorable" word like *father* has negative emotive value in the Western world if its referent is a boy of fourteen. Moreover, all this applies only for the presumable majority of people. For if I should prefer rocky beaches because they provide more shelter or pebble beaches because they are cleaner, the phrase *sandy beach* may carry a negative emotive load for me; and the phrase *my father* may have a frightening ring to the son of a drunkard. With a gangster the word *steal* may be music to the ears, and so may the word *criminal*. Mellitta Schmideberg (1949: 186) records the following conversation with a criminal who, in speaking appreciatively about a certain policeman, said: "he was quite a criminal himself". In answer to her question he added: "you could talk to him about his children and wife, he was quite human, he was like one of us". She concludes:

To him being "*human*" *was synonymous with* "*criminal*". Hardly surprising, since often all reactions these men encountered from respectable society are retaliation and inhumanity, or at best patronizing charity and moralizing hypocrisy (italics mine).

As an example of the different emotive values of a nonlinguistic sign, Goffman reminds us of

the shoulder-patches that prison-officials require escape-prone prisoners to wear (and that) can come to mean one thing to guards, in general negative, while being a mark of pride for the wearer relative to his fellow-prisoners (Goffman 1963: 62-63).

(Cf. also Zimbardo and Ebbesen 1969: 87ff.)

Having got to this point, one begins to wonder if the case of the four-letter words mentioned in the first section really belongs to that section only, if it is purely a social case, of entirely the same nature as the U vs. non-U distinctions dealt with by Nancy Mitford. The case of the four-letter words rather seems to be one halfway between the first and the second category in that it has a little of both – social as well as emotive load. Incidentally, this intermediate category may well cover quite a bit more than the groups of four-letter words only; it is a universal tendency of linguistic categories, especially of semantic and connotative ones, to be the opposite of clear-cut.

As for the case in hand, it should be noted that it is not all the four-letter words indicating body parts that are taboo; we can freely mention a person's *hair, nose, chin, lips, hand,* and *foot,* or say that he has broken the *bone* of his *shin.* The taboo four-letter words are only those that refer to sexual or digestive organs, parts that apparently tend to awaken the said "feelings of revulsion or disgust" (Nida and Taber 1969: 91) all over the world, for the words for them are taboo words in a great many languages. That the taboo is against the referent can be seen from the fact that in primitive societies like the Masaba in Uganda there are no parallel innocent terms that can be used in polite society; there are only the vulgar words that make the informants giggle when you ask for them; in polite society such matters are not mentioned. Moreover, this unanimity in the use of vocabulary in widely different languages could surely not exist if it were not for a unanimity of attitude towards the

things meant, the referents. This conclusion is supported by sociological
and anthropological investigations, as we shall see below.

"EMOTIVE MEANING"?

It might be objected that we do not only have socially unacceptable
words with their acceptable counterparts, and emotively unfavorable
words with their euphemisms, we also have generally acceptable sets of
a negative and a positive word to refer to one and the same thing.
Compare for instance *wench* and *girl*, and in Dutch *Mof* and *Duitser*
for a German: surely the difference in emotive value is in the words
themselves then, for it cannot be in the referents?

Indeed, of each set both members can be applied to the same person,
but the two words of each set do not mean the same. A *wench* (*Concise
Oxford Dictionary* 1964), is a *particular kind* of girl: the word is used
"esp. of rustics or servants", probably implying unpolished manners
and behavior. And a *Mof* is a *particular kind* of German: a noisy and
loud-spoken one who behaves as if he owns the world. Thus here again
any negative feeling concerns the thing meant, the referent.

If I now call a nice and decent German a *Mof*, I use a small-scale metaphor to express that I do not like him, maybe because he has a loud
voice. And if I call a well-mannered, polished college girl a *wench*, I
use another small-scale metaphor to express that I do not approve of
her, maybe because of her rustic clothes or her plump and inelegant shape.
In those metaphoric applications the negative emotive value of the words
is strengthened because only certain negative aspects of the usual referent
are transferred to the new one; it is like calling a stupid boy an *ass* or
a naughty one a *monkey*. In this metaphoric type of use the words seem
to answer Black's definition of words with emotive *meaning*. Black's
example of such words is *hurrah*! (quoting Stevenson 1944), but the
metaphoric words discussed here are also "*interpreted*, as a *sign* of
feelings and attitudes *expressed* by the speaker or *intended* to be aroused in
the hearer" (Black 1963: 219, italics mine; cf. above). However this may
be, Black rightly makes little of the difference with descriptive (Stevenson's term = denotative) meaning in stating that it can be expressed
"in terms of differences between the respective *designata*", which means
that linguistically the concept of *emotive meaning* is redundant, also
for the cases described in this section.

This is further supported by facts like the following. If one considers all Germans as "Moffen", there is no difference in emotive load in Dutch between the word *Mof* and the word *Duitser*. It was like that in Holland during World War II. When there were house-searching raids for hidden Jews or young men or radio apparatus, the warnings "the *Moffen* are coming!", "the *Duitsers* are coming!", or simply "*They* are coming!" all carried the same negative emotive load. It is only now, with a new generation, that the old value differentiation between the two terms is regaining its ground. Similarly, once a particular girl is known for her unpolished country manners, it makes no difference in emotive value whether she is referred to as "that Saunders *girl*" or "that Saunders *wench*"; the difference is only there for those who do not know her. It is our knowledge about the referent that loads the sign for it, any sign, with emotion.

LINGUISTIC STIGMATIZATION AND SAPIR-WHORF

It is the emotive load of words that is of importance for an evaluation of the idea of linguistic stigmatization and de-stigmatization. A linguistic stigma is an unfavorable labeling word attached to a person or thing as a mark, comparable to the mark formerly branded on a slave or a criminal. In recent years the importance of such labels, e.g. *thief*, *criminal*, has drawn the attention of authorities in three main fields of study concerned with deviant behavior: punitive justice, social work, and psychiatry. The belief seems to be gaining ground in these circles that the linguistic labeling of a person needing help may be an obstacle to his progress or improvement.

Basically, this belief is a further development of the Sapir-Whorf hypothesis of so-called linguistic relativity; in fact we find these two authors quoted repeatedly in studies of the problem. The crucial passage is one in Sapir's well-known paper on "The Status of Linguistics as a Science":

Human beings do not live in the objective world alone, nor alone in the world of social activity as ordinarily understood, but are very much at the mercy of the particular language which has become the medium of expression for their society. It is quite an illusion to imagine that one adjusts to reality essentially without the use of language and that language is merely an incidental means of solving certain specific problems of communication or reflection. The fact of the matter is that the "real world" is to a large part unconsciously built up on the language habits of the group.... We see and hear and otherwise experience very largely as we do because the language habits of our community predispose certain choices of interpretation (Sapir 1960: 69).

Whorf was fascinated by this idea of Sapir's (which in fact goes back to Plato and was already fully worked out in the nineteenth century by von Humboldt), and applied it freely in the many links he laid, without a hint of any doubt or hesitation, between the grammar and vocabulary of American Indian languages and the world view and mentality of their speakers (Whorf 1956). Although the hypothesis of such a direct link has often been refuted by linguistic studies of meaning (cf. Carroll 1963; Thielemans 1969; Siertsema 1970; and the literature they refer to), it has a strong romantic appeal and many a scholar, especially outside the field of linguistics, still succumbs to it when he gets acquainted with it.

In the above-mentioned sectors of society that concern themselves with deviant behavior, mental disease, and criminality, the Sapir-Whorf theory has naturally attracted attention, although several leading scholars in these fields, too, either have carefully stood aside ("I do not intend ... to get involved in that particular quagmire" [Bernstein 1972: 161]) or have actually expressed their scepticism towards it. Several authors have pointed out the circularity of the reasoning which derives language from world view and then world view from language. Among them are Osgood and Sebeok (1954: 194), Carroll and Casagrande (1958: 21), Kluckhohn (1961: 903-904) and Triandis (1964: 37). Kluckhohn recommended that the hypothesis should be investigated at the hand of "genuinely independent variables", because "No validation can be obtained by pointing on an ad hoc basis to correspondences, however actual, between features of language and features of non-linguistic culture."

Earlier, Charles E. Osgood, trying to reconcile pro- and anti-Whorfians, suggested making "a distinction between two general classes of cognition ... *denotative* and *connotative*". This would conveniently rid the pro-Whorfians of "the phenomena which seem to display generality across human groups regardless of language or culture", because these "are essentially connotative – the affective 'feeling tones' of meaning which contribute to synesthesia, metaphor, and the like" (Osgood 1960; quoted by Kluckhohn 1961: 906).

H. C. Triandis' anthropological investigations led him to the same conclusion, that there are "panhuman factors" operating in the "similarity of associations and stereotypes obtained from subjects from different cultures" (1964: 26), and that

... though subjects in different cultures use different categories and different organizations of lexical fields, there is considerable similarity in the ways they evaluate key concepts, make judgments of emotion, desirability, and morality. Human life, for instance, is valued in all cultures... (1964: 41).

He summarizes the consequence of these findings in the short statement that in the field of "connotative meaning ... the Whorfian hypothesis is not relevant, because ... the structure of connotative meaning in heterogeneous cultures is very similar" (1964: 39).

Among those who have hopefully accepted the Sapir-Whorf theory, it tends to be linked up with proverbs like "once a thief, always a thief". They point out that verbal labels like *thief, criminal, psychopath*, etc. will stick to a person long after he has left the prison or the mental hospital and in fact may stigmatize him for the rest of his life, making it difficult or even impossible for him to get a job or a house or in general to get back to normal and "start a new life". Thus the punishment for a crime, for instance, becomes much heavier than the judge who pronounces the verdict is aware of.

Lawyers, social workers, psychologists, and psychiatrists are rightly concerned about this, and in their search for means to remedy it some of them have hit on the idea that if there is this linguistic stigmatization, there should also be the possibility of "linguistic de-stigmatization". Their hopes have increased when they came across that other statement of Whorf's, that "a change in language can transform our appreciation of the Cosmos" (Whorf 1956: 263). Interpreting the word *language* in this statement as "choice of words within one language" – which is not what Whorf meant! – they put forth with conviction that if only we would stop calling a thief a *thief* and a psychopath a *psychopath* but would refer to them with "neutral" words, these people would be better off.

The advocates of this method do not seem to be aware of the fact that it is the time-honored method of euphemism dealt with above – camouflaging an unpleasant referent with a different name. In any case they do not *call* it "euphemism", they call it "changing the label"; but as the new label is always meant to be a better looking one, it is what in linguistics is known as a euphemism. If they realized this, they might become more realistic about the effectiveness of their new labels. That these are also subject to the same ever returning ineffectiveness as euphemisms, with regard to the change of feeling aimed at, will be shown below.

As evidence supporting the method of label changing one finds references to basic experiments such as Doris Dietze's, in which Kluck-hohn's recommendation of "independent variables" is observed. Dietze found that four- and five-year-old children would learn to discriminate between slightly different objects more readily if they were named by completely different nonsense words than they would if the nonsense names differed by one phoneme only. If the ideal of the experiment, which was optimal discrimination of objects, is reversed into that of the Whorfian social worker – minimal discrimination – it does seem to follow from the experiment that this ideal could be attained by naming objects (actions, persons) that should not be discriminated from others by the same word as those others are named with. Those who draw this inference, however, tend to forget that in Dietze's experiment the referents were entirely without emotional value (Dietze 1955).

APPLICATIONS IN PSYCHIATRY

Thus, in the psychoanalyst J. Rosen's book *Direct Psychoanalytic Psychiatry* (1962) terms such as *doctor, patient, symptom, diagnose,* and further medical language were left out intentionally. His patients are *clients* taken up in a *house* and treated not by a *psychiatrist* but by a *psychotrophist,* a "feeder of the mind" (Foudraine 1972: 369). Earlier, K. T. Erikson, wanting to create a more realistic position for those who were "finding living difficult" (as he preferred to view it), had pleaded for an atmosphere in which the patient would be rather a *student* than a *medical patient* (Erikson 1957; quoted by Foudraine 1972: 368 without page reference).

The "school" and "student" idea was found attractive; in 1964 K. L. Artiss also suggests to do away with the "medical model" in psychiatry and with the whole vocabulary that belongs to it, especially with the "patient role" with its connotations of helplessness and passivity and absence of responsibility for getting better. By the time this is realized the future nurse "may have dropped off part of her role, to be replaced by an appellation that suggests *teaching* or *tutoring*" (Artiss 1964; quoted by Foudraine 1972: 379 without page reference, italics mine).

Finally, the Dutch psychiatrist Jan Foudraine tells us of his experiment as a member of staff in the psychoanalytical sanatorium Chestnut Lodge (Rockville, Maryland, U.S.A.). One of the "Cottages" of this sanatorium was turned by him into a *school for living,* where the *students* were *taught* by *assistant educators* and where they could *learn* what had gone wrong in their lives and how it could be changed. They were no longer *mentally ill* but simply *ignorant*; the psychiatrist was their *educator*, and the nursing office was labeled *educational office* (Foudraine 1972: 345-346, translation mine).

It is important to note that this change of terminology was part of a radical structural change in other respects in the whole set-up of the Cottage as well as in the treatment. The change of terminology was simply the linguistic reflection of what was going on in the place. This is no doubt why it was accepted and thus could contribute its small share to the completion of the drastic reforms made. It is also important to note what the head nurse reported about the effect of the introduction of the word *students* on the morale of the Cottage, namely that this was very positive, "especially *in the beginning*" (Foudraine 1972: 349, translation and italics mine).

APPLICATIONS IN LAW AND JUSTICE

A parallel development has somewhat later set in in the area of penal law and punitive justice, and it is interesting to see how the very "illness" and "patient" concepts that psychiatrists are trying to get rid of are now being embraced in this field as the means to solve the really serious problems of ex-delinquents and those who try to help them. V. Eisner, in his study of the delinquency label, summarizes those problems succinctly when he observes that

the mechanism that society had set up to "understand, protect, and help the child or youth" [the juvenile courts] was often the very mechanism that, by labeling him as a delinquent, made him unemployable and thus sentenced to a life of poverty.

For

... there is no way to reverse the labeling process: Once the delinquency label has been applied, a boy remains either a delinquent or a former delinquent (Eisner 1969: 15, 16).

As a possible way out of this sad circle, Eisner states that the delinquency label can be prevented by providing a youth with the alternative label of *psychiatric patient*, so that he will not act his role as delinquent but as patient and try to *get well*. Eisner does not seem to be aware of the fact that this view draws rather heavily on the stigmatizing effect of the "patient" label on the die-hards and tough guys in the criminal world. For we have seen that psychiatrists object to this same label for real mental patients because of its connotation of passivity and absence of responsibility for getting well.

Other scholars in this field make similar suggestions: "As a precedent and illustration of [the required] transformation we are often referred to what happened in the treatment of the insane... some day we shall look upon prisons as we do upon the psychiatric institutions of a century ago", writes Wilkins (1969:140), and on the abolition of prisons: "instead, new institutions... are called *reformatories, bridewells*, etc., and therefore their inmates are not called *convicts*, but *inmates, wards*" (1969: 184). Earlier in the same book, Wilkins has pleaded for the *illness* view as a means also to differentiate punishments for different offenders: "... there is no generally good treatment ... for all types of offenders". But if delinquency is seen as an illness, then it becomes necessary to find the nature of the different types of ailments that have thus far been classified together. "If we accept this analogy [with medical treatment], it immediately appears that what is effective treatment for one offender is dangerous for another." In an experiment, two treatments made use of intensive "living group therapy" (Wilkins 1969: 95).

Besides label change, there are also suggestions for a kind of label generalization in the sense of D. Chapman's "operational definitions". These are general descriptions that should "present behaviours without their moral referrents". Thus theft, burglary, larceny, embezzlement, fraud, then become "The transfer of goods or rights from one person to another without the former's full knowledge and consent" (Chapman 1968: 177-178). Assault would become "actions which cause pain and/or injury to the health of the subject". Afterwards the approval or disapproval of such behaviors in certain circumstances could then be accounted for (Chapman 1968: 177). The author realizes that "this model would [only] be useful in discussing the general case", and that "for crimes in highly specific circumstances ... a more complex model is needed". He will need the latter model in all cases, it would seem to me, because the "circumstances" will be vitally important in order to distinguish the criminal from the noncriminal varieties of the actions thus described. Chapman seems to be aware of this when he says that "for any behaviour thus defined there exist condemned, neutral, and approved forms, the valuation of each depending on factors independent of the action".

The reverse way towards linguistic de-stigmatization is advocated by H. Bianchi and J. de Back who, on the contrary, propagate the use in law courts of more specific terminology and the avoidance of general terms. Bianchi compares the information of a word like *cow* to that of *heifer* and holds that the latter word gives less, but more specific, information ("it only says something about the age of the cow..."). The more general term "evoke(s) in the hearer a number of associative patterns ... from which he can choose at will according to his own ... world view" (1971: 51, translation mine). Hence the more specific kind of term is to be preferred in the sphere of the law court, he says.

Having already dealt with Bianchi's brochure *Stigmatisering* elsewhere (van Reenen and Siertsema 1972), I will here restrict myself to de Back's *Taal en Afwijkend Gedrag* [Language and Deviant Behavior] (1973) which in more than one respect is typical of this kind of approach. In this book the writer illustrates Bianchi's proposition with an example of an "abstraction ladder" applied to a Mr. Johnson who because of his shop-lifting could be described as a *criminal*, a *delinquent*, or a *thief*. Instead, he should be described as a "shop-thief" or better still, with an even more specific label like "Johnson, fined twice for shop-lifting" (de Back 1973: 79). De Back summarizes his ideas about linguistic destigmatization in a number of suggestions for what he calls "our everyday moral speech (use of language)", by enumerating several kinds of words we should avoid, such as words with a dominant emotive value (replace *criminal* by *deviant*), words which "contain facts [*sic*] and at the same time a [moral] judgment of these facts" (replace Dutch *misdadiger* 'wrongdoer' by *delinkwent*), and also words which "contain one or more presuppositions" (an example might be this, found on page 76 in the book: *psychopath* = 'dangerous person' = 'criminal' = 'sexual violator') (de Back 1973: 87-88, translation and examples mine). It is de Back's firm belief that

the attempts at decriminalization and de-stigmatization within the systems of punitive justice and medical psychiatry will only have a chance of succeeding if in future the rendering of reality through language will be done in a fundamentally different way (de Back 1973: 79, translation mine).

THE LANGUAGE USER KNOWS, AND LIKES OR DISLIKES, THE THING MEANT

Leaving aside for the moment the question if not our feelings, too, are part of "reality", we realize that of de Back's suggestions for our future use of words, the last one is the most intriguing and of great importance for our subject, viz. that we should use "words that contain [no] presuppositions".

Whatever a lawyer may mean by this, linguistically speaking there are no such words. The use of a lexical word is always based on at least two presuppositions: that the speaker and hearer know what the word means, and that they have some amount of knowledge about the word's referent, the "thing meant". In other words: they know which referent is referred to and they know (something about) this referent, i.e. they have both got to know (some of) its properties and implications, have both formed an opinion as to its value, moral or otherwise, and have both developed some feelings towards it, positive or negative depending on the first two factors. All of this is always involved in speech. "All language has some emotive value", said H. Delacroix, "if what I say were indifferent to me, I would not say it" (quoted by Ullmann, 1962: 128).

In further elaboration of what was said above, therefore, we may now specify that it is the hearer's knowledge, opinion, and feelings about the referent of a sign that cause the positive or negative emotions in him when the sign is given. When a red light over the road I am driving on in a hurry irritates and annoys me, this is not because I dislike red lights, nor because I disapprove of red traffic lights indicating danger, but because I dislike what it implies at that moment: that I have to stop and wait; I dislike its referent *hic et nunc*. If red traffic lights throughout the country should be replaced by "neutral" white lights, it would at once be the white light that would cause my irritation in similar circumstances, as I would similarly have to stop and wait, which I dislike.

It is no different with language signs. If the word *murderer* should be replaced by a "neutral" word such as *eliminator* or *abolisher*, it would at once be the new word that would awaken my negative feelings whenever it should be used to indicate that person who has killed someone: that referent which I fear and dislike.

PROOFS FROM THE "HISTORY OF LABELING"

If viewed in their historical setting, several of the suggestions made by the writers cited above are in fact illustrations of what I have been saying. Thus T. R. Sarbin traces the development of terms indicating mental illness. In the sixteenth century the view was that the patients were *bewitched* or *possessed* (*by demons*) and had to be killed. To save them from this fate they were then declared to be *as if sick*, from where it was but one step to just *sick* or *ill* with its physical connotations now objected to (Sarbin 1969: 12-13). Naturally, this linguistic change could not have succeeded so well if it had not reflected the fundamental change in outlook, the new insight that deviant behavior had nothing to do with witchcraft. What is disappointing but of interest for our subject, however, is that the emotive value of all those different words has remained the same; the reactions to mental patients still are the same old negative ones of fear and dislike, and there is not much hope that they will be any different towards the *students* of the *schools for living.*

We see a similar succession of terms in the names of the places where mental patients are lodged. The *madhouse* became *lunatic asylum* when people thought that the moon had something to do with the disease, and this – when that idea was dropped again – became *asylum for the insane* and then *mental hospital* or *mental home*, and as we saw above, there is a new suggestion for a change in the recent term *school for living*. But the negative feelings towards this kind of institution remain, whatever the changes of insight and whatever new label is attached to it.

Although "in the beginning" (see the remark of the head nurse quoted above) each new label has a mitigating effect in so far as people are not immediately aware of what it indicates, even then the camouflage is only partial, owing to the destructive effects on it of the context and the situation in which it is used. There is a mental hospital in Holland which used to bear the neutral name *Merenberg* 'Lake-and-hill'. When I first came to live near there as an eight-year-old child, I did not know what *Merenberg* was but gathered at once that it must be some unpleasant place where people were kept, from the expression "he is ripe for Merenberg", used by my classmates for our teacher when we thought he had been unreasonable in his demands or punishments. Ten years later the place had changed its name into *Provinciaal Ziekenhuis* 'Provincial Hospital'.

Similar examples could be adduced of a succession of vain attempts at linguistic destigmatization in the circles of penal law and punitive justice. The change from Dutch *misdadiger* (lit. 'wrongdoer') to *delinkwent* has been mentioned above, but it must be added that linguistic destigmatization advocates are already suggesting that the latter word should be changed into *deviant* because *delinkwent* is too much of a stigma. The same has happened to Dutch *beklaagde* '(the) accused' (lit. 'the one complained about'); it had to disappear from the books of penal law because of its stigmatizing effect and was replaced by *verdachte* 'suspect'. But it was not long before this word acquired the same unfavorable emotive value and some insiders are already suggesting in irony that it might be replaced by the former word (Mulder 1971: 14).

As a final example, one from the field of social work in a wider sense, the term for foreign laborers in Holland may be mentioned as a case of rapid development in this respect. Within a few years, the first word *gastarbeider* 'guest-laborer', specially designed for its favorable meaning so as to prevent linguistic stigmatization, had to be replaced by *buitenlandse werknemer* 'employed (person) from abroad' in official documents, and this in its turn is now being abbreviated to its initials *b.w.*, just as we in Dutch say *c.a.* for *cancer* and *t.b.* for *tuberculosis*.

As for what I have called label generalization and label specification, there are no instances from practice known to me, but it would seem to me that both could have either positive or negative effect, depending on the seriousness of the crime committed. As a generic label would hide the details of the crime by subsuming it under a much wider class, the perpetrator of a major crime is likely to benefit by such a label, but the petty offender may well suffer from it; inversely, a label specifying details will have positive effect for the latter (see de Back's example of *shop-lifter* above), but it will evoke stronger negative feelings if the crime thus specified is a serious one.

In the case of label generalization there is an additional problem. I have already pointed out that with such general behavior descriptions as proposed by Chapman, the "circumstances" become extremely important in distinguishing the criminal from the noncriminal varieties of an action. In fact, it all depends on what is to be called "the action". Bashing in some round object with a sledge hammer because you want to get rid of it is a legitimate action, but if the object happens to be somebody's head, is that fact to be relegated to "circumstances", to "factors independent of the action" (Chapman 1968: 177)? I have a strong suspicion that the "more complex model" foreseen by him, which is to link the decisive "circumstances" to the behavior first described in general terms, will in the end prove to contain such distinguishers again as *theft, burglary, larceny, murder*, etc., or their substitutes, if it is to work at all. If those words – as well as the generic ones condemned by the opposite party pro label-specification – were not needed in our community they would have disappeared from our language long ago. They have not; they are there as distinguishing signs available for immediate use. So why make such detours to reach them?

Instead of using neutral, generic, or specifying terms, we could still go one step further in our attempts to camouflage our negative feelings about certain persons or things by speaking about them in words of praise. But this attempt would also fail, for our praising words would in those circumstances immediately be interpreted as irony: "Here is a *nice* mess!". The existence of a phenomenon like irony is crucial, and to my mind devastating, for the concept of linguistic destigmatization. Only if an unfavorable referent changes, and with it the negative opinion of and attitude towards it, only then will the word by which it is named lose its negative emotive load. And then there will be no need any more to replace it.

CONCLUSION

We must conclude that there are no lexical words capable of destigmatization or incapable of stigmatization. Linguistic stigmatization is the inevitable outcome of two facts: (1) that there are persons and things around (and within) us which we fear, dislike, or disapprove of because they have done harm to us or to others, and (2) that we sometimes speak about them.

An attempt at linguistic de-stigmatization can only have a chance of success if at least one of these two factors is changed; so either we must stop being ill and stop harming each other, or we must stop speaking about it. As for the first change, this is what the Bible promises us for the future, when "the former things have passed away" – a new world where all tears will be dried, "neither shall there be mourning nor crying nor pain any more" (Rev. 21: 4). And a linguist might add: so there will be no need of the words for them any more, nor of names for ourselves when we cause these things for we shall have stopped doing so.

One of the purposes of Bible translation and all that contributes to it – Eugene Nida's works, for instance – is that people may get to know this *Gō(d) spel(l)*, this "good news", be comforted by it, and take heart to work at the change. As long as it is still this present old world of ours, however, *with* its tears and its pain and its mourning, as long as we continue hurting and harming each other, there can only be linguistic de-stigmatization in the second way mentioned: by hushing things up, by not speaking about them. But we cannot stop speaking about them if we want them to be changed. So we need the words for them, clear, unambiguous words such as the Bible uses, to point out the things in our lives that we have to get rid of, the things that, some day, are to "pass away".

REFERENCES

Artiss, K. L.
1964 "Environmental Therapy", in J. H. Masserman (ed.), *Current Psychiatric Therapies* 4 (New York), 46-54.
Back, Jan de
1973 "Taal en Afwijkend Gedrag" [Language and Deviant Behaviour] (Meppel, Holland: Boom). Doctoral dissertation.
Bernstein, B.
1970 "Social Class, Language, and Socialization", in P.P. Giglioli (ed.), *Language in Social Context* (Harmondsworth: Penguin Books), 157-179.
Bianchi, H.
1971 *Stigmatisering* (Deventer, Holland: Kluwer).
Black, Max
1963 *Language and Philosophy*; *Studies in Method*, 4th printing (Ithaca, N. Y.: Cornell University).
Carroll, John B.
1963 "Linguistic Relativity, Contrastive Linguistics, and Language Learning", *International Review of Applied Linguistics in Language Teaching* 1, 1-21.
Carroll, John B., and Joseph B. Casagrande
1958 "The Function of Language Classification in Behaviour", in Maccoby, Newcomb, and Hartley (eds.), *Readings in Social Psychology* (New York: Henry Holt).
Chapman, Dennis
1968 *Sociology and the Stereotype of the Criminal* (London, New York: Tavistock Publications).
Concise Oxford Dictionary of Current English, The
1964 5th ed. (Oxford: Clarendon).
Dietze, Doris
1955 "The Facilitating Effect of Words on Discrimination and Generalization", *Journal of Experimental Psychology* 50, 255-260.
Edgerton, R. B., and S. C. Plog (eds.)
1969 *Changing Perspectives in Mental Illness* (New York, Chicago: Holt, Rinehart, and Winston).
Eisner, Victor
1969 *The Delinquency Label: the Epidemiology of Juvenile Delinquency* (New York: Random House).
Eissler, K. R. (ed.)
1949 *Searchlights on Delinquency*; *New Psychoanalytic Studies Dedicated to Professor August Aichhorn, on the Occasion of his Seventieth Birthday, July 27, 1948* (New York: International Universities).
Erikson, K. T.
1957 "Patient Role and Social Uncertainty, a Dilemma of the Mentally Ill", *Psychiatry* 20, 263-275.
Foudraine, Jan
(1972). *Wie is van Hout... een Gang door de Psychiatrie* [Who is (made) of Wood... a walk through Psychiatry], 12th printing (Bilthoven, Holland: Ambo). First printed in 1971.
Giglioli, Pier Paolo (ed.)
1972 *Language in Social Context* (Harmondsworth: Penguin Books).
Goffman, Erving

1963   *Stigma: Notes on the Management of Spoiled Identity* (Harmondsworth: Penguin Books). Reprinted in 1970.

Kluckhohn, Clyde
1961   "Notes on Some Anthropological Aspects of Communication", *American Anthropologist* 63, 895-910.

Mitford, Nancy (ed.)
1956   *Noblesse Oblige; an Enquiry into the Identifiable Characteristics of the English Aristocracy* (London: Hamish Hamilton).

Mulder, G. E.
1971   "Laus Iudicis (Lof des rechters)" [Praise of the Judge], *Dordrecht, journal of Law Students of the Free University* 3, 10-16.

Nida, Eugene A.
1964   *Toward a Science of Translating, with Special Reference to Principles and Procedures Involved in Bible Translating* (Leiden: Brill).

Nida, Eugene A., and Charles R. Taber
1969   *The Theory and Practice of Translation* (Leiden: Brill).

Osgood, Charles E.
1960   "The Cross-Cultural Generality of Visual-Verbal Synesthetic Tendencies", *Behavioral Science* 5, 146-169.

Osgood, Charles E., and T. A. Sebeok (eds.)
1954   *Psycholinguistics; a Survey of Theory and Research Problems* (= Supplement to the *Journal of Abnormal and Social Psychology* 49: 4, Part 2) (Baltimore: Waverly Press).

Reenen, P. T. van, and B. Siertsema
1972   "De-stigmatisering", *Delikt en Delinkwent* 2 (Leiden: Brill), 399-411.

Rosen, J.
1962   *Direct Psychoanalytic Psychiatry* (New York).

Ross, Alan S. C.
1956   "U and non-U; an Essay in Sociological Linguistics", in Mitford (ed.), *Noblesse Oblige; an Enquiry into the Identifiable characteristics of the English Aristocracy* (London: Hamish Hamilton), 11-36.

Sapir, Edward
1960   "The Status of Linguistics as a Science," in David G. Mandelbaum (ed.), *Edward Sapir, Culture, Language and Personality, Selected Essays* (Berkeley, Los Angeles: University of California), 65-77. First printed in *Language* 5 (1929), 207-214.

Sarbin, T. R.
1969   "The Scientific Status of the Mental Illness Metaphor", in Edgerton and Plog (eds.), *Changing Perspectives in Mental Illness* (New York, Chicago: Holt, Rinehart, and Winston).

Schmideberg, Melitta
1949   "The Analytic Treatment of Major Criminals: Therapeutic Results and Technical Problems", in Eissler (ed.), *Searchlights on Delinquency* (New York: International Universities), 174-189.

Siertsema, Berthe
1970   "Morphemic Make-up and World View", in Roman Jakobson and Shigeo Kawamoto (eds.), *Studies in General and Oriental Linguistics presented to Shirô Hattori on the Occasion of His Sixtieth Birthday* (Tokyo: TEC Company), 525-535.

Stevenson, Charles L.
1944   *Ethics and Language* (New Haven: Yale University).
1963   *Facts and Values; Studies in Ethical Analysis* (New Haven: Yale University).

Thielemans, J.
1969 "Taal en Relativiteit; de hypothese van Sapir-Whorf, dertig jaar later" [Language and Relativity; the Sapir-Whorf Hypothesis Thirty Years Later], *Handelingen Kon. Z-Nederl. Mij v. Taal- en Letterk. en Gesch.* 23 (Brussels), 357-375.
Triandis, H. C.
1964 "Cultural Influence upon Cognitive Processes", in L. Berkowitz (ed.), *Advances in Experimental Social Psychology* (New York: Academic Press), 1-48.
Ullmann, Stephen
1962 *Semantics, An Introduction to the Science of Meaning* (Oxford: Basil Blackwell).
Whorf, Benjamin Lee
1956 *Language, Thought, and Reality; Selected Writings,* edited by J. B. Carroll (Cambridge, Mass.: M. I. T.).
Wilkins, Leslie T.
1969 *Evaluation of Penal Measures* (New York: Random House).
Zimbardo, Philip, and Ebbe B. Ebbesen
1969 *Influencing Attitudes and Changing Behavior; A Basic Introduction to Relevant Methodology, Theory, and Applications* (Reading, London, Ontario: Addison-Wesley).

RESTRUCTURING TRANSLATIONS OF THE
PSALMS AS POETRY

WILLIAM A. SMALLEY

The difficulty of translating poetry is notorious.[1] However, discussion of this complex question usually takes place on too many levels and from too many angles at once. For some critics and translators the translation of a poem must match every feature of the original: phonological sonority must match phonological sonority, meter match meter, rhyme match rhyme, image match image, idiom match idiom, and so on up to overall effect matching overall effect. But they realize that this ideal is impossible to attain, so they weigh endlessly the compromises which have to be made, and feel defeated by those points where the whole tour de force cannot be carried off (van der Veen 1952: 212-213). Furthermore, most of them are talking primarily about translation from European languages (classical or modern) into other European languages, with the common ground of literary and linguistic tradition which that area shares, digressing no farther than an occasional discussion of translation from Chinese, Japanese, or a major language of India.[2]

Linguists, on the other hand, sometimes take far too simplistic a view of the capacity of the latest linguistic insight, or fad, to provide a valid basis for a linguistic theory of the nature of literary language, including poetry, and of its translation. Many of the points made are individually useful, often perceptive, yet they must on the whole seem relatively trivial to the literary critic who has the advantage of looking at literary phenomena in a broader perspective, and the disadvantage of not having been trained in discovering and using the kinds of linguistic and socio-

William A. Smalley is a Research Consultant for the United Bible Societies, Wallingford, Connecticut.

[1] I am grateful to Daniel C. Arichea, Jr., Robert G. Bratcher, David J. Clark, Jan de Waard, Howard A. Hatton, Norman A. Mundhenk, Barclay M. Newman, Alfredo Tepox, and William L. Wonderly for excellent comments on an earlier draft of this paper.
[2] For two important bibliographies on translation see Nida 1964:265-320 and Morgan 1959.

linguistic distinctions which linguistics ultimately has to offer. However, until a model really broad enough and complex enough to have explanatory and predictive value for literary art is produced, it is only those who are predisposed to be convinced who will be convinced by linguists' piecemeal offerings. At present the most popular linguistic theories are still undeveloped for those upper levels of linguistic and cultural phenomena where discourse – let alone literary discourse – lies.[3] Nowhere do we have anything like a comprehensive model into which the enormous variety of phenomena relevant to the literary use of language can be integrated in any kind of satisfying or convincing way.

Even without such a comprehensive theory (but hopefully contributing something to its development), Eugene A. Nida, his colleagues, some scholars in the Summer Institute of Linguistics, and others, are working on variations of a theory of "dynamic equivalence translation". This work has the important advantage of being tested constantly through application to large quantities of widely varied text (the Bible or parts of it) being translated into several hundred languages, with cultures ranging in complexity from those underlying English or Chinese on the one hand to tiny groups in interior New Guinea on the other. Translation is done in some cases by highly trained linguists or Biblical scholars (both expatriate and native speakers), and in other cases by native speakers trained in the literary skills of scores of different languages. All have had exposure to dynamic equivalence theory and the principle of its application. Their work is monitored by a team of specialist translation consultants who, among other things, look for the problems which emerge in the application of the theory.

An adequate theory of translation should be suitable for guiding translation from any natural language into all other natural languages. At the same time it should help to define just what is possible and what is impossible in translation, separating out the many variables of language structure and use, and determining how they fit into translation process (Longacre 1971). It should not only be linguistic in its orientation, but requires roots in sociolinguistics (the use of language), cognitive theory, and literary criticism.

Statements on the theory of dynamic equivalence translation do not

---

[3] For a varied but incomplete sampling of linguistic work on the problems of poetic structure and of discourse in general, see some of the essays in such collections as Chatman and Levin (1967); Fowler (1966); Freeman (1970); and Garvin (1964); see also Cromack (1968); Fowler (1972); Grimes (1972); Halliday (1964; 1967-1968); Jakobson (1960); Longacre (1968; 1972); Stennes (1969); Taber (1966); and Young, Becker, and Pike (1970).

yet fill all of these requirements. They acknowledge the place of literary form, for example, including poetry,[4] and point in the direction of practical solutions to its translation, but do not otherwise say much on the subject. In its initial stages the theory has understandably been concerned with the INFORMATIVE function of language, and has focused on developing explicit principles for rendering the information content of the source message clearly intelligible in the receptor language medium, most particularly within individual sentences, where linguistics in general has been most comfortable.

The results of this emphasis can be clearly seen in the Today's English Version (TEV) of the New Testament, the translation in English which most explicitly follows the principles of dynamic equivalence translation. The great popularity of this translation has been due to its plain, straightforward sentence structure, in which a sober exegesis of the meaning of the Greek text has been rendered in unadorned English.[5] However, the poetic nature of the original in some passages has been completely lost, as may be quickly seen by a comparison of the "poetic" passages of Luke 1 with the surrounding "prose". Aside from the visual distinction created through printing the *Magnificat* and Zechariah's prophecy in indented lines beginning with capital letters and unjustified right margins, one would hardly know he had reached a "poetic" section.

But this lack of attention to the poetic aspects of language is a result of the fact that not all problems can be resolved at once in the working out of any theory, and in the translation of the New Testament the problem of the communication of equivalent information in translation is by far the most pressing one. As solutions to the more knotty problems of the translation of information are being more fully developed, attention is turning to other aspects of language, and I believe that Nida's basic theoretical framework provides the foundation for understanding the linguistic factors in translation there also.

---

[4]   See the indices of Nida (1964) and Nida and Taber (1969) for references to "poetry" and "poetic language". See also Nida and Taber (1969:145-152) on "special effects" in language. The following papers in *The Bible Translator* deal with poetry from this point of view: Culshaw (1968); Crim (1972); Bierwisch and Ellingworth (1973); Hatton (1974).

[5]   Philips (1967). The fact that the TEV follows an unusually simple level of English is not required by dynamic equivalence theory, but choosing a readership level and restructuring to the readership ability of the level chosen are requirements.

An Example

To get a feeling for the issues discussed in this paper two restructurings of Psalm 2 should be read and compared. Comparison will be facilitated by the use of the traditional verse numbers which have been included in the left margin.

Version 1 is not a new and independent translation of Psalm 2, but is my further RESTRUCTURING based on version 2. The term restructuring is from Nida's model of translation (Nida and Taber 1969:33-34, 120-162). It refers to the final stage in the process of translation, the stage of writing the translation is a style suitable for achieving the appropriate effect in the receptor language.

In preparing version 1 I followed the ANALYSIS reflected in version 2 as far as possible. Analysis refers to the first stage in Nida's model, that of determining in as precise detail as possible just what the purpose and cognitive meaning of the source message is. I assumed the analysis made apparent in the TEV to be one of the possible correct analyses insofar as the information content of the Psalm is concerned, and on that level tried to follow it in every detail.[6] However, I did do some further analysis of the mood and emotional thrust of the Psalm.

I also followed the TRANSFER displayed in the TEV as much as possible. Transfer refers to the problems of matching semantic areas, grammar, vocabulary, idioms, etc., between source and receptor cultures and languages. I did need to consider further the problem of the matching of poetic form.

Primarily, however, what I did to produce version 1 was to take version 2 and rewrite it in the light of such minimal additional analysis and transfer. I tried not to change any detail of information content, but only to recreate the mood which I felt was likely in the original. I experimented with "writing the same thing in a different way" (i.e. restructuring) to produce that mood in English.

In this paper, which is dedicated to Eugene A. Nida on his sixtieth birthday, I would like to explore the implications of restructuring like that shown in version 1 for the translation of Biblical poetry in general, and the Psalms in particular, within the framework of the dynamic equivalence theory of translation.

---

[6] There are differences of interpretation on the part of Biblical scholars as to whether, for example, the Psalmist is speaking (as here), or the King himself is speaking. Adoption of the latter interpretation, which may be the majority opinion (Arichea 1973), would cause some changes in the restructuring.

Version 1

1a The subject nations are planning rebellion...
1b   Their people are plotting...
2a   Their kings and rulers join in revolt...
3   "Freedom!" they say,
       "Freedom from rule!"
       "Off with control
2b   of the Lord
       and the king he has chosen."

1b   Plotting
     Useless plots.
1a   Why?

4 The Lord laughs on his throne.
     Mocks them in heaven.
5b Furious, he terrifies them,
5a Speaks to them, angry.
6b "I have installed the king,
6a   Placed him on Zion,
     My holy hill."

7 And the king announces
     What the Lord has declared to him:
     "You are my son.
     Today I became your father.

Version 2

1 Why do the nations plan rebellion?
   Why do these people make useless plots?
2 Their kings revolt,
     their rulers plot together
     against the Lord and his chosen king.
3 "Let us free ourselves from their rule", they say;
     "let us throw off their control."

4 From his throne in heaven the Lord laughs
     and makes fun of them.
5 He speaks to them in anger,
     and terrifies them with his fury.
6 "On Zion, my sacred hill", he says,
     "I have installed my king."

7 "I will announce what the Lord declared",
     says the king.
   "The Lord said to me: 'You are my son;
     today I have become your father.

8 Ask me for the nations,
  and I'll give you them.
  Ask for the earth,
  and the whole world will be yours
9 to rule.
  Break the nations in pieces
    like a clay pot smashes.
  Rule them with a harsh king's rule."
10 So listen closely, rebel kings.
  Watch out, you plotting rulers.
12 The Lord becomes angry quickly.
11 Tremble!
12 Bow down!
11 Serve him with fear
  or you will die!
  But people are happy
  who go to the Lord
  for protection.
                (Psalm 2, my restructuring)

8 Ask, and I will give you all the nations;
  the whole earth will be yours.
9 You will rule over them with an iron hand;
  you will break them in pieces like a clay pot.'"
10 Now listen to me, you kings;
  pay attention, you rulers!
11 Serve the Lord with fear;
  tremble 12 and bow down to him;
  or else he will be angry, and you will die,
  for his anger is quickly aroused.
  Happy are all who go to him for protection!
                    (Psalm 2, TEV)

SOME SOCIOLINGUISTIC FACTORS RELEVANT TO POETRY

The factors to be discussed in this section are ones which have been weakly emphasized in dynamic equivalence theory (and in linguistic theory). Further study will doubtless reveal more such factors.

The Expressive Function of Language

Under the heading of the expressive function of language I include a wide range of phenomena which arise out of the pleasure people get from creating special effects with language. In any one instance such phenomena may or may not be associated also with music, which, in the case of vocal music, is another way of creating special effects with language. Of the several functions of language, the expressive function is certainly one of the most important, and yet so far one of the most difficult to analyze linguistically.[7]

In the expressive function of language there is psychological effect intended or created. The same information content, handled in expressively different ways, can reveal sharply different emotional states in the user of language, and create equally different reactions on the part of the receptor: anger or joy or tears or disgust.

The expressive function of language is not restricted to poetry by any means. An orator like Martin Luther King or John Kennedy could move an audience with his expressive skill in a way that a more pedestrian Ralph Abernathy or Richard M. Nixon cannot. A John Steinbeck short story will excite a perceptive reader by its expressive perfection, but normal magazine fiction arouses interest in nothing more than the

---

[7] By the communication functions of language I refer to what the use of language accomplishes as intended by the speaker and/or as understood by the addressee. Some important functions are the informative (where the speaker assumes the information is true, whether or not it is), deceptive (where the speaker believes the information is not true and seeks to mislead the other person), expressive (under discussion), evocative (to follow in the discussion), imperative (where the speaker tries to stir the addressee to action), permissive, interrogative, performative (where the language act has power: "I pronounce you man and wife"), phatic (to provide a link with another being for the sake of community of feeling, recognition, keeping the communication going, etc.: greetings, expressions of sympathy, "I love you"), interpretive (saying the same thing in other words), mystery (to create a sense of the unknown, the religious, awe, dread, fear, etc.), and doubtless many others. Jakobson (1960) who did pioneer thinking in this area refers to what I am calling expressive function as "poetic" function. It may be that what I am calling the expressive function would better be divided into two functions (self-) expressive and emotive, but that distinction has not been made in this paper.

plot. The emotional force of J. B. Phillips' (1958) translation of many New Testament passages places it a step above most other translations in expressive power.

Expressive language draws attention to itself, to the communication event, as well as, or instead of, to the information content; it draws attention also to the mood of the communication as well as, or instead of, to the information itself. In so doing, it may enhance or obscure the information, and what may enhance it for one reader may obscure it for another. Expressive language seeks a conscious effect. It says something not in a straightforward, unadorned, or most direct way, but it highlights, accentuates, and draws attention by the unusual, the emotionally laden, the colorful,[8] and even the ungrammatical (Mukařovský 1964).

Some of the devices used to create expressive language look almost mutually contradictory until we remember that they are examples of the higher, overriding device of the force of the unusual. Both conciseness and elaboration are characteristic of expressive language, for example, as are both regularity and discontinuity, understatement and overstatement. And these can apply on all levels: to sound sequences, words, grammatical constructions, ideas, and larger units of discourse.

For example, Psalm 2, in version 2 above, starts off with a pair of questions. "Why do the nations plan rebellion? Why do these people make useless plots?" In the Hebrew original the two questions are combined by "and". If we were to take these questions as being purely informative, we would learn (a) that certain nations are planning to rebel against someone, and (b) that the writer wants to know why. Our interpretation of (b), however, is not completely accurate. When we read the Psalm as a whole we see that the questions are rhetorical, and that the information content really is (b) these people are stupid to try such an impossible thing. The use of the rhetorical question permits the communication of (a) and (b) more concisely, more indirectly, more expressively than would a straightforward informative version: "Some nations are planning to rebel, and I think it is utterly futile to do so."

On the other hand, the two questions redundantly have the same information content (with the slight addition of "useless" in the second). This is an example of the parallelism which characterizes Hebrew poetry (Gray 1915; Robinson 1947: 26-31). Characteristically the same information content is carried two or three times in succession with slight

---

[8]   One of the questions on which linguistics will have to throw some light before there is an adequate theory of literary language is the meaning of such concepts as "emotionally laden" and "colorful" as applied to linguistic forms.

additions or deletions of detail and the extensive use of synonyms. So that while the rhetorical questions themselves compress the information and carry some of it only by implication, the parallelism repeats much of what is said more than once. But both are done for expressive purposes, to highlight, to attract attention, to create mood within the characteristics of Hebrew style and/or universal language features.

The Psalm then goes on to state (a) again, with the additional information that (c) the rulers are involved in the plots, and that (d) the rebellion is against "the Lord and his chosen king". The nature of the rebellion follows: (e) they want to be free of God's control. After that the theme changes, and we can consider that we have come to a new stanza.[9]

The information structure of the first stanza, then, is

1	b		a		
2	b		a		
3		c	a		
4		c	a		
5				d	
6			a	d	e
7			a	d	e

The dominating theme (a) of the nations in rebellion is included in almost every line. We could even argue that it is in line 5 by implication. Lines[10] 6 and 7, coming at the end of the stanza, complement lines 1 and 2 by giving the nature of the rebellion left unstated earlier, and doing so in the rebels' own words. Lines 3, 4, and 5 are the heart of the stanza, stating the point in the most direct fashion. The emotional focus is in line 5 – the line which has no strict parallel – where we find that the revolt is against God. In a heavily parallel style such lack of parallelism is unusual, calls attention to itself, and serves the expressive function of highlighting the fact that the rebellion is against God. This point again is then reinforced in the following parallelisms. Thus, the parallelism of meaning is unusual in comparison with the non-expressive use of language, and draws attention to itself, and the lack of parallelism at this point in a poem made up of parallelisms is unusual for the poem and draws attention to itself.

[9] In this model I am dealing with the semantic parallelism and to some extent lexical parallelism. Grammatical parallelism, as well as phonological regularity of meter, etc., are part of the Hebrew original, but are not necessarily apparent in the translation. All of these discourse devices involve types of linguistic agreement (Pike 1974).

[10] "Lines" in this sense are parallel numbered units reproduced from version 2, not the units so called in discussions of Hebrew poetic structure.

Hebrew poetry, furthermore, is metered, and although meter does not in itself guarantee an effective expressive use of language, its skillful use may contribute greatly to expressive quality. The regularity of meter helps to make the language move smoothly and easily. The regular occurrences of stressed syllables (or long syllables in those languages which work on that system) helps to accentuate the key words. And the changes in meter, when skillfully handled, may highlight shifts, bring something to attention, or alter the mood.

Hebrew meter is based on the regular occurrence of stressed syllables, with the varying numbers of unstressed syllables between being read so as to take roughly the same amount of time, no matter how many there are (Fitzgerald 1968), a phenomenon which can be referred to as stress-timed meter rather than syllable-timed meter.[11]

In addition to parallelism and meter, a third major characteristic of Hebrew poetry (and of most poetry everywhere) which contributes to the expressive function is imagery. In this category we include figures of speech, colorful turns of expression which evoke vivid ideas, vivid pictures, emotionally laden words which carry not only their primary components of meaning but also supplementary associations.

At the beginning of the second stanza of Psalm 2 we have a radical shift in imagery: God laughs, derides, is angry, terrifies the plotters. This picks up theme (b), the futility of the plotting, and, with the imagery of God laughing, accentuates it.

Trying to get a complete inventory of the information content implied here would be more difficult because the heavier the imagery, the more possible implications which different readers can see in it, as will be discussed below under the evocative function of language. Certainly, however, the ridiculousness of the rebels' pretentions is emphasized, and this in a highly expressive as well as evocative way, not an informative one.

Both the above versions have already toned down some of the imagery of the Hebrew because of the deliberately plain style of the TEV already mentioned. "Let us free ourselves from their rule" in version 2 is a translation of "Let us break their fetters" (cf. NEB). The effect of the reduced imagery is something more directly informative, less fully expressive.

---

[11] English is structurally a stress-timed language rather than a syllable-timed language (Pike 1947:13). However, classical forms of English poetry tend to require a restriction of the stress timing in the direction of equal numbers of unstressed syllables between stressed ones in any one poem. Modern poetry, and especially free verse, is often more freely stress-timed.

I would make no attempt to mention all of the devices which contribute to the expressive function of language even if I knew them all, but one more is crucial – the use of appropriate transformations (Fowler 1972; Ohmann 1964; 1966). Of the various grammatically different ways of saying the same thing, some are in context more expressive than others, more suited to mood or theme. To illustrate this point we take the beginnings of the second stanza of Psalm 2 in versions 2 and 1:

Version 2: From his throne in heaven the Lord laughs
            and makes fun of them.
        He speaks to them in anger,
            and terrifies them with his fury.

Version 1: The Lord laughs on his throne.
        Mocks them in heaven.
        Furious, he terrifies them,
        Speaks to them, angry.

The information content of the two renderings is the same. There is some difference in imagery, as *mocks* is more vivid than *makes fun of*.[12] There is a more pronounced meter in version 1, coming heavily on the key words, and accentuating them. However, the biggest differences are in the grammatical transformations. In version 1 I used short, clipped sentences which would lend themselves to a staccato effect, contributing to a reflection of the explosion of laughter and the surge of anger. The word *furious*, brought to an initial stressed position by a normal grammatical transformation, is balanced by an equally prominent *angry* at the end, prominent in this case partly because it borders on the ungrammatical, if we limit grammaticality only to the transformations typical within the informative function.[13]

Along with the reordering of components due to the use of different transformations goes the difference of order between sentences or clauses, as seen in version 1. The effect of this kind of linguistic phenomenon needs serious study.

In version 2 the first three lines are almost purely informative, and the fourth line picks up some expressive function through the use of emotional supplementary components (Nida 1973), but does not reinforce the effect through any other device. The total effect is primarily informative.

---

[12] At least to the more educated reader of English. It may be too high a level of English vocabulary for the audience at which the TEV is aimed.

[13] This produces a syntactic chiasmus in the two lines. Keyser (1973) points out the turbulent, wrenching effect of chiasmus in the poem "Poetry is a Destructive Force", by Wallace Stevens (Matthiessen 1950:661).

In illustrating a few of the linguistic bases of the expressive use of language, however, I should most emphatically not leave the impression that their use will necessarily produce effective expressive quality. Doggerel and purple prose are both samples of expressive language. Just as some people can convey information clearly in the informative function of language, while others are not so skilled, so some people can use language expressively with high skill, and others cannot. People also differ both in capacity to respond to the expressive use of language, and in the kind of expressive language to which they do respond. The student who is left cold by his high school class in poetry may respond with great enjoyment to a well-told story, a good joke, or a protest ballad.

Creativity

What was referred to as high skill above, and discussed in other terms in preceding paragraphs, I would now like to define a little more closely under the term CREATIVITY. For present purposes I will use the word creativity to mean the functionally effective stretching or breaking of rules, or what Mukařovský (1964: 43) calls "deautomatization", consciously taking the nonautomatic course so far as language is concerned. Ogden Nash's (1945: 212)

> Or better yet, if called by a panther,
> Don't anther.

is a functionally effective breaking of a rule for phonological realization.

> We speak Volkswagen here.

as a sign outside a service station is a functionally effective breaking of a semantic collocation rule.[14]

The lunch counter sit-ins were functionally effective in breaking the cultural segregation rule. Chomsky's *Syntactic Structures* was functionally effective in breaking the rule for practicing structural linguistics whereby you had to look at language taxonomically, not dynamically.

By functionally effective I mean any function of communication, but the expressive function of language will usually be involved to some degree because the breaking of a rule draws attention to itself and is sometimes highly emotionally charged. And I mean that it fulfills one

---

[14] Cf. Larson and Smalley (1972:262). However, there we used the term "creative" in a broader sense than that given in the present paper.

of the functions of communication better than could be done without breaking the rule.

Some rule breaking leads to nonsense, but Wheatley (1970: 25) has rightly pointed out that when a rule is broken we follow a higher rule, which is to "look for the explanation, and act sensibly in light of it". When Chomsky suggested

Colorless green ideas sleep furiously

as being "nonsensical" and

Furiously sleep ideas green colorless

as "ungrammatical" (Chomsky 1957: 15), some people began looking around for poetic contexts in which to use them and to give them sense (Voegelin 1960: 59). Mary Jonathan's poem, "You, Noam Chomsky" (Young, Becker, and Pike 1970: 306-307) is an example, and succeeds in making the sentences functionally effective through breaking the rules of semantic collocation and grammatical transformation.

For the translator, the creative use of language to achieve expressive function is significant not so much because of the fact that it draws attention to the medium, to the language itself, as because it creates such important nonlinguistic meanings as a sense of worship, of praise, of protest, of humor, or of any emotion. To translate in such a way that the original writer's mood of worship, praise, or anger is not carried through is to mistranslate, no matter how clearly the information in the original poem is conveyed in the translation.[15]

The Evocative Function of Language

Another extremely important function of language, frequently found in poetry, but by no means restricted to poetry, is the EVOCATIVE. It derives from the capacity of language to be ambiguous or vague, but represents a constructive, sometimes creative use of that capacity, stimulating the receptor to respond with ideas, associations, and feelings out of his own experience and background.[16]

[15] This is true even though we often cannot be sure of such subtle features in ancient documents. The translator's only recourse is to make the best possible evaluation of what they probably were, and restructure accordingly. He may, of course, sometimes be wrong, but probably not more wrong than as though he paid no attention at all to the expressive qualities.

[16] Ullmann (1962:133-135) uses the term "evocative" in a narrower way than I do here, but his usage would be completely included in mine.

For the terms AMBIGUOUS and VAGUE I follow Lachenmeyer (1972: 97-106):

... An expression or statement is ambiguous if it has multiple, specified interpretations: if any user of it can specify a limited range of interpretations for it which agrees with the limited range of interpretations of it extant in the language community in which it occurs....

... An expression or statement is vague if it has multiple, specifiable interpretations: if any user of it can specify some, but not all, of the possible interpretations of it that are extant in the language community in which it is used (1972: 97).

Lachenmeyer goes on to point out that ambiguity and vagueness are to be avoided in scientific language systems; there is, however, much greater tolerance in conventional language systems, and they are essential ingredients in literary language systems:

... the receiver of a vague message must arrive at his own interpretation of part of the semantic content of that message. This occurs because the possible interpretations are unspecified. In searching for these interpretations the receiver is likely to become introspective, and in being introspective he is likely to self-generate the "feeling" that is elicited ultimately by the vague expression or statement... the use of vague expressions or statements elicits a state in the receiver in which he must arrive at some of the interpretations of that expression or statement, and in so doing, he is likely to probe his personal background, thoughts, and emotions. In this probing lies the intended objective of the literary artist. Of course, the process is not random; it is guided by the total context of the particular literary work... (1972: 105).

It is this stimulation to introspective search for meaning on the part of the receiver, through the effective manipulation of vagueness and ambiguity, the creation of multiple associations, that I am calling the evocative function of language.

The evocative function is carried to its greatest development in English in short lyric poems densely packed with imagery – various images reflecting different, sometimes clashing literal referents, but, juxtaposed in the structure of the poem, they evoke a vague sense that there is always something more there, some deeper layer of meaning to be uncovered. And critics vie with each other in their efforts to unravel the strands.

In some cases the author may have had a limited cluster of meanings which he sought to evoke. In others he may have been taken up in his own artistry with words, playing on his own subjective introspections, and may have had no more clear impression of any one single meaning than do the readers.

This kind of densely packed evocative quality in poetry, highly admired as it is by its devotees, is completely lost on many other people, and is one reason why many students are completely turned off in poetry classes. However, everyone employs the evocative function of language on other levels. Epithets like "racist", "Nigger", "capitalist", "Commie", and limitless others are evocative. Their meanings are vague as they are used, and they produce a response in the receptor based on his own background, introspection, and interpretation. The same applies, of course, to some uses of otherwise technical terms, as when some transformationalists use the term "taxonomic" in an evocative way, and the structuralists earlier referred to "traditional" grammarians. The language of the propagandists and the hucksters is highly evocative. On the other hand, myth, fiction, drama, and many other literary forms are frequently built up with evocative effect, stretching the reader's imagination to draw his own inferences.

There are many examples of passages in the Bible with important evocative function. The parables of Jesus were simple stories, but they always had some point to make, usually concerning the way it should be when God ruled peoples' lives. Jesus' disciples frequently asked for explanations of what he meant by his parables. Sometimes he obliged them with explanations, and sometimes not.

Jesus' speech was frequently evocative, in fact. The Beatitudes (Matthew 5: 3-11) have been endlessly interpreted and reinterpreted. Jesus' talk with Nicodemus (John 3: 1-11) left that presumably well-educated man puzzled as Jesus used imagery which has been interpreted and reinterpreted since.

The "apocalyptic" literature of the Old and New Testaments was probably highly evocative to the original readers. Written in times of political stress or danger, it alluded to these events in oblique fashion with faith in God's intervention and better times to come. And people of many generations since have found meaning for their own time and situation from the multiple interpretations which such use of language makes possible.

Evocative function is often produced through figures of speech. I think it would be possible to develop a graded system in which, other things being equal, metaphor is more evocative than simile, and various forms of metonymy could be ranked into vaguer and vaguer associations. In considering the translation of Old Testament poetry on this point I operate at a complete disadvantage because I do not know which of the figures of Old Testament poetry were powerful new figures as they were used, and which had undergone the process of automatization and become accepted clichés.[17] Certainly many Biblical expressions, evocative in their original setting, have been automatized by the faithful at various times, until someone once more opened his mind to the other possible meanings, and a new freshness in the understanding of the passage became possible.

The evocative use of imagery is not the same as the expressive use of imagery. The latter enlivens, makes more clear, more vivid. The former teases by opening up multiple possibilities. And the use of grammatical transformations, so central to the expressive use of language, can at other times contribute to evocative function. The passive, with its lack of an explicit agent is sometimes used that way, as are deletion transformations. The rhetorical questions in Psalm 2 have an evocative function as well as the expressive function already discussed.

In the Psalms which I chose for my illustrations of restructuring, the evocative function is only moderate. Imagery is used, but within the context of any one of these Psalms the implication of the imagery is usually fairly clear. But even then, the fact that imagery is used helps to create an evocative tone in contrast to what would be true of a purely informative function; there is quite a history to the interpretations given Psalm 2, for example. It was probably used as a song on the occasion of the coronation of a new king. But its mildly evocative nature helped to make it possible for it later to have Messianic meanings when the Jews no longer ruled themselves, and it was eventually reinterpreted by many Christians to refer to Christ as the king chosen by God.

The Communication Functions of Poetry

I have discussed the relationship of the expressive and evocative functions to poetry, but before I get back to the question of translating poetry we must think also about its other functions. Here the experience of Westerners can be quite limited in comparison with people of certain other cultures. We do not consider poetry a suitable medium for our history, our laws, moralizing, socialization of the young, major governmental and religious pronouncements, etc. Many other peoples down through the history of the world have and do. We have other examples in our literary history, but for modern Westerners poetry comes mainly in songs, and secondarily in other forms where the expressive content is

---

[17] Mukařovský (1970:43). Possibly study of such factors as frequency of occurrence in relation to date of authorship would throw some light on this question for ancient documents (cf. de Waard 1974).

high, including humor. In many such cases there is important informative function as well, usually an attempt to communicate a creative idea. There may be some imperative function from time to time, as in the attempts of protest movement writers in the recent past to stir people to action. Frequently there is some minor phatic function in expressing and reinforcing the bonds of relationship between members of an in-group – members of the counter culture or of a religious group. For the initiated poetry addict, forms with high evocative function may be supreme. But most of this is quite marginal to the mainstream of Western culture.

Poetry in the Hebrew Old Testament occupies a far more central place in the total body of literature than does poetry in modern English; and functions other than expressive and evocative are far more important in Hebrew, including functions which we would not realize in verse at all. Performative function can be seen in the blessings and curses (Gen. 3: 14-19; 9: 25-27; 14: 19-20; 27: 27-29). There is a recurring predictive function (Gen. 49: 2-27, and passages in some of the prophets). A clear case of phatic function can be seen in I Chron. 12: 18:

> We are yours, O David:
>   and with you, O son of Jesse!
> Peace, peace to you,
>   and peace to your helpers!
> For your God helps you. (RSV)

There are frequent poetic passages of praise, worship, and rebuke which might be considered related to phatic function throughout the Old Testament. The imperative function is prevalent (such Psalms as 6 and 7, Proverbs, Isa. 1: 2-31). The list could be extended considerably. Expressive and evocative functions are usually also present in much of the poetry of the Old Testament, and, frequently, informative function. Expressive and evocative function predominate in such major parts as the Psalms and the Song of Solomon, and many passages of worship and praise. Sometimes the function that seems to predominate varies from stanza to stanza and even from line to line.

However, the fact that other functions, ones which are not normally expressed in poetry in English, are of major importance in major sections of the Old Testament suggests the decision that for English these passages should not be translated as poetry at all, but as prose more suitable to their function in English usage. In doing so, a toning down of the expressive function is also required so that the prose will not seem overblown. This has been the decision of the TEV commitee for parts of the Old Testament, especially many of the prophetic oracles (Crim 1972: 105-106).

The Psalms, however, are a case where the expressive function predominates, and (together with the Song of Solomon) most of the material seems most pertinent for translation into English poetry.

IMPLICATIONS FOR THE TRANSLATION OF POETRY

Dynamic Equivalence Theory of Translation

There are some assumptions in the dynamic equivalence theory of translation which apply importantly to the translation of poetry.

1. *Translation is not a surface linguistic phenomenon.* Nida deals with deep structure in terms of SEMANTIC COMPONENTS and KERNELS. The use of his kernels begs the question of just what the nature of the deep structure[18] is, but has the real practical advantage of making it possible to talk to nonlinguists about many kinds of deep structure relationships without a complicated abstract apparatus.[19]

Nida's identification of OBJECT, EVENT, ABSTRACT, and RELATIONAL as the archilexemes of four different hierarchies of referential meaning on the highest level of abstraction (Nida 1952; 1964: 59-69; Nida and Taber 1969: 41-55; Nida 1973) helps to avoid the temptation to confuse grammatical structure verbs with semantic structure events, etc.[20] This becomes particularly useful in translation when used to sort out semantically complex phenomena realized in similar surface structures. Here is one of Nida's examples:

In *our beloved ruler,* the object *(our)* performs the event *(beloved, ie., love),* of which the goal is the object element in *ruler.* But this same object performs the event of ruling the first object, *our.* This may be paraphrased as "we love the one who rules over us".

[18] My use of the term "deep structure" and of other terminology from generative grammar is sometimes somewhat metaphorical and is motivated partly by the practical consideration that this metalanguage is better known than that of other theories. A more sophisticated theory of deep structure than that usually proposed by generative grammarians is required to account for translation, however (Fowler 1972; Makkai 1971; see also the interesting non linguistic treatment in Lefevre 1970). Under this term I will simply lump together a variety of different phenomena of function, meaning, and structure for the purpose of this paper.

[19] For Nida's use of kernels and transforms in analysis see Nida and Taber (1969:32-55).

[20] This is one of the problems of Chafe (1970).

In *his old servant*, the first object *(his)* may be said to "command" or "direct" the object element in *servant*, but this same object also is the subject of the event of *serving* the first object *(his)*. At the same time the abstract *(old)* may be described as attributive to the object contained in *servant*. It is also possible for *old* to designate the length of time during which the serving was done or to specify that it was the one who served at a previous time, in which case *old* is attributive to the event element in *servant*.

In *three good bakers*, however, *three* qualifies the three objects, but *good* qualifies not the men but their capabilities in baking.

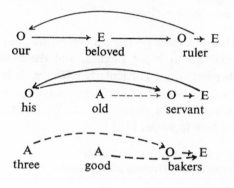

(Nida and Taber 1969: 41-42)

In the above diagram, 0 = object, E = event, A = abstract.

As the above example shows, one of the important implications of the assumption that translation is not a surface phenomenon is that it provides the basis for the redistribution of semantic components through the selection of different transformations:

> Your wedding gift is beautiful.
> What you gave me for our wedding is beautiful.
> What a beautiful gift for our wedding!

or through the reordering of sentences to fit better the textual order of the receptor language. For example,

> I meditate on all that Thou hast done. (Ps. 143: 5, RSV)

presents problems in languages where temporal sequence is not easily expressed in reverse order. The translation can then follow the temporal order:

> There are so many things you have done, and I think about them constantly.

Because translation is not a surface phenomenon, it follows that linguistic devices such as puns and plays on words which depend heavily on surface similarities are not usually translatable. Once in a while there will be an appropriate corresponding possibility in the receptor language, but usually not. Pierce (1954: 66, following Moffatt 1922) tries his hand at some plays on words in the translation of Mic. 1: 10 ff:

> Tell it not in Telltown (Gath)
> In Weeptown (Bochim), weep.
> Grovel in dust in Dusttown (Beth le-Ophrah).

The effort reveals the otherwise unsuspected play on words, but there is nothing remotely "natural" about it for English, and the breaking or stretching of the English rules is not particularly effective. It is usually impossible to get a natural equivalent of surface structure phenomena.

The situation becomes worse when Pierce (and Moffatt) add an imitation of the Hebrew alliteration in verses 11, 13:

> Fare forth naked, O fair ones of Fairtown (Shaphir)...
> Harness the horses, O habitants of Horsetown (Lachish).

There are times, of course, when surface forms in two languages do carry the same function, and so the source and the translation are somewhat similar in this respect. When the surface forms are successfully similar, however, it is because the deep structure can be realized effectively in such forms in both languages. This may be coincidence, or it may represent some fairly common pattern from language to language.

Moffatt (1922) translates some jingles in the book of Judges by restructuring as English jingles:

> If you hadn't used my heifer for your plough
> You wouldn't have guessed my riddle now. (Judg. 14: 18)

> Our God has now put
> the foe in our hands,
> who wasted our lands
> and slew us in bands! (Judg. 16: 24)

Moffatt did this because these are two of the rare instances of elaborate rhyme in the Hebrew verse of the Old Testament (Pierce 1954: 66). By the principles of dynamic equivalence translation the motive may have been wrong (matching rhyme with rhyme), but the effect was not too bad because the original function works out well with a jingle-like effect in English.

2. *In the translation of literary materials* (texts which are judged to be pieces of literary prose, or poems) *the objective is to achieve a translation with literary quality*. Note that the canons of the "literary", what is valued as art, may be quite different in the two cases. To the degree the original was artistically effective, so the translation should be also, but to the reader of the translation, not the original reader. This is implied in the term dynamic equivalence. However, some translations are to varying degrees formal correspondence translations (literal translations) either because the translator did not penetrate deeply enough behind the surface structure and mechanically reproduced the form, or he did not do sufficient restructuring into the surface patterns of the receptor language in spite of the fact that he understood the deep structure relationships. Special types of translation (like interlinear translation) for special purposes by linguists and anthropologists have their legitimate purposes (Phillips 1959; Lefevre 1972: 113) but are not dynamic equivalence translations. They lack at least the restructuring stage.

In a dynamic equivalence translation the level of restructuring depends on the intended audience of the translation. The TEV translation of the New Testament was referred to above as a plain, straightforward translation in simple English. It was originally intended as a translation for the many speakers of English for whom English is a second language, and whose knowledge of English, while functional, is not advanced. Phillips' (1958) translation was intended for university students in Britain. To the degree that the translators were successful, these two translations should have different styles on this basis alone.

The application of this principle to materials with strong expressive and evocative use of language is enormously complicated by the fact that in the original writing the specific details of content were often selected or modified by the requirements of the expressive or evocative function (Stankiewicz 1960: 73; Richards 1960: 14-23). The poet was working on the communication of ideas and feelings together, and neither of these may have been clearly formulated ahead of time. As he worked he adjusted one and then the other until he felt a coherent unity between them.

This the translator cannot do by the requirements of dynamic equivalence translation. He must recreate the original author's content as it is in his final product, building it into a new form which also recreates the original expressive and evocative functions. He can restructure, redistribute the semantic components in many ways, select new forms which will carry the informative, expressive, and evocative content, but his first responsibility is to be faithful to these. As a translator he cannot do what the original author did and modify these deep-structure meanings to make them fit together in the translation.

3. *Faithfulness in a translation is measured by its effect on the intended receptor, measured against the content and character of the original document.* From this perspective no literary document is fully translatable in an absolute sense, any more than a paraphrase using different transformations in the same language is an exact replica of that which it paraphrases. It is also true that it is easier to translate from English into French than from English into Fulani, with its very different history, world view, and assumptions.

For the informative function of language there has been a relatively high degree of success in translating the Bible, especially the New Testament, in many varied languages. Readers in an enormous range of different languages have read with understanding and appreciation. There is, of course, always some information loss and intrusion in translation, but the principles of dynamic equivalence keep this minimal by the transfer of meaning rather than surface structure, and specifically by making explicit in the translation many components of meaning which are implicit in the original.

The fact that tax collectors were despised by Jesus' contemporaries is an important bit of background which was known to the original readers who read of Jesus eating and drinking with "tax collectors and outcasts" (Luke 15: 1-2, TEV). Such people were hated for collaborating with the Roman authorities, and for their brutality and unfairness in collecting the money, of which they kept a good share. All this is not usually known to the reader in most other cultures, so the point of some stories about Jesus is partially lost without such background. Part of this implicit information can be made explicit if it does not change the character, the thrust, the focus of the text. To put in two or three lines of explanation would usually be a distortion. The author was referring to tax collectors, not describing them. However, to bring in some of the implicit components by translating "tax collectors, and other such people who were despised and bitterly resented" would supply much of what is needed to get the implications of the story without altering the character of the document.

A dynamic equivalence translation, then, is a literary translation which is the "closest natural equivalent to the source language message, first in terms of meaning, and second in terms of style" (Nida and Taber 1969: 12-32). It is achieved by analyzing the author's purpose and informative function and preserving it by rendering it in the different surface structure of a different language. The "first in meaning" part of this definition has rightfully predominated, but more needs to be said about the styles appropriate to the expressive and evocative function of poetry.

Dynamic Equivalence Translation of Poetry

In applying the principles of dynamic equivalence translation to poetry I think it is essential to expand "meaning" to be the author's overall purpose in the broadest sense. I think that is true for prose as well, but it is especially important here. If we do so, the assumptions of dynamic equivalence translation apply well.

Why did the original writer write in poetry? What was the original effect? We have already discussed some reasons, such as the achievement of strong emotion or mood, but not all poetry is like that. Sometimes the reason was simply that the conventional form for the subject matter or occasion was verse form. Or, among the Psalms, for example, there are several in which each line begins with a different letter of the alphabet, in order. Psalms 25 and 34 have an additional final line beginning with *pe* so that the first line begins with *aleph*, the middle line with *lamed*, and the last line with *pe*, giving the consonants of *aleph* written out in Hebrew (Fitzgerald 1968: 243). Psalm 119 has a separate section of eight lines, all beginning with the same letter, for each letter of the Hebrew alphabet, giving 176 lines of not very subtle variation on the theme of the value of the Torah, each line standing as a virtually independent aphoristic-like statement.

Devices of this kind certainly belong within the category of the expressive playing with language but often do little more than demonstrate the cleverness of the author.[21] In much of this type of verse there is no free movement of thought or imagination (Kraft 1938: 9). Such formal gimmicks may not combine harmoniously with other devices such as the selection of transformations or the imagery to produce any particular valued effect. When that is true, they illustrate a kind of discourse where the surface form is dominant in the author's purpose, and where both emotion and content are completely overshadowed by it.

In such a case I believe that the poetry is not translatable in any meaningful sense of the term, at least not into present-day English. There is no close natural equivalent. To begin the first eight lines of an English

[21]   Clearly one of the functions of language! However, I do not mean to imply that such cleverness is necessarily or entirely divorced from feeling.

translation with A, the second eight lines with B,[22] etc., would not be a close equivalent of the Hebrew, as acrostic structure was a common discourse type of Hebrew poetry, but not of English. Fortunately, within the acrostic form, Psalm 119 is unique in the lengths to which it goes. The best solution for it is probably to translate the informative function of the Psalm into a long, loose collection of aphorisms with considerable coalescing of excessive redundancy. I do not believe it is possible to make a really dynamic equivalence translation of Psalm 119, any more than it would be possible to make one of the "Mouse's Tale" from *Alice in Wonderland* without showing it on the page printed in the shape of a tail. The surface aspects of the form are too much a part of the author's purpose.

The better the poem, of course, the more subtle and powerful is its text structure (Hendricks 1969), the tightly knit interplay of many elements on many levels of deep and surface structure. This cannot be preserved as such in translation, but the elements of deep structure which the translator keeps must be formed into a new intricate text structure in the receptor language. In a sense, the acrostic form is one kind of manifestation of such text structure, a special case, and in poetry of a higher quality the formal restrictions may be even more elaborate. Translatability depends on the degree to which meanings can be identified and restructured into a new, equivalent text structure.

A careful reading of Psalm 5 will show two intermingled themes, a structure sometimes true of other Psalms also: (a) commitment of the writer to worship, prayer, submission to God, and (b) preoccupation with the writer's enemies who are also enemies of God.

---

[22]   Knox (1955) in his prose translation of Psalm 119, begins all the sentences of the first paragraph with A, those of the second with B, etc.

Version 3

1 Listen to my words, O LORD,
    consider my inmost thoughts;
2 heed my cry for help, my king and my God.
3 In the morning, when I say my prayers,
    thou wilt hear me.
  I set out my morning sacrifice
    and watch for thee, O LORD.
4 For thou art not a God who welcomes wickedness;
    evil can be no guest of thine.
5 There is no place for arrogance before thee;
    thou hatest evildoers,
6 thou makest an end of all liars.
  The LORD detests traitors and men of blood.
7 But I, through thy great love, may come into thy house,
  and bow low toward thy holy temple in awe of thee.
8 Lead me, Lord, in thy righteousness,
    because my enemies are on the watch;
  give me a straight path to follow.
9 There is no trusting what they say,
    they are nothing but wind.

Version 4

1-2 Listen, Lord, I call!
    Hear me, God, I cry!
    Help me, King, I pray!

3   *Lord, I pray in the morning;*
    At sunrise I wait; will you answer?

4   Pleased with wickedness?
    Not you, God—
    No evil around you!

5-6 No proud where you are,
    Destroyer of liars,
    Hater of wicked,
    Despising the violent, the deceitful.

7   *Because you love, I come, Lord.*
    I worship, bow down in your temple,
    do reverence in your holy house.

8   *Lead me right, Lord.*
    Make your way plain to follow.

9   Lord, my enemies are many:
    Murdering liars,

Their throats are an open sepulchre;
    smooth talk runs off their tongues.
10 Bring ruin on them, O God;
    let them fall by their own devices.
    Cast them out, after all their rebellions,
    for they have defied thee.
11 But let all who take refuge in thee rejoice,
    let them for ever break into shouts of joy;
    shelter those who love thy name,
    that they may exult in thee.
12 For thou, O LORD, wilt bless the righteous;
    thou wilt hedge him round with favour as with a
        shield.
            (Psalm 5, NEB)

Angry destroyers,
Smoothly, deceptively hateful...

Because they sin,
    Condemn them, Lord!
Because they plot,
    Thwart them!
10   Punish them!
    Banish them!
Because they rebel against you.

11 *We will be glad, Lord,*
    who find safety in you.
    We will sing – with joy,
    the protected who love you.
    Happy because of you!

12 *You bless us, –*
    your obedient ones, –
    And shield us with kindness!
        (Psalm 5, my restructuring)

The informative function is relatively small. The significance of the poem is its expressive function. The NEB translation (version 3), however, is flat. "The Lord detests traitors and men of blood" is said with the same even tone as "For thou, O Lord, wilt bless the righteous". If we assume expressive function to be the author's purpose, a major part of the meaning of the poem, what do we do?

A dynamic equivalent translation must evoke the two moods, and although the information content should be fully preserved in the translation, it should be integrated with the expressive function, which is primary. As with all translation, this can only be done in English by changing the poetic form, and translating the meaning in terms of another surface structure than that of the original. This has already been done to a limited degree in the NEB, but translations of the Psalms into English often seem terribly ponderous and verbose, directly damping any expressive quality in English. Dynamic equivalence translations of Hebrew poetry into English should usually be considerably more condensed than the original, just as translation of prose with informative function is usually expanded (Nida and Taber 1969: 163-168). In my own attempt at restructuring Psalm 5 I have also marked the shifts in mood typographically (version 4).

By the third assumption of dynamic equivalence translation described above, the evaluation of these two restructurings is made by comparing their effect on the intended reader as measured against the content and character of the original. This is an evaluation best made by others than those who were involved in the restructuring, but it should have a little discussion. For the reader in the case of versions 3 and 4 we can assume an educated native speaker of English. Version 3 was translated by Britishers who use many Britishisms elsewhere in their translation. I am an American and assume American readers. Beyond that it is hard to go. For the reader, then, however he is defined, are the expressive and evocative functions of the translation substantially the same as those of the original? And is this done with the same information content, the same highlighting, implication, etc., factors referred to earlier as the "character of the original document"?

The question of the expressive and evocative function is, at least at the present state of our knowledge, a subjective question. I leave it to you to judge. An examination of the content of versions 3 and 4 seems to turn up discrepancies, however. Some of these are only apparent. The deep structures are the same. Thus, there is no "call" specifically in the surface structure of version 3, but there is "cry for help". For the sake of balance and parallelism in version 4 "cry for help" has been split into "call" and "cry". I contend this does not alter the meaning relationships of the original.

Other cases are not so clear. Version 3 says "I set out my morning sacrifice", which does not seem to be matched in version 4, which has "I pray in the morning". But that could be the equivalent of "In the morning, when I say my prayers" in version 3. The TEV, from which I actually did my restructuring, has "at sunrise I offer up my prayer", If version 3 is better than version 4 in representation of the Hebrew. then the restructuring in version 4 should be modified also:

With sacrifice I wait; will you answer?

or, a more extensive restructuring may be required to achieve flow and harmony.

Then there is "their throats are an open sepulchre" in version 3 which is hard to find in version 4 because the imagery is reduced. This comes in a context with other imagery which seems ponderous for modern English: "they are nothing but wind", "smooth talk runs off their tongues". In version 4 all of this has been rendered in clipped descriptive phrases with little imagery, but reflecting the irritation and impatience of the mood. Any evocative function is thereby lessened, though the vocabulary is somewhat generic. The meaning of "their throats are an open sepulchre" can be seen by the semantic parallel in the next line of version 3: "smooth talk runs off their tongue", which is further clarified by the preceding context: "There is no trusting what they say". Some of the evocative imagery of "sepulchre" is preserved in "murdering". So the information content is all there in version 4, but in a different surface form.

On the other hand,"Angry destroyers" of version 4 has no real counterpart in version 3 which takes a different interpretation from RSV ("their heart is destruction"), JB ("deep within them lies ruin"), or TEV ("they only want to destroy"). As before, my restructuring follows the information content of the TEV.

What does this reduction in imagery do to the evocative quality? In this case I am not sure, because I am not sure how evocative the original imagery was. Certainly, if the original imagery of "their throats are an open sepulchre" was strongly evocative, the restructuring with "murdering liars" may represent a loss. And in all instances where we can be sure of the evocative function, to translate with only the most likely meaning out of the many possibilities may be distortion of a serious kind. It limits the horizons of meaning, whereas the evocative function serves precisely the function of enlarging them in an open-ended way.

Under the principles of dynamic equivalence, translators are told that in cases of ambiguity they should translate with the meaning that the original writer probably intended, that ambiguity is in the mind of the receptor and in the surface structure, not in the intention of the writer. And for information function this is usually correct, but it is not correct for evocative function, where the ambiguity and vagueness is part of the purpose and leads the perceptive reader beyond itself.[23]

Occasionally the fairly direct transfer of evocative imagery into other languages is successful. Imagery from other languages is sometimes assimilated easily and quickly because the imagery is related to common experience or common humanity. Jesus' talk with Nicodemus about being "born again" has been evocative to Christians in many cultures all over the world as they have thought about the restructured character which Jesus said was a part of obedience to God.

But other times such transfer produces no evocative effect whatsoever in the receptor language. "The horn of my salvation", with its pastoral and originally phallic overtones, has no evocative power in English. The best that dynamic equivalence translators have done in such cases is to rescue the most obvious information value: "my mighty savior", and wash out the rest.

Translation sometimes involves moving down the scale of imagery from the less vague associations to more precise ones. Metaphors frequently have to be translated as similes, or without any figure at all. The loss is not particularly great when the function of the figure of speech was fairly well frozen, but when it was fresh and effective in the original the loss may be significant, sometimes critical. Ideally we would seek to find a corresponding figure in the receptor language, a figure with the same expressive and/or evocative quality, but with the time and culture difference from the Biblical culture this can sometimes be well beyond the ingenuity of any translator. On the other hand, some of the Biblical imagery is more evocative in some cultures which share more of its superficial cultural features than does modern Western culture.

But whether versions 1 and 4 are successful or not, I think that there

---

[23] Here I am of course not referring to extrinsic factors which could also cause ambiguity or vagueness – the loss of the original context, changes in culture and custom through time, etc. Such factors are part of the present reader's problem, but were not problems to the original writer or user of the piece. Sloppy writing which produces ambiguity of no valuable function is also excluded.

can be translation of expressive function as well as informative function, and that a significant level of evocative function can be reproduced within dynamic equivalence translation. The rules are not different from those of the translation of informative function, but they need to be applied radically.[24] To the degree that there is a poem in the original there should be a poem of nearly equivalent value in the receptor language if the other functions involved are also suitable to verse form in the receptor language.[25] If the informative or imperative functions are more important than the expressive function, or if the type of content is not suitable to verse form in the receptor language, then the balance of conflicting characteristics would probably best lead to a decision in favor of prose, and a muting of the expressive function. If the verse is primarily a device of surface structure significance, this cannot be translated any more than a pun or a play on words can be translated unless there is some analogous surface structure device in the receptor language, which is rare.

Finally, a word to those who believe that some tightly-knit works of art have an absolute unity and perfection such that to change one detail is to destroy them, or at least weaken them seriously, or change them into something else.[26] Translation is not an interlingual xerox process which produces the same work of art in another language. Every piece of literary art, whether a poem or a piece of literary prose, is in some respects unique. It is a unique combination of deep and surface structure elements, and has a gestalt all its own. This artifact, as a total piece of art, cannot be translated as such. Its deep structure elements, its semantics, its communication functions, its purpose, can usually be effectively translated within the terms of dynamic equivalence translation unless the evocative function is too strong. And if the restructuring is done by an artist equivalent to the original artist, presumably he can produce an equivalent piece of literary art with a different surface structure, but the same content and function.

---

[24] There are, of course, limits to restructuring, beyond which the resulting text is no longer an "equivalent" of the original, but something new. There is not room to pursue this question here.

[25] I am not saying that my restructurings are of equivalent value. I say that somebody should be able to produce them.

[26] See discussion and references in Fowler (1972:19-22). Compare also Hirsch (1972), which ends, "If it is great poetry it communicates in unique forms, forms that cannot be reduced to anything more basic than themselves." I agree with the first part of this statement but not the latter, although Hirsch's arguments against attempts to do this are well taken.

And this is an extremely important service in our multilingual world. We can have access to the verbal productivity of other peoples without knowing their languages if someone will do a good translation for us. In so doing we won't get everything. Particularly the surface structure, which may be fascinating and highly significant, is mostly lost. But the power of ideas, the force and mood, can usually be substantially recreated, and we benefit by these informative and expressive functions, among others.

The ideas in this paper, and the samples of restructuring a few Psalms, have been useful in helping several poets redo their translations of the Psalms or other Old Testament poetry, giving it new life and expressive function. This is, of course, not something in which any translator can ever "arrive". His work may become more expressive or less expressive, the information content may be transferred with less loss or more loss, one translator's work may be a more natural equivalent than another's, but we can never say that any one translation is the correct translation. The variables are multiple, and they are subtle, and the reader's reactions are partly buried in years of reaction to the emotive use of language. But we are untangling some of the elements, and to the degree that we can do so, translators can be stimulated, and critical evaluation of their work can be more precise because of an increasingly sharp theoretical framework.[27]

REFERENCES

Aland, Kurt, et al. (eds.)
  1966   *Greek New Testament* (London: United Bible Societies).
Arichea, Daniel C., Jr.
  1973   Personal communication.
Bierwisch, Aleksander, and Paul Ellingworth
  1973   "Psalms in Serbian Popular Verse", *The Bible Translator* 24:2 (April) 234-240.
Brower, Reuben A. (ed.)
  1959   *On Translation* (Cambridge, Mass.: Harvard University).
Chafe, Wallace L.
  1970   *Meaning and the Structure of Language* (Chicago: University of Chicago).
Chatman, Seymour, and Samuel Levin (eds.)
  1967   *Essays on the Language of Literature* (Boston: Houghton-Mifflin).

[27]   When I wrote this paper I had not yet seen Halliday (1973) and related publications cited there. Halliday's work has considerably deepened my understanding of the functions of language, so that I would change my presentation somewhat if I were to do it over again. However, the implications for translation remain the same.

Chomsky, Noam
1957 *Syntactic Structures* (The Hague: Mouton).
Crim, Keith R.
1972 "Translating the Poetry of the Bible", *The Bible Translator* 23:1 (January), 102-109.
Cromack, Robert Earl
1968 *Language Systems and Discourse Structure in Cashinawa* (= *Hartford Series in Linguistics* 23) (Hartford, Conn.: Hartford Seminary Foundation).
Culshaw, Wesley
1968 "Translating Biblical Poetry", *The Bible Translator* 19:1 (January), 1-6.
Fitzgerald, Aloysius
1968 "Hebrew Poetry", in Raymond E. Brown, Joseph A. Fitzmyer, and Roland E. Murphy (eds.), *The Jerome Bible Commentary* (Englewood Cliffs, N. J.: Prentice-Hall), 238-244.
Fowler, Robert
1972 "Style in the Concept of Deep Structure", *Journal of Literary Semantics* 1, 5-24.
Fowler, Robert (ed.)
1966 *Essays on Style and Language* (London: Routledge and Kegan Paul).
Freeman, Donald C. (ed.)
1970 *Linguistics and Literary Style* (New York: Holt, Rinehart, and Winston).
Garvin, Paul L. (ed.)
1964 *A Prague School Reader on Esthetics, Literary Structure, and Style* (Washington: Georgetown University).
Gray, G. B.
1915 *The Forms of Hebrew Poetry* (New York). Republished in 1972 (New York: KTAV Publishing House).
Grimes, Joseph E.
1972 *"The Thread of Discourse"*, duplicated prepublication version (Ithaca, N. Y.: Cornell University Department of Modern Languages and Linguistics).
Halliday, M. A. K.
1964 "The Linguistic Study of Literary Texts", in H. G. Lunt (ed.), *Proceedings of the Ninth International Congress of Linguists* (The Hague: Mouton). Reprinted in Chatman and Levin (eds.), *Essays on the Language of Literature* (Boston: Houghton-Mifflin, 1967).
1967- "Notes on Transitivity and Theme in English", *Journal of Linguistics* 3,
1968 37-81, 199-244; 4, 179-215.
1973 *Explorations in the Functions of Language* (London: Edward Arnold).
Hatton, Howard A.
1974 "Translation of Poetry: A Thai Example", *The Bible Translator* 25, 131-139.
Hendricks, William O.
1969 "Three Models for the Description of Poetry", *Journal of Linguistics* 5:1 (April), 1-22.
Hirsch, David H.
1972 "Linguistic Structure and Literary Meaning", *Journal of Literary Semantics* 1, 80-88.
Jakobson, Roman
1960 "Linguistics and Poetics", in Sebeok (ed.), *Style in Language* (Cambridge, Mass.: MIT), 350-377.
JB
1966 *The Jerusalem Bible* (Garden City, N. Y.: Doubleday).

Keyser, Samuel J.
 1973 "A Theory of Poetic Form and Content", lecture delivered to the Yale
  Linguistics Club.
Knox, Ronald
 1955 *The Psalms: A New Translation* (New York: Sheed and Ward).
Kraft, Charles Franklin
 1938 *The Strophic Structure of Hebrew Poetry* (Chicago: University of Chicago).
Lachenmeyer, Charles W.
 1972 "Literary, Conventional, and Scientific Language Systems", *Journal of
  Literary Semantics* 1, 95-106.
Larson, Donald N., and William A. Smalley
 1972 *Becoming Bilingual: A Guide to Language Learning* (New Canaan, Conn.:
  Practical Anthropology).
Lefevre, Andre
 1970 "The Translation of Literature: An Approach", *Babel* 16, 2.
 1972 "The Translation of Literature: An Approach", *The Bible Translator* 23:1
  (January), 110-115.
Longacre, Robert E.
 1968 *Discourse, Paragraph and Sentence Structure in Selected Philippine Languages*
  (Santa Ana, Ca.: Summer Institute of Linguistics).
 1971 "Translation: A Cable of Many Strands", *Working Papers in Linguistics* 3:4
  (April), 283-293.
 1972 *Hierarchy and Universality of Discourse Constituents in New Guinea Languages*
  (Washington: Georgetown University School of Languages and Linguistics).
Makkai, Adam
 1971 "The Transformation of a Turkish Pasha into a Big Fat Dummy", *Working
  Papers in Linguistics* 3:4 (April), 267-273.
Matthiessen, F. O. (ed.)
 1950 *Oxford Book of American Verse* (New York: Oxford University).
Metzger, Bruce M.
 1971 *A Textual Commentary on the Greek New Testament* (London: United Bible
  Societies).
Moffatt, James
 1922 *A New Translation of the Bible* (New York, London: Harper).
Morgan, Bayard Quincy
 1959 "Bibliography", in Brower (ed.), *On Translation* (Cambridge, Mass.: Har-
  vard University), 271-293.
Mukařovský, Jan
 1964 "Standard Language and Poetic Language", in Garvin (ed.) *A Prague
  School Reader on Esthetics, Literary Structure, and Style* (Washington:
  Georgetown University), 40-55.
Nash, Ogden
 1945 *Many Long Years Ago* (Boston: Little, Brown).
NEB
 1961, *The New English Bible* (London: Oxford and Cambridge Universities).
 1970
Nida, Eugene A.
 1952 "A New Methodology in Biblical Exegesis", *The Bible Translator* 3, 97-111.
 1964 *Toward a Science of Translating* (Leiden: E. J. Brill).
 1973 "Componential Analysis of Meaning", prepublication manuscript.
Nida, Eugene A., and Charles A. Taber
 1969 *The Theory and Practice of Translation* (Leiden: E. J. Brill).

Ohmann, Richard
  1964   "Generative Grammar and the Concept of Literary Style", *Word* 20, 424-39.
         Reprinted in Freeman (ed.), *Linguistics and Literary Style* (New York:
         Holt, Rinehart, and Winston, 1970), 258-278.
  1966   "Literature as Sentences", *College English* 28. Reprinted in Chatman and
         Levin (eds.), *Essays on the Language of Literature* (Boston: Houghton-
         Mifflin, 1967), 231-240.
Phillips, Herbert P.
  1959   "Problems of Translation and Meaning in Field Work", *Human Organization*
         18, 184-192.
Phillips, J. B.
  1958   *The New Testament in Modern English* (New York: MacMillan).
  1967   "Review of TEV", *The Bible Translator* 18:2 (April), 99-100.
Pierce, Ellis E.
  1954   "The Translation of Biblical Poetry", *The Bible Translator* 5:2, 62-73.
Pike, Kenneth L.
  1947   *Phonemics: A Technique for Reducing Language to Writing* (Ann Arbor,
         Mich.: University of Michigan).
  1974   "Agreement Types Dispersed into a Nine-Cell Spectrum", in this volume.
Richards, I. A.
  1960   "Poetic Process and Literary Analysis", in Sebeok (ed.), *Style in Language*
         (Cambridge, Mass.: MIT), 9-23.
Robinson, T. H.
  1947   *The Poetry of the Old Testament* (London).
RSV
  1946, *The Holy Bible,* Revised Standard Version (New York: Thomas Nelson).
  1952
Sebeok, Thomas A.
  1960   *Style in Language* (Cambridge, Mass.: MIT).
Stankiewicz, Edward
  1960   "Linguistics and the Study of Poetic Language", in Sebeok (ed.), *Style in
         Language* (Cambridge, Mass.: MIT), 69-81.
Stennes, Leslie H.
  1969   *The Identification of Participants in Adamawa Fulani* (= *Hartford Series in
         Linguistics* 24) (Hartford, Conn.: Hartford Seminary Foundation).
Taber, Charles R.
  1966   *The Structure of Sango Narrative* (= *Hartford Series in Linguistics* 17)
         (Hartford, Conn.: Hartford Seminary Foundation).
TEV
  1970   *Psalms for Modern Man* (New York: American Bible Society).
  1971   *Good News for Modern Man* (Today's English Version of The New Testa-
         ment), third edition (New York: American Bible Society).
Ullmann, Stephen
  1962   *Semantics – An Introduction to the Science of Meaning* (Oxford: Basil Black-
         well).
Veen, H. van der
  1952   "Use of Literary or Poetic Language in Poetic Parts of the Bible", *The Bible
         Translator* 3:4, 212-218.
Voegelin, C. F.
  1960   "Casual and Non-Casual Utterances within Unified Structure", in Sebeok
         (ed.), *Style in Language* (Cambridge, Mass.: MIT), 57-68.

Waard, Jan de
   1973   Personal communication.
   1974   "Biblical Metaphors and their Translation", *The Bible Translator* 25, 107-116.
Wellek, René, and Austin Warren
   1956   *Theory of Literature* (New York: Harcourt, Brace, and World).
Wheatley, Jon
   1970   *Language and Rules* (The Hague: Mouton).
Young, Richard E., Alton L. Becker, and Kenneth L. Pike
   1970   *Rhetoric: Discovery and Change* (New York: Harcourt, Brace, and World).

THINK METRIC

GEORGE L. TRAGER

On a wall of my office at the University was tacked a large glossy photograph of a very prepossessing young woman, entitled "Think Metric".[1] The picture shows the subject dressed in the skimpiest of bikinis, and at the three crucial levels of measurement are the figures 914 mm, 610 mm, 914 mm. in easily read black type; the usual inch measurements, 36, 24, 36, are also to be found on the picture, but they are in light grey, barely visible.

The intentions of the compiler or composer of the photograph were good, the title attracts attention, and the picture is worth looking at. But the rendering of the English measurements in millimeters just possibly misses the point of the cogent title, because users of the metric system in ordinary daily life (i.e. all of the world – or the "civilized" world – except the English-speaking countries) usually give such measurements in exact centimeters – say, 91, 61, 91. These figures would make the point better, and they have a certain pleasing lilt to them. Of course, 90, 60, 90 would be even better mnemonically, though they might make more stringent dieting necessary.

The change of the system of weights and measures from the customary English (or "imperial") one to the metric system involves psychological and linguistic problems of considerable magnitude, not to speak of the technical aspects of "exact" as against approximate equivalents alluded to in our perhaps trivial initial approach above.

I do not know of any studies of what happened in France after the French Revolution, or in the rest of Europe during the nineteenth century, or in Russia after 1917, or what is taking place in Great Britain now (and in the other British countries). I do know that so far in the United

George L. Trager is Professor of Anthropology, Emeritus of Southern Methodist University, and Research Associate of its Fort Burgwin Research Center at Ranches of Taos, N.M.
[1] The picture is distributed by Reactor Experiments, Inc., San Carlos, California.

States the problems have been approached almost entirely from the technical point of view even when the intention is "practical". The United States Bureau of Standards has long had a publication dealing with equivalent measures.[2] Since that time there have been updatings, and recently, after the congressional approval of conversion to the metric system within a limited number of years, there have been some specific studies of the problems by the Bureau. There have also been suggestions from time to time to change the values of the customary measures into exact metric equivalents (say, 1 inch = 2.5 cm, 1 pound = 450 grams, 1 mile = 1.6 km, etc.).

The technical or "exact" equivalents are comparatively easy to handle, and American engineers and scientists have long been provided with tables of equivalents and devices for finding the equivalents easily. But what I wish to discuss here are the nontechnical, nonexact equivalents for ordinary use by nontechnicians. In some areas of activity exact equivalents will continue to be in order, but in others it will be necessary to "think metric" from the start. The word CONVERSION seems particularly appropriate, because what is involved is a really deep change in the ways of handling the part of the universe that we subject to measurement by fixed tables of weights and measures. And TRANSLATION becomes practical only after the conversion has taken place.

It is because of the conversion and translation aspects of the matter that I offer this paper to Eugene A. Nida in his Festschrift.

It seems appropriate to begin with some remarks on orthography and pronunciation.

In the United States it has been the custom to spell *meter* and *liter* as given here. In Great Britain (and presumably all the other British countries and former colonies except possibly Canada) the spellings are *metre* and *litre*. It would really be a good idea for the American spelling to be replaced by the British one in these two items; there is a word *meter* as in *gas meter*, and it would be nice to distinguish the unit of measurement from the instrument. As for *litre*, this would at least prevent the ill-educated from saying LIGHTer. (I may add in passing that the English-speaking world really ought to hold a conference and unify its orthographies, instead of muddling through as it does now.)

About pronunciation I need only say that I hope the pronunciation kiLOMeter will be eradicated before it leads to *cenTIMeter and

[2] The one I happen to have is *Units of Weight and Measure* (*United States Customary and Metric*): *Definitions and Tables of Equivalents* (= *National Bureau of Standards Misc. Publ.* 214) (July 1, 1955).

*milLIMeter; and let us remember that a miCROMeter is an instrument, while a MIcrometer is a millionth of a meter. (If I write *metre* in all that follows, I wonder, will the editor of this volume edit it out?) Another pronunciation point regards the form *kilo* used as a short form for *kilogram*: should one say KEElo, or will KILLo do nicely, if one says KILLo in *kilometre, kilogram, kilocycle*, etc.? (I prefer KILLo, finding that I've always said this in English, even when in Europe and using the metric system.)

There are no grammatical problems that I can think of. If something measures seven feet (plural) then it measures two metres (plural). And a seven-foot man would be a two-met*re* man (while someone possessing both a water meter and an electric meter would be a two-met*er* man). At this point I think of *six-footer*, and I really don't know how I'd convert that into metric, but this will be treated below.

The last remark leads directly to some of the things I'd like to say that may be of real importance in the discussion of the effects of metric conversion.

Many people watch the weather reports on television, and are fed fairly exact statistics in considerable quantities. There are measures of rainfall or snow in inches, of barometric pressures in inches, and of temperatures in Fahrenheit, not to speak of wind velocities in miles per hour. It seems reasonable to believe that here the conversions will be for the most part into fairly exact equivalents, tempered only by the kind of wisdom that a good translater shows in departing from literalness to achieve stylistic elegance.

A rainfall of an inch will become one of 2.5 centimetres; a snowfall of a foot will become one of 30 centimetres. Barometric pressure of 29 inches will be converted to 746 millimetres, or perhaps – more elegantly – to 75 cm. Of course, the listener is going to have to learn the new system, and the TV weathermen might help him by slowing down their chatter and giving the metric equivalents, at first; then the metric first with an English equivalent, and finally (after five years?), leaving out the English measures.

The temperatures themselves will be converted "exactly", since the weather predicters all fancy themselves as exact scientists and insist on their "normal" figures – normalcy in this case being simply the constantly changing average. But in training the public, common sense will have to be used. The centigrade (or Celsius) temperatures at ten-degree intervals equal whole-number Fahrenheit temperatures – $0° = 32°$, $20° = 68°$, $40°$

$= 104°, -10° = 14°, -40° = -40°$. The other way around is not so neat $- 40°F = 4.44°C, 70° = 21.11°, 100° = 37.77°$, and so on, with only a few cases $- 32°F = 0°C, 50° = 10°$, and $212° = 100°$ – giving whole numbers. Since the conversion will be made from °F to °C, we will all have to learn that 40°F is about 4°C, 100° is about 38°, 70° is about 21° and so on. Exact conversions can be made by using the following formula: to convert from Fahrenheit to centigrade, subtract 32 and multiply the remainder by 5/9; to convert from centigrade to Fahrenheit, multiply by 9/5 and add 32.

The hardest part of learning new temperature figures will be the reaction to them as meaningful statistics. Many years ago I was in Yugoslavia, on the Adriatic coast, in the summertime. Walking into the town, I passed a wall thermometer which had the bright sun shining directly on it. The temperature read 50°, but I didn't really react to it until I took out my conversion table and found that it was 122°F. Then I suddenly knew it was hot and rushed into the first establishment I saw where I could get a cooling drink. With the passage of years, I have learned – inside of me, so to speak – that normal body temperature is 37°C, that 20°C is a good temperature to keep your house at (= 68°F, too cool for many Americans), that freezing is 0°C, that in the high mountain area where I do research, water boils at about 90°C (which is about 195°F), and so on. But getting the feel of these things is a long and possibly painful process, and unless constantly warned, the general public will find itself wearing coats when the temperature prediction is 30°C (86°F) or leaving them home when the prediction is 15°C ("That's pretty warm, isn't it?" "I guess so." – forgetting that it's under 60°F). Moreover, what will "zero weather" mean, freezing or 15° below freezing (F zero)? And what will become of the record so-many days of "over 100°" in Phoenix, Arizona or the like? "Over 37° weather" doesn't quite have the same effect; and will we then take 35° as pretty hot (95°F), or talk about the long hot spell only when it stays over 40° (104°F)?

In the realm of lengths, heights, and distances, the conversions from English to metric measures result in uneven numbers with decimal fractions, and here translation, with common sense, is necessary. Moreover, the public will have to adjust much of its vocabulary and its "thinking" to new sizes and quantities. It is to be hoped that the manufacturers of things – clothing, appliances, containers, and so on – will take advantage of this situation to eliminate some of the present confusion and reduce the number of different sizes as well as bring some system and reason into the packaging and sizing problems.

Sizes in inches can easily be converted into centimetres by the formula 1 inch = 2.5 cm. So a two-by-four becomes a 5 × 10, and since such artifacts are rarely exact in size, the new size need bring about no actual change. Stationery that is 8½ × 11 becomes 21.5 × 28 by actual measurement. Book sizes are not always exact, so it is easy to convert 6 × 9 into 15 × 24, 7 × 10 into 16.5 × 25.5, and so on, and to talk about a book 2 cm thick (or 3 or 5, if necessary). In these examples, the only problem is that of learning the equivalents or quasi-equivalents, and getting a feel for them. However, how do we convert "to inch along"? Maybe this is a case where *inch* is to be retained as a kind of indefinite and old-fashioned measure (like the Biblical *cubit*).

Feet and yards are more troublesome. A foot can be thought of as 30cm, but the inexactness grows quickly. And yards and metres, though of the same general order of magnitude, are sufficiently different to cause some problems. The rooms of houses are sized in feet for length and width and square feet or square yards for floor area (yards mostly for carpeting or other floor covering). A room that is 10′ × 12′ will have to be converted to one that is 3m × 3.7m (that's not quite exact), and its floor space of 120 sq.ft. becomes 11.163m² (exactly). When houses start getting built by metric measurements, such a room will probably be 3 × 3.5m exactly, and its floor space will be 10.5m². This is a considerable difference from 11.163m². If a square yard of carpeting costs, say $6.00, a 10′ × 12′ room takes 3⅓ sq. yd., and costs $80. The price per square metre will have to be $7.17, which will probably be rounded out to $7.20, for a total of $80.37 (sale price $80!). For a 10.5m² room, the cost will be $75.60 (perhaps an even $75?). The customers will be even more confused than they are now – especially when sales tax, installation costs, etc., are added.

In a recent article in *Science*, altitudes were given in metric units, but depths of seawater were in fathoms. The author explained that most charts were in fathoms, and he could not, for the purposes of the article, convert most of the floor of the Pacific from fathoms to metres (1 fathom = 6 feet = 1.83 m). This is obviously a problem for the chart and map makers.

A person's height is measured in feet and inches: 5′ 4″ = 163cm; 5′ 10″ = 177cm; 6′ 7″ = 201cm. So far, so good – people learn the equivalents. But how do we speak of a "six-footer"? Above we equated seven feet to two metres; now we should perhaps equate "six-footer" to "two-metre [person]". Or should we? Only time will answer this – time and whatever habits people develop after they get a feel for the metric system.

As is well-known, in sports the English system has been in use along with the metric system, since so many athletes are from English-speaking countries. John Lotz[3] has discussed the matter of "ideal targets" for records in the two systems. He makes precisely the same points about round numbers and exact equivalents that we are making. "The four-minute mile" is untranslatable; as Lotz says, "to try to run 1609 meters in 4 minutes is not the same thing as shooting for the 4-minute mile". In this article we are extending Lotz's main point that it is language that controls the formulation of the "ideal targets", and not other factors, to all the matters involved in the conversion from English to metric measures. For mere exact translation mostly doesn't work. I could aptly quote the whole of Lotz's article, but obviously will refrain from doing so, and refer the reader to it for examples of "round numbers" in various linguistic systems and subcultures. English-speaking people consider 16 a round number – 16 oz. in a 1b., but in metric system countries it would be 15 or 20; however, 12 and 60 are round numbers everywhere because of the time-measuring system.

The number 60 is a round number in the measurement of distance in setting speed limits in English-speaking countries. When the metric system takes over, the equivalent round number to 60 miles will be 100km, for the exact translation of 60 miles is 96.56km, and that will clearly not do as a speed limit. We speak now of going "a mile a minute", and that's pretty fast on the ground even in today's world of 600 mile-an-hour airplanes. But how are we going to translate that expression? This is one that's going to need conversion, and I don't know what the result would be, though I've known about 60 miles "equalling" 100km for many years. (In Paris once I was being driven to the airport in an embassy car when I remarked to the French driver that we seemed to be doing awfully fast for 60km – and through city streets, and his reply was, "No, monsieur, that's 60 miles, which is 100km.") All other speed limits are going to have to be converted in this manner: 15mi. to 25km; 25mi. to 40km; 70mi. to 115km (?). Fortunately, these metric measures are nearly the same as the English ones. But when it comes to the distances to named places, exact (but, let us hope, whole-number) measurements will be called for, and here confusion will reign for years, unless the signs

[3] John Lotz, "On Language and Culture", in Dell Hymes (ed.), *Language in Culture and Society* (New York: Harper and Row), 182-184.

bear both the English and metric figures, and some real educational effort is applied to the problem. And let us remember that while "a miss is as good as a mile", it can't possibly be as good as a kilometre!

Measures of capacity are already thoroughly confused and confusing for Americans. Dry measure – quarts, pecks, bushels – is completely unused these days except for bushels in measuring farm products, and these commodities are sold by weight (see below). Liquid measure, in pints, quarts, and gallons, differs in the United States from the same-named units in the British countries, and many a motorist has found that his car's gas-tank will not take 15 gallons in Toronto even though it takes the 15 gallons in Buffalo 90 miles away. And those Americans who have driven in Europe or Mexico have learned to buy gasoline by the litre. The conversion here is not difficult, if one thinks of a litre as approximately equal to a quart, but it's a conversion, not a translation. "Let me have five gallons of gas" converts to "twenty litres of gas", but that translates into 5.28 gallons, so the motorist will have to learn not to be surprised at the greater cost.

For Americans, the not too close conversion suggested here will affect their buying not only of gasoline, but also of milk and all the other beverages they consume. The opportunities for quick profits will probably not be lost on the packagers and bottlers of beverages, and it will certainly be necessary to insist, for some time, on exact equivalents (both ways – 1 quart = .946 litres, 1 litre = 1.056 quarts) for the protection of the public.

Difficult as the conversions and translations so far discussed may be, those having to do with weight are probably the hardest to deal with. Ounces and pounds are in a different universe from grams and their multiples. One ounce = 28.35g; one pound = 453.592 + g; one gram = .035 ounce; 1 kg = 2.204 + pounds. Approximations are not easy to state, and this will probably be the area in which the greatest amount of conversion, as we are using the term here, will be necessary. For a beginning, we could start with the notions that 30 grams are a little more than an ounce (maybe a percentage would help – about 5 percent here), and a pound is a bit less than half a kilogram (about 9 percent). Eventually we might do as the French do, and use the term *pound* (*livre*) to equal a half-kilo. When I was in France in the late '30s, I never quite got used to buying a "half-pound" of something and calling it "un quart" (a quarter of a kilo). But for the present, we're going to have to learn a number of approximate equivalents: 5 lbs. $=$ $\sim$ (read "about") $2^1/_4$ kilos, 50lbs. $=$ $\sim$ 23 kilos, 100 lbs. $=$ $\sim$ 45 kilos, 200 lbs. $=$ $\sim$ 90 kilos, 2000 lbs. (1 ton) $=$ $\sim$ 907 kilos; and, the other way, 5 kilos $=$ $\sim$ 11 lbs., 50 kilos $=$ $\sim$ 110 lbs., 100 kilos $=$ $\sim$ 220 lbs., 1000 kilos (1 metric ton) $=$ $\sim$ 2200 lbs. $=$ 1.10 tons; and so on. The "long ton", 2240 lbs., is pretty close to a metric ton, but is not a unit too many of us are familiar with; if we have to go back to burning coal for heat, let's say, we'll have to learn what a metric ton is, at least.

If the United States had really adopted the metric system in 1866, instead of merely legalizing it (U. S. Code, title 15, section 205), all the problems here cited would have been ever so much smaller in number and effect because of the smaller population and the much smaller development of industry and commerce. However, this was not done, and it is now necessary to impose the change on a public which is inclined to resist all government impositions. The resistance takes the form of lack of interest, assertion of one's rights to freedom of choice, decrying of violations of civil liberties; it seems in very way to be analogous to an imposition of a state religion. Americans have never had the latter problem, for even in those parts of the country where everybody – or nearly everybody – is a fundamentalist Protestant, this is a historically determined condition and not a government-imposed situation.

Some of us will probably not be around any longer when the actual use of the metric system begins on a large scale. But the younger readers of this paper should prepare themselves, by anguished soul-searching, for the conversion. All the cherished values in size, shape, weight, distance, will have to be changed, and if, when these younger citizens are themselves elderly, they still continue to talk in terms of the old units of measure, they will encounter a frustrating and aggravating generation gap, for the young of that day will simply not know what their elders are talking about.

BIBLICAL REFERENCES

OLD TESTAMENT

APOCRYPHA

NEW TESTAMENT